D1453921

My Home
Sweet ROME

*Living (and loving)
in Italy's Eternal City*

*My Home Sweet Rome is a no-holds-barred
exposé of the country's stifling bureaucracy,
its dead-end politics and contradictory social
customs, recounted by Sari Gilbert, an Italy
expert and a former foreign correspondent for
Newsweek and the Washington Post.*

Praise for *My Home Sweet Rome*

"Beguiling, infuriating, intoxicating: this is what Italy is really like, written by someone who has lived it from the inside while still being able to write about it from the outside. Ever wondered what it would be like to wake up every morning surrounded by a cast of Roman characters straight out of Fellini? Sari Gilbert is the ultimate insider-outsider, a journalist who knows what's really going on and has a wonderful ability to describe what it looks like, smells like, feels like, to live like a Roman. As good on Italian food as on Italian politics and politicians, this is the book to take with you if you're going to be on holiday in Italy, thinking about a holiday in Italy, or just dreaming about it." – Robin Lustig, UK newsman and BBC commentator

"I can't imagine a better introduction to Rome than this – a first-hand account with lots of illuminating and often amusing anecdotes. It is the most perceptive analysis of the Italian way of life – social, political, and cultural – that I have read since Luigi Barzini's The Italians fifty years ago." – Katherine, former US diplomat in Rome

"Sari Gilbert brings a unique vision to these stories: the outsider's distance plus the do-it-yourselfer's hard-won knowledge of life as it is really lived in this extraordinary city. A stunning writer, she amuses us as she enlightens us--no mean feat, but one that is all too rare. A giant Thumbs Up--a custom begun in ancient Rome--to this witty, perceptive, highly clarifying book." – Vera Loquor "scripsit"

"Sari Gilbert knows Italy like the back of her hand and has woven a fascinating portrait. The country, its people – neighbours, colleagues, the mighty and the rest. Not forgetting a lifelong devotion to in depth study of Italian men, morals and manners! There is no aspect of italian life that she has not described, analysed, And decrypted with affection humour and lucidity. If you want to know what Italian life is like from the inside you should read her book!" – Neko

"… the author manages to eloquently convey both the magical and the exasperating aspects of life in Italy. In true memoir fashion, she reminisces about the colorful (and oh-so authentic!) denizens of her beloved Trastevere, she patiently unravels the complicated

political evolution of the past four decades, and she allows us to eavesdrop on the emotional vicissitudes of her love affairs. All this adds up to the real story of what life in Rome is like…" – Amerina

"I really enjoyed this nicely written look back at the author's fascinating expat life as an American journalist in Rome. What a great way to learn about modern Rome and Italian politics and culture, especially the changes that have taken place over the past 30 years. Highly recommended as pre-trip reading for visitors to Rome!" – Barbra L Goering

"As one would expect from a seasoned journalist, a well written, interesting read, a personal peek into the past with titillating descriptions of adventurous day to day life (and love life) of a young, independent woman living in Roma in the 70s-80s-90s. Thanks Sari for your insights into Italy's politics in those years: that part of life was always just a mystery to me. Brava!" – Mary Jane

"A book with great knowledge of and great affection for Rome. Sari Gilbert knows Italian politics and the Italians. She writes about their customs and idiosyncrasies with great wit." – Elisabeth Erlanger

"It is a truly remarkable memoir, unfolding Sari's unique perspective on Italian life, gained through her several intimate relationships with Italian men – wittily and tellingly recounted here. But there is much more than the loving element: her take on the political and social history of this fascinating country – where I spent only about 17 years compared to her more than four decades – is full of valuable insights." – Nick Parsons

"You should read this book to get a flavor of how uplifting, exciting and bright Italy and its inhabitants used to be before they fell into the current state of terminal moral and material decline. You should also read it as a manual for how to live, how to be accepting, open, curious, exploratory and non-judgmental. I commend the author for her autobiographical honesty and historical observation, and recommend this book." – Conor Fitzgerald

My Home Sweet ROME

Living (and loving)
in Italy's Eternal City

Sari Gilbert

Perigord Press, London

Credits

Cover design: Petar Silobrcic www.petar.org

Book design: Dean Fetzer, GunBoss Books www.gunboss.com

V 1.2

*To all those who not only love Italy but
who really want to make an effort
to understand it*

Intrepid Girl Reporter (circa 1975)

Contents

Introduction

When I was an adolescent, I fell in love. But the principal object of my affections (along with James Dean, a little known Italian-American crooner named Teddy Randazzo and Yannis, the Greek who owned the pizzeria on Broadway and 94th Street) was a place, not a person. At an early age, I became enamored with the Mediterranean in general and, more specifically, with Italy. I had no Italian or Mediterranean blood (both sides of my family were Ashkenazim, Jews from Lithuania and Ukraine) and no one in my immediate family had ever been to Italy, my father's wartime experiences having been limited to England, France and Germany. But there it was. A veritable passion.

You remember how it was. Some of the books you read as a teenager, some of the films you see, turn out to be real eye-openers or at least leave an indelible impression. In my case it was works such as D.H. Lawrence's *Sea and Sardinia*, Hemingway's *A Farewell to Arms* and *The Sun Also Rises*, Laurence Durrell's *Bitter Lemons*, Mary Renault's books on Greek mythology and authors such as Henry Miller, Albert Camus and Nikos Kazantakis that stirred feelings in me that were hard to explain, but nevertheless real, for countries like Spain, Greece, and Italy. Movies of the Fifties like *Never on Sunday*, *Rocco and his Brothers* and *The Bicycle Thief*, or performers I saw at the New York City Center such as the Spanish flamenco dancer, José Greco, or Marcel Marceau, the French mime, were those books' counterparts and like them, had persuaded me that surely I had some Mediterranean blood of my own.

The art and history courses I took in high school and college had taught me that Italy was a cradle of civilization, the repository of innumerable treasures of painting, sculpture, artifacts and architecture. So when, as a freshman, I learned that Syracuse University offered a junior-year semester abroad in Florence, I didn't have to think twice. Four months of study in the shadow, figuratively speaking, of the David and the Ponte Vecchio, followed by a three-month trip by scooter throughout Europe, only whetted my appetite. Two years later came a year of graduate school at the European branch of an American university, felicitously situated in the lesser-known (to foreigners) northern Italian city of Bologna, where medieval arcades in tones of reddish-orange protect you from the inclement weather. And once I had completed by M.A. in International Relations, I moved to Rome for almost two years to research my doctoral thesis. Finally, my studies concluded, a research grant brought me back to Rome once again; it was another prolonged visit to Italy, or so it seemed, but this time it was one that turned out to be permanent.

Like many foreigners throughout the ages, I came to Italy already bewitched by the country's beauty, already entranced by reports of its slow and sensual Mediterranean life-style, and already inebriated by its wealth of archeological and artistic treasures. In addition, intrigued as I was by both its past and recent history, I felt energized by the impression that my arrival seemed to have coincided with a watershed period in the country's postwar economic and political growth. In other words, it seemed to me – a political scientist – that I had moved here at a time when – finally – the forces of change would endow this magical place with a political structure suitable for survival and progress in the modern world.

So with my own personal choices apparently dovetailing with my intellectual interests, it seemed to me I had it made. This is where I want to be, I told myself, more or less on a daily basis, barely believing in my good luck. This is the place – amid crumbling Roman columns and Byzantine tiles, the remains of Greek temples, whitewashed houses, vineyards, stone walls, centuries-old fig and olive trees, black-clad women on recalcitrant donkeys and grizzled old men sunning themselves in empty piazzas – where it all comes together, I thought. The place where the things that really count in life – beauty, sensuality and emotion – predominate over all the rest. Where time slows down, allowing one to truly feel life's pleasures. I am "home", I concluded, having convinced myself that my ancestors must have been Sephardic Jews expelled from Spain in the late 15th century. Yes, this is where I was meant to be and where I surely would find love, happiness, fulfillment and a sense of belonging.

To make things even more exciting in this adventure I embarked upon in the early 1970s was the fact that, after years of study initially designed to lead me to a career as a researcher or a university professor, I had instead chosen to earn my keep as a freelance journalist. Working as a reporter for American, British and Canadian news organs, I had found myself a *mestiere*, a profession, which allowed me to follow Italy's development closely. In effect, I had won myself a front-row seat for the ongoing and dramatically animated theater of Italian political and economic events that I shall talk about later in this volume.

Needing to earn a living, my days, alas, were spent not at the corner café sipping Campari and soda, but following heretofore-unimaginable events in Roman Catholic Italy such as the legalization of divorce, first, and later abortion. Yes, now and then one would indeed find time for that sparkling aperitivo at Piazza Navona's crowded tables or at one of the two cafés in Piazza del Popolo, under the shadow of the Pincio hill (the *Collis Hortulorum*, for its ancient Roman wealthy inhabitants) and the location of the charming early-19th century park where Henry James's Daisy Miller rode in her carriage. But for the most part, my days, and those of the other foreign correspondents I palled around with, were spent covering frequent government crises and, even more important, the parabolic rise of the Communist party and the U.S. government's attempt to block it from coming to power.

Rather than sunning myself on the pebbled beaches of the Amalfi coast (that delight was limited to a couple of weekends a year), I was on the spot at the onset of Red Brigades terrorism and witnessed up front the group's deadly ability to reach ever more highly placed targets, like former Christian Democrat Prime Minister Aldo Moro who, shockingly, was kidnapped and then pitilessly murdered 55 days later. When a previously little-known Polish cardinal was elected Pope in 1978, I was in St. Peter's Square to hear the crowd puzzle over the unintelligible name and listen to the new pontiff choose the appellation John Paul the Second. And soon thereafter I was once again back in St. Peter's Square in the hours immediately following the 1981 attempt on John Paul II's life and then, like all my colleagues, was kept busy for months, if not for years, trying to figure out who was behind the attempted assassination, attributed by some to the Soviets through the so-called Bulgarian Connection. Furthermore, as the accredited correspondent for such important American newspapers as *Newsweek*, *The Washington Post* and *The Boston Globe*, I had a nearly unique opportunity for a young American woman living in Rome to get to know, personally, many of the principal players on the Italian stage. "*La vita è bella* – life is beautiful," I concluded, and it seemed obvious that I was in the right place to realize my expectations of overall happiness.

There was, too, another side to my life in Italy. As a well-connected foreign reporter, I had access to lots of highly placed *personaggi*, a great many of whom were men – politicians, policemen, public prosecutors, prelates and – of course – playboys. And as the reader will see from the accounts I chronicle in this manuscript, relationships often shifted dramatically from the professional to the personal. For along with being a journalist and a political scientist, I was also a sensual young woman with an active libido and a particularly pronounced penchant for slim, dark-haired men of medium stature. And I was for many years single and less interested in having either a husband or children than in passionate love affairs. And that, of course, was not difficult in a country where the pleasure principle dominates and where foreign women were viewed as particularly enticing.

So while I was covering the news and trying to put current events into a political and historical context, I was also engaged in a series of affairs of the heart (and the hormones) with some of those politicians, policemen, public prosecutors and, more occasionally, playboys. (No prelates, of course, although I do remember that after several viewings of the TV mini-series, *The Thornbirds*, we female reporters did look at our sacerdotal contacts with renewed curiosity.) But although I was living in what many consider to be the realm of romantic love, it was hard not to be disappointed.

Part of this had to do with my apparent and perhaps unfortunate preference for men who were married or otherwise unavailable. But although I would love to corroborate the myth of the Italian lover that has inspired women all over the world, I'm afraid that, overall, my own experience led me to conclude that the late Helen Lawrenson was right when she wrote: *Latins are Lousy Lovers*. As readers will see, Italian men are highly seductive and overwhelmingly affectionate but often too much concerned with themselves. It's not so much a question of sexual performance, which despite their reputation is, I suspect, not much different from that of men elsewhere, but their overweening need to be loved and adored.

So things turned out not to be all that simple. Gradually, over the years, I began to have some doubts as to whether this was a place where someone like me – who loves beauty and thrives on sensuality, but also believes strongly both in responsible citizenship and in responsible government – could find total fulfillment. When did these thoughts first begin surfacing? During the 1980s anyone covering

Italian news had little time to think. The "*anni di piombo*", the period of home-grown terrorism called the "years of lead" (because of all the bullets that were fired), and which killed hundreds, destroying families and causing heartbreak, ran parallel to years of tremendous Mafia violence, the attempt by the Italian state to fight back against organized crime, and the heroic efforts in this endeavor of the country's courageous magistrates, several of whom were to lose their lives in the process. Then, too, there was the revolving-door succession of Italian governments and the ongoing concerns about THE COMMUNISTS (eek!) to keep us journalists busy. But gradually, with terrorist bloodshed dwindling and the new Pope firmly ensconced at the Vatican, there was more time to pay attention to life on a day-to-day basis.

To be honest, it really hadn't taken me anywhere near that long to realize how complicated and wearying – *faticosa* is the perfect term in Italian – daily life was (and still is) in Italy. The stories I've included in this book show how, right from the start, I was forced to deal with a very Byzantine bureaucracy in all walks of life. Strikes – trains, buses, air traffic controllers, pilots and teachers – were often almost a daily occurrence, with the Rome city government (and here little has changed) almost always incomprehensibly giving strikers and other demonstrators permits for a *corteo* or protest march and thereby generating significant collateral damage such as enormous traffic jams for those of us who were simply going about our business. Stores and gas stations closed at very inconvenient hours, and this is true even today in non-central Roman neighborhoods and in the majority of small towns and cities. Payments for utilities and other services or taxes then had to be made in person. People didn't stand in line at the post office (or for that matter, anywhere else). Construction had run amok, ruining countless shorelines. And in the big cities, where new residential housing was built without provision for underground garages, the streets were (and are) a jungle of creatively parked cars; with their front wheels on the sidewalk, and cars double- and triple-parked even at intersections, the sidewalks were (and are) such that no visually impaired or disabled person could even think of trying to navigate them.

What I discovered after not much time was that laws, in general, tended to be ignored and honored more in the breach than in the observance. Increasingly, I would find myself growing very impatient with the labyrinthine methods of banking and bureaucracy, the difficulties of dealing with utility companies, the delays in renewing important documents like driver's licenses, the feelings of helplessness when the street lights in your street have gone off for the fifth time in three months and you need to carry a flashlight in your purse to find your way home in the dark. Perhaps this is not the right place for me, I would find myself thinking. In other words, there were (and to some extent still are) difficulties in getting through the day that make problems in the U.S. pale by comparison.

And what were my feelings about ordinary Romans? They are witty, funny, *simpatici*, and – when they know you – remarkably generous. But the average person here, perhaps taking his cue from the people he has elected, still seems to have a very fuzzy idea of that very basic concept of the common good. The Golden Rule seems to be largely unknown. And as for loving thy neighbor as thyself, at least where this concerns not a friend or relative but simply a fellow human being with whom one is not acquainted, well, all I can say is take a look at this city's ubiquitous driver rudeness and reckless driving and all one can say is "*Mamma mia!!!*" So *tutto sommato*, all in all, at some point I began to have a sneaking suspicion that Italy was not all I had cracked it up to be.

The reasons for this are many and varied. A legacy of centuries of feudalism, warring city-states and foreign domination has left Italians convinced that self-interest, and that of their families, should be their major concern. Two more-recent postwar periods had infelicitous results: in the first case, 20 years of Fascism; in the second, an overload of ideology and, perhaps in response to the destruction wrought by World War II, an excess of materialism. The Roman Catholic Church, born and bred right here on Roman soil and which until not all that long ago ruled much of Italy, preaches the need for salvation and, compared to Protestantism, places relatively little emphasis on personal responsibility. An elitist tradition of government has engendered a widespread sense of helplessness among the governed, which encourages the focus on the individual, his pleasure and satisfaction.

And then, too, it occurred to me at some point, it may also be that finding yourself surrounded from day one by so much beauty – natural and man-made – might not, in the end, be totally positive. Could it be, I asked myself, that the long-term effects of a surfeit of sunshine and of centuries of experiencing beauty and of recreating it, in cooking, clothing, style and architecture (think of all those monuments, churches and *palazzi* and their décor) might not be totally positive? I adored living in a place where beauty occupies a place of honor, but I also wanted to be in one where human beings were also able to use their God-given intelligence to effectively organize modern life. When combined with a lack of what one might call "northern angst", might it not be that too much beauty can have been bad for Italians, dulling the edge of their need for making good on everyday accomplishments?

At some point, all this had the overall effect of making me feel increasingly American and reluctant to consider myself "Italian". When acquaintances would purr, "By now you're more *romana* than American," I tended to demur, smiling and saying "*Veramente, mi sento americanissima* – I really feel very, very American." And indeed, at this writing I have so far declined to request Italian citizenship, relying on my *carta di soggiorno* (the equivalent of a green card), which so far has proved sufficient for all my needs. True, my inaction has partly been motivated by a disinclination to take on Italian bureaucracy and deal with its unending cavils. But it went even further: perhaps this is not the right place for me, I would find myself thinking.

But, then, there was always some charming incident to change my mind: a warm, welcoming *incontro* downtown with someone insisting we have a coffee, an illuminating chat with the barista downstairs at my local café, with other neighbors chiming in with their opinions, a wonderful meal overlooking a medieval village, or a stroll among second-century tombstones, to make all thoughts of pulling up stakes fade into the distance. Perhaps, I told myself, this ambivalence was just something to which I would simply have to get accustomed.

Part One

A Home in Rome

*I*t is 1972 and I have come back to Rome to live after a four-year absence, if you don't count a few brief visits in between. I am 30, have received the doctorate which makes me a bonafide "italianista" and – after a failed attempt at becoming a Foreign Service officer or an analyst for ACDA, the now defunct Arms Control and Disarmament Agency – I am about to launch myself into a new adventure. I have a place to live (an apartment in the "it" area of Rome, Trastevere), a $10,000 grant from the Council on Foreign Relations in New York which has named me as one of the year's International Affairs Fellows, and I am supposed to do research on Italy's recurring non-compliance with Common Market directives. Even better, I shall be doing an informal internship with Paul Hoffman, the veteran bureau chief in Rome for the New York Times. I don't know where any of this will lead and, looking back, suspect I hadn't thought all that much about the long-term prospects. For me, it was more than enough that I was back in Rome with enough money to support myself, a highly interesting if low-paying job and ample opportunity to see where life would lead, even if there were some unintended complications I could have easily done without.

Chapter 1 – Arrival: A New Life

The taxi is careening down narrow streets, taking hairpin turns, backing out of mistakenly entered one-way streets, weaving around parked cars while the pastel façades of low, crooked buildings – seemingly identical despite their different colors – flash by. The driver, who will shortly take advantage of my confusion by pocketing the 100,000-lire bill I give him instead of the 10,000-lire note I should have chosen, is not happy navigating the narrow streets of this labyrinthine neighborhood where, I am quick to notice, flapping, third-world-like laundry-lines alternate with fashionable boutiques. "*Imbecilli, idioti,*" he mutters as pedestrians meandering down the middle of the narrow roadway make little effort to get out of the way, repeatedly forcing him to come to a full stop. Although I am soon to come to agree that this is, indeed, an extremely irritating Roman habit, for the time being I am content to sit and observe. In fact, I think, the small knots of local residents chatting calmly on street corners confirm that, yes, the pace of life is definitely slower here than back in New York or even up in the Italian North.

By now, I am convinced that the taxi driver himself is lost even though, he has confessed, he was born only a few blocks away. ("But we moved, *grazie a Dio*, to someplace modern: Two bathrooms and a garage!" he exults.) But he can't stop bemoaning the fact that this or that one-way street ran in the opposite direction only a few weeks before, or so he says.

We slow down as a blue *motorino* (a moped) comes up the one-way street towards us, its driver, who is clearly in the wrong, nevertheless motioning us aside to make room for him. A Vespa, driven by an unshaven, middle-aged man in an undershirt with a small boy standing precariously on the running board between the driver's seat and the windshield, unexpectedly darts out of a side street that doesn't look wide enough for motor traffic. A thick-set woman in one of those shapeless, flower-patterned summer dresses favored by middle-aged southern Italian women, particularly by the *portiera* – the generally portly, female concierges who sit in a small room just inside the main doorway of a residential building and tell you where to find this or that tenant – steps out of a doorway without looking and narrowly misses a premature trip to the *camposanto*, the "holy field", as many Italians call a cemetery.

I am starting to feel frantic and crane my neck, peering out the window in the hopes of seeing, somewhere, the name of Olivia's piazza, "Sant'Egidio". In this ancient part of town, street names are written, or rather chiseled, on stone tablets placed high on corner buildings – but not on all corners, I notice, as yet unaware that this lack of semiotic consistency will turn out to be quite indicative of the Roman method of urban organization. We pass a seemingly endless number of grocery shops, a restaurant with paper tablecloths and, but I could be wrong, a tiny gray-haired woman walking a Siamese cat on a leash. Where are we? Where is Olivia's apartment? I am totally confused and wonder how I will ever find my way around this maze-like neighborhood.

But why am I so worried? This is not the first time I will be living in Italy, or for that matter in Rome. Although I am not even 30, this is to be my fifth extended stay in this country. Perhaps it is because the other times I had lived in more central or "bourgeois" neighborhoods. There was the summer, for example, that I housesat a penthouse apartment or "*attico*" near the Policlinico, the sprawling hospital managed by Rome's major university, La Sapienza, although "managed" may be a misnomer given the frequency of health-care scandals.

There, where I lived free in return for watering the plants regularly, my only problem was making sure I had enough of the tinny, ten-lire pieces needed for the elevator. I certainly had no desire to walk up eight flights. But even more importantly, I wanted to be prepared for any visits from Tommaso, the gorgeous, green-eyed assistant television cameraman I had met the year before in New York, when I was working for Italian television. Tommaso was engaged, but his *fidanzata*, his girlfriend, was a virgin, which may have explained the frequency of his visits to my place. "*So' io*, – It's me", he would say into the intercom in *romanesco*, the Roman dialect which is often guttural but which sounded to me like music when it came from Tommaso, a guy who otherwise seemed not to have a vulgar bone in his body. Goodness! What if he didn't have a ten-lire piece? I certainly didn't want him using up his energy on the stairs. So out I would rush onto the terrace, pop one into a plastic bag, and throw it down into the street.

When I next returned to Rome, this time to do my doctoral research on Italy's tormented post-World War II decision to join the NATO alliance, I also lived in more upscale areas. For a brief time, I moved in with four young (male) Italian diplomats – in a fancy, upper middle-class, terraced apartment in a suburb called Vigna Clara, an area where only Sardinian housemaids went out early in the morning – primarily to walk the dogs and buy milk and newspapers for their *padroni* – and where well-dressed *signore*, the well-heeled ladies who employed the Sardinian housemaids, went out only later in the day to shop or have their hair done. Next, I moved to a narrow, furnished apartment in Via Gregoriana, a charming street running down from Trinità dei Monti and therefore only a couple of blocks from the Spanish Steps. There my roommate was a young Florentine woman named Lucia Cencetti whose last name could be translated into "little rags", and this in fact was the undiplomatic way in which the young diplomats with whom I had remained friendly used to refer to her. Lucia was blond and blue-eyed and at first the other people who lived in the building thought she was the American and I, with my dark curly hair, the Italian. Of course, that ended when they heard me speak.

Even back then, I spoke Italian reasonably well and have always had less of an accent than many other Americans have. But my slight inflection nevertheless has always seemed to be enough to send even the politest of Italians into paroxysms of delight. Proving once again that the rules of good manners are not universal, they would immediately launch into an imitation of my harder "r"s and broader Anglo-Saxon vowels. In effect, I soon learned, this was mostly fall-out from comedian Alberto Sordi's brilliant portrayal of a fanatically philo-American Roman bully, Mericoni, in the 1953 film *Un Giorno in Pretura* (shown in the U.S. as *A Day in Court*), a true Italian classic which, like Billy Wilder's *Some Like it Hot* for many Americans, has remained impressed on the Italian consciousness. Needless to say, I found this terribly annoying, even offensive, and it was to take years before I could accept that what seemed to me downright rude was, to Italians, only affectionate teasing which allowed them to show off what they thought was their linguistic sophistication. Actually, most Italians *love* the American accent. To them it sounds exotic (perhaps like a French accent sounds to many of us?) and they love to imitate it, maybe not realizing that doing so may not be terribly polite from the point of view of others. I can only imagine what would have happened to me if someone in my family had brought home a Venezuelan or a Russian and, if, immediately after saying hello, I had started imitating them. My mother would have had me over her knee in a minute.

On the other hand, I had no difficulty in joining in the Italians' laughter at some of my mistakes in Italian, although at some times it took me a while to catch on. The most memorable? I recount a complicated dream that begins, I tell them, with me sitting under a weeping willow tree and everyone bursts into laughter. What have I said, I wonder. The problem, Gabriele's friend Marco finally manages to gasp out between guffaws, is that I have called the tree a "*salsiccia piangente*" (a weeping sausage) rather than a "*salice piangente*". On another occasion, another friend of Gabriele, the young diplomat, who has become my boyfriend, looks at me uncomprehendingly when, after he mentions someone who is "*presbite*" (pronounced *prez*-bi-tay, far-sighted), I interject, "Really? I thought he was Catholic." But at least I never did anything so public as one friend who once ran through the Florence train station calling "*Tacchino, tacchino* – Turkey, turkey!" instead of "*Facchino, facchino!* – Porter, porter!".

It was great fun to be with Gabriele and his friends, who for the most part would grow up to become Italian ambassadors. There were lengthy, five-course dinners at a cheap, smoky *trattoria* behind Piazza Navona, the long, oblong piazza (once a Roman stadium) where crowded sidewalk cafés spilled out over the pavement and two-bit artists offered to do your portrait in the shadow of one of Bernini's magnificent river gods. There were the Sunday "*gite*", excursions, sometimes to the Castelli Romani, the rolling hill-towns to the east of Rome which are known for their castles, their white wine and *porchetta*, or to Tarquinia and Cerveteri northwest of Rome with their splendid Etruscan tombs, other times to flashy Porto Ercole and Porto Santo Stefano on the coast of Tuscany's Argentario peninsula where I repeatedly marveled at the Italian woman's ability to look elegant and chic even when she's practically naked.

Everything was fine once I learned not to have any expectations. I don't mean as far as Gabriele was concerned. He would soon be leaving for his first foreign posting. And, ambitious as he was, it was clear that an American girl (Jewish to boot) and with no family money was not what he wanted in *una sposa*. As for me, at that point in time I was concentrating on finishing my research and getting my degree.

Sure, every once in a while I found myself daydreaming about marriage and *bambini*, but it was largely recreational. No, I'm talking about everyday expectations. In the world I grew up in, if someone says, "I'll call you Wednesday," they generally do. If a friend says: "Let's have lunch on Saturday," it's practically a done deal. Not in Rome. And it was to take me years to catch on, years of countless disappointments before I figured out that there was a considerable disparity between what was said and what was meant. In fact, what seemed to me to be commitments more often than not turned out only to be expressions of intent. Indeed, getting used to the fact that in Italy the warmest of words may often turn out to be meaningless may be the hardest adjustment any Anglo-Saxon has to make.

"You've never been to the Rome stadium to see a soccer match?" Piero, another of Gabriele's friends, was incredulous. We were sitting around the table in one of our usual haunts eating *rigatoni all'amatriciana* and swilling *vino rosso sfuso* (the cheaper, unbottled variety of red wine) and the subject of Italy's national sport (and obsession) had somehow come up. When I confessed I had never seen a live *partita* (which is still the case), Piero, who not long ago served as Italian Consul General in Boston, was adamant. "We'll go next Sunday," he said, putting an arm around my shoulders. So when next Sunday came I got dressed and waited for him in my Via Gregoriana flat until, finally – sometime after the kickoff – I realized that he simply wasn't coming. Looking at it now, I can see how silly and disingenuous I was, but back then I had no idea of just how inflated the use of words can be in this part of the world. Maybe it's a vestige of all those centuries of feudalism when currying favor with the powers that be, flattering the duke or duchess and making oneself agreeable to their courtiers, were the most important communication skills one could have. Whatever. The fact is that somewhere along the line Italians became really good at creating a warm, fuzzy atmosphere. It may even be what they do best. So they tend to say pleasant things and make enticing promises that allow people – including themselves – to feel good. And it's great! Just as long as you realize that the words may not really mean anything.

Mind you, they're not faking. Far from it. It's just that the emotions of the moment often have little to do with making real plans. In fact, what Piero really had meant was, "Wouldn't it be nice if one Sunday I were to take you to the stadium to see a soccer match?"

It took me ages, but after years I finally got it. You simply say "*Benissimo,*" and promptly forget about it. And *tanto meglio,* so much the better, if someone surprises you by actually following through.

The apartment in Via Gregoriana was a foreign student's dream. From there I could walk to Via Veneto, the Trevi fountain, the main post office at Piazza S. Silvestro, the Pantheon or Piazza Venezia. I was only a short distance away from Palazzo Chigi, the seat of the Italian government, and from Palazzo Montecitorio (most people just call it Montecitorio), the Italian Chamber of Deputies, where the library quickly became my second home. That's where I was, in fact, reading the parliamentary debates from the postwar period, when I learned that my then hero, Robert Kennedy, had been gunned down in the Ambassador Hotel in Los Angeles.

This time, in contrast, I would be living in Trastevere, the "in" area on the left bank of the Tiber River. For centuries Trastevere had been somewhat isolated from the rest of the city; it was only in the late 15th and early 16th century that two popes, first Sixtus IV and then his nephew Julius II, finally got around to building bridges and roads linking Trastevere to what was then Rome proper, thereby enabling pilgrims and other visitors to get to the Vatican more easily.

By the time I got to Trastevere, of course, connections from and to the rest of Rome were no longer a big deal; then, in fact, there were two direct bus lines, the 56 and the 60, that ran from the beginning of Viale Trastevere down to Piazza San Silvestro, where the main post office is located, and beyond, and others that went to the main train station, Termini. If you liked walking, you could simply cross Ponte Sisto (literally, Sixtus's bridge) by foot, carry on through the Campo de' Fiori area and down Via dei Giubbonari with its bargain-oriented clothing and shoe stores, to Piazza Argentina, where sunken ancient ruins were home to countless Roman cats. From here it was only a few blocks more to the Pantheon where, thrillingly, one could sip *espresso* and soak up the sun in the shadow of this 1,900-year-old Roman temple which, rebuilt in the second century AD by the Emperor Hadrian, is still standing, thanks no doubt to centuries of use as a Catholic church. Alternatively, you could, as I did, buy a *motorino* and join the legions of Romans who – to the despair of environmentalists and fuddy-duddies – prefer darting speed to the leisurely saunter.

Ever since Roman times, Trastevere has been a favorite of foreigners; never mind that in those ancient days that meant mostly

Jews and Syrians (Arabs) and, somewhat later on, Christians (in large part former Jews and gentiles who had converted to the new faith but who were still a tiny minority). In later times, Trastevere became the site of many artisans' workshops and, still later, of early cigarette factories, becoming a largely working-class neighborhood. But after World War II the area's winding streets and narrow passageways held great appeal for American and European expatriates as well as for "arty" Italians, and it quickly won a reputation as Rome's Greenwich Village.

"*Dove abiti*? Where do you live?" "Trastevere." "Oh, of course. You're American." How many times was I to hear that in the coming months and years? To be truthful, I had ended up in Trastevere by chance. As I was getting ready to move to Rome, ostensibly to do research for the Council on Foreign Relations fellowship I'd been awarded, I'd met Olivia, a fellow New Yorker then living part of the year in Rome, who wanted a roommate to share her Roman apartment. It was only much later that I would realize how desirable a neighborhood I lived in.

When the taxi finally pulls up in front of number 14, Piazza Sant'Egidio, I am exhausted and somewhat apprehensive. Olivia is out of town and has told me that the key sometimes sticks. Who knows if I will like the apartment? What if she and I don't get along? And suppose there's not enough room for me to work on my research project? The taxi driver, muttering audibly about the absence of an elevator, hauls my bags up two flights of very steep stairs and in return for all his trouble decides not to tell me that I have vastly overpaid him. The supposedly troublesome key, on the other hand, gives me no problem and even though the apartment has no real view, I decide I like it; in fact it occurs to me almost immediately that (as will shortly happen) I would like it even better if I had it all to myself.

Olivia's room is the large and spacious bedroom on the quiet, inner court. I get, instead, what a few years hence will become my small but cozy living room, a smaller space that looks out over the long, trapezoidal piazza below and the *bar-latteria* directly underneath. Thanks to all the time I've already spent in Italy, I know this means a café that also sells fresh milk. Unfortunately, as I am to discover the following morning, it opens at six a.m. when its first clients, the neighborhood garbage men, meet before starting their shift. They make a lot of noise, not least because they all share that particular

Trastevere hoarseness which must come from a combination of smoking and a lifetime habit of loud speech, so loud that you think most everyone you meet must have had at least one close relative who was hard of hearing. The café owner, Umberto, a portly, gray-haired fellow, is however quite nice. In fact, following his suggestion, after only a few days I fall into the habit of lowering a basket from the window into which he will put my morning *cornetto*, Italy's unbuttery version of a croissant.

Between the two "bedrooms" there is a central space which the landlord, a well-known art-gallery owner who was married to a famous actress but is understood to be gay, has divided into two rooms, a kitchen with a window and the entrance hall. The front door is made of heavy dark brown wood with large nail heads visible on the inside and an iron knocker on the outside. It looks like something out of the Middle Ages and, indeed, the first two floors of the building are very old, (although not Middle Ages old). One later occupant of the building, Signora Andreoli, a maddening octogenarian with a gray page-boy haircut who will become the bane of our tenants' meetings, was given a 17th-century print in which you can see the original, two-storey building quite clearly. Back then it had a conical roof which some time later was replaced by two more stories, bringing the total number of apartments up to nine.

Olivia's apartment has a stone floor made up of a pattern of red, black and cream tiles, a combination that apparently has long been very much in vogue because along with her apartment and our building's four landings, I keep running into it in a variety of downtown Rome apartments and hallways. Many of the tiles are cracked but nevertheless have a certain charm, and once I see what the gallery owner has done to the floors of the other apartments he owns in the same building (shiny, white tiles that look as if they belong in a public lavatory), I realize how lucky I (whoops! I mean Olivia) am. In addition, all the rooms have magnificent, dark wood-beamed ceilings, in Rome considered almost as much a prize as a terrace.

Back then, many Romans used to complain that foreigners were taking over Trastevere. And after I moved in I saw it was hard to fault them. In my building, a four-floor walk-up, I quickly discover that six of the nine apartments are occupied by "*stranieri*", foreigners. On the first floor, which for Europeans is not the ground floor but one flight up, the right-hand apartment is occupied by Lloyd and Bill, two

American men who have been living together for years and who moved to Rome in the sixties. Lloyd has a PhD in Classics and teaches at one of the several foreign universities in the city. Bill, a Texan who is considerably younger, has taken up cooking and has become a successful caterer for diplomats and institutions like the American Academy on the nearby Janiculum Hill.

Across the hall from them lives David Henderson, a delightful young American priest from California with a passion for archeology, who has managed somehow to get approval for his non-priestly living arrangements. Normally, foreign priests in Rome are expected to live within an institutional format, but David – who for a time will become one of my closest friends and with whom I will later take a memorable trip to Israel – has a mind of his own and can't abide regimentation.

When he lived at North American College, an American seminary, he repeatedly got into trouble when his rector caught him sneaking in way after curfew. No, he wasn't out with women or anything like that. He was just out, exploring this fascinating city. This flexibility regarding David's living arrangements appears to be one of the relatively few instances when the Church has showed itself to be capable of bending the rules to keep a sheep within the fold. Alas, at least for the Church, it was not to suffice. Eventually, David was to fall in love with a young American widow and, though on one level it broke his heart to do so, he would end up leaving his vocation and marrying her. He apparently felt the need to cut all ties with the past and our friendship did not survive this trauma.

One floor above me lives Jacques Herlin, a slim, gray-haired French movie actor who came to Rome in the early sixties and has already played every conceivable role – from Roman centurion to debonair man of the world. On the fourth floor there is Leonardo, a tall North African believed to be one of the gallery owner's lovers, who will move out after an embarrassing stairway tussle with a transvestite for which the police will have to be summoned. Across from him lives Howard Johnson, a Canadian economist who works at the UN's Food and Agricultural Organization (FAO) and is married to a French-Canadian painter (a marriage destined not to last). They have a magnificent view of the Janiculum Hill from his terrace. I, alas, have no view at all.

Italians of various ilks occupy the remaining apartments. A feminist journalist and her live-in boy friend inhabit one of the flats on the top floor, across from Howard and next to Leonardo. Above me, on the third floor is Paola, a young economics researcher from the northern Friuli region who is rooming with Grazia, a very attractive blonde (dyed) whose dream is to become a TV or radio producer but who is well aware that she will need help to get there, be it a recommendation from a politician, an influential friend in the Italian state broadcasting company, or a well-positioned lover. On the second floor, across from Olivia, and now me, is Fulvio, a friendly, dark-haired guy with glasses who is a systems analyst at the Rome branch of IBM.

This was the residential line-up for the first several years of my life at S. Egidio. (Today the proportions have shifted sharply and only one of the apartments in the building is occupied full-time by foreigners, although two others are now often rented out as short-term holiday lets.)

But after only a short time, there was one significant change. Grazia, who in the meantime had become a close friend, moved out of Paola's apartment and into Fulvio's, an arrangement that would last only until she met someone who had a more "interesting" job, and who was, in fact, just what she had dreamed of, a top TV executive who could give her career a boost. In the end, however, Grazia's primary accomplishment turned out not to be work-related, as she never attained her professional dreams, but rather in convincing her married Italian lover to leave his wife and set up house with her. No easy task, that.

Having finished my initial surveillance of the apartment, I am too excited to unpack and decide to go out and experience some of the local atmosphere. It's perhaps a bit soon to attempt a detailed exploration of my new neighborhood, so I settle for a *cappuccino* and a *cornetto* at Di Marzio, one of the two outdoor cafés in Piazza Santa Maria in Trastevere, the physical and spiritual center of this neighborhood or *quartiere*.

From the outside, the Basilica of Santa Maria is lovely, a largely Romanesque construction with just a hint of early gothic peeping out in the windows of the many-tiered bell tower, the *campanile,* with its large, round clock. The somber mosaics on the facade, women holding lamps and surrounding the Virgin Mary and the infant Jesus, are, like much of the early religious art in Italy, Byzantine in style and impart a sense of quiet spirituality. At 11 a.m. on a weekday morning, the café is almost empty except for a small group of workers (more garbage collectors?) who appear to have finished their shift. They are talking politics and at one point break into a chorus of the stirring Communist *Internazionale*. Catholics and Communists, I think, wondering what kind of life I will end up having in this country of stark contrasts, passion and emotionally charged conflicts.

Chapter 2 – And It's Every Woman For Herself

T he cat was pregnant, and so was I, but we seemed to be taking our common predicament rather differently. She, a black stray that I'd brought home a few months earlier, roamed lazily around the apartment, languidly stretching herself out along the cool, red, black and cream floor tiles and contentedly licking her fur. I, though pleased with the unusual size of my breasts, was frantic. Carried away by a temporary passion for a young, up-and-coming, seemingly socially-committed journalist for a major Italian daily whom I'd met a year earlier in New York, I had neglected to use my diaphragm, even though I had been well aware that what turned out to be our last encounter was occurring on a day not likely to be a safe one. And the reaction of my bed partner (actually, the act was consumed consummated in the kitchen) was, like something out of a 1950s *True Romance* magazine story, all too depressing. *"Chi mi dice che è mio?* – Who says it's mine," he had queried heatedly when I told him the news, clearly eager to wash his hands of the whole business.

So it was every woman for herself and I had to assess my options. Abortion was to be legalized in Italy in May 1978 by a center-left government and reconfirmed three years later in a landmark popular referendum, a rush to the polls by an overwhelming majority of the Italian electorate that can be seen as a high point in the frontal clash between the Christian Democrats, the giant Catholic political party that had dominated much of the postwar era, and the Italian left. In the blink of a ballot box, Roman Catholic Italy, a place where until 1971 contraceptives other than condoms were actually outlawed, would boast one of the most liberal abortion laws on record; women over 16 were given the right, after consultation with both the doctor and the state psychologist, to terminate a pregnancy up until the 12th week and, in addition, to have it paid for by the National Health Service. Interestingly enough, private doctors were forbidden to perform abortions. This latter part of the law was to create problems in areas such as parts of the Italian South, where a large number of doctors, fearful of condemnation by their bourgeois neighbors or the local parish priest, were given the right to declare themselves conscientious objectors, thereby forcing women "in trouble" to have unwanted children or to travel northwards to a more open-minded part of the country. But it is still an extremely liberal law that allows abortion more or less on demand up to the end of the third month and owes its existence to the unflagging pressure that had been exerted for years by the gadfly Radical party and its now aging leader, Marco Pannella.

But this was 1972 and my choices boiled down to a trip to London or Scandinavia or going the illegal route. Someone, I can't remember who, gave me the name of a Via Veneto gynecologist, and a few days later I found myself in a fancy, carpeted office, sitting across the desk from Dr. X, a tall man with a patrician mien, a somewhat snooty manner and an Elmer Fudd pronunciation because of what the Italians call *un'erre moscia*, a barely pronounced, slightly "French" "r". I have never been very keen on Italian male gynecologists. For one thing, almost none of them give you a gown to put on. This serious lacuna can be dealt with by going to a woman doctor. Otherwise, all you can do is wear a full skirt, if you still own such a thing; in this case, you just slip off your underpants and use the skirt as that symbolic but psychologically important barrier between your genital nudity and the doctor. But should you forget, or habitually wear trousers as I do, you are out of luck. And so I found myself in the middle of the snooty doctor's office, naked from the waist down and more vulnerable than I needed to be, given the circumstances. But I didn't have the energy to quibble. "Why have you come to me?" he asked, looking balefully down his Roman nose, once we'd established that I was indeed pregnant. "I certainly can't (read that as "won't") help you," he said sternly. "However," he added as I sat there mutely, "maybe *he* can help." He scribbled a name and an address on a piece of scrap paper and told me to pay his outrageous fee to the receptionist.

This was certainly no way to start off my new life in Italy. I had arrived only two months earlier to start work on my research project for the Council on Foreign Relations and to help out as a part-time local assistant at the *New York Times* Rome bureau. It hadn't been easy picking up and moving from the U.S. and I therefore had been eager to re-establish a connection with the young, up-and-coming, seemingly socially-committed journalist, no matter that he was married with two children and an extremely jealous wife. And thanks to that lapse of judgment, I was now pregnant and rather embarrassed about it – I who had known the facts of life since the age of 10 and had always been very, very careful.

The office of the abortionist, a more fatherly, gray-haired gynecologist who wanted either to help women or to supplement his income (or both), was on the western side of town, in a less central, middle-class residential area called the Balduina. And for a fee that was not exorbitant, but still high enough that I would be forced to ask the seemingly socially-committed journalist to chip in, the doctor, whose name and face have totally faded from memory, was indeed willing to help. He set the procedure for a Saturday morning and gave me the address of what turned out to be a near-empty apartment in a nondescript building somewhere in the same district. To my horror – and this was before the suction technique had been introduced – I discovered there was to be no anesthetic, although this shouldn't have surprised me since only in late 2006 was it decided that hospitals in Italy would stop expecting women to deliver their babies without anesthetic. The whole thing was depressing and scary but it would have been even worse had it not been for Umberto, who was in the waiting room next door waiting for me.

No, Umberto was not the father of my baby, the latter having disappeared from the scene after agreeing to share the cost of the operation and who was to let five years go by before apologizing. Umberto was someone I had met for the first time the night before the D&C. At a dinner with a group of people he zeroed in on me, having noticed that I was depressed and possibly close to tears. When he asked me what was wrong – "*Che c'è, cara?*" – I found myself blurting out the whole story, including the part about the seemingly socially-conscious journalist's rejecting manner. "So who will be accompanying you?" he asked me softly as we sipped some courage-building *grappa* at the end of the meal. "No one," I said, gulping back tears. "Well, then, I will come with you," he said. And he did.

Umberto Giovine, whom I haven't seen since, went on to become a businessman in Northern Italy, a passionate federalist and, for a while, a member of Parliament and an undersecretary of Industry, having been elected on the ticket of Forza Italia, the first party founded by media magnate Silvio Berlusconi. Back then, however, Umberto was a Socialist and a journalist, perhaps best known for a rather un-Italian exploit: hijacking an Olympic Airlines plane in 1968 to protest against the ongoing rule of the Greek colonels. Now he was playing the paraclete and helping out *una giovane americana,* a young American woman, whose passionate nature had gotten her in trouble.

Why do I say that Umberto's hijacking, carried out without bloodshed and designed to dramatize the cause of Greek democracy, was unusual for an Italian? If you count out extremists, either of the murderous or less murderous type, one doesn't run into very many people here who seem willing to take action which could be risky – physically or professionally – in the name of principle. Of course, there are exceptions, particularly in times of war and political crisis. There are Italian doctors in Médicins Sans Frontières and Italian priests and nuns in the deepest jungles of Africa who put sacrifice before all else. Goffredo Mameli, the author of the patriotic poem whose words would later be set to the Italian national anthem's music (although, as I have often noticed, no one seems to know them), died in 1849 before reaching the age of 21 while fighting with Giuseppe Garibaldi's Red Shirts on the Janiculum Hill to free Rome from the papacy. Under the Fascist regime, socialist Giacomo Matteotti paid with his life for his commitment to free speech. The anti-Fascist Resistance spawned many a hero. Salvo D'Acquisto, a 23-year old *Carabinieri* corporal, in September 1944 confessed to a crime he did not commit to save 22 people held hostage held by the Germans. And in the early 1990s, Sicilian anti-Mafia magistrates Giovanni Falcone and Paolo Borsellino, and their police escorts, paid for their commitment to justice with their lives.

But in general, principle does not seem to play a large part in the Italian consciousness, and one rarely hears anyone talking about ethical considerations. Consider the story told to me years ago by the now deceased Bruno Trentin, for decades the leader of Italy's left-wing trade union, the CGIL. He grew up in France because his father Silvio, a university professor, had been forced to emigrate after he refused to sign a loyalty oath to the Fascist regime. "Guess how many of Italy's professors refused to sign?" Trentin asked me during the course of an interview. The answer? Thirty-one. And that included his dad.

Political passions rage strong in Italy, of course, but are largely verbal. Sexual passion, on the other hand, is something that motivates a lot of people here, leading many, particularly men, to do some very daring and probably foolish things. Naturally, not all Italian men cheat. Although probably only a small minority of married Italian men would say "no", were an appealing woman to slide in between their sheets, many are faithful. Some are Catholic and really believe in the sanctity of marriage. Some are profoundly in love. A few, I suppose, are simply reluctant to risk hurting a loved one. Some are simply too shy or sexually insecure, and others don't have the time or the energy to engage in the subterfuge required for serious adultery. But for every man who says "no", there are many more who say "*sì, sì, sì*". And this appears to be true more or less across the social board.

Indeed, in Italy the pleasure principle rates so high that adultery, by men or women, is frequent and has long been more openly acknowledged than in many other societies. In part, the highly charged sex and passion of adultery may be facilitated by the flexibility of the Italian life-style, which lends itself better to sexual dalliance than the more regimented workplace of northern countries. Although nowadays in Rome almost no one with a full workday goes home to eat at midday, lunch breaks for many people are still longer than in the United States, and many government offices shut down at 2 p.m. It's also easy to meet for steamy coffee breaks if you both work and live in the relatively small historic center. And a large number of the small apartments around the Pantheon, Piazza Navona and Campo de' Fiori appear to have been bought as *pieds-à-terre* by well-off married men with just that in mind. But a very large proportion of Italian men, including those who, like the seemingly socially-committed journalist, are married, seem to be afflicted primarily with that extreme narcissism that renders them unable to resist any woman who appears to love or desire them.

When I came to live in Italy in the Seventies, I was in my twenties and there were still a lot of single, non-gay Italian men in my age group. But no doubt because of problems of my own – like growing up in a very unhappy marriage – I tended to shy away from relationships likely to become something serious. Instead, I always seemed drawn to men who were already someone else's boyfriend, husband or *fidanzato*, someone in other words who in the end was likely to reject me. The fact is that for my own reasons I, too, was hooked on that rush of sexual adrenaline one gets when attracted to someone new and also unavailable, the *amore impossibile*. And since many married Italian men don't seem to have too many scruples about infidelity, I – now sadly pregnant – was apparently in the right (wrong) place.

Chapter 3 – Journalism 101

The *New York Times'* Rome Bureau was located on the top floor of the *ANSA* building on Via della Dataria, a 14th- century ocher-colored palazzo that the Italian National News Agency had recently bought and renovated, moving from its previous site near Piazza di Spagna and the Spanish Steps. At the new location, alas, it was no longer particularly convenient to stop into Babington's Tea Room for a quick fix of hot, buttered scones or, at a later hour, for a chicken curry with chutney, both of which constituted highly welcome comfort food for us displaced Anglo-Americans, people who adored pasta and all the rest of the wonderful Italian cuisine but still suffered from nostalgia. Back in those days, there was exactly one Chinese restaurant in Rome, and if you wanted variety you got it from sampling different regional Italian cuisines, not by going to foreign restaurants.

But since the *ANSA* building is just down the hill from the hulking Quirinale Palace, right around the corner from the magnificently Baroque Trevi Fountain, only five or six blocks from the Parliament and from Palazzo Chigi, the seat of government, and within walking distance of the headquarters of Italy's top political parties, it was ideal for covering the news. Along with the *Times*, the British news agency *Reuters* had also hurried to move in and was subletting half of its space to a variety of foreign news organs: *Newsweek*, the *Toronto Star*, the Israeli paper *M'aariv*, *Westinghouse Radio* and others.

I had grown up on the *New York Times*, practically the closest thing to a family bible since my mother, a teacher, and my father, a lawyer, just about swore by it (although in pre-Murdoch days they did also have a weakness for the *New York Post*'s then-liberal columnists). So I had been delighted when, during a previous visit to Rome, veteran correspondent Paul Hofmann, upon learning that I planned to return after finishing my PhD at the School of Advanced International Studies in Washington, D.C., had asked me if I'd like to help him out at the bureau. Now, with my grant in hand, I was back in Rome and raring to go.

The idea of being a foreign correspondent had appealed to me even as a youngster. So Paul's unexpected and exciting offer was looking better and better. Helping out at the *New York Times* would also give me a close-up view of contemporary Italian politics which, from the academic point of view, was my principal interest. But it also meant learning how to be a journalist.

Most reporters in America start out by working for local papers, sometimes even in lowly jobs such as the mailroom. Others go to journalism school after college. And some, inspired even at an early age, gain initial experience by working for high school and college rags. I had done nothing but *read* newspapers. And though I had been told by many professors that my term papers and essays were extremely well written, I knew next to nothing about writing a news article, except for the proverbial who, what, when, where and how. Fortunately, I had Paul Hofmann to teach me, and teach me he did.

My part-time job involved making phone calls, collecting statistics, reading the Italian papers and doing some research. But right off the bat Paul also had me writing, doing those brief, unsigned three- to six-inch filler articles you might see at the bottom of a *New York Times* newsprint column, articles with concise headlines that say things like: "Italian admiral gets NATO post", "Rome Coliseum to be cleaned", or "Bus strike paralyzes Rome". I'd bash these little things out on the typewriter and put them on Paul's desk and wait till he gave them back to me with his corrections: bright-red, penciled arrows instructing me to move one paragraph up and another down, more red lines crossing out this or that, and decisive red question marks next to ideas that seemed unclear and so on. It was depressing, but it was also quite helpful. And one day, in fact, I "graduated". I took an article into his room to have it vetted, and Paul, without even looking up from his typewriter, waved a hand at me and said in his inimitable, Austrian-accented English, "Ah, chust go ahead und file it!" What a thrill!

It was 1972, and Italy was in a phase of sharp political and social ferment that had begun with the student movement in 1968, moved on to the hot autumn of 1969 when the militancy of Italian trade unions was revved up to unprecedented levels, and – in December of that year – escalated to the first of what would turn out to be a long series of acts of real political violence. The unprecedented and murderous bombing of the Banca Nazionale dell'Agricoltura in Milan's Piazza Fontana, in which 16 people died, was attributed first to an anarchist and later to neo-Fascists. It sent a shockwave through the country and heralded the appearance on the scene of a variety of radical groups, leftist and rightist, some of which opted for normal political activism while others gradually swung into the spiraling terrorist activity that for more than a decade was to set Italy apart from most of its European neighbors. In 1969 alone, there were over 300 bombings, mostly with political targets (persons and places). By the end of 1975 that number had reached 4,384, with the majority ascribed to right-wing groups including New Order, National Vanguard and myriad others.

The extreme right made ample use of dynamite, and people of that political persuasion have been convicted for the bombings of the Italicus train (12 dead, 48 hurt), the explosion in Piazza della Loggia in Brescia (8 dead, 108 wounded) in 1974 and a bomb placed in a waiting room at Bologna railroad station in August, 1980, killing 85 people and wounding countless others. The groups on the extreme left were also increasingly busy at wreaking havoc. But they soon developed a more sophisticated but cruel and murderous strategy that used kidnappings, kneecappings and outright killings of carefully selected human targets in a vain and unrealistic attempt to stimulate widespread police repression and eventually, or so they hoped, a popular uprising by the Italian people.

On October 5, 1970, an initial episode of left-wing "armed struggle" took place when the so-called "October 22 Group" briefly kidnapped the son of a Genoa industrialist and then, the following year, killed an armoured guard in the course of a botched robbery.

Then, only two months before I arrived in Rome in May, 1972, the well-known left-wing publisher, Giangiacomo Feltrinelli, then known primarily for being the first in the West to publish Boris Pasternak's *Dr. Zhivago*, was found dead and dismembered at the foot of an electricity pylon outside Milan that he had been in the process of sabotaging.

Italy was changed, if not forever, then for much time to come. For this was more or less the start of the escalating violence that was to culminate, although not terminate, in Moro's 1978 abduction and murder. And if a significant portion of the members of the Red Brigades was destroyed following the December, 1981 kidnapping (and subsequent liberation by the NOCS special operations unit of the *Carabinieri*) of U.S. General James Lee Dozier, remnants of the terrorist organization have continued shedding blood. Fortunately, the last of their headliner killings dates back to March, 2002 with the murder of labor jurist Marco Biagi, a consultant to the Italian Labor Ministry. But dozens more were arrested as recently as early 2007.

The social and political conditions that spawned the unrest that lay behind this growing political unrest and violence were increasingly obvious – that is, to anyone who *wanted* to see them. And indeed the center-left government led by the Christian Democrats and the Socialists that was then in power did make a stab at introducing some much-needed reforms. Chief among these, and more than 20 years after it was called for in the 1948 Italian Constitution, a decentralized, regional system of government was introduced. A new Workers' Statute introduced far-reaching labor legislation. And a law was passed allowing popular referenda on a variety of subjects, thereby opening the door to important social changes in the early 1970s such as the legalization of both divorce and abortion.

But if some things were changing, others were not. My personal hope was that the unresponsive government that contrasted sharply with the first, positive reactions (with Marshall Plan help) to right some of the destruction wrought by starting out on the wrong side in World War II, would turn out to be little more than growing pains. After all, the country was still young; unification had occurred only little more than 100 years earlier, and the Mussolini era was still a recent memory.

But the situation was not promising. After 30 years – we are talking about the mid-1970s – the Christian Democrats (DC) were still the country's dominant force, albeit an extremely fragmented one. Their grip had loosened to the extent that the Social Democrats and the small but influential Republican party, both of which were substantially pro-American and anti-Communist, had to be called on to join the DC in coalition governments.

Starting in the early sixties, after they had broken with Moscow over the invasion of Hungary, the Italian Socialists also were brought into the fold while, with the Cold War in full swing, the Communists were kept moored tightly on the sidelines, to a large extent because of an informal but effective American veto on their possible participation in a government. Then the most powerful Communist party in the West, and coming close to overtaking the Christian Democrats in popular support, the party was *partito non grato* to the United States. Because of this, most analysts agreed, Italy was *una democrazia bloccata*, a blocked democracy.

In this context, it was not surprising that the Christian Democrats were having a hard time dominating the situation. In December 1971, it took a record 23 ballots for the Italian Parliament to elect Giovanni Leone President of the Republic. Leone, an extremely short Neapolitan lawyer with a very thick local accent, was a well-known Christian Democratic politician and a former Prime Minister who was – it was clear from the start – unlikely to bring much stature to the role of Italian Head of State. From the media's point of view, he appeared to have only one really distinguishing asset: a young, dark-haired wife, Donna (Lady) Vittoria, who stood at least a head taller than he and who was beautiful, elegant and fashion-conscious. In other words, she was "good copy".

So despite my lack of experience (or, who knows, perhaps because of it?), Paul decided that this should be my first "major", bylined piece for the *Times,* and off I went to interview her in the decorative splendor of the sprawling 16th-century Quirinale Palace. Because it stands on higher ground than the Vatican, this magnificent palace originally was a summer residence for the Popes. Later it became the residence of Italy's Savoy monarchs and, once Italy was transformed into a Republic in 1946, it became home to the Italian Head of State, the *Presidente della Repubblica.*

I don't remember much about the interview. And I recall being much more impressed with the imposing *palazzo* than with Mrs. Leone, a pleasant enough woman but one who did not seem particularly remarkable. What she did seem was dignified and chaste, making it impossible to believe the rumor that she, much more attractive than her tiny, white-haired, bespectacled husband, was having an affair with a Quirinale *autista* or chauffeur. Leone, much like prime minister Silvio Berlusconi more than 20 years later, once embarrassed the more enlightened part of the country when he was caught on camera trying to ward off the evil eye by using that centuries-old Neapolitan *corna* gesture, in which only the index finger and the pinky of the hand are stiffened and pointed downward. (More recently, Berlusconi used the same gesture – at a meeting of European heads of government – but with the fingers pointed upward which, instead, means the person indicated is wearing horns, in other words is a cuckold.)

But what really bowled me over was the fact that all of a sudden, just because I had been sent there by the *New York Times*, even huge, carved monumental doors guarded by towering *corazzieri* (the helmeted Quirinale honor guard, minimum height 6'3") would open. The day before I was just an ordinary New Yorker, albeit with two graduate degrees. And the next day I was having tea with and interviewing the First Lady of Italy. And this was to be the story of my life for the next couple of decades. Even though I was always to be a stringer, a local hire, often looked down on by staffers and editors at the major newspapers and broadcasters I worked for (smaller outfits were, instead, generally grateful for your services), my accreditation as a foreign correspondent with the Foreign Ministry assured me an enormous amount of highly enjoyable upward mobility and a great deal of possibly undeserved clout with Italian contacts and colleagues.

There was no doubt that I had quite a bit to learn about journalism. However, I had two major advantages over the scores of other foreigners trying to make it in Italy as freelance journalists and even over some of the "staffers" stationed here in the Seventies by U.S., Canadian or British news organs. First of all, after years in Italy as a student – undergraduate and graduate – I already spoke near fluent Italian. Secondly, as a "Europeanist" with a specialization in Italian studies and a 600-page doctoral dissertation on Italian foreign policy under my belt, I kind of knew what was going on here. This does not mean, however, that it was an easy matter informing American readers, used to our own fairly simple two-party, presidential system, about the intricacies of Italian parliamentary politics.

At the time, Italy had a strict proportional electoral system, meaning that the seats in both the lower house, the Chamber of Deputies, and the upper house, the Senate, were divided among the country's nine largest parties, ranging – from right to left – from the neo-Fascists to the PSIUP which then stood to the left of the Communists. To govern, since it was no longer strong enough to do it alone, the DC had to look for coalition allies among Italy's small centrist groups and the country's "acceptable" leftists. As a result, governments were highly unstable. They collapsed so frequently that at one point I remember being sorely tempted to use the same piece I'd written during the previous government crisis, simply changing the names and the day of the week. *La crisi,* as it was called, was often followed by long, extenuating negotiations that generally resulted in the formation of an equally unstable successor government, sometimes headed by the same prime minister who had just been unseated. It was complicated, Byzantine, and hard for most readers to digest. But it had to be reported and because of my academic credentials I had something of an advantage. Or so it seemed.

The city then appeared to be swimming in Anglo-Saxon would-be freelance journalists, some of whom were simply people who for some reason had traveled to Rome, liked it enough to stay, and were trying their hand at writing as a way to support themselves. I at least had some background and consequently almost every time I wrote to an American newspaper offering to be its local correspondent, the answer was a "yes". For a time, I was sending articles to daily papers that included the *Washington Star*, the *Toronto Star*, the *Chicago Sun-Times*, the *San Francisco Chronicle,* and *Newsday*. And not long after, I also started doing 30-second news-spots for *CBS Radio*. None of these news organs paid stringers anything significant, maybe $30 for a radio spot and between $60 and $100 for a news article, depending on its length. And it was frustrating since sometimes a newspaper would ask for 800 words and then use only 400, paying you only half! But in those days, life in Italy was still quite inexpensive and I was able to live quite well. My apartment cost under $100 a month, food was cheap, and it wasn't long before I could even afford to have someone come in and clean the house and to enjoy such other luxuries as a weekly massage and a monthly pedicure. One of the first things I discovered about Italy, in fact, was that services cost much less here than back at home, enabling me to enjoy a life-style that in the U.S. I would never have been able to afford.

Primarily, however, I was having fun. By the time I stopped working for the *New York Times* (if I remember correctly, this came about because the paper's then foreign editor, the late Jimmy Greenfield, decided to terminate my arrangement with Paul, because, it was implied, there was concern – unwarranted I might add – that I might take advantage of strict Italian labor laws and try to make the position permanent), I had lined up enough other jobs to be able to move to my own office downstairs on the ANSA mezzanine. This was part of an area of the building rented out to the British news agency, *Reuters*, and my first office was that which the *Toronto Star* had rented a year earlier for its then correspondent, the late Stuart Troup, who was on his way to Paris to join the *International Herald Tribune*. Next door to me on the left was Robin Stafford, who worked for London's

Daily Express. Phil Caputo, the *Chicago Tribune's* correspondent, a former marine who later wrote the much admired *A Rumor of War* about his tour of duty in Vietnam as a young lieutenant, occupied the office on the right, and we generally kept the adjoining door open to exchange information or perform, along with *Reuters* staffer Robin Lustig (later a major *BBC* commentator) impromptu faux Shakespearean dramatizations. Phil's assistant, Daniela Petroff, was dating the *Associated Press's* Victor Simpson, whom she later married. And further down the hall, another room housed Don Larrimore, an extremely hyper but kindly man, who worked for *Westinghouse Radio* and also for *Newsweek*. He shared his office with David Willey, the *BBC's* veteran Rome correspondent who at 80 is still producing unparalleled copy. In the other direction, beyond the stairwell and the elevator, was the *Visnews* office, then manned (womanned?) by Janet Stobart, who quickly became one of my closest friends, and the *Reuters* office itself, where Alexander Chancellor, subsequently editor of *The Spectator* and now a columnist for the *Guardian*, played chief to a staff of four or five reporters. Other news people worked at home but came in to *Reuters* to file their stories and pass the time of day.

It's hard to fathom this, now that computers are an integral and essential part of our lives, but in those days one still worked on a typewriter and filed one's copy by phone or through the telex. The *New York Times*, of course, had its own telex machine and operator (as well as a full-time chauffeur named Giorgio, whose everyday gray suit was the exact same shade as his pompadour). But lesser mortals had to use the services of agencies such as *Reuters*, the *Associated Press* (AP) or the *United Press* (UPI). Many foreign journalists, especially freelancers or staffers for smaller papers or broadcasters, worked out of the Stampa Estera, the Rome Foreign Press Association, then located a few blocks away in Via delle Mercede, close to the main branch of the central Post Office. The Postal Ministry provided the Stampa Estera with phone and telex services and there was a small auditorium for press conferences and a bar that served light lunches and snacks. One Stampa Estera member back then was Joaquin Navarro-Valls, a former doctor who somehow had ended up in Rome filing for the Spanish daily *ABC*. Following the surprise election to the papacy of Karol Wojtyla in 1978, Navarro-Valls, a kind, handsome man with a serious mien that belies his quiet sense of humor, was asked to head up the Vatican press office (a post he relinquished only in mid-2006, following the election of Pope Benedict XVI). He was thus to become the chief object of attention for all those other journalists – foreign and Italian – who were *vaticanisti*, that is, journalists based in Rome specifically to cover the Vatican. They had desks and phones at the Vatican Press Office in Via della Conciliazione, the wide avenue that leads directly to St. Peter's and its massive dome, the one designed over 500 years ago by Michelangelo.

Journalists may have many defects, but as a group they are notably quick-witted and amusing even when they are covering difficult and depressing events. As foreign reporters for American and British publications, we all tended to cover the same stories – elections, government crises, papal deaths and papal coronations, Mafia trials and terrorist assassinations – therefore spending a considerable amount of time together. Reporters who work together on the same story, particularly on foreign soil, develop a strong sense of complicity and what might at times appear to be questionable forms of cooperation.

For example, sometimes after a press conference or a court session in Italian we would huddle together to agree on the best translation, or even the best quote. One episode demonstrated the difficulties for women in working with male colleagues. After a press conference by a U.S. ambassador to the Vatican, a group of us were trying to remember the diplomat's exact words. I was covering the conference for radio and explained, to no avail, that I had recorded the ambassador's speech. "Sari has it on tape," a woman colleague also kept saying to all and sundry, without ever getting any reaction. Then up walked Phil Pullella, then of *UPI*, a man, saying "I've got it on tape," and all the guys rushed off with him as if my friend and I had never even opened our mouths.

But there were also a lot of laughs, generally over long, winy lunches or dinners. Here, too, there was a difference between staffers and stringers. The former, who had generous expense accounts, would be wont to go off to lunch at places like Nino's, a somewhat snobby Tuscan restaurant near Piazza di Spagna or to the Bolognese at Piazza del Popolo.

For obvious reasons, we freelancers preferred somewhat cheaper places, and for a time those of us who were based at *Reuters* in Via della Dataria would congregate at lunch time at a nearby *trattoria* called La Sciarra. That came to an end when one of our number, Chris Winner, who was then writing for the *Daily American*, a local English-language rag, and whose usual lunch consisted of a large plate of *spaghetti alla carbonara*, was made *persona non grata*. Why? The *padrone* said he was using unheard of amounts of *parmigiano* cheese and told him he was no longer welcome.

Chapter 4 – Lost (In a Roman Love)

It is evening and I am with a group of people walking towards a restaurant not far from the Pantheon. The balmy early summer air is filled with the clink of glasses and the chatter of Romans sipping their *aperitivi* in the shadow of this magnificent and ancient temple, the pediment of which still bears its original inscription: "Marcus Agrippa, son of Lucius, consul for the third time, built this". Agrippa was the right-hand man of Octavius (later to be the Emperor Augustus); in 31 BC he led the latter's forces to victory at Actium in Greece, defeating Mark Antony and Cleopatra. First built in 27 BC in the form of a rectangle, the "current" in-the-round version was erected about 100 years later by the Emperor Hadrian, and we can probably thank the Roman Catholic Church, which for centuries used it as a church, for its survival.

It's hard not to be distracted by this imposing edifice each time one crosses the busy Piazza della Rotonda, but as we walk along I do notice that there is one fellow whom I don't know trailing along at the end of our group. "*Sei dei nostri?*" ("Are you part of our group?") I ask, casually. He looks at me, dark curly hair falling over his forehead, soft lips smiling, says "*Sì,*" and right then and there I fall in love.

I was 30, above average attractive, and sexually eager, but I had always prided myself on the fact that unlike many of my women friends, I had never gone to bed with someone I had just met. No "zipless fucks" for me, I thought later when I read Erica Jong's *Fear of Flying*. But in Luca's case my former resolve had fallen by the wayside. After the long, noisy dinner in a *trattoria* known for its vast selection of *antipasti*, I asked him if he wanted to come home with me and in the end he spent the night.

Surprisingly, since it was the first time, the sex was fairly good. And he was sweet and affectionate. But even if he hadn't been, I still would have been smitten. Luca, then 33 and a programmer at *RAI*, the Italian public television broadcaster, had looks I just couldn't resist. He was the right height (5'10"), slim with pale skin, hazel eyes and tousled dark hair, adding up to a look that brought the word "Byronesque" to mind, a mental tag that seemed even more appropriate when I learned he had some (misplaced, I later discovered) artistic ambitions. At the same time, there was something about him – the nice clothes, the terraced apartment bought for him, an only child, by his doting parents, the green sports car – that reminded me of all those fraternity boys who had never looked at me twice. And if all this was not enough, after not too long Luca and I discovered that we had some mutually compatible sexual fantasies, something that had never happened with any of the other men I'd known. To put it bluntly, I was, as they say here, *veramente cotta*, truly "cooked".

And was to remain so for much longer than I should have. For if that night in the *trattoria* Luca was on his own – his willingness to stay overnight telling me he wasn't married or living with someone – alas, things in Italy are often not what they appear. After a few weeks of hot and heavy dating during which I was feeling oh, so *innamorata,* Luca announced at lunch at a *trattoria* overlooking the lower part of the muddy Tiber (the Romans use the phrase, *il Tevere biondo*, the blond Tiber, which is a nicer way of saying muddy), that he and his estranged wife, Daniela, with whom he had a small daughter, had decided to reconcile; that is, they had decided to start "seeing" one another again. My heart plummeted when I heard those words but I tried to appear nonchalant. And then I did one of the stupider things I have done in my life. "Well, what does that mean for us?" I asked, it never entering my mind until years and years later that I might have simply wished him well and told him to come back if things didn't work out with his "ex". The fact is, that I was so hooked, maybe sexually more than anything else, that I couldn't bear the idea of not seeing him any more. And he, being a true son of a country in which ambiguity and ambivalence are the principal breakfast foods, said: "*Nulla*" – nothing. "If you're willing," he continued, "we can keep on seeing each other. I just have to be careful." So there, once again, I'd gone and gotten myself into one of those famous situations in which I would be the *other woman* rather than the official one.

Only a few weeks earlier, having finished my fellowship year and my apprenticeship at the *New York Times*, I had started working for *Visnews*, the now largely defunct British TV news service then owned jointly by *Reuters* and the *BBC*. My job was to coordinate the coverage filmed by Visnews's two cameramen, Pino and Enzo, and get the films shipped to London. I had inherited this job from my friend Janet who had been hired away as office manager for *Newsweek*, and, since I worked just down the hall, I was quite familiar with the *Visnews* "office", although the latter was really little more than a desk and a phone situated in the anteroom of the *Reuters* office. The job fit in with the other part-time jobs I had; it brought in a small but steady basic salary and had rather flexible hours.

But there were deadlines to be met and shipments to be made and I have to admit that several times, because of my infatuation with Luca, I did not do my job in a 100-percent responsible fashion. This was not at all like me, a kid who had practically never been in trouble, who had done her homework religiously, studied for exams regularly, had always gotten good grades and who had then put herself through several years of graduate school. But love, for that's what I thought it was, can make you crazy. And I was crazy. So crazy that I more or less would drop anything, including work, if Luca would call and say he was free. So crazy that I didn't realize just how boring I'd become, regaling my friends constantly with talk about Luca. And crazy enough not even to blink the night he told me, at midnight, that I'd have to get dressed and go home because Daniela, who'd been out of town, had called and said she was coming over.

There was one thing, however, that I really didn't like about Luca; he was what in Italy one would call *un raccomandato*, someone who had gotten his or her job through connections rather than through merit. A *raccomandazione* Italian-style has little in common with a recommendation back in the United States. To get into grad school or to get a job it is normal in the United States to ask for letters of recommendation from people who know you and think highly of you because you've studied or worked with them. In Italy, instead, it is a kind of cronyism which unfortunately is the rule rather than the exception, especially whenever the public sector is involved. So-and-so gets a job, even one that requires special talent, like a violinist with a major orchestra (which gets state subsidies), not because he is the best, but because his father is owed a favor by a politician who sits on the orchestra's board; in some universities, particularly in the Italian South, relatives make a point of hiring relatives who hire even more relatives. A repertory theater (funded by a city government) may choose an assistant director not because he was the top in his graduating class in drama school but because his mother is the daughter of a bishop's brother. A recent economics graduate whose uncle is a politician beats out another candidate with higher grades for a job in a branch of a major bank, the president of which belongs to the same party.

Cilio and Rosanna Rossetti brought up four children on the proceeds of a small but popular grocery store on the main street of Sabaudia, a town built by Mussolini on reclaimed swampland running between the Mediterranean and the Apennine mountains, and which has now become a very desirable beach resort. After years of doing my summer shopping here – they sell wonderful, crusty *pane di Lariano* and the most succulent *mozzarella di bufala* in the area – I came to know them well. The eldest child, Ruggero, now married with two children, was earmarked from the start to take over the grocery, which, it was thought, would bring in enough income to support only one family. The Rossettis' youngest, daughter Rachele, decided early on to become an architect and graduated from the University of Rome (although she has yet to find a full-time job).

But the other two children, Romano and Ada, like many Italian young people, have found life difficult. Both decided to become bookkeepers, *ragionieri*, hoping that a high-school diploma in that field would be the best way to get a job. But such was not the case. Ada, the second born, found a job in nearby Latina working for a local accountant who refused, however, even after she'd been there for years, to put her on the books as a regular hire; she has momentarily "solved" her problem by marrying a young *carabiniere*, moving to Rome and having a baby. Romano, the other *maschio* (male) of the family, has taken every entrance exam for local banks or governments that has been held in the last ten years, has always passed, but has never been high enough up on the *graduatoria*, the ranking list, to get a job. "I have no one to give me that extra *spinta*," he says – the extra push. He is still working in the store.

Stories like this are a dime a dozen, with the result that Italy is filled with thousands of discouraged and embittered youngsters whose lives are spent working at fallback jobs rather than following through on their career of choice. And indeed, it is this kind of frustration that has led so many young people to become politically disaffected, causing them years later, in February 2013, to vote en masse for the rambunctious gadfly comedian, Beppe Grillo, who, as I re-edit this chapter, has done much to cause a total breakdown in government here.

True, in recent years, the job market has become more flexible so that companies are now allowed to hire people on short-term contracts that at least allow the newly employed to put some money in their pockets. But even if there weren't a recession, there would be considerable dissatisfaction, given that most young people's dream remains that of the *contratto a tempo indeterminato* – the contract for an indefinite period, basically a lifetime job – which, because of Italy's high social charges, Italian companies are increasingly reluctant to offer. Today in Italy, as in other economically troubled European countries – in particular Greece and Spain – more than 35% of young people are unemployed while others are in what are seen as precarious jobs, jobs that can be terminated at any time. The unemployed and the "*precari*" haven't fared any better following the austerity package introduced in 2012 and are now pinning their hopes, assuming they still have any, on the new government headed by 39-year old Matteo Renzi. On the other hand,, it is rather discouraging to note than many immigrants have managed to find jobs, but those are in fields – restaurants, domestic employment, agriculture – that most Italians now refuse to do.

A few years ago, a Harris poll in the United States showed that 92% of 20-plus-year-olds hoped to go through life with a flexible work schedule; 96% wanted their jobs to involve some amount of creativity, and an even higher number dreamed that the work they do will allow them "to have an impact on the world". Such wishes may prove impossible to satisfy but are indicative of the way young Americans envisage work: they want to leave ample room for self-expression, change and multi-tasking. In Italy, instead, the dream remains that of the proverbial *posto fisso,* the full-time, permanent position from which, thanks to highly protective labor laws, you can probably never be fired unless you do something really drastic like embezzle money or knife your boss. (In the public sector, not even recidivist absenteeism appears to qualify as a cause for getting fired, as several stories that recently appeared in the press would indicate.)

Wanting a steady, full-time job may sound normal, but the fixation with lifetime security has meant, among other things, that creativity gets pushed into second place. Giancarlo, a talented carpenter, closed his workshop to become a maintenance man for a government agency (a job he got through a powerful client). Fausto, a highly skilled apprentice upholsterer, gave it all up for a job at the Vatican. The fixation with lifetime jobs means many young people fail to develop much get-up-and-go. Their lives revolve around the search for what has now become a chimera, a type of job that has less and less relevance to the flexibility of a services-oriented economy. Even worse, this kind of permanent job, when paired with the country's overly protective labor laws, has tended to breed rampant absenteeism or on-the-job sluggishness. Not long ago *Corriere della Sera*, the country's major daily, began following the story of Signor M., a high school teacher who for years had been absent from work some 70% of the time but because of union support was fired only after years of court cases. What kind of an example does a system characterized by extreme laxity set for new-entry jobholders?

In some ways, however, Italy's Generation Y has been wising up. For years, thousands and thousands of applicants would crowd exam halls for this or that entrance exam, called a *concorso,* in the hopes of getting such a permanent job. More recently, they've been staying home. According to the prestigious Rome research organization, Censis, only 8.2% of Italians now think there is any point in taking this kind of test if you don't have what the Italians would call *un santo in paradiso* – a saint in paradise – or what Americans might call a "rabbi". Over the decades, Italians have come to accept this wink-and-nudge hiring system. Surveys have shown that six out of ten young people in Italy get their first jobs through family and friends and that 65% of Italian parents think it is up to them to find a job for their offspring.

The country's major business paper, *Il Sole 24 Ore,* until December, 2007, my employer, not long ago conducted a poll which came up with similar results. Seven out of ten people queried (the sample included 1,000 Italians between the ages of 18 and 79) said they were all too well aware that *raccomandazioni* were widely used in both the public and private sector. Some 63% recognized that such a system often led to the hiring of people not necessarily suited for the job. Almost the same number insisted that *raccomandazioni* were useful and often indispensable for getting a job. And only 51%, including a high number of the younger people polled, said that *raccomandazioni* were wrong and immoral. And a couple of years ago, an Italian news weekly published a computer file leaked by someone at the Italian Post Office. It contained a list of thousands of names of the employees who had been *raccomandate* by politicians, trade unionists, high-ranking civil servants and even a smattering of cardinals.

In Luca's case, things were similar, albeit at a "higher" level. He graduated in Lettere (literature) from a second-string university and must have had a fairly easy time of it since something he once said led me to believe that he – or perhaps his parents – had paid for someone else to write his thesis. As for most young Italians, the main thing on Luca's mind when he started job-hunting was to get a *posto fisso*. Since he was interested in the arts, he thought the best place for him was *RAI*, the Italian state broadcaster, which, since its five-member board is chosen by a special parliamentary commission largely on the basis of their political affiliations, has always been run more like a government ministry than a profit- or efficiency-oriented network. Luca's father, a businessman, had excellent contacts in the then-ruling Christian Democrat party but also had several good personal friends who were high-level Socialists. The result was that after Luca took the *RAI concorso*, he was able to leapfrog hundreds of others to find himself behind a much-desired desk at *RAI* headquarters, the hulking, glass-walled modern building in the residential Prati section fronted by a massive sculpture of a rearing horse named *Cavallo morente*, the dying horse. (Given the network's ongoing financial and political problems, the sculptor, Sicilian Francesco Messina, may have been prescient.)

When Luca got his job, the state-run *RAI* had a monopoly on television and radio broadcasting in Italy, and it is not surprising that the country's political parties saw "Viale Mazzini", as insiders refer to *RAI* because of its street address, as a source of political influence and an instrument of useful political patronage. And since along with radio and TV news broadcasts, some good documentaries and a never-ending series of appalling but popular quiz and variety shows, *RAI* was also a major film co-producer, it had become a sort of Mecca for hundreds of young, middle-class, left-leaning, *soi-disant* Italian intellectuals infatuated with the idea of becoming film makers, movie critics or TV documentary makers. For young men like Luca it was the place to be, even if many of those who did get in just ended up sitting around doing very little.

(Nowadays, thanks to the deregulation which was introduced in the late 1980s, *RAI* is no longer alone but shares the airwaves with the three channels belonging to Silvio Berlusconi's *Mediaset* network, a fourth channel, *La 7*, until just recently owned by Telecom, the former state telephone monopoly, and dozens and dozens of local stations. In addition, Rupert Murdoch arrived on the Italian scene about ten years ago and gave Italy its impressive *Sky* Italian TV satellite channel.)

But back then, *RAI* was the place to be. Luca had been hired as a *programmista*, someone whose job was supposed to involve working on parts of the weekly scheduling, but he spent most of his time writing essays he sought to publish in literary magazines, plays he thought some experimental theater group might be willing to put on stage, or organizing small, avant-garde poetry festivals. I found his career path somewhat disturbing, but when a woman is in love, she can glorify any man's existence. So, determined to hold on to my infatuation, I pushed all this to the back of my mind, at least for the time being.

Gradually, however, I became well aware that even if he should break up with Daniela, Luca was not the man I wanted for a long-time partner. But no doubt out of pride I wanted to be the one to make the decision. Ironically, this was not to be possible because when, finally, the marriage finally did fall apart, an Italian girlfriend of mine, Maria, seduced Luca and, as they say, took him away from me. No doubt, this was partially my fault since I'd been singing his praises to her for years. Needless to say, that was the end of the friendship with Maria as well my relationship with Luca. My only consolation was that after a year or so, their *storia,* as a love relationship is called here, also disintegrated. Maria had been bisexual for years, and Luca, who had always himself demonstrated a degree of sexual ambiguity, gradually became a full-fledged, practicing gay.

Chapter 5 – Amerigo (Part One)

Amerigo – the accent is on the "i" – is sponging the counter-top, and he is doing it very, very slowly. On the other hand, Amerigo, the owner of the "bar" that after only a few months in my new apartment I have chosen as my morning coffee hangout, does everything very, very slowly, and we customers often tease him for being the slowest barman in town. A pleasant-looking man of average height with dark hair, an unlined forehead and a regular hairline that encourages him to keep his hair cut neatly short, Amerigo does not like to rush. But despite occasional but vociferous complaints from customers wondering when their coffees are arriving and expostulating that they are in a hurry – "*Ma quand'è che arriva questo caffè? Dai, Amerigo, ho fretta.*"("Where's my coffee? Come on, Amerigo, I am in a hurry!") – no one seems to mind all that much.

Back then, fast food had yet to come to Italy, and by the time it does begin to make significant inroads, Amerigo will have retired and turned the café over to Alessandro, his nephew. At that point, Alessandro, a university graduate who has lived in London and traveled extensively, will spruce up the place, install a computer for would-be net surfers, install a big screen for music videos and soccer games, diversify the menu and introduce a variety of imaginative salads and Brazilian cocktails. But he will prove smart enough to know that to maintain his daytime trade (in the evenings the clientele is different), the bar must never lose its neighborhood character.

In the meantime, however, there is absolutely no risk of that. Remember the theme song from *Cheers!* as in "sometimes you want to go where everyone knows your nay-yay-yame...."? I often think of it when I walk the 80 yards to the bar every morning to have my two consecutive *espressos*. In fact, the days when Amerigo or any of his employees or successors would address me as "*Signorina*" are long gone. Whether the person on duty is Amerigo, Alessandro, Domenico, Giancarlo, Bruno, Alex, Michele, Sandro, Romina, Ana or Anna, depending on the shift and the year, I am just plain old Shari (Sari is pronounced thusly), or better yet Sha', since one characteristic of Roman dialect is to hack off the last syllable of almost every word. My particular *espresso* habits – extra water, no sugar or sweetener, a bit of cold milk but, remember, she wants to pour it in herself – are so well-known I don't even have to speak when I walk in the door. And so it is for all the other regulars. Furthermore, since this is our home away from home, rather than the formal "*Lei*", we mostly use the "*tu*", the familiar form of address. Of course, this is Trastevere where informality reigns. For although today's Italians may be more inclined to move on to the "*tu*" more readily than, say, their French neighbors, the older generations of Italians in more "bourgeois" neighborhoods, would still consider it inappropriate for the barman-customer relationship.

This type of linguistic distinction disappeared from modern English long ago. As an American used to the extreme casualness of our own language (Mr. Smith immediately becomes John or Robert, and even your gynecologist is likely to start using your first name when you're lying, legs spread open, on the table), my inclination when I arrived in Italy was to use the "*tu*" with almost everyone, be it Orlando, the garage attendant, Giacomo the plumber, Rita at the dry cleaner's, or Nello, the concierge at my office building. However, as I quickly came to see, the indiscriminate use of the "*tu*" does have its drawbacks. In particular, an incautious use of the "*tu*" with an Italian man, particularly of a "different" social standing, can send the wrong signals, signals that you may regret as I did when the cook from the restaurant downstairs mistook my friendliness for something else and took to ringing my doorbell at two a.m. and begging me to let him come upstairs. At the very least, it can remove what can be a very useful distance between you and someone who is working for you. This was a lesson that it took me some time, and some embarrassing situations, to learn. But none of this applied at Amerigo's where all social or educational distinctions seemed to disappear, just like those at *Cheers!* between Lilith the psychiatrist and mailman Bert.

When I first started going there, Amerigo's small bar (in Italy *un bar* is a café which also serves alcoholic beverages) was little more than a counter and a few scattered tables. And although Alessandro insists the place does have a name (supposedly, it is called *Il Bar del Parente,* the Relative's Bar) the sign outside simply reads "BAR" in capital letters. Situated at the intersection between the cobble-stoned Vicolo del Cinque and the even narrower Vicolo del Bologna, and roughly only a minute's walk from my then apartment, it served only the basics – *espresso, cappuccino, caffelatte,* the usual *aperitivi* and *digestivi,* beer, juice and liquor and, like Umberto's, milk from the *Centrale del Latte*, the municipal milk company. In the morning there were *cornetti* and other sweet rolls, and at lunch time an assortment, albeit limited, of *panini* (sandwiches on rolls), *piadine* or *pizzette* (sandwiches on flat bread or pizza which, ideally, should be toasted) or *tramezzini*, those triangular half sandwiches on white bread you see all over Italy.

And in the seventies, when most people in Italy are still going home for lunch, this is what suits. Amerigo's customers – for the most part people from the neighborhood – come here day after day for "breakfast", generally a *cappuccino* and a *cornetto*, and also seem to consider repeat visits, for an *espresso*, a *spremuta d'arancio*, an *aperitivo*, an essential part of their daily routine. And what we all find extremely gratifying, although no one talks about it, each of us preferring to believe ourselves to be someone special, is that Amerigo, like the best of Italian barmen, seems to have an unlimited capacity to remember what his customers generally order. "The usual *cappuccino* with extra foam and a sprinkling of cocoa?" he once asked a friend of mine, another New Yorker, who unexpectedly reappeared after a two-year absence from Rome. She was moved to tears.

This kind of customer attention is more or less par for the course in a place like Rome, where one's neighborhood bar or café has an importance that neither the Automat (remember those?) nor Starbucks could ever acquire. But some barmen have made it into a fine art. Amerigo was a master, but what about Giancarlo, the barman Amerigo will eventually hire and who will remain for another 25 years until finally retiring, with his two dogs, to his apartment in an outlying area? As far as I'm concerned, Giancarlo won the barman's Oscar when he demonstrated the ability to prepare my *caffè Hag* (for a while I drank only decaf espresso) before I even got there. Looking out the window, he would see me coming from about a half a block away and would *mettere il caffè in macchina* so that it would be steaming on the counter in its small demitasse cup when I walked in the door. The only problem was that occasionally I would get distracted and decide to go first to the *fruttivendolo* (the fruit and vegetable store) or the grocery. *Mamma mia*, would I catch it when I finally made my appearance! But despite his sharp tongue, Giancarlo does not hold grudges and after a stagy glare or two he would smile and make me a fresh cup.

When I first moved into the neighborhood, Amerigo was on duty in the mornings while in the afternoons the counter was manned by

Domenico, better known as *Il Lepre*, the hare, for his past as a sprinter, and whose quick service was always compared, admiringly, to Amerigo's dawdling. When the "hare" is tending bar, the cash register or *cassa* is handled by Natalina, Amerigo's mother, a stern-looking, older woman with gray hair in a bun, who chats with the local ladies and keeps track of anyone who's had his or her previous breakfast or *aperitivo* on credit. She's also there to keep an eye on Domenico, not because he's dishonest – heaven forbid! – but on principle, because you never know. Other employees, left on their own, have been known to help themselves to some of the *lire* in the till.

I chose this bar over Umberto's as my morning coffee haunt in part because of Amerigo himself, and in part because of his clientele, which has always been a beguiling mixture of the old Trastevere and the new. On an average day, I would find myself sipping my *espresso* (Italians tend to gulp theirs. I can't help it, I sip mine) next to Benito the mailman (now retired) or Teresa (now dead) who ran the tiny fruit and vegetable store in my piazza where she kept on view a large photo of her deceased *mamma* even though this woman, with her evident moustache, must have been one of the ugliest women in the world. Olga, the butcher's wife, sometimes pops in, as does Lina, who works at the bread counter in the grocery shop across the street. Within walking distance – I am pleased to discover – there are four grocery stores, two butchers, two bakers, three greengrocers and no supermarkets at all. (Who knew then how radically this would change? (Today, instead, there is one all-purpose grocery, no fruit store and no butcher. You have to walk several blocks to the outdoor market in Piazza San Cosimato and a tiny bit farther for one of several *supermercati*.)

Other habitués of the bar include various officials of the Comunità of Sant'Egidio, a grassroots Roman Catholic organization that has its headquarters in my piazza. Among them, too, are Mario, who runs a small (one truck) transportation service and Nino (now dead), owner of *Cencio La Parolaccia*, the restaurant a few doors away that caters to locals and tourists who (inexplicably, to my mind) enjoy the bawdy songs, jokes and insults spewed out by its waiters while serving *rigatoni all'amatriciana* and *coda alla vaccinara*. Teresa, from the fruit store, is Nino's sister-in-law, and therefore her sons, Sergio and Attilio, are cousins of Ettore, Nino's son. Attilio is earmarked to take over the *frutteria* when Teresa dies and Ettore and his sister Simonetta, will inherit the restaurant. In the meantime, Ettore has become a hairdresser and together with his heavy-set, bleached-blonde wife, Paola, will turn the barbershop next to the restaurant into a tiny, downscale but perfectly adequate unisex *parrucchiere,* or hairdresser, where for the equivalent of about $15 (recently raised to $17) I can get my hair done and pick up all the local gossip.

Another regular "customer" of the bar is Nicolina, (also now deceased), the small, wizened old woman I espied the day I arrived, walking her Siamese cat on a leash. Having been forced to give up her apartment in nearby Vicolo della Frusta, Nicolina is living in a *"basso"*, a small, ground-floor room across the street from Amerigo's which by day she turns into a sort of store, selling contraband cigarettes and odds and ends people give her. It is rumored that some of these things are stolen property, which would make her a sort of a local, low-level fence. And some say she also lends money, although where she would get it is anybody's guess since her old-age pension is no more than the equivalent of $400 a month. She sometimes runs errands for the bars and restaurants in the neighborhood or finds parking spaces for their owners and in return they give her coffee and *cornetti* on demand and at least one square meal a day. Nicolina, who is a widow, always wears an apron and has her steel-gray hair pulled back in a tight bun. Since her only son has died, she lives with her nephew, Roberto, a loafer who has never worked a day in his life, says Alessandro. But blood is blood and Nicolina has already told Amerigo and Alessandro that when she dies, she expects him to keep giving Roberto his morning coffee, free, and they say they will do so.

Nicolina's other "nephew", Giancarlo (years later I will discover they are not actually related), is a highly talented upholsterer, although you'd never guess this if you walked in, cold, to his small, overcrowded *laboratorio* around the corner from the bar on Vicolo del Bologna. Here, old chair frames left who knows how many years ago by former clients, hang on the walls, vying for space with piles of foam rubber and bags of goose feathers as well as stacks of textile sample books which are constantly getting misplaced. After an unhappy, failed marriage, Giancarlo met Stella, a blond seamstress in similar post-matrimonial straits, who was working for one of his rivals. They fell madly in love, married, set up shop together and at one point decided that from then on they would dress identically. "What do you notice about these two?" I once asked Daryl, my Filipino godson when we were all at the bar one morning. I was sipping yet another *espresso*. Daryl, who was seven, drank his *latte tiepido* (warm milk) with cocoa sprinkled on the top, and watched the happy couple drinking identical fresh-squeezed orange-juices. "They've got the same clothes!" he shouted laughing, after a couple of minutes of observation. And then, in a giggly whisper to Giancarlo, "Are your *mutande* (underpants) the same, too?"

Another person who often came into the bar was Maria, a dark-haired, half-Roman, half Neapolitan woman with a slight moustache and a pronounced limp who cleans for me and frequently makes me furious; at least a couple of times a month, she fails to show up without letting me know. Once, when I had invited a visiting foreign correspondent for dinner, I was mortified to come home to find the kitchen filthy and the bed unmade. Maria, who will work for me for 12 years, is one of a veritable army of unskilled Italian women able to eke out a living by cleaning houses for middle- and upper-class *signore* who, it must be said, are so fanatical about having their homes cleaned that they think everyone else – the French, the British, the Americans – are dirty.

Although many Italians think nothing of littering or of allowing their dogs to leave their droppings anywhere they please, they are horrified by the home cleaning habits of others: they find wall-to-wall carpeting disgusting because it can't be lifted and cleaned underneath on a regular basis, and they are also horrified by the absence of bidets in other people's bathrooms, apparently unaware that Italy is one of the few countries in the world in which bidets are a normal part of every bathroom, not just those in upscale hotels or luxury villas. This is an obsession that a Freudian might trace to some kind of unhealthy fascination with defecation or to that part of the body that is related to that function. For although many non-Italians think the primary function of the bidet is related to sex, this is not the case. It is a question of post-bowel movement hygiene.

Today, the major beneficiaries of this obsession with daily housekeeping are the tens of thousands of foreign immigrants who now make Italy their home. One Spanish woman I know – and the Spaniards are reportedly more or less as high up on the housecleaning scale as the Italians – says it's because there is more dust in Mediterranean countries, by which I think she meant that there is more light and thus more dust is visible. That may or may not be logical, but the fact remains that Italian women, or their hired proxies, apparently clean much more than almost anyone else. According to a study by Proctor and Gamble, which – like other multinationals – has had to adapt cleaning products to the mania of Italy's women, the latter spend on average 21 hours a week on household chores other than cooking – compared with just four hours for Americans. The study showed Italians wash their kitchen and bathroom floors at least four times a week, compared to once a week for Americans. They iron nearly all their wash, even socks and sheets. And they buy more cleaning supplies than women elsewhere do.

When I first meet Maria she is living in a tiny, ground-floor apartment down the block, where she shares a creaky double bed with her illegitimate adolescent son, Franco, who suffers from a mild form of epilepsy. The apartment is dark and dank and her attempts to spruce it up haven't helped much. Not surprisingly, then, when she finally gets to the top of a list of people eligible for subsidized, low-income public housing, she jumps at it, even though it means leaving the neighborhood and, in particular, her best friend Gianna, a miniscule woman with a ponytail known as *la gattara*, the cat lady, because her life, despite her own evident poverty, is dedicated to feeding the neighborhood's then numerous stray cats. (Nowadays, stray cats are a relative rarity thanks to the free sterilization offered by many vets and government veterinary offices.)

In fact, the ties forged in the neighborhood are so strong that years later when Maria dies, Franco will not be able to stay away. Dubbed *Marruzzella* by the neighborhood after a well-known Neapolitan song, he can be found most days either at the bar, where he sweeps up, clears tables or runs errands, or – before it was replaced by a restaurant – at Attilio's *frutteria* where he makes deliveries in return for small sums of money that supplement his disability pension. Franco does disappear for a couple of months starting every August when he visits Maria's relatives in the Naples area. But he makes sure to return to Rome each year at the end of October so he can visit his mother's grave on November 2, *il giorno dei morti*, the day of the dead.

The few times I have asked him for a favor, he rushes to help. "I'd do anything for you, Sha'," he insists, "because after all you knew Maria." Recently, he offered me a picture of her which, of course, I took but tucked away somewhere out of sight. Although he sleeps elsewhere, he tells me he has kept his mother's apartment intact. "I can't bear to throw out anything that belonged to Maria," he says. Furthermore, he seems determined to look as much like her as possible even though it makes him look quite peculiar. He has let his hair, still mostly black but now graying, grow very long and wears it in a ponytail as she did. "I know why you don't want to cut your hair," I said to him not long ago in a burst of intuition. "*Zitta, Sha'*," he replied. "*Non ne voglio parlare.*" "Hush, Sha'. I don't want to talk about it."

Part Two

Settling In

*S*ince I have already spent so much time in Italy as a student, I
know a lot more about Italian habits and customs than most
foreigners who for one reason or another decide to settle here.
But that doesn't mean there aren't things to learn and things to get
used to, things as basic as shopping, cooking and preparing food,
relationships with the opposite sex and, perhaps all-importantly, the
best ways to maneuver through and around the obligations of Italian
bureaucracy: this was, something I'd been substantially sheltered
from as a student, living more or less outside the realm of permanent
residency. I am also now working as a full-time journalist and thus
find myself increasingly busy following current events and ever more
involved in political developments and, on a personal level, with
politicians and other public figures. It is the seventies and Italy is an
economically thriving European nation but one which seems unable
to find any kind of a political balance in its daily life. I have already
discovered that the Cold War is still being re-enacted daily on
Italian soil, with Christian Democrats and Communists regularly
locking horns. Popes are dying and new ones are being elected. And
terrorism has reared its ugly head, reaching a high point, or rather a
low point, with the bloody kidnapping and murder of Aldo Moro, a
former prime minister and top Christian Democratic leader, an
event that leaves people stunned and increasingly uncertain about the
future.

Chapter 6 – The Bureaucratic Tangle

"**A**nd don't forget your screwdriver!" Janet's words echoed in my ears and, pausing on the doorstep, I ran back into the apartment for a set of *cacciavite* and shoved them into my shoulder bag. I was about to embark on the yearly pilgrimage to renew my EE license plates, the *escursionisti esteri* tags the Italian motor vehicle bureau gives to people who bring a car into the country temporarily and then, when they leave, re-export it. The Italian foreign ministry extended this courtesy to foreign journalists living in Italy as well, even if they bought their car right here in Italy as I did, in my case a metallic dark gray Fiat Uno. I wasn't planning to ever re-export my car, but at the time I saw the EE plates as a way to steer clear of the oppressive bureaucracy that then characterized all walks of Italian life and even now can cause you to waste huge amounts of time on senseless requirements. Driving with the EE plates also allowed you to be a bit "different" and, I must admit, to get away with some minor traffic violations, such as driving in special bus and taxi lanes.

It also meant that I could drive a car without having to register as a resident at the Rome *Anagrafe*, the City Registry office, one of the few rules that it otherwise seems impossible to get around unless you want to live in partial hiding. Since my arrival here in 1972, I myself have never been without a *permesso di soggiorno*, the "residence permit" foreigners need to live here legally. But out of instinct I had balked at going to the Registry Office located just down the street from the hulking, gray ruins of the Teatro di Marcello, the massive (15,000 spectators!) ancient Roman theater built by the Emperor Augustus in 11 B.C. as the *Theatrum Marcelli* in honor of his nephew Marcus Marcellus, who interestingly enough was also his son-in-law! Why bother getting a *residenza*, I asked myself, justifying this legal lapse with the fact that I already had a sojourn permit. The last thing I wanted was to make myself subject to God-knows-what-other time-consuming obligations. With the EE plates, I could drive with my American drivers license and thus didn't need to go to an expensive driving school and get an Italian driving license. And indeed, this was something which I managed to put off until 1991 when, after being hired by an Italian newspaper, I had no choice but to become a bonafide *residente*.

Naturally, this being Italy, having the EE plates didn't mean that life as a driver was without red tape. Quite the contrary. In the first place, unlike the regular Italian tags, these plates were valid for only one year and, even worse, had their expiration date, month and year printed right on them. This meant that if, as once happened to Janet, you ran into one of the few authentically vigilant *vigili,* or traffic cops, in this all-too-laid-back city, he could stop you and confiscate your car until you paid your fine. Also, the procedures for renewal were hardly simple. But luckily for me, Janet's plates always expired a couple of months before mine, so I could always phone her and ask for a reminder as to which documents were needed and in what order one needed to do things.

Janet, blonde and blue-eyed, had come to Rome in the late 1960s as an *au pair,* something British girls from good families – often dissuaded from following their brothers to Oxford or Cambridge – were once encouraged to do. Far too smart to remain in such a menial position, she soon landed a research job with an eccentric American newsman, and gradually worked her way up to becoming office manager, first for the local *Newsweek* bureau and then for the *L.A. Times.* Among more noble pursuits, this job required nursemaiding a series of American correspondents, resolving their bureaucratic problems and helping them unravel the red tape of daily Italian life. This made her an ideal advisor for a more scatterbrained me. "*Ufficio informazioni?*" I'd query in an attempt at a Roman accent when I phoned her at her office to ask her something: "Information Office?" "*Spiacente, siamo chiusi* – Sorry, we're closed," she'd reply, launching into a near-perfect imitation of a disgruntled Roman civil servant at one of those myriad government offices that closed at unreasonably early hours, generally after being open to the public for only an hour or two.

Each year she would patiently re-explain to me the drill for renewing the EE plates. First came the annual trip to the working class/student neighborhood of San Lorenzo on the northeast of the *centro storico,* the historic center, where one would find the old *Dogana,* or Customs House, a sprawling building with peeling, sickly-green or yellow walls inside, sagging metal shelving and speckled concrete floors. It was important to telephone first to check on the office hours, which were always changing, before making the trip across town, knowing in any event that at least two hours would be needed to get your "*protocollo*", or authorization. You had to go armed with the papers for your car, a letter from the Foreign Ministry confirming your accreditation as a foreign journalist, and a statement from the U.S. Consulate saying I can't remember what, but one which they never wanted to give you and, indeed, eventually stopped handing out.

Once you got over that hurdle, the next step was to make an appointment with Signora Carla Palombaro (not her real name) at the EE office at the new branch of the motor vehicle bureau, clear on the other side of Rome between the Via Laurentina and the Grande Raccordo Anulare or GRA, the great, connecting ring-road that circles this sprawling city. Signora Palombaro was very accommodating and perhaps inadvertently would encourage the feeling that the EE plates (or was it the journalists' accreditation?) made you somewhat special. She always suggested that to save time you might prefer to come after regular hours, which ended at about noon, or on Tuesdays or Thursdays when the office was not open to the public at all.

The big problem was that to get the plates, you had to go first to the post office and make three separate payments, and since the new post office branch planned for the *Motorizzazione,* the motor vehicle bureau, was not yet operative, after filling out the forms you would have to drive back into town. The solution was to get Signora Palombaro to send you the pre-printed forms or *bollettini* by mail or, alternatively, to tell you over the phone how each one should be made out, not an easy task in itself since the account numbers – the *conti correnti* – of two or three different government agencies were involved and the three payments consisted of small, odd-number *lira* sums. That way, you could then pay them at the post office of your choice before you made the trek out there, simply bringing her the receipts. But, of course, none of this would do you a bit of good if you didn't hand in your old plates, hence Janet's warning not to forget my screwdriver.

Mrs. Palombaro seemed to feel bad about all this and was almost apologetic when one staggered in with the old plates in one hand and the postal receipts from the *bollettini* clutched in the other. But there was nothing she could do. An employee of the Transport Ministry since the age of 21, at 40-ish she was already the head of the department dealing with the EE plates and the CD plates for members of the *corpo diplomatico*, the diplomatic corps, and was used to dealing with the city's scores of embassies, media bureaus and individual foreigners. Pleasant looking, with her streaked blond hair casually pulled up, she appeared to be the epitome of efficiency and calm detachment. But oh, what dark secrets lurked behind this civil servant's exterior mild appearance! Not long before, she had fallen in love with a colleague and left her husband of six years to set up house, alone, with her two children. In a clear indication of the degree to which many Italians had stopped paying much mind to the precepts of the Roman Catholic Church, a third child was sired out of wedlock by the new love, who was not – however – a live-in companion. This unconventional arrangement was Carla's choice, but it meant that lots of overtime (largely the giving and grading of driving tests) was necessary to keep the small household afloat.

And how did it all end up? As she told me recently, just as she was getting ready for retirement, Gianni, the man for whom she'd sacrificed all, at 65 had fallen in love with a Bulgarian woman 20 years his junior and had gone off to live with her. The presence and the sexual availability of Eastern European women immigrants has been one noticeable consequence of the fall of the area's Communist regimes and recent membership in the European Union. Many of the prostitutes now working in Italy are Eastern European, but just as many are normal women, many of whom seem to have found it even easier to find a man than a job. Italian men like them, several of the latter have told me, because they are more feminine and not "feminists".

Not to overly digress, the *conto corrente* requirement to which Signora Palombaro involuntarily subjected us has been an integral part of the Italian payments system since 1917, when it was introduced to allow people and companies to more easily make and receive payments. But it is enough to drive many foreigners to distraction and getting used to it was not easy. The first thing you learn when you come here to live is that in Italy, as in many other European countries, the post office has always performed banking services along with the traditional postal functions. In the early 20th century, the Italian banking system was rudimentary. So, long before the average Italian had access to a bank, he or she was opening a savings account, called a *libretto di risparmio*, at the *Ufficio Postale*. And since checking accounts did not yet exist, the post office developed the *conto corrente*, literally a "current account", as a relatively simple means of making a money transfer.

In other words, a company, a store, a public utility, a cultural association or a government agency could open an account with the post office that customers or clients would use when they needed to make a payment. In most cases it works like this: your bill from the electric company arrives with a pre-printed *bollettino* and you take it, together with your money, to the payments window at the post office. (Blank forms are also available, unless of course when they've run out, which happens often.) For only a tiny supplementary charge, the post office credits the money to its final destination, the original advantage being that you could pay all your utilities at the same time rather than going separately to the electricity, phone, gas companies and what not. The problem is that even at the approach of the third millennium, the Italian establishment appeared to be unaware that in other countries, common sense or technological advances had been used to invent even more timesaving alternatives, like personal checks and credit cards. And Italian lawmakers and civil servants, rarely inclined to give top priority to the goal of making life easier for the country's citizens, weren't much help.

One huge difference between Italy and other countries like the United States, the United Kingdom and France, is that the use of personal checks has never become truly widespread here. In a country where fraud is commonplace and where organized crime is always looking for ways to launder money, personal checks have always been considered unreliable, and the suspicion that originally attached to them seems to have contaminated primarily the Italian government, its various agencies and public utilities. So although I can now use my checks to pay most repairmen, I – like the holders of the other more than 33 million checking accounts in Italy – cannot pay utility bills, driver's license fees or driving tickets simply by putting a check in the mail. Increasingly, of course, you can now do some of these things on line. But even at the end of 2012, only about 50 percent of Italian families was "connected" to the internet. That said, the banks themselves make it difficult for their clients to use checks by giving out only ten (checks, not checkbooks) at a time, insisting that you come in and pick them up in person, no doubt after more than a little time spent standing in line.

Janet was one up on me when it came to dealing with many aspects of daily Italian life because her "significant other" at the time, Umberto, tended to take care of many of her everyday problems.

Umberto, a Sicilian journalist with a passion for World War I history, was extremely solicitous when it came to anything involving Janet's car, her checking account or her investments, mainly – she suspected – because he probably considered her, a woman, incapable of dealing effectively with such things. "But let him think whatever he wants," she chuckled. "This way I've got more free time for myself."

Her free time, such as it was, was devoted largely to her horse, Enzai, a white Arab gelding she'd bought and boarded at a stable run by an American woman in Campagnano, a village about 35 kilometers north of Rome. In an earlier period, we'd gone riding together at a different stable located on the east side of Rome off the Appia Nuova highway and not far from the ancient Appian Way of Roman times. That place was run by an eccentric ex-military officer named Mario, who would either put us through drills in the ring or take us out on long rides through the surrounding countryside, but with whom it was hard to have a personal conversation. Only once did Mario and I have an intimate talk and, strangely (or perhaps not), he chose to confide in me about his family problems only on the night of our Mardi Gras party when I was dressed as a frog, or rather a frog-prince – you know, the one waiting for the princess who, with a kiss, would release him from an evil spell. Wearing a green velvet doublet, green tights, a green velvet plumed cap and with green makeup on my face, I sat and listened while Mario told me about his unhappy marriage and a daughter's unfortunate marriage to a man who was chronically unemployed.

Janet went as a Dalmatian, the dog, not a resident of the former northeastern Italian province which today is part of Croatia. She wore a full body suit that was white with black spots and had made herself up with whiskers and a big black spot over one eye. We'd gotten dressed in the deserted *Newsweek* office before heading into the Roman night and making the longish drive out of town to the stables. It was teeming with rain, and we couldn't believe it when, despite the awful weather, we were flagged down at a roadblock for one of those random police checks that are a fact of daily life here. The uniformed *carabiniere* who had stopped us and who, after the usual initial salute, asked for the car's registration and her driving license, didn't blink an eye when he saw her costume. "*Dogumenti,*" he said, deadpan, with the thick Southern accent that led him to pronounce the "c" in *documenti* as a "g"; a classic scene that has been repeated countless times in Italian movies or comedy sketches.

But Janet, more burdened than I was by office bills and those of her generally helpless foreign correspondents, was on her own when it came to the post office. And with a *conto corrente* form, or *bollettino*, necessary for everything from charitable donations to newspaper or magazine subscriptions, property taxes, the obligatory state television "subscription fee", and the so-called "*bollo*" or vehicle ownership tax, she spent more time at the post office than most of us. Now, of course, there are simpler ways. Since 1983 it has been possible to have utility bills and other regular payments directly debited to a bank account, a process that for some unknown reason is known as *domiciliazione,* a word that normally means establishing a residence or domicile. As for traffic tickets and other fees such as the annual state TV tax, they can now also be paid through an electronic system that links many tobacconists who also sell lottery tickets.

But although the number of people who take advantage of these options is growing (there are over 300 million *domiciliazioni* a year now compared to only 60,000 ten years ago), the force of habit is strong and a huge number of people still seem to prefer standing in line at the post office and paying cash, and this even though the introduction of the euro means there are eight distinct coin denominations to deal with, as compared to the four that existed with the *lira.*

Of course, even if you get your bills "domiciled", or if you are computer-savvy enough to pay bills online, you will still find it impossible to avoid making at least some payments at the post office. You are bound to get the occasional *bollettino,* be it for a traffic ticket, the housekeeper's social security payments (although now you can pay on line), your condo maintenance or the *tariffa rifiuti,* or garbage tax, the latter unavoidable if you own or rent an apartment. This tax is calculated on the basis of the number of square meters you inhabit (but singles get a discount), and is now the ace up the sleeve of Italy's municipalities. You can do almost nothing legally until you've paid it. Indeed, nowadays when you go to the *Anagrafe* to establish a residency, to change your legal address or apply for an official I.D. card, the first thing you have to show is that you have registered with the garbage tax department and paid your bill. In the old days, however, you could get away with a lot. When I finally registered at the *Anagrafe* in 1991 after I'd been hired by an Italian newspaper and had no choice but to become an official Rome resident, I was asked how long I'd lived at my then address. Fearful of what would happen if I were to tell the truth, which was 19 years, I lied and said "six months". And no one even blinked. Today, this would be impossible.

Since, try as you will, you can't avoid the post office altogether, one can only be glad that in more recent years *le poste italiane* have made major strides into the 21st century. About ten years ago, the system was revamped, with separate teller windows (and thus separate lines) for postal and financial operations. Since 2001, you can use your ATM card (*Bancomat*), but not a credit card, to make payments, thereby eliminating the need to first arm yourself with a wad of cash. At long last, you can purchase mailing boxes and padded envelopes (not to mention a series of books or gadgets) right at the post office, eliminating the need to stop first at a stationery store. And perhaps most importantly, almost all post offices now have a numbers system to establish precedence, forcing people to accept the first-come-first-serve rule. In the old days, going to the post office almost always meant doing battle with someone trying to crash the line or get ahead of you. Italians have an instinctive aversion to standing in line, and even when they acknowledge that you are ahead of them, they seem to feel compelled to take up a position at your side rather than behind you, inevitably creating the impression – and a hefty dose of accompanying anxiety – that they plan, or hope, to sneak ahead.

Speaking of ATM cards, the reluctance to adopt new technologies can also be seen in the long lines that still form at the tollbooths on the Italian *Autostrada*. The unmanned lanes where you can use your *Bancomat* or credit card to pay the toll are almost always clear, or have very short lines, while the cash lanes are backed up. Interestingly enough, while Italians with an ATM or credit card or a computer are still a minority, and while Italy still lags in Europe where internet access is concerned (only 55% of families have it) almost every Italian has a cell phone and many have more than one. Presently, close to 93% of Italians have at least one cell phone and, since many people own more than one, there are reportedly 122 cell phones per 100 inhabitants, possibly the highest level of cell phone penetration in Europe.

This love story between Italians and their cell phones exploded as soon as the little boxes arrived here in the early nineties. In fact, there was a veritable frenzy; people didn't want to be without their new toys even for a minute. Way before Americans got hung up on those useful little gadgets, Italians were laying them on the table when they went out to dinner, hanging them around their necks, taking them to the movies, concerts, lectures and so forth. And if things have calmed down slightly – mainly in restaurants – many Italians seem to need to be phone-connected all the time. People riding motorbikes wedge them under their helmets so they can talk while weaving in and out of traffic. Automobile drivers use them constantly despite a law that makes a headset obligatory. That law, like many here, is largely unapplied. But if you do get a ticket for this offense you will both lose points on your license (in Italy, you start with 20 points and lose them for infractions) and be forced to go in person to pay your fine…guess where…at the post office.

Punishment enough, perhaps, since despite the positive changes mentioned, part of the post office organization appears to be firmly stuck back in the 19th century. Let's say someone sends you a registered letter but you're not at home when it comes. The postman leaves a small, postcard-sized notice and as soon as you can, you trot off to the post office to pick up your letter. So far so good. But when – and if – you get to the front of the line, the fun begins. The postal worker takes your notice and then leafs through packs of envelopes, which are supposedly in alphabetical order but are not necessarily well sorted. When he finds the right letter, he then hauls out an enormous sheaf of handwritten papers and thumbs through those until he finds the page where you are listed. You show identification, sign on the ink-stained page (sometimes I think a quill pen would be more in order) and, finally, you get your letter and can leave.

In my case, these are almost always parking tickets, and sometimes the process gets even more convoluted. The last time this happened, when I opened the registered letter I'd gone to pick up, inside I found not a ticket but yet another notice card, this one stating that I had to go to a police station downtown which is open only weekday mornings until 12 noon and Thursday afternoons. When I finally found the time to go there, I found that the ticket had a *bollettino* attached and – you guessed it – I had to go back to the post office to pay it. Maybe this kind of disorganization can help to explain why Italy consistently shows up in near last place in European productivity surveys.

Chapter 7 – Left Meets Right (In Bed and Out)

When we went to bed at night, the first thing Fabio did was to put his 38mm revolver on the night table. It's embarrassing to admit, but I found this very sexy, even though I knew that: a) guns are dangerous; and b) there were very serious reasons why he had started carrying a gun; two years earlier he had been "kneecapped" by the Red Brigades as he was leaving his office and since terrorists were now killing people, and no longer just shooting at their legs, there was ample reason to be scared.

Fabio was a first-term member of parliament, one of a small group of young Christian Democrats who, appalled and scared by the soaring fortunes of the Italian Communists, were hoping to reform Italy's ruling party from within, and, at the same time, to carve out space for its younger, supposedly more modern-minded members. The DC (pronounced *dee-chee*) had never been a monolith; almost from its creation in 1946, it had been a conglomeration of factions of various political shadings and in some ways resembled the Democratic or the Republican Party in the United States, each of which includes conservatives and liberals who often appear to have little in common. But for good reason it had almost always been perceived as a primarily conservative party and blamed by the leftist opposition, and not by them alone, for having failed to help Italy along the road to the political modernization that would have allowed it to keep pace with the developments brought by and accompanying its postwar economic boom.

With fear mounting that significant political change might be on the way – in other words, that the Communists might actually succeed in clawing their way to power at the ballot box – there were signs of new ferment within the DC. And although this was to prove largely illusory, Fabio and a group of his colleagues were making names for themselves as a potentially new breed of Catholic politician who might have been able to change the party's image.

Fabio, however, had also drawn particular attention to himself, first from the press and later from the terrorists, because of his outspoken and visceral anti-Communism. Slim and blue-eyed with dark, neatly combed hair, he looked mildly anal-retentive and gave the impression of being priggish and sexually uptight. So after I interviewed him and accepted an invitation to dinner at Passetto, a venerable Roman *trattoria* near Piazza Navona at the time favored by businessmen and politicians, I couldn't stop teasing him ferociously. And it turned out that if I disregarded his politics, he was charming and extremely interesting, with eclectic tastes in reading, hobbies and travel that despite his somewhat stuck-up image made him rather appealing. I couldn't help it. When I was driving him back to his apartment our hands touched and, zowie, sparks flew.

Happily married with six kids, a practicing Catholic and, until our meeting, a faithful husband, he turned out to be a highly affectionate, touchy-feely man with a lot of pent-up desire and sexual fantasies and the result was that he fell rather headlong in love with me and, along with the good and enthusiastic sex, did all those things that *un uomo innamorato* is supposed to do: shower you with gifts, take you to fine restaurants and spirit you away for that romantic weekend whenever he has the chance. Once he surprised me by preparing a romantic Sunday breakfast, featuring champagne, strawberries and cream, fresh-squeezed orange juice, croissants and other pastries.

Since his family was used to his frequent travels – whether for political campaigning or for his work as a financial consultant – spending time together turned out not to be all that difficult; my own steady man was also on the road a lot and since he himself had more than once been guilty of cheating, I myself didn't feel all that bad about my peccadillo. The difference between male and female cheating, it seems to me, is that even if the man is, or believes he is, fundamentally committed to the main relationship, he often somehow lets his wife or significant other find out that he is being unfaithful whereas we women, whether it is because we are more deceitful or simply more careful, can hide an affair for a very long time, if not for ever.

Of course, having an affair with a somewhat well-known politician poses its own challenges, especially in a small country like Italy in which everyone seems to know one another, or knows someone you know and where the gossip mills work overtime. The main government and party buildings, mostly imposing, late-Renaissance structures converted to modern-day use, are located in the heart of downtown Rome, where major newspapers and news weeklies also have their offices. In other words, the entire area stretching from

Piazza Colonna, where the Prime Minister has his offices in Palazzo Chigi, and the nearby parliament, over to the Pantheon and on to Piazza Navona, which itself is across the street from Palazzo Madama, the Senate, was out of bounds for any illicit billing and cooing. And if you cared about your privacy, and your reputation, even genuinely chaste dinners or lunches in this area were risky. As I had already discovered.

In Rome, as in most capitals, political gossip runs rampant, and it is only too easy for a girl's reputation to be "ruined"; at one point, I discovered that a small group of conservative intellectuals were telling people (falsely) that two American women journalists, one working for the *New York Times* and one (me) working for the *Washington Post*, were having affairs with well-known Communists. In my case, my "lover" was supposed to be Senator Ugo Pecchioli, now deceased, a former partisan fighter and orthodox Communist party member who at the time, with the PCI still barred from formal government participation, was known as the Party's "shadow" defense minister. I knew and liked Pecchioli, who was about 30 years older than I and had a reputation as a womanizer. But I certainly had never been involved with him in any way, nor had he ever made any kind of a pass. My "sin" had been to have dinner with him a couple of times in this downtown area which, precisely because of this plethora of government and parliamentary office buildings, is knee-deep in nosy reporters and sententious politicians (or, if you like, sententious reporters and nosy politicians). And for many Italians, including politicians and intellectuals, if you dine with a man you are, *ipso facto*, automatically assumed to be having an affair with him! Ridiculous!

Strangely enough, this relatively small geographical area was one which Italy's terrorists also seemed to consider off limits. True, in May 1978, the Red Brigades terrorist group decided to abandon the bullet-ridden body of former Prime Minister Aldo Moro in a car parked just about halfway between Via delle Botteghe Oscure and Piazza del Gesù, which placed it just two blocks from both Communist and Christian Democrat party headquarters. But that was still outside this political "in-zone" and, despite all the bloodshed of the 1970s and 1980s, the terrorists never actually attacked anyone in what seemed to be considered a *terra franca*, a safe zone. Or maybe it was simply a potentially more difficult one from which to escape, since the Italian terrorist, unlike today's Islamist fanatic, had no desire to die. Thus, even in the darkest days of all that home-grown Italian political violence, you could run into some of the country's top leaders strolling around, arm in arm, conferring among themselves *sotto voce* with, apparently, not a care in the world.

But precautionary measures of a more mundane kind were necessary in the day-to-day aspects of my relationship with Fabio. Like most Italian legislators, he generally spent Tuesdays, Wednesdays and Thursdays in Rome, attending parliamentary sessions, committee meetings and less formal parleys in the massive 17th century Palazzo Montecitorio, the original design of which can be traced to the Baroque sculptor Gian Lorenzo Bernini, who originally was commissioned to build it as a private residence.

The lower house of the Italian parliament, the Chamber of Deputies, has been meeting in this building since 1871. The front piazza, with the obelisk erected here in the late second century by Emperor Marcus Aurelius to commemorate the Romans' victory over the Germanic barbarian tribes, is a wide, cobblestoned expanse where tourists, MPs, reporters, and ordinary Italians amble by on more or less pressing business. The back entrance, in Piazza del Parlamento, is more discreet. And it was there, in the evenings, that I would pick up Fabio in the battered, blue Volkswagen Beetle a colleague who was leaving Rome had sold me for a pittance, largely because its out-of-date British plates meant it was totally illegal. We'd have dinner in some more outlying neighborhood or, in the good weather, at the beach resorts of either Ostia or Fregene. Or else we'd go directly to my place. Fabio was a terrific cook and could always be counted on to whip up something delectable such as *pasta con melanzane* (eggplant), *risotto alla milanese* with saffron or, using my wok (and back then he may well have been one of the few Italians to even know what a wok was), stir-fried chicken with porcini mushrooms.

Things were somewhat easier the few times we managed to enjoy a weekend outside the capital, but one could never totally relax. Fabio was so affectionate that he was wont to forget where he was and start hugging me passionately right in the middle of the street. Walking down the street in some small medieval town, or meandering along the wooded shores of Lake Como, he'd simply stop and kiss me as if nothing else in the world counted. Inevitably, since the newspapers most Italians read are national papers and politician who makes headlines can have an extremely high recognition level, now and then someone would recognize him. But since Italians are generally world-wise they probably didn't care, or didn't realize I was not the official woman.

But there were some near misses. One spring weekend on the wooded Gargano peninsula of Apulia in the Italian South we found ourselves being greeted by a hotel manager who rushed up to me saying, "Cara Signora, I know your father." I put on a *pro forma* smile and said something non-committal, but once we got up to our room, Fabio went almost crazy with fear and I had to convince him to tell the hotel manager the truth, that the woman he was with was not his wife.

"Non ti preoccupare," I said, "Don't worry. After all, hoteliers are used to this kind of thing and are well-schooled in discretion." In the end he got his nerve up and went to have a man-to-man talk with the manager who, guess what, gave us a private dining room, and afterwards they became friends and, even later on did business together.

The relationship with Fabio was very satisfying. From time to time, however, there were crises: periodically, Fabio would start feeling guilty and/or sinful; as long as our affair went on, he felt couldn't take communion when he went to church, no doubt raising eyebrows, at least those of his wife and his parish priest.

The only other dark spot in our relationship reflected our diametrically opposed political views. He was conservative, violently anti-Communist, a man who saw no difference between Italy's Marxists and Stalin's henchmen. I had a more open point of view, one with which my friends at the U.S. Embassy, troubled by the PCI's longstanding relationship with the Soviets, did not agree and no doubt classified as wrong-headed or, at best, naïve. But it was shared, instead, by tens of thousands of Italians, and not just the ones who voted Communist. I had lots of friends and acquaintances in Italy who voted PCI but who were by no means dyed-in-the-wool Marxists. Furthermore, the party officials I met during my work as a reporter generally struck me – paradoxically, I suppose – as a stimulating mélange of Marxism, democracy and American-style liberalism.

It was hard, at least for me, not to have some sympathy for them. By the 1970s, after all, it was clear that Italy's postwar economic boom had not been accompanied by the hoped-for significant social or political change. Fabio's party, the Christian Democrats, had proved adept at manipulating the Cold War international climate with the result that the effective ban on the Communists' participation in an Italian government, backed by an informal U.S. veto, lasted well into the late 1980s. This meant that for decades the same three or four centrist and center-left parties were in power with no real fear of being unseated. At the same time, the West's largest Marxist party was in power in many of Italy's local and regional governments and, perhaps ironically, was gaining credibility at home as a largely reformist body.

So when I started working as a journalist here, it was already clear that a very significant number of Italians had become convinced that the coalitions led by the Christian Democrats had failed to produce good, honest and effective government. They consequently had come to view the legitimization of the Communists – or the Eurocommunists, as the latter were then calling themselves – as the only possible way to give Italy a truly functioning democracy, one in which at least two serious contenders vie for power and government and the possibility of alternation between them is a real one. Not surprisingly, then, in the local elections of 1975, held to renew the governments of most of Italy's 20 regions, its then 90 provinces and many of its 8,000 cities, the PCI did amazingly well. Although it hadn't been in power nationally since the end of World War II, when tripartite coalitions of Christian Democrats, Socialists and Communists briefly governed, the party won close to 35 percent of the vote, almost overtaking the Christian Democrats, and winning control over such cities as Bologna, Florence, Venice, Pisa, Siena, Rome and Milan. Significantly, only a small percentage of those voters were actually PCI party members.

When a woman has an affair with a married man, most arguments are about the usual things: "You don't spend enough time with me," or "If you really loved me you'd leave your wife." But what we argued about was what I saw as Fabio's political blindness. The PCI's success at the polls drove him mad, and he simply couldn't appreciate why it was that for millions of other Italians, it was a time of enormous exhilaration. As the results of the 1975 elections were being broadcast on televisions and radios around the city, tens of thousands of Romans, many waving red flags, rushed elatedly to party headquarters in Via delle Botteghe Oscure (in English, perhaps aptly enough, "the Street of the Dark Shops"), about midway between the Capitoline hill, the *Campidoglio,* and the cat-friendly Roman ruins at Piazza Argentina. I watched and took notes as they jammed the street outside party headquarters, cheering wildly and clapping rhythmically until Enrico Berlinguer, the small, dark Sardinian who was then the party's leader, made his appearance on a balcony. As self-effacing as ever and somewhat rumpled (he always seemed to be wearing the same shabby gray suit, of which, I liked to imagine, he had a closet full), he was there to greet the crowd. But he shook his head as the crowd yelled, "*Enrico, il pugno, il pugno*" ("the fist, the fist"), hoping – vainly – to see him make the Left's clenched-fist salute.

Despite his unprepossessing physical appearance – or perhaps because of it – Enrico Berlinguer, who died in 1984, was extremely charismatic and beloved by many. Born into an aristocratic Sardinian family, the son of a militant anti-Fascist, he joined the party when he was only 21 and rose so quickly in the ranks that people joked he had been appointed at birth to a top position in the party hierarchy. Berlinguer became the party's effective leader in the late sixties when the health of the then party leader, Luigi Longo, failed. And it fell to him both to deal with the confusion caused by the continued crumbling of Moscow's hold over Eastern Europe and to marshal the Italian left's attempts to make a breach in the Christian Democrat's stranglehold over the Italian government. His solution, then considered inventive by some and subversive by others, was the so-called "*compromesso storico,*" a solution he posited as a "historic compromise" between Communists and Christian Democrats.

For the next decade, therefore, he was to be hot copy for the foreign press, and the PCI was only too happy to oblige. One Saturday afternoon some 50 foreign correspondents allowed themselves to be bused (I drove my own car, however) from Rome to L'Aquila in the Abruzzo region where Berlinguer was delivering an electoral speech. "And then you're all invited to dinner with Berlinguer," drawled press secretary Martha Galli, an American from the somewhere in the south of our country who was married to a party official. Sure. Tell me another.

Yes, Berlinguer had dinner in the same restaurant as we did, but *upstairs* with all the local party pols. The rest of us ate downstairs and had to make do with a brief handshake from Enrico. Fortunately, my friend and colleague, Thea Lurie, who was then writing for the *Washington Star*, and I did somewhat better: We at least were seated at the same table as Tonino Tatò, Berlinguer's witty and engaging "*chef de cabinet*", and others from the press office.

I myself was to have two other real chances at dinner with Berlinguer. One occasion was in Turin where, after a major show of union strength calculated to impress the ownership and management of the giant FIAT automobile company, the Party and the Communist-dominated CGIL trade union – *Confederazione Generale Italiana del Lavoro*, Italy's national labor confederation – gave a dinner honoring the French Communist party leader, George Marchais. I got myself seated right across the dais from Berlinguer. But to little avail, since I could see that he, extremely wary of the press, was not pleased.

The next time was for real. In August, 1976, I was invited by a colleague from Italian state radio to have a few days summer holiday in Stintino, a lovely fishing village of 700 people on the northwestern corner of Sardinia, an island that boasts beaches of incredibly white sand and a bluer-than-blue sea. This was the place where Berlinguer, who came from the inland Sardinian city of Sassari, regularly spent his August holidays.

To my good fortune, he was friendly not only with my host, who belonged to the small but then influential Republican party, but with the village's other habitué VIPs – various Christian Democrats, some mainstream and radical Socialists, a few Republicans and even a Trotskyite. Again, when he saw me, he was not happy, but I think he then took my measure and quickly realized I was not there for gossip. What I noticed about him, having finally gotten up close was, in the first place, his curiosity.

At a dinner at my host's villa, he was the only one who asked about the details of my visit the previous day to Asinara, an offshore island that was once a leper colony but which for a time hosted a maximum-security prison. It had then only recently been transformed into a jail for big-time *mafiosi* and I had found it interesting, almost amusing, that the Calabresi and the Sicilians housed there lived in different barracks and were not on speaking terms. Second, he was kind: he seemed very concerned by the severe seasickness that the return trip in the tiny fishing boat I had rented to make the visit had given me. "It's the *onda lunga*," he explained, referring to the slow, rocking waves that characterized that part of the Mediterranean in the late afternoon. Third, that he couldn't for the life of him carry a tune, a fact that became painfully clear when, one evening, the group gathered to sing Sardinian folk songs after a fireside dinner of awful boiled mutton prepared by some local peasants.

And then there was the sense of humor that no one looking at this slight, dour-faced man would ever have suspected. He laughed heartily when I recounted a dream I'd had in which Communist party headquarters had been transformed into a trendy department store. And at yet another dinner, this time at the nearby villa of Demetrio Volcic, then Italian state TV's man in Moscow, he made what I thought was, for the leader of a party that was struggling between its European and Soviet identities, a droll and charming remark. The food that evening was particularly yummy because every course included caviar that Volcic had brought with him from the USSR. "And then they ask me why I don't want to break our ties with the Russians?" he quipped, avidly dishing himself a second portion of *penne al caviale*. It hurt me to do so, but out of respect for the off-the-record nature of the evening, I left that quip out of the piece I wrote for the *Washington Post* and which was entitled "Enrico Berlinguer's Summer in Stintino: Popular Politics on the Island of Sardinia".

Chapter 8 – L'Appetito Viene Mangiando
(Eating Makes You Hungry)

I have always loved Italian food. Who doesn't? Nevertheless, when I moved to Italy I ran up against a series of mind-sets that were either contrasted with my own or to which I had to adapt. Take frozen food, like it or not for decades now a welcome shortcut for the harried American housewife. When I first mentioned it to anyone here – probably because I was planning on freezing something so I could use it the following week – I quickly learned from their horrified expressions that frozen food was a "no-no" for any Italian worth his or her salt, and I remember being told by Cristina, the wife of the Southern Italian-born custodian of a gated beach community in Sabaudia where I used to rent a summer house, that frozen foods were "poisonous" and unfit to eat. When I first met her, Cristina, a seriously overweight woman with messy blond hair tied back in a short ponytail, spent an entire week at the end of summer "putting up" tomatoes in various forms but mostly making jar after jar after jar of *sugo di pomodoro*, tomato sauce, designed to last the entire winter. Practically every day but Sunday, the family ate spaghetti with tomato sauce, so they needed a lot of it.

Things change of course, and recently I noticed that Cristina had installed a huge, free-standing freezer on her back porch and had signed up as a regular customer of Bo-Frost, a German frozen foods company that now operates in 12 European countries and makes money by home delivery of things frozen – cakes, ice cream, pizzas, pastas, French fries, meat dishes, vegetables and so on. In the meantime, she had given up on the tomato sauce because, she explained, the process exhausted her, "and anyway, you can now buy ready-made sauces that are just as good as mine." Today, in fact, there are huge frozen food displays in every Italian supermarket, specialty frozen-food stores where you can buy individual frozen fish or un-packaged frozen vegetables by their weight. And most big-city Italian food stores now carry things like parboiled rice, pre-cooked minestrone and fast-cooking pasta dishes – there is even a delicious fast-cooking *polenta* which means you no longer have to wear yourself out stirring constantly for 40 minutes.

Today's younger Italians go to McDonald's, eat *panini* (sandwiches on rolls) even while walking on the street (once an unacceptable practice that only barbarous Americans engaged in), line up outside other, Italian, fast-food places to save time and money, go to Chinese restaurants and, although less frequently, eat falafel, couscous or shwarma at one of the growing number of Arab takeouts that now exist. But it is reasonable to imagine that, tradition being what it is, when they grow up they'll be just like their parents with a rather long, must-do, or must-eat, list.

One of the first things you learn is that many Italians are very particular about olive oil and will simply not be satisfied with the store brands bought by most; they are always on the lookout for friends or acquaintances who live in the country and make their own. For years I bought mine from two retired journalists, Beppe and Cristina, who until recently lived almost full-time on a *podere* or farm in Fabbro in Tuscany with 600 olive trees and a donkey named Nellie. Beppe and Cristina produced about 500 liters a year and sold most of it to friends and acquaintances.

But I could have also gotten a yearly supply from Gino, the contractor-engineer in the lake town of Bolsena, north of Viterbo, where I have a weekend apartment; Gino has several plots of land with olive trees and every year organizes the *raccolta* and the *spremitura* – the harvest and the pressing – so he can sell some and give the rest away to deserving associates and clients. Another supplier might have been Antonio, the waiter at one of my favorite restaurants in downtown Rome, whose father makes his own olive oil every year and supplies not only his son's boss, but several other local trattorias with what many in the Mediterranean believe is – along with bread – truly the staff of life. Some people, especially well-off people who have migrated to the countryside, will invite you to take part in their *raccolta*; gathering olives is downright backbreaking but seems to fill some people (not lazy me, I confess) with a sense of being part of the overall scheme of things.

Olive oil can be deep yellow or green, and when it's recently pressed, somewhat *piccante* or peppery, and the best way to sample it is on a piece of *pane casareccio*, the crusty, wood-oven baked bread that I prefer to others in Italy, or on bread toasted for *bruschetta* (a word most Americans continue to mispronounce, the proper pronunciation being brusketta!). When the new oil arrives, everyone is desperate to taste it and it's always a welcome gift. The American reader should keep in mind, however, that no restaurant here that caters to a genuine Italian clientele would *ever* give you a dish of oil to dip your bread in while you are waiting for your meal. And if you do eat bread and oil at home as a snack, the oil gets poured *on* the bread and not, please God, dipped, never ever.

I quickly discovered that Italians who live in the country or who have homes out of the city also had other seasonal, food-related activities. Starting in September and extending through November, depending on the weather, Marcello and Angela, a couple who moved to Bolsena when Marcello retired, get up at the crack of dawn almost every day to look for *funghi*, mushrooms, preferably of the *porcini* variety, but also the white and red *ovoli*, which are so good with *parmigiano* shavings and walnuts, *galetti,* also known as *finferle, chiodini* (little nails), *mazze di tamburo, russole* and *trombetti del morto* ("trumpets of the dead"!), all of which can be used in pasta dishes or in *frittate,* Italian omelets. Naturally, you have to be careful picking mushrooms, and even the most expert sometimes make mistakes. Another couple I know, Stellino and Carola, who consider themselves *funghi* experts, ended up spending a week in the hospital after making a soup of mushrooms known as *cromati,* which they had picked in a forest a few hours out of Rome. Unlike in neighboring Abruzzi, where you are supposed to go to a forest ranger station and have your mushrooms checked for safety, in Lazio, although a license granted after special courses has been required since 2000, it seems to be a free-for-all, and probably a lot of people have been very, very lucky not to poison themselves.

March and April, on the other hand, are the season for wild asparagus, another vegetable delicacy that some people believe is worth getting up at 5 a.m. for but which, before coming to Italy I, a city girl, didn't know even existed. My friend Guido, a writer and university professor who has a weekend home at Lenola, a small hill town near the coast below Sperlonga, never misses a season. He uses the small, delicate stalks in omelets or, alternatively, with risotto.

Then of course, there is wine, which is one of the reasons for which many foreigners move to places such as Italy, France or Spain. Happily, I discovered that although Italians love wine, drink – per capita – about 42 liters of it a year, their affection for the grape rarely gets transformed into the kind of fanaticism and devotion expressed by the wine-crazed characters in the 2004 American film, *Sideways.* Yes, most educated people here make a point of opening red wine well before serving it and a few even decant it. But there seems to be more concern with superstition (it is bad, bad luck to pour with your left hand or, even worse, backhanded with the right hand) than with rolling it around in the mouth, inhaling the bouquet and claiming to identify myriad components. By the way, in 2010, according to that year's statistics, Italians – as drinkers – had fallen behind to fourth in the world, coming after (believe it or not), Vatican City, Luxembourg and France, in that order. But when all the numbers are in for last year, the country appears likely to emerge once again as the world's number-one 2012 wine producer.

Interestingly enough, many of the strongest views, or perhaps it is better to call them prejudices, about wine seem to be held by the less sophisticated part of the population. My friend Dino, a contractor who started out as a mason and who has since moved out to the country to be closer to nature, believes that all bottled wine is to be avoided because it contains additives and in some way has been altered. He drinks only homemade wine and will drive miles to get some from this or that peasant supplier. Sometimes the stuff is good and other times, at least in my view, undrinkable, but he and his friends will not drink anything else.

Another discovery for me was first, mozzarella, and then buffalo mozzarella, one of the few things some Italians *would* fight traffic and drive across town to get. Normal mozzarella, that made from cow's milk rather than from the milk of the Mediterranean water buffalo, often goes by the name *fior di latte*, which literally means the curd of the milk, and is sold either in large, orange-size balls, or in smaller, bite-size balls called *bocconcini*, or cherry size, *cigliegini*, which are good primarily as antipasti or in salads. This kind of mozzarella is also good sliced and served with *prosciutto* and often is used for the topping on some kinds of *pasta al forno* as it melts well. I couldn't believe how good this mozzarella was, above all compared with the rubbery stuff that was used in Italian restaurants back in New York when I was growing up. But in terms of pure taste and succulence it pales next to *mozzarella di bufala*, my next discovery.

This is truly one of Italy's major and unique delicacies, fantastic when served with just a little bit of good oil and pepper, or else with tomatoes and fresh *basilico*. Campania, the region of which Naples is the capital, is the part of Italy best known for its succulent *mozzarella di bufala* (sometimes also sold in the form of a braid, or *treccia*). It should be eaten within a day or so and, in the meantime, must be kept in its own *siero*, or serum. But other Italian regions such as Puglia, Abruzzo and Molise are also renowned for theirs. Other famous Italian cheeses include *parmigiano reggiano* and the less precious (but I find very tasty) *grana padano*. These, too, had little in common with the stuff one got back home, at least when I was growing up. A chunk of *parmigiano reggiano*, eaten with a pear or some kind of fruit compote, is truly a dish fit for a king. But although it may not compare to France, Italy cheese production does not stop there. There are myriad types of local *cacio* or *caciotta* cheeses made from cow or sheep milk, dozens of hard and soft cheeses the tastes of which change more or less subtly from region to region. There is *pecorino*, a hard cheese like *parmigiano* but made from sheep's milk, more tangy and considered more suitable for grating on most Roman pasta dishes. And let's not forget, *gorgonzola,* although that luscious cheese is really too fattening for me to eat more than once a year, if that.

I learned, too, that every area of Italy has its specialties. If a friend were going to Calabria I might ask him to bring back some *ricotta salata*, which is wonderful, grated very coarsely, on some kinds of baked pasta; if he were going to Puglia, I might beg for some *burrata,* leftover pieces of mozzarella and cream combined in this delicious and maddeningly fatty cheese. In Palermo's bustling outdoor Vucciria market you can buy, by the gram (bring your own jar!), the most incredible tomato concentrate.

In Piedmont, all sorts of products are laced with white or black truffles. In Bologna you can get fabulous *mostarda*, a condiment of candied fruits that is served with *bollito*, a mix of different boiled meats. Livorno has *pesto* that no one anywhere else can duplicate although many, including me, have tried. *Luganica* sausage, although originally from Lucania in the south (it is thought that Roman soldiers brought it northwards) has been turned into an art by the Milanese, who use it in *risotto*. And the best *prosciutto* comes either from Parma or from San Daniele in Friuli. All this, of course, is a matter of opinion.

At one point, Janet's family organized a two-week Tuscan holiday reunion and a Spanish brother-in-law arrived from Madrid with his car full of bottles of Spanish red wine, Spanish olive oil and an entire Spanish prosciutto, the latter being, according to him, other

Spaniards, and even to one of my local grocers), even better than that made in Italy.

But even if they don't often go rushing across town to buy this or that foodstuff, primarily because they can usually find what they want in the corner *alimentari*, or grocery, Italians definitely have some very strict dos and don'ts that you simply cannot ignore if you want people to accept a second invitation to your house. As I knew even before I arrived, Italy's major contribution to culinary lore is *pastasciutta*, of which there are countless shapes, lengths and thicknesses, most of which can be cooked with an apparently unlimited number of condiments or *sughi* (sauces), be they made with vegetables, fish, shellfish or meat. Primarily, pasta (like rice) must absolutely not be overcooked and must be taken off the flame when it is still *al dente*. This requires a lot of hovering over a pot of boiling water and fishing out strands of pasta that at least one person (if not more, if you've got guests for dinner) will sample, saying "quick, it's ready" or else, "one minute more", "30 seconds more" and so on.

There are also strong feelings in some quarters about how much water you should use in the pasta pot and whether or not it is admissible to recover the pot temporarily once you've put the pasta in so that it will boil up again. A few drops of olive oil in the boiling water will also keep the pasta from sticking together, but purists are against this, too. Second, and contrary to what some foreigners seem to think, not every pasta dish should be doused with grated cheese: you must not sprinkle cheese on pasta with any kind of fish; purists believe porcini mushrooms should also be left in their natural state, and most Italians would rather die than put grated cheese on a pasta dish made with fresh tomatoes.

I have come to appreciate most of Italians' dos and don'ts, but not all of them. I still think garlic salt is a major invention, I consider eggs to be a light meal not – like the Italians – a heavy one, and cannot for the life of me tell the difference in taste between a battery-raised chicken and a *pollo ruspante,* a barnyard chicken. *Me, poverina* (poor me!). Furthermore, although I grew up knowing that Italians were famous for their veal (every time my parents took me to an Italian restaurant, they ordered veal *Marsala* or veal *piccata*), I have definite reservations about their beef. As far as I am concerned, you can't give an A for beef to any populace who has spent decades serving and eating the so-called *fettina*, a boring, dry, tough tasteless cut of *manzo*.

Probably designed to use as much of the cow as possible, the *fettina* has remained the meat mainstay in a country that long ago left the worst of wartime poverty behind it.

And then, of course, there's coffee. In the home, coffee is usually made in the *moka*, the three-piece Italian percolator coffee pot, which when heated on the flame, forces water up through the coffee grounds and into the top portion. In the Italian South, people use the *napoletana*, which works on the drip principle and must be turned upside down before being poured out. The key thing to remember in either case, under pain of total ostracism, is that neither must ever be washed with soap or any other detergent, only rinsed with water.

The mainstay of Italian coffee lore, *la tazzina di caffè*, or an *espresso*, as served by one's local bar and during the day consumed – generally – standing up, is another one of those things about which Italians have very strong feelings. The purists want it very dense, *ristrettissimo*, which is the way they serve it in Naples, generally laced with so much sugar so that it is almost more Turkish than anything else. A whole segment of the population wants it *al vetro*, in a small glass (another Arab legacy), while others prefer it in the classic *tazzina*, where they can swirl it around so as to get all the sugar mixed in.

Many Italians want their coffee *macchiato*, literally "stained" with milk; some – especially heavy laborers who start work at 7 a.m. or before – want it *corretto*, corrected, or shall we say "spiked", with something alcoholic. Others – like me – want it *lungo* (the Florentines say "*alto*") which means it has more water in it. And then there are those who prefer *cappuccino*, which in turn can be served in several varieties, although not of the Starbucks type. Some want it *scuro,* with less milk, some want it *chiaro*, with more milk, some prefer it without foam, *senza schiuma*, and there is generally a shaker of cocoa powder somewhere available for those eager for a bit of chocolate. *Caffelatte*, a hot drink we Americans mysteriously have dubbed a "latte" (which in Italian simply means "milk"), comes in only one variety and is a morning drink, as is a *cappuccino*.

In fact, many Italians consider a *cappuccino* or a *caffelatte* to be breakfast; nowadays they'll give their kids cornflakes or some other kind of cereal but they, themselves, as their morning meal will have only *caffelatte* or *cappuccino* with a *cornetto* or some kind of cookies. (Be aware that the generic word for cookies in Italian is *biscotti*, and that this has nothing to do with what in the U.S. are now called

79

"biscotti" and which, instead, are an oversized version of the *tozzetti* or *cantuccini* some Italians like to dip in *vin santo* and eat at the end of a meal. *Tozzetti* are quite common in Tuscany; elsewhere, not all restaurants have them. By the way, although nowadays your average Italian waiter will no longer flinch when an American or a German asks for a *cappuccino* after or even with dinner (he knows what side his bread is buttered on), be advised that he thinks it's pretty disgusting. No Italian would ever drink *cappuccino* with, or immediately after, a meal and finds the idea repulsive as, at this juncture, I confess, do I.

Chapter 9 – La Mano Morta

(And Other Intercultural Complications)

Common wisdom had it that in Italy women always got pinched, particularly while riding on Italian buses. I regret to report that I myself have never been pinched (by a stranger, that is). And so when I first started living in Italy, I had to disappoint a lot of uncles back home and their friends who every time I visited, or they came to Italy, would ask me, chortling or winking, about this, as in, "I guess – heh, heh – you've been pinched a lot, right?" To console them, I would relate some similar experiences: the time that on the way to my office in the *ANSA* news agency building, about a block from the lusciously Baroque Trevi Fountain, a teenage boy, probably on a dare, ran by and squeezed my right breast before disappearing down a narrow *vicoletto*. Or about the time a white-jacketed waiter, after helping me up after I fell because the wheels of my motorbike got caught in the trolley tracks in front of the restaurant where he worked, attempted insistently to medicate my unblemished inner thigh. Or about the passenger in a moving car who slapped me on the rear while I was biking, alone, along the *lungomare*, or coastal road, in Sabaudia, an hour south of Rome.

But, no, I have never been pinched, on the bus or elsewhere. Furthermore, or so I am told, the real technique is different; *la mano morta*, or dead hand, is used in crowded quarters when the molester's hand is allowed to rest, immobile, alongside a fellow passenger's derrière or other body part. And although sexual violence is on the rise in Italy, as is violence against women in general, there is still much less danger here for women than in many other countries, including in particular, the U.S. Indeed, if you travel on Rome's crowded buses, you are much more likely to be the victim of a pickpocket than a sexual deviate.

In general, it has also been hard to explain to people that it wasn't men that led me to Italy in the first place (much less the idea of being pinched); this is something that people, Italians and Americans alike, often take for granted. If a foreign woman has lived here as long as I, it must be – they think – because she met and married an Italian. This, of course, is not uncommon. Over the years I have met a lot of foreign women who came here to visit, fell in love, and got married. And a lot of them married, or at least got deeply involved with, men who turned out to be totally unsuitable. This happened to my friend Christine, an American with a degree in Fine Arts, who married a Sicilian telephone operator whose family, whom she met only at the last minute, expected her to be a traditional wife and daughter-in-law and who ended up in a very messy divorce when she decided to take the kids back to the States. Or take Clarice, an Englishwoman who came to Rome, she thought, for a year of language study but got married and stayed. The man she married, a fairly well-known Socialist intellectual, did speak some English. But not enough for her to realize – before she married him – what a bully he was.

Intercultural relationships can, of course, work out fine. Despite the Italian conviction that one should always choose "*moglie e buoi dei paesi tuoi*" that is, pick your wife and cattle from your own hometown, cultural differences can sometimes help to keep boredom at bay. But when such relationships are bad, they are really bad. It's not necessarily a language problem, although that can be a contributing factor. The fact is that when you meet someone at a time when you are still basically unfamiliar with the country he or she comes from, you are unable to make all those subtle distinctions you unconsciously rely on at home – accent, pronunciation, mode of dress, physical bearing – to give you what is often vital information about a new acquaintance.

This was bound to be particularly difficult in a country like Italy where people were (and are) particularly conformist in their way of dress. However, even in the sixties and the seventies, when all Italians dressed far more formally than they do today, there were clues.

For example, almost any man who wore an Austrian style, full-length loden overcoat in the winter, almost always dark forest green (although personally I preferred the less frequent navy, or the even rarer dark gray) was likely to be "un borghese", that is, of upper middle class provenance. Men with short, well-trimmed beards were generally conservative or even right-wing, whereas longer hair and messier facial hair generally was a sign of a left-wing affiliation. Low-level government bureaucrats were much more likely to wear white shirts and checked sports coats than *dirigenti*, management-level employees. And a rough accent, Roman or otherwise, is something you can't hear until your language ability is at very high levels, quite a shame since it is and was a very reliable indication of background and cultural level.

Understandably, then, it can take a while to catch on. But once you do, it is a great help. Even though today people dress differently (almost everyone, except top entrepreneurs and government officials, dresses more casually than in the past), I can read most Italian men at a glance. Over the years, in fact, I gradually became able to rule out a whole stratum of men as unsuitable prospective partners. True, this can have its downside. Not long ago I found myself momentarily taken aback when a woman friend, newly arrived from the United States, gushed on about all the gorgeous men she was seeing on the street.

"Really?" I remember saying in a somewhat incredulous tone. And then, thinking about it, I remembered that I, too, had once voiced such thoughts, and realized that over the years my built-in filter must had been working overtime and screening out a lot of men who at one time had seemed to be potential candidates. For the same reason, when you can't read – or hear – the signs that tell you about a person's educational level or background, your attraction to a person becomes above all physical. The result? It can be only too easy to get sexually involved with – and possibly married to – someone who when it comes to a long-term relationship turns out to be totally unsuitable.

Fortunately for me, and perhaps because I never married, there were never any major errors. But this doesn't mean that getting it right was not a challenge. As a junior-year abroad student in Florence, I had fallen head over heels in love with a remarkably good-looking law student without realizing that he had one major strike against him, especially for a woman of Jewish origin: he was a bona fide member of the Italian Neofascist party and president of the city's Neofascist youth group. Love, they say, is blind, and in fact I was so enamored of Guglielmo, called Mino by his friends, that even once I had the whole picture I decided to ignore this political blemish.

In my defense I should point out that in postwar Italy, the Neofascists have never been actively anti-Semitic and he certainly wasn't, otherwise he certainly wouldn't have asked me to marry him and introduced me not just to his parents but to his *nonni*, his grandparents. For my part, I wasn't interested in tying the knot. This was partly because at that point I wasn't interested in marriage, period. But even more significant was the fact that he wasn't much good in bed. Back then, I myself didn't have much sexual experience; he was only the second man I'd made love with. But I knew from my reading – and from instinct – that his performance was not what it ought to be and that sex was one area in which two people either clicked, or didn't.

There were other mistakes in that period. Take Lapo, another terribly handsome Florentine fellow – green eyes, olive skin and thick, dark blond hair that made my hands itch with the desire to caress it. Like most students abroad, I tried to divide my time between my studies and getting to know the country or city I was living in. Lapo picked me up one day at Piazza della Repubblica and we had a pleasant day driving through Florence and its environs – Fiesole, San Domenico, Settignano – on his Lambretta. But then something went wrong and at midnight I found myself abandoned, alone, on the grassy bank of the Arno River, when I wouldn't "cooperate". Since it was well after midnight and the buses had stopped running, I had to walk all the way home and slink into the apartment where I was boarding with the Niccolinis, a middle-class Florentine family that supplemented its income by taking in American students.

And what about Giorgio, the owner of a tiny jewelry store on the Merceria San Zulian in Venice whom I fell for (temporarily) while pricing a necklace of seed pearls and gold? Attractive without being downright handsome, a shock of dark brown hair falling onto his forehead, Giorgio was wearing a large Jewish star around his neck and, knowing how far back in history the Venice Jewish community goes, I was intrigued – as I was meant to be. I was in Venice as the guide for a group of college girls who weren't much younger than I, so I couldn't spend that much time with him. But I was so smitten that after the tour was over I returned to spend a few days with him. Not long after, and for reasons that would be obvious to any woman who has grown up Jewish, it became clear that Giorgio wasn't a member of the tribe at all, something he more or less readily admitted once the Star of David had served its primary purpose, that of making a "sale". Generally, its function was to encourage the affluent American Jewish tourists who visited the city to buy a piece or two of gold jewelry. But if my example was anything to go by it also worked on single American women. However, his lovemaking, too – an overly hasty and unnecessary five in a row – paradoxically wasn't much to write home about. But he did take me to some wonderful restaurants where I could explore the Venetian variations on Italian cuisine.

Fortunately for me, most of my serious involvements in the Mediterranean have been with men who were more or less on the same intellectual wavelength as I, and the one exception would turn out to be with a manual laborer named Paolo, a person whose humanity far outweighed his cultural limitations. As for the less serious involvements, well, they were fun. Think, for example, about the inside gossip you can pick up from having an affair with one of the Interior Minister's bodyguards, especially if you're a reporter.

The fact is that as a *straniera* you had an inside track. The Italian man's fascination with foreign women had flourished in the immediate postwar era, when Italian life-style and morals were significantly different from those in northern countries like Germany and Scandinavia and, to a lesser degree, in the United Kingdom and the United States. Even when I first visited Italy as a *studentessa* back in the sixties, our orientation program aboard the SS. Cristoforo Colombo had included a lesson explaining that whereas in the U.S. a long period of time could elapse between a first kiss and a full sexual encounter, in Italy kisses were a considered a near-immediate prelude to *rapporti sessuali*.

Our group leader drew a very telling diagram on the blackboard in the port-holed stateroom we had been given for our lectures. Next to the words "United States", there was a long chalk line separating two points; the first "x" was labeled "the kiss" and the second, way, way over to the right, stood for sexual intercourse. Below, a second chalk line illustrated the situation in Italy. Under the American "kiss" there was nothing written at all. Far over to the right you saw the word "*il bacio*", the kiss, and only a few inches away you got to the final act itself.

The message was clear: Watch out whom you kiss in Italy because once you've done that you'll soon be expected to go all the way. This was particularly useful for me since at the time I was coming under heavy "attack" by a junior ship's officer, also named Giorgio, whose "dress whites" made him appear more attractive than he actually was. Despite the warning, I did go back to his cabin with him where, however, he made a major tactical error. Before making a real pass, he opened a drawer to show me an enormous collection of postcards from other "*straniere*". The more fool he, I thought as – determined not to be part of someone's stable – I quickly headed back to the cabin I shared with three other women students.

The orientation lecture had been directed at all of us, men and women alike. But it was quite clear that in the sixties, even more than in the U.S., nice Italian girls didn't go to bed with anyone until after marriage, or unless *matrimonio* loomed on the horizon. This could have well explained the attraction of *le straniere*, foreign women, particularly those from Germany and points north, who, along with being, for the most part, blondes (blondes have always had an inner track in Mediterranean countries, as can be seen immediately by the vast number of Italian girls and women, natural brunettes, who lighten their hair), were freer about these things than the average *italiana*. Whenever Italian men had the opportunity to meet a *straniera,* their systems were all go. And if they benefited from the fact that the willingness of foreign women meant not too much work was needed to carry out a seduction, they were also helped by their reputation for being warmer, more demonstrative and better lovers than the foreign men that the *straniere* had left back home. And of course they, the Italian males, also had the wine, sun, the blue sky and the incredible beauty of this country on their side and all working for them.

Today, this has all changed. Italian women and young, and ever younger, Italian girls, make love as freely as their Scandinavian or American counterparts. Sex and nudity are everywhere: on billboards, on television, on newsstands and even on the covers of mainstream newsmagazines such as *L'Espresso* and *Panorama*, the Italian equivalents of *Newsweek* and *Time*. Although there seems to be more restraint in neighboring countries such as France and Greece, women here increasingly dress more like streetwalkers than anything else. Even female newscasters often look less like journalists and more like what we in the U.S. or the U.K. would call "bimbos" (by the way, in Italian the word "bimbo" simply means a small boy and has nothing to do with women) with lots of cleavage and, if they are standing up, bare legs ending in "fuck-me" slingbacks with five-inch heels.

So sex is high up on the daily menu, much more so than when I first came here. But does this really mean that the Italian male's sexual prowess lives up to his reputation? Perhaps I've been unlucky, but my experience, and that of those few women I know here who are inclined to discuss such things openly and graphically (à la *Sex and the City*), has led me to the sad conclusion that here, just as elsewhere, many men are far from the skilled Latin lovers that legend would have them. Perhaps, with so much flesh around, Italian men know they are operating in a "buyer's market" and no longer feel they have to try harder? Or maybe it was all a myth from the start and Italians are no different from men anywhere else, some being good lovers and others not? Who knows?

In some ways, of course, Italian men *are* different and in my opinion got – and deserve – their reputation because of their extreme warmth, actively affectionate nature and sentimental romanticism, not necessarily because of their sexual bravura. As was always clear from the hordes of *pappagalli*, pick-up artists, who once hung around the Trevi Fountain or lurked in the shadow of Michelangelo's David outside the Palazzo della Signoria in Florence, Italian men – like men all over – have always wanted to score.

But contrary to the Latin lover image they have always enjoyed, maybe they never really cared about how well they did it, or didn't know they were supposed to care. And maybe Italian women have fewer expectations or are less demanding. From my own experience, only a very few of the Italians I have made love with would classify, in my mind, as really good lovers from the point of view of both technique and stamina. They also appear to be less "generous" than men from some other cultures. Obviously, there are no statistics available, but from what I can tell, from personal or second-hand experience (and from what my Italian male friends tell me about the talk in the locker rooms of the city's *palestre*, or gyms), Italian men love being on the receiving end of oral sex but generally shy away from giving it. "Oh, there are a few older guys who like it," says one male friend, "but most men think it's kind of icky."

One theory, now bandied about in most Western countries, is that the liberation of women has made men everywhere less secure in their lovemaking, and that would appear to be even more true in Italy, a country where there is a long-standing tradition of men as stalkers and women as prey – probably willing, but prey all the same. Surely the enormous number of female prostitutes out on the streets is an indication that there is some sort of a disconnect between what men expect from sex and what goes on in a normal, everyday relationship. Sometimes it would seem that when it comes to their day-to-day relationships, Italian men care more about being loved, desired and admired than about the various intricacies of lovemaking? Could it be that they care more about romance than about sex, especially when they are on the receiving end? Certainly, this would explain why many of them feel far more comfortable when they are the ones who take the initiative.

This at least is my experience. One protracted period during which I was in between men, and thus significantly horny, comes to mind. Unattached and unsure when, or if, true love would arrive, I was on the lookout for some good sex, an attitude that led colleagues with whom I then shared an office, Federico and Gerardo, to say that I was "the only real *maschio* (male) in the room". Both claimed that they only care about sex and want it when they are in love. And while I agree – and who wouldn't? – that being in love is the optimum, I have learned that what we call love, or at least what I called love, was often only a ferocious physical attraction.

During this hormonal rush I was going through, I had several encounters that might have made me doubt my attractiveness but could also have seemed to confirm that many *maschi italiani* were too sexually insecure to accept either a direct proposition by a woman or her taking the lead in bed, especially if she is (horrors!) older than they. I used to hang out at the gym with a group of three younger Italian dentists with whom I exchanged a lot of amusing repartee. At one point, I invited them to dinner at my apartment. Not for group sex (although looking back I am increasingly sure I missed a once-in-a-life occasion) but because I hoped that one of the three, whom I found particularly attractive, would stay on after the others had left.

Domenico was a well-built guy with green eyes and floppy light brown hair, the color that passes for blond here in Italy. After a dinner characterized by riotous laughter and the startling revelation that it was not impossible for an American woman to be a good cook, two of the guys left and Domenico indeed did stay on, but afterwards I wondered why. I tried snuggling up to him on the couch but he didn't take the hint. And when I asked him, as beguilingly as I could, to *darmi un bacio*, to kiss me, he not only demurred but then started shouting. "You don't understand," he snarled as he walked to the door. "It is I who am supposed to take the initiative." He never spoke to me again.

This fiasco was followed by several others of the same type, leading me to believe that some, or maybe all, of my antennae simply were not working. At a party in Rome I had met Alberto, a headhunter who was based in Milan, and we had become friends; he spoke excellent English, had a good sense of humor and was tall, blond and decidedly attractive, although not my usual type. In that period I was doing a lot of financial reporting and spent a lot of time in Milan where Alberto was always extremely generous with his contacts, his friends, and his spare bedroom. But he never made a pass, not even when we arranged to spend a three-day weekend together in Istanbul, a city we both adored, and where – although we were staying in different hotels – I was still hopeful "something" might happen.

Finally, at one point, having clearly not learned my lesson, I tried to force the issue by taking his hand. A few seconds later, to my extreme embarrassment, he gently withdrew it, allowing me to experience a glimpse of what men go through when they make a pass and are rejected. But maybe they are more used to it than I was. No, he was not gay, as some of my friends charitably suggested; he probably just wasn't attracted to me.

The same probably was true for Marco, a red-haired artisan in my neighborhood who played calcetto (soccer with a team of only seven players) several times a week and as a consequence had a fantastic body. He always seemed delighted to see me (now as then), and always invited me to the bar for a coffee, but once when he'd come to the apartment to see if he could fix a faulty cabinet door and I tentatively put my arms around him, he moved away. Was this because I didn't appeal to him, because I was taking the initiative or because I was older than he? Perhaps all three.

Years later I had some further insight into why when I mentioned to Sergio and Claudio, two brother jewelers in my neighborhood with whom I am very friendly, that I had once had the hots for Marco. Their reaction was to gasp (in unison) in what I can only describe as horror. "But he's our age," one of them, 15 years my junior, exclaimed. "So?" I asked. "Senti, if we want something on the side, we're going to look at 20-year-olds," continued Sergio, confirming my theory that in this country men confuse sex, or rather sensuality, with window-shopping for things that are new (that is, young) and pretty.

And what about Enzo, a publicist, which in Italy means someone who operates as a journalist but has not taken the state exam still required in Italy to become one? Enzo worked for a publishing house and also did part-time PR work for an important church group. We met at a dinner hosted by a mutual friend, a Vatican correspondent, and no doubt thanks to the wine and the candlelight developed a strong mutual attraction. It turned out that Enzo was married and that his wife had stayed home for the evening with their children, but that wasn't going to stop him (or me, naturally). As soon as he could arrange it he asked me out: I invited him for dinner but when we repaired to the bedroom it seemed he was too shy even to take off his underpants and believe me I am not *that* aggressive.

Chapter 10 – Amerigo (Part Two)

Amerigo has a small blackboard pegged to the shelves behind him, shelves that hold a myriad of bottles containing liquids ranging from the usual wine or whisky colors to the more peculiarly shaded *aperitivi*, such as the bright yellow Crodino, the raspberry-red Campari and the more exotically green Coca-Buton or light blue Curaçao. Generally, Amerigo uses the blackboard to keep track of the results of Rome's two soccer teams, Roma and Lazio, which, not surprisingly, make for boisterous discussions between those who, like Amerigo are *romanisti*, supporters of the Roma team, and the neighborhood *laziali*. Over the decades, Lazio has generally been the underdog, but in 1974 it had finally won the national championship (something that was not to happen again for 26 years!), creating great exhilaration among its fans. But sometimes Amerigo's cryptic remarks are linked to current events, as in "*La Roma*, just like Jimmy Carter," or some such slogan, giving even a person like myself who is not a sports fan an opening to angle in on the conversation among *i tifosi,* the fans.

One of the reasons Amerigo moves so slowly is, in my opinion, because of the time he spends listening to others and thinking about what they've said. One day, for example, he wanted to know my opinion of the film *Carnal Knowledge*, which he had recently seen, although of course like almost all foreign films here it had been dubbed into Italian. I, myself, had seen the movie here in Italy, at the now defunct Pasquino movie theater, the only movie house Rome has ever had that was dedicated full-time to showing English-language films in the original version. Named after the so-called "talking statue" near Piazza Navona (where 19th-century dissidents opposed to the Papal State used to leave revolutionary messages), the theater was located round the back from my apartment, which made movie-going extremely convenient. It has some disadvantages, too, as I discovered shortly after moving into Olivia's apartment; in those days there was no air conditioning and to counter the effects of the summer heat, the Pasquino's owners had built a sliding roof that could be opened to let in air, and the occasional inexperienced kitten. This, unfortunately, meant that in Olivia's bedroom (soon to be mine) one could hear dialogue, music, gunshots, screams… the works.

"Is that really what life is like on a university campus?" Amerigo asks me, pronouncing it "campoos". Amerigo has other American customers, but sometimes I have the feeling I may be the only one with whom he has what can be classified as real conversations, perhaps because my Italian is so fluent, perhaps because when I have the time I am a grade-A chatterer. Although he has never been out of Italy, Amerigo seems genuinely interested in other people's lives and viewpoints. And this seems to be particularly true where Americans are concerned.

Although World War II has been over for almost 30 years, after moving here I quickly discover that internal Italian politics are still in full 1950s Cold War swing. Here, as elsewhere in Europe, people are divided among those who love Americans, those who hate them, and those (probably the majority) who feel both sentiments. This means that then, probably less so than now, as an American you were going to find yourself on the receiving end of a lot of finger pointing, no matter what your own personal politics. The first time I did a national radio program with audience call-ins, I was baffled, staggered and, yes, depressed by the degree of anti-Americanism that seemed to be directed against me as an individual. True, this was the post-Chile, Vietnam era, and there were many things about American foreign policy I, too, found abhorrent. But I also got tired of hearing my country described as a nation of imperialists and racists, especially since at the time Italians were hardly in a position to preach, particularly on the latter point. It's probably ridiculous to expect Italians to remember their own past imperialism, the Roman Empire having been extant for a couple of millennia. But what about Mussolini's nasty exploits in Africa? Furthermore, it was all too easy for them to point fingers at the U.S. for its unsolved racial problems. When I moved here in the early seventies, as far as I was concerned there was nothing credible the Italians could say about racism since anything but a white face was a real exception; Rome, like the rest of the country, was wrapped in a blanket of homogeneity that to a born-and-bred, Rainbow-Coalition New Yorker was simply stifling. In fact, often the only thing I could come up with as a retort was to point out that Italian-Americans as a group – at least those in New York or New Jersey – certainly had a less than a sterling record on racial tolerance.

Amerigo also likes talking to me, I imagine, because I am a reporter and in Italy there has always been an undue amount of admiration and pedestal-placing for *il giornalista*. By the time I got here, many of the trappings first accorded journalists as a group, for example, under Fascism, had gone by the boards. But others were still in place. True, you could no longer ride the buses free or get into movies for nothing (unless you were a film critic), but there were special train and airfare rates for journalists, discounts for the *Autostrade*, the big national highways, and – as a rather enterprising New York girlfriend of mine discovered – if you had the nerve, there were many stores you could walk into and ask for a *sconto per giornalisti*, a journalists' discount, and actually get it!

Not surprisingly, then, journalism is a profession that in Italy has often attracted a lot of people with a penchant, and a skill, for what one could call pontification. As a journalist, you are expected to know something, even a lot, about more or less everything, something which is of course impossible. So this may explain why Amerigo was so interested in my answers to his questions. For my part, even though I have plenty of opinions, I am not afraid of admitting when I don't know something and therefore I was always fearful of disappointing him. More than once, listeners to the call-in radio program I hosted, the one during which I was sometimes targeted for being an ugly American, expressed dismay that I had admitted to not being up on this or that subject and would have to check and get back to him or her. "But," they would say in aggrieved tones, "you're a journalist!"

Another day it's the issue of political assassination. "Listen, Sherry," he says, as usual mispronouncing my name (but by now I've given up correcting him). "No one really believes that Oswald (or "Osvald" as the Italian pronounce it) acted alone, do they? And what about Sirhan Sirhan? The two surely are linked, no?" I tell him that public opinion in the U.S. is divided on the issue but that much of the evidence seems to indicate that "Osvald" acted alone and that Sirhan Sirhan's murder of Robert Kennedy appeared to be unconnected to President Kennedy's murder. Amerigo, clearly skeptical, looks at me with raised eyebrows. Like many Europeans, and some Americans as well, Italians are convinced there is always a plot behind everything, that chance simply does not exist, and that the high-ranking and powerful are always up to no good. Thus, in 1978, it took only moments for almost all of Italy to decide that Pope John Paul I had been murdered in his bed rather than having suffered a heart attack. Many also unkindly – and disrespectfully – joked that when death arrived, the newly elected pontiff was probably reading pornography rather than *The Imitation of Christ* as the Vatican insisted. In the same way, in the summer of 1999, many Italians immediately decided that *forze oscure*, "dark forces", had deliberately sabotaged John F. Kennedy Jr.'s plane.

It's not hard to figure out that this kind of mind-set has a lot to do with Italian history – a succession of invasions, alliances, broken alliances, betrayals, court intrigues and so on – and I am also willing to concede that I, myself, am probably a bit naïve. But the Italians' unwavering *dietrologia,* a word coined to mean the "science" of figuring out what's behind – *dietro* – this or that event, is depressing. So pervasive a conspiratorial outlook says very negative things about a society. It says, for example, that people believe they are only pawns in the game of life and that nothing they do will make any difference. Which may go far to explain why Italians, and the Romans in particular, are so passive, putting up quietly with so much inefficiency and government unresponsiveness. Only a few weeks earlier, I had been to the local post office to pick up a package of books that had arrived while I was away on a three-week visit back home. "It's been destroyed," the clerk told me without a trace of sorrow or regret. "What?" I cried. "I go away for a month and come back to find my personal property destroyed by the Italian Post Office?" I was furious, but what amazed me more was that I didn't get a word or glance of sympathy or encouragement from anyone else standing in line. For them, all poker-faced, it was just business as usual.

Although I didn't know much about his politics, Amerigo seemed to belong to the group of "pro-American" Italians rather than the hostile ones; although clearly not overcome with adulation, he was honestly curious about life in these United States. Once you are living over here, the impact that American society has had on Italy quickly becomes obvious; for if gratitude for the U.S. wartime military presence and the generosity of the postwar Marshall Plan have faded, the country was (and is) awash in the sound of American music, the impact of American movies, and countless images of the American life style, be it, back then, that of Fonzi in *Happy Days*, or now by the characters in *Desperate Housewives* or *CSI*, not to mention fast or frozen food, huge supermarkets, drive-in burger joints or giant malls. Our defects, too, be they racism, spiraling domestic crime and violence, the scourge of handguns, and the unwarranted or unwise interventions abroad that more than once have characterized our foreign policy have also left their mark on Italian views, often producing a real love-hate relationship.

On my part, I must confess, I find Amerigo interesting more for "sociological" reasons than for his political views. At 41, unmarried and living with his mother, he seems like a stereotype come alive. "But I am happy like this," he says when I ask him if he minds not being married. "I have everything that I want and need," he insists. Still, it was unusual, even in Italy, where grown men publicly address their mothers as "*mammina*" ("Mommy"), where people who barely know you will say things like, "Today I took Mamma for a check-up," or "Mamma had a fall this week," and where *la mamma* is always sacred. "*Ma la mamma è sempre la mamma,*" people will say to you chidingly when you try to explain the bad relationship you might have had with yours – "But your mother is always your mother," they keep saying.

Amerigo and his mother, Natalina, live in a large apartment in the residential Prati area of Rome together with his sister, Lella, her husband Aldo, a watchmaker, and that couple's two children, Luciana and, of course, Alessandro. Amerigo has been working in the bar almost his entire life, starting right after the war when he began by helping out his father, Guido, behind the counter. And by now, with his calm and kindness, he has become a neighborhood fixture, or at least for that part of the neighborhood – really just a block-long radius running from the bar halfway up Vicolo del Cinque, the first bit of Vicolo di Bologna, the first half of Via della Scala and part of Piazza S. Egidio – that constitutes our turf. (Only one piazza away in Piazza De Renzi, the locals head in an entirely different direction for their caffeine fixes and other refreshments.) In our small area, in fact, everyone seems to know everyone else's business. After an incident for which the police had to be called, Teresa, the *fruttivendola*, immediately informed me that strangers (actually, they were policemen I had called) had been peering under and in my car and that I should be careful. When someone dies, word gets around immediately. And when someone wins the lottery, that news travels even faster.

What almost no one knew, and what I myself found out only several years later, was that there was more to Amerigo's life than met the eye. Although it only came out after Natalina's death in 1992, it turned out that Amerigo had a long-standing *relazione*. Catty-corner to the bar, at the intersection between Vicolo del Cinque and Via della

Pelliccia where today there is a restaurant, there was once a car mechanic's *officina*, or garage, and unbeknownst to almost all there was *del tenero*, that is tender feelings or sentiment, between Amerigo and Gabriella, the mechanic's wife. A heavily made-up, improbable redhead who despite a large mole on her face is not unattractive, Gabriella apparently was attracted by Amerigo's kindness and calm, a sharp contrast to her difficult and sometimes violent husband. No one seems to know exactly when their affair began. The official story is that they ran into one another in a hospital corridor when Amerigo's mother was dying and Gabriella, by then divorced, was visiting a sick friend. But still waters run deep, and Alessandro is sure that the two had been seeing each other for years before that. Two months after Natalina's funeral, they wed, and Amerigo finally got to see something of the world – Paris, Egypt, London, Vienna – places about which he'd been limited beforehand only to asking questions. But alas, his new life was not to be lengthy. His heart gave out and after a series of attacks he passed away, leaving Gabriella as the bar's owner and Alessandro as its manager.

Part Three

Days of Wine… and Bullets

We are now into the 1980s and no one quite knows why, but alone among European countries, with the exception – for a briefer and less bloody period – of West Germany, Italy has been murderously afflicted with the scourge of home-grown terrorism. This violence compounds that wrought by the Mafia, engaged in a bloody attempt to repel efforts by the Italian government and judiciary to bring organized crime under control, and the first signs of international terrorism have surfaced. All these things are beginning to have a particular relevance to my own life. Not only do I myself appear, inexplicably, to have become a target of terrorists, but with some Italian investigators having laid the attempt on Pope John Paul II's life at the feet of the Bulgarians, work increasingly revolves around these themes. Life as a freelancer continues to have both pluses and minuses and my personal life is getting complicated. I have had an unhappy break-up with someone I really cared for and am trying to distract myself with new lovers. Luckily, I have been able to buy the apartment I have been living in and have come to love and I am making an effort – although this will inevitably prove impossible – to become more "Italian", generally putting pleasure first and foremost.

Chapter 11 – Terrorism Threatens (me)

He was probably not much older than 22 and, with his khaki green *eskimo,* an anorak or sort of hooded parka that was in vogue then, a knitted cap pulled down low over his forehead and the scuffed, tan leather shoulder bag known as a *"borsa di Tolfa"*, he looked no different from thousands of other European male students. The only difference, a big one, was that he was a terrorist, probably an embryonic one, but there he was nevertheless, standing on my doorstep with a gun (cum silencer) pointed quite noticeably in the direction of my navel.

Terrorism was not far from my mind on that morning in spring, 1981, when, as I sought to ease into the new day, I sat drinking my Lapsang Souchong tea and catching up on the previous day's *Corriere della Sera.* Ever since the 1969 Milan bank bombing, political violence and terrorism had become a major issue and one that journalists in Italy simply had to cover. The explosion that year in the Banca di Agricoltura, in which 16 innocent people died for no other reason than that they were in the wrong place at the wrong time, sent shock waves throughout Italy.

The incident's most likely political matrix – Anarchism? Fascism? Communism? – or was it renegade secret service plotting? – was to be the subject of unending debate and a mind-boggling number of criminal trials stretching out over the decades. But if you look at the photos taken in the immediate aftermath of the explosion, the shattered expressions on the faces of the *milanesi* gathered in Piazza Fontana to watch the bodies being carried out said it all with silent eloquence, they register dismay and horror at scenes of destruction they thought they had left behind them at the end of World War II. Over the next 20-odd years, spiraling violence was to kill and maim hundreds in this country, and yet Italians today seem to have emerged from this violence largely unscarred, and no more introspective than before about what it was in their society that had encouraged the emergence of so much bloodshed.

But back in 1969, it was just the beginning. Who could have imagined then, for example, that in March, 1978, left-wing terrorists would have successfully organized the kidnapping of Aldo Moro, an erudite, courteous politician and master tactician, whose melancholy southern Italian mien and dark hair with its curious streak of white running back from the forehead were stamped indelibly on the Italian collective consciousness?

Indeed, almost ten years later, on the morning of March 16, 1978, a commando unit disguised as flight attendants or pilots (it has never been entirely clarified) ambushed the motorcade accompanying Moro to his downtown office. For their venue, the attackers chose Via Mario Fani, a normally quiet street in the residential Camilluccia neighborhood on the eastern side of the city. Slaughtering all five of Moro's police bodyguards with machine-guns – purchased, it was later discovered, in Eastern Europe – they threw the former prime minister into the back seat of a blue Fiat sedan and spirited him away.

I heard the news on my car radio while I was driving up Via Baldo degli Ubaldi on my way to a dry cleaner in another, more outlying, neighborhood that unlike the one near home was willing to store my winter coats on their premises. I was so stunned that I had to pull the old blue VW over to the side of the road to catch my breath and stop trembling. I hadn't felt that way since Robert Kennedy had been murdered and felt particularly shaken since only a few nights before I had had a strange dream in which I had been riding in an old U.S. Army jeep together with Eisenhower and Moro, both dressed in wool, khaki-colored, World War II U.S. army uniforms.

The kidnapping was to have significant political repercussions. Shortly after, at ten o'clock that morning, the Speaker of the Chamber of Deputies, Communst Pietro Ingrao (his recent election to that post in itself an explicit recognition of the party's notable parliamentary strength) formally announced that the kidnapping had taken place.

Within an hour, Italy's three major trade unions had called a general strike and began organizing a giant outdoor rally against terrorism. Ironically, Moro's kidnapping brought the Communists and the Christian Democrats closer than they'd been in a long time. That day for the first time, Italy's Marxists actually voted "yes" in a vote of confidence for a new Christian Democratic government headed by Moro's frequent party rival, Giulio Andreotti.

But Moro was just the most illustrious of Italian terrorism's victims. Among the dozens of others the terrorists – right wing or left wing – had killed (or were to kill) were Guido Rossi, a union organizer, Vittorio Occorsio, a Rome magistrate, Vittoro Bachelet, a

Rome University law professor, economist Ezio Tarantelli, who was married to an American psychotherapist, Carol Tarantelli, and Fulvio Croce, the president of the Turin Bar. Many politicians, including my friend Fabio, had been kneecapped.

Terrorists had also blasted a fatal hole in the brain of Walter Tobagi, a leading young journalist of the country's most authoritative newspaper, *Corriere della Sera*, and murdered Carlo Casalegno, the veteran editor of the Turin daily, *La Stampa*, owned by the Fiat automobile company (where, incidentally, about a dozen executives or workers had also been shot, although none fatally). The situation had gotten to the point that when I awoke in the morning, I immediately turned on the radio to learn if there had been any incidents and, if so, how serious they were. Indeed, there were so many terrorist acts (and, in general, acts of political violence) that the *Ministero dell'Interno*, the Interior Ministry, which is in charge of police and internal security matters, routinely released monthly and yearly statistics listing all episodes, large and small, everything from rock-throwing and arson directed against right-wing or left-wing party branch offices to kidnappings, kneecappings and outright murder.

So it was probably no wonder, given the political climate and the subjects I was dealing with professionally on a daily basis, that even three years after Moro's death, I had terrorists on the brain. But if during the so-called *anni di piombo*, the "years of bullets", several Italian journalists had been targeted, foreign reporters had been exempt. So when the downstairs buzzer rang, it certainly didn't occur to me that I might be on someone's hit list. "*Chi è?*" I said into the intercom. "Who is it?" Still in my pajamas, and by now used to living in a city where there is relatively little everyday violence – so little that more often than not I forget to double-lock my door when I go to bed at night – I was perfectly willing to believe the man when he said that he had an envelope for me from Romana Recapiti, one of the first messenger services in the city to capitalize on discontent with Italy's then highly inefficient mail system and provide a private way to satisfy the need for a rapid delivery system for letters and documents. "*C'è una busta* – there's an envelope – per *Lei*, for you," the disembodied voice said. "I'm not dressed," I replied, "leave it in the mail room, please." But, he said, they needed a signature. So I buzzed him in.

I thought nothing of it when, once I'd opened the door, he handed me a bulky envelope, a ballpoint pen, and an open, oversized register with a red-orange cardboard cover, similar, or perhaps identical, to those the Italian post office then used for *espressi,* the now-discontinued special delivery letters that despite their name generally took the longest to arrive.

It was after those first few seconds, while I was unsuccessfully trying to click what was a defective ballpoint into action, that I found myself looking into a gun barrel, or rather into the silencer that was attached to it. Probably on his first "mission" and no doubt as frightened as I was, my unwelcome visitor neglected to give me any orders of the kind you'd expect to accompany a pointed gun: *"Mani in alto!* – Hands up!" or *"Tieni la bocca chiusa!* – Keep quiet!" So instead of cowering and stepping aside to let him come in, my reaction, in retrospect probably highly unwise, but nonetheless happily effective, was to scream, *"Aiuto! Terroristi!"* – Help! Terrorists!" throw the book at him (literally) and slam the door.

He ran down the stairs and, I was later told, jumped on the back seat of a waiting scooter, and disappeared. Fleeing, the two men lost – or tossed – the shoulder bag containing the gun and two pairs of handcuffs, the latter a detail which, when I learned of it, left me retrospectively numb with fear. In the meantime, I had rushed to the window, opened it (or so I thought; actually my arm went right through the glass) and continued to call for help. "Terrorists, terrorists," I yelled, it never entering my mind for a second that my assailants might have been ordinary robbers.

It was, of course, a very heady time. The political fallout from the Cold War had turned Italy into what some called a *democrazia bloccata,* a democracy in which a genuine alternation of power was impossible, in part because of the U.S. veto on the Communists' participation in government. The result was widespread frustration. And if normal people on the left of the political spectrum realized that they had little immediate recourse but to grit their teeth and bear it, the same could not be said of those with an extremist bent.

That group could be divided into two components. On the one hand were the students and other young people who in the late 1970s were joining Marxist collectives and running amok in the streets to protest against the "regime". Pointing fingers of blame at the world's big multinational corporations, they were convinced that most of the evil in the world could be laid at the doorstep of the CIA and the U.S. government, which had succeeded in blackening our country's name with its backing of government repression in places like Chile and tarnishing its reputation with our own misguided Vietnam War.

But these extreme leftists were equally furious with the PCI, the Italian Communists, and to signal their disaffection with and independence from the official left, they called themselves *gli autonomi*, the autonomous ones. And if, at the start, they limited themselves to disrupting university life, 1968-style, increasingly there were Molotov cocktails being hurled and ever-more violent skirmishes being provoked with the police. In Rome, the streets around the university were often dense with clouds of tear gas and if you had to be there as I often did, doing radio spots for *CBS News*, you really had to be careful.

The second, and fortunately far-smaller, group consisted of somewhat older people who, whether on the left or the right, shared the conviction that the only effective strategy for political change would be to create widespread terror. Leftist extremists, who saw themselves as the only true Marxists in Italy and some of whom had founded or joined the Red Brigades or groups such as Front Line or the Party of Communist Combatants, were convinced that ongoing terror would stimulate a *coup d'état* by the military that would then lead the Italian Communists and other leftists to re-discover their true calling: Revolution. Rightist terrorist groups like the NAR (the Armed Revolutionary Nuclei) theorized instead that terrorism would lead to the installation of a strong, autocratic government, the only kind that in their view could put the country back on its proper course.

Although they came from different ideological backgrounds, these two groups were equally committed to what they called *la lotta armata*, the armed struggle, and as kneecappings escalated into assassinations, subjected the country to pervasive political violence. The real danger, given the widespread political disaffection that existed in the country, was that these extremists, particularly those on the left, would be able to use sympathizers, the so-called *fiancheggiatori,* as a reservoir to be tapped for new recruits.

Moro had been held prisoner for 55 days when, on May 9, 1978, he was murdered, his limp, lifeless body abandoned in the trunk of a dark red Renault 4 car, that had been parked – deliberately, the pundits suggested – in a street almost equidistant from the headquarters of both the Christian Democrat and Communist parties. During the preceding period, tensions had run incredibly high. As the correspondent for the *Washington Post*, I had an inside line to the Home Minister's chief spokesman, Luigi Zanda, a charming and friendly 36-year old with black hair and a ready smile (now, a grey-haired left-of-center member of parliament) who would call me with a last-minute update every night before leaving the office, basically providing information for the next day's story. One night he told me about the report of a handwriting analyst on the most recent of the many letters written from captivity by Moro as he sought desperately to mediate between government and terrorists in what proved to be a vain hope of saving his own life. Another time, Luigi told me, there had been a séance with a medium who, it was hoped, might have had something helpful to say about where the veteran leader was being kept prisoner. (Interestingly enough, the medium appears to have come frustratingly close, coming up with the name "Gradoli". The small town of that name above Lake Bolsena in Northern Lazio was searched fruitlessly from attic to cellar. After Moro's death, captured terrorists revealed that the apartment where he'd been held prisoner in Rome was located instead in the capital's Via Gradoli!)

The Italian police's inability to find Moro was a severe blow for the then Home Minister, Christian Democrat Francesco Cossiga, a Sardinian university law professor turned politician who was later to become President of the Republic. Cossiga was probably ill-equipped in terms of experience or worldliness to deal with the kidnapping crisis, but was clearly frantic to save the life of Moro, one of his closest friends. When the latter's body was found he resigned his office, a relatively rare occurrence in Italian political life.

In comparison to all this, my own run-in with the terrorists was just a little blip on the monitor, even though it was written up by my colleagues at the *Associated Press* as a kidnapping attempt ("What did you think they were going to do, spirit me off on a Vespa?" I joshed my colleagues when, some time later, I was able to joke about it.) The story made the Italian papers and got me a lot of short-lived attention, including a telegram from Prime Minister Andreotti congratulating me on my escape, an offer of a gun permit (turned down) from a high-ranking officer at Rome police headquarters, and some much appreciated day-after support from the police who, when I became obsessive in the attack's aftermath, patiently examined my car for explosives and sent someone over whenever I felt threatened. All this helped assuage the terrible fear that I felt for several months afterwards every time I returned to my apartment and saw young, long-haired men hanging around downstairs in the piazza, which was all the time, because in those days most young Italian men in my area *looked* like left-wing activists (whereas today they tend to have shaved or gel-embossed heads, earrings, and goatees). "Why don't you move?" Henry Tanner of the *New York Times* asked me when I referred to my fears. But that seemed unacceptable to me.

Looking back, some of the related episodes were ludicrous. One day shortly after the incident, I had just gotten out of the shower when the downstairs doorbell rang. The would-be visitor announced himself as a *Carabiniere* officer from the neighborhood station. It sounds perfectly reasonable – now – that I should have had such a visitor. But in the aftermath of the incident, I was in the grip of post-incident terror and feared, albeit irrationally, that my attackers were back with yet another ploy. So I called the police. The *Carabinieri*, easily recognized by their black uniforms with a red stripe down the pant legs or their dark blue police cars, originally a police division of the Italian army that is both highly esteemed for its discipline and loyalty as well as the butt of many Italian jokes, as in "How many *carabinieri* does it take to screw in a light bulb?" Answer: "Two: one to stand on a chair to hold the bulb and the other to turn the chair." But they are also the fierce rivals of the Polizia di Stato, the Italian state police corps, which reports to the Home Ministry. I had told my would-be visitor that I was busy washing my hair. But when he rang the bell a second time, I told him to go away and that I had called the police. He was aghast when he learned a rival was on his way to check him out. "*Dio mio!* Couldn't you have called the *Carabinieri*?" he wailed almost plaintively when we finally talked.

For the record, the young *carabiniere* was convinced the incident had only been a robbery attempt, despite the evidence pointing to the contrary: – the handcuffs, the silencer and also the fact that there was no reason for anyone to imagine that I, low-paid as I was, would have much worth stealing. Indeed, the *Carabinieri* Anti-terrorism unit at the Piazza Bologna station across town disagreed. Although they could offer no plausible reason why I, in particular, might have been chosen as a target, they believed my visitors were members of some small, neophyte terrorist group. My own theory as to "why me", was that the terrorists had confused me with the late Claire Sterling, an older American woman, who had written for the *Washington Post* before me, and as the author of the Bulgarian Connection theory that sought to explain the attempted assassination of Pope John Paul II, was known to be politically conservative and strongly anti-Communist. The anti-terrorism unit asked me to help build an identikit of my would-be attacker. But after having done that and, incidentally, after having turned down a request to spy on my fellow journalists, I was to hear no more. Fortunately, the fear soon gave way to some amusing memories.

Along with the *carabiniere* episode, my favorite memory of an incident that could have had tragic consequences for me, was the interview with the *dirigente,* or top plainclothes officer, at the Trastevere police precinct who just happened to speak with the same heavy Sicilian accent as a fictional character, also a policeman based in Rome, in a wonderful 1970 movie directed by Elio Petri called *Investigation of a Citizen Above All Possible Suspicion*, a movie about the politically-charged sixties. When I was accompanied to the precinct to be debriefed after the incident, he seemed to have only one important question to ask me. He slowly tore open the manila envelope my unwelcome pistol-toting guest had brought with him, clearly just to give credibility to his claim he had a delivery for me, only to find that it held nothing more than a rolled- up copy of the leftwing daily, *La Repubblica*, today one of Italy's two best-selling newspapers but then a new, outspoken daily which, to conservatives, appeared almost subversive. It was clear to me, as it would – I think – have been to anyone, that the newspaper had been chosen at random merely to give my putative missive its proper bulk. But the *dirigente* seemed set on finding a deeper, darker reason. "Tell me," he said, in a portentous tone, staring at me intently and narrowing his eyes with suspicion, "are you a subscriber to this paper?"

Chapter 12 – Paolo

Winter in Rome is happily temperate. Since I moved here in 1972 there have been only three major snowstorms. Even in January there are often Sundays when it is possible to eat outdoors, on a friend's terrace or in one of those small trattorias around the Campo de' Fiori where the waiters always seem happy to drag a few tables outdoors to satisfy those desperate to enjoy the sun's feeble rays, together with a view of the flower market and the statue of Giordano Bruno, the "heretic" burned at the stake on that spot in 1600. In November and December, in contrast, the rain can pour down incessantly, day after day, washing down the long-neglected ancient cobblestones, backing up the sewer system (parts of which date back to Roman times) and filling the Tiber to the brim.

After 20 days of constant wet, I was down in the dumps. But the weather was only partly to blame. I had just broken up with the man I had been seeing for ten years, who at 45 had become enamored of a 25-year old TV woman broadcaster (it didn't last), and I was greatly in need of consolation. My mother had offered to come over from New York to comfort me, but given our tortured relationship, I was sure that wouldn't make me feel much better. So the only solution, other than seeing friends – primarily other American or British correspondents – was to throw myself into work.

Early that fall (I remember the exact date, September 2, 1982, because I was on the ferry returning to Rome from a vacation in Sardinia), Italy's anti-Mafia "Czar", Carabiniere General Carlo Alberto Dalla Chiesa and his young wife, Emanuela, had been assassinated in downtown Palermo, their small, white Autobianchi 112 reduced to Swiss-cheese status by hundreds of bullets from one or more Kalashnikov machine-guns. As usual in Italy, it was difficult, if not impossible, to separate fact from fiction, always the first step in doing any serious reporting from here. Some newspapers were suggesting Dalla Chiesa been set up by someone in the Italian cabinet and that his secret diaries, containing God knows what, had been stolen. Others said the diaries had never existed and blamed his death on the Mafia's ability to take advantage of the general's carelessness; rumor had it he so wanted his adored bride to enjoy a normal life that, as on this occasion, from time to time he would forgo his bodyguards and armored limousine in favor of an ordinary car. In any event, there were lots of stories to do. Only three years after the Moro kidnapping and killing, the country was again in shock, and at the *Reuters* office where I was still renting my small space, the climate was uncharacteristically somber. Even Claudio, the burly traffic cop on duty near the presidential palace, the Quirinale, seemed to be unusually subdued. When I would arrive at the entrance to Via della Dataria, flashing my driving permit for the *centro storico*, he'd wave me on cheerlessly with an uncharacteristic lack of interest in the usual rambling chat.

To keep my mind off my break-up, I was also busying myself with the renovations I had decided on for what now really was *my* apartment. A few years earlier, when the landlord had become concerned that his lessee, Olivia, who was spending almost all of her time in New York, was someone with whom he no longer had any direct contact, I had taken over the lease. And then, in 1982, I had taken him up on his offer to sell the place to me, paying not much more than around $40,000 for what would be my home for the next 20 years. I had decided to replace the old stone floor with deep red-orange Tuscan *cotto* and to re-do the tiny bathroom, installing a bidet, putting in bright blue faucets and towel racks, and totally re-tiling. The floor and wall tiles I chose were simple: slightly off-white and edged with blue. But I had splurged and chosen a beautiful, hand-painted and very expensive design, tiles with a blue and turquoise, iris-like flower with a curving dark green stem that were to be placed in a seemingly random pattern on the walls. I had also decided to demolish the non-weight-bearing wall delimiting my too-small kitchen and had ordered a wonderful wood-paneled, marble-topped Italian *cucina,* the kind that for some unknown reason, Italians like to refer to as a *cucina americana*, an American kitchen.

So too much moping would have been impossible. The three workers I had hired, Paolo, Alberto and Mimmo, arrived every day at about 8 a.m., broke for lunch sharply at noon when the cannon on the Janiculum Hill boomed, and resumed working at one p.m. until about four p.m. Afternoons, I was always in my office downtown. But try as I may, getting out of the house early is always a problem for me. And even when, to escape the dust and debris, I would sleep at a girlfriend's house a few blocks away, I still had to come home in the morning to change clothes, pick up phone messages and see if I needed anything from my files. The upshot was that I ended up spending a lot of time with these guys. And, little by little, I realized that I was becoming increasingly aware of Paolo and looking forward to seeing him each day.

When he was young, Paolo was very attractive. Unusually for a Roman, he was blonde and blue-eyed. Not tall – but then again I have always found myself attracted to men on the shorter side of the height spectrum – he had a great-looking body. So what if his powerful shoulders and arms (the result of years of hefting bricks and bags of cement) were slightly out of proportion with his slim legs and thighs? Most intriguing was his apparent centeredness. Quiet, calm and with an enormous capacity for concentration, he seemed happy to be who he was. That, and the fact that, except when he was explaining a structural or decorating problem, he rarely looked at me, combined to make me feel increasingly captivated. I had no idea if the attraction was reciprocal. But I was sure he was too shy, and too professional, ever to make a pass at a client.

We spent a lot of time discussing whether the beige, four-by-four wall tiles in the kitchen should be mounted on the straight or on the diagonal (in the end we opted for a mix, which looked terrific). Then there was the problem of the sink; I wanted a brown one and it took ages to find one, but the chocolate-brown double sink he came up with was perfect, although I did have to settle for beige rather than brown faucets. And after long debate, I decided (a serious mistake) not to have the apartment totally rewired. Throughout all this, things had never become even remotely personal, but nevertheless I was becoming obsessed. So one day when he returned from lunch ahead of his partners, I decided to take matters into my own hands. We were standing on the small black and red-tiled landing outside my door and, summoning up my courage, I decided it was now or never. "*Mi piaci* – I like you," I blurted out without much ado, my heart thudding away under my off-white Max Mara sweater. "*E tu?* And you?" I queried. Paolo has always been a man of few words and that day was no exception. And, as he later admitted, he was quite surprised. But he quickly rallied, putting his arms around me and kissing me warmly on the lips.

Needless to say, Paolo was married. Then 30, he'd been married for 10 years – that is ever since he'd gotten a 15-year-old neighborhood girl named Annamaria pregnant. Abortion was illegal and terminating a pregnancy was risky as well as expensive. But Paolo was happy to get married, even though it meant dropping out of high school and finding a job. Getting hitched allowed him to leave his family's cramped apartment in the working-class San Lorenzo neighborhood and to set up a household of his own. It wasn't that he didn't get along with his mother, a tiny, over-solicitous homemaker, and his father, a small, wrinkled stonemason from whom he had learned his craft. "But getting married made me feel grown up, as if my life had finally begun," he told me once.

This did not mean, however, that at the outset he particularly enjoyed married life or was even particularly involved in the arrival of little Chiara (today a stunning 35-year-old, pocket-sized Venus with a flawless olive complexion, waist-length chestnut hair, her own husband and two little boys). Hardly. So while Annamaria was suffering the pangs of pregnancy, Paolo was out with his buddies, playing pool; while she was giving birth at one of those Italian hospitals staffed with nun-nurses who refuse to give you painkillers, he was out with his makeshift band, strumming on his guitar. And for the first few years after this modified version of a shotgun wedding he was a lousy husband. "I went right on as if nothing had changed in my life," he later confessed. "If I wanted to go out with my friends, I did. If I wanted to go to bed with another girl, I did. In fact, I spent most of my free time outside the house, while Annamaria stayed home and fumed, or cried."

At some point, however, he doesn't remember exactly when or why, he sobered up and became something at least resembling a family man. And by the time I met him his small contracting firm was doing very well – well enough for him to have built a three-story, semi-detached villa in a northern Roman suburb where he lives with Annamaria, Chiara and two sons, Gianmario and Bruno, and into which my tiny Trastevere lodgings could fit several times over. They have two cars and a motorbike, a large Maremmano sheepdog named Gertrude, an enormous game room complete with stereo equipment, a pool table, a wood-burning pizza oven and a wine cellar. There is also a large garden with several fruit trees and a vegetable garden where the family grows peppers, eggplants, chili peppers, strawberries and tomatoes and where two large turtles crawl about. All this is a far cry from the deprivations of Paolo's childhood and adolescence. When he was growing up, entertainment consisted of hanging out at the local café, taking a girl out for pizza or riding two buses and the subway for two hours to get to the beach at Ostia.

Growing up in a working-class family in an outlying district of Rome, Paolo knew next to nothing of the city he'd been raised in. To this day, largely because of a deep-seated, instinctive anticlericalism that for a long time led him to vote Communist, he has never been inside St. Peter's or the Vatican.

What he can't swallow, he says, is the Church's wealth and its contrast with the poverty that exists not just in Italy but also in many parts of the world. "There are plenty of priests doing incredible work with the poor, at great personal sacrifice," I, would argue with him, since over the years I have met many Roman Catholic religious whom I consider to be highly principled individuals. "If you say so," he'd answer skeptically, probably to keep the peace, since he is convinced that priests are part of the privileged class. But that has nothing to do with the fact that he was 18 before he saw the Coliseum for the first time, and only got to Venice and Naples at 20 because he was sent to those places to do his military service. Yes, he'd heard of Shakespeare and remembered a bit from his school days about major Italian authors such as Dante, Boccaccio and Alessandro Manzoni. But otherwise his education was limited. I had read Italo Calvino, Alberto Moravia, Umberto Eco and Leonardo Sciascia, all Italian writers he'd never heard of. And forget about foreign authors. Mention Dickens, Tolstoy, Proust, Hemingway or William Faulkner and he'd look at you blankly.

This was understandable given his family's background and limited economic resources, and I mention it only because the relationship made me realize how much we who have had the good fortune to get more education take for granted in normal interpersonal discourse. "Who do you think you are, Lady Macbeth?" I can say to my Italian girlfriend Minni, who works at the Ministry of Foreign Trade and she knows just what I mean. "You're acting like Dr. Strangelove," I can say to my colleague and he gets it immediately. "He's a modern-day Abraham Lincoln," would be easily comprehended by most of my friends, Italian or not, as would references to Woodstock, the Sphinx or the Colossus of Rhodes. But such things had no significance for Paolo, which meant that either I had to curb myself (which is tiring) or, each time, explain myself (which is also tiring). I felt, often, as if I were constantly translating, shifting from one conceptual framework into another. All this meant that I didn't really mind that he was married. I needed warmth, sex and affection to get my mind off my recent break-up. But it was clear that a bricklayer and a New Yorker with two graduate degrees had little in common on which they could base a long-term relationship.

Paolo had not always been faithful to Annamaria, but he was hardly a man on the prowl; after a long day pouring concrete, plastering walls and laying *parquet*, a man's energy is probably limited. Nevertheless the kiss on my landing changed things. "When can we see each other alone," he asked me shyly, as we broke apart? "Why don't we have dinner together tomorrow," I countered. And so we did, Paolo having invented some story about having to meet with a homeowner who wanted an estimate for re-paving a leaking terrace.

I remember we ended up eating at my place; Paolo is one of those Italian men who won't lift a finger at home but who, when stimulated, can turn out an excellent dish of pasta, in this case *fusilli* with tuna, mushrooms, tomato and capers. And then I was to be doubly surprised, since in the bedroom I had expected passion, but not such delicacy and responsiveness. Long live D.H. Lawrence! Paolo had never heard of the Kama Sutra or of Masters and Johnson. Yet there was a world of difference between him and those Italian intellectuals who despite all their reading seem convinced women should have instant orgasms and, should this not be the case, are unprepared (or perhaps unwilling and/or unable) to do anything about it.

Not surprisingly, Paolo's tastes were more "earthy" than mine; he preferred homemade wine, I the more sophisticated *grand cru* variety; he was more comfortable in inexpensive local *trattorie* with paper tablecloths and hearty pasta or meat dishes heavy in oil, while I who have always been weight-conscious preferred more ascetic cooking, except on special occasions. Once when we went to a somewhat "better" restaurant out on the Appia Antica and the waiter poured some red wine into Paolo's glass for him to taste, I could see that he was in trouble – but only briefly. After hesitating for a few seconds, he tasted it and nodded his approval. "You know, at first I didn't understand what I was supposed to do," he'd confided afterwards. "Then, I remembered I'd seen it in a movie."

Like many working-class Italians in those days, Paolo was also uncomfortable with anything but Italian cooking, whereas I, a native New Yorker, was delighted when foreign restaurants began opening in

Italy. But we shared a love of eating and drinking, and often would cook together, ending our meal by savoring several after-dinner glasses of *grappa* and then tumbling happily onto the bed or, more frequently, onto the living room couch. Everything he did was uncomplicated, direct and without shame; still naked, after making love he would fall soundly asleep, sprawled, arms, legs – and penis – akimbo. In addition, he was unremittingly affectionate; prone to those lengthy, rib-crushing hugs that make you feel you are not, after all, alone in the world.

Chapter 13 – Vacation Frenzy

In spring, as the British poet Alfred, Lord Tennyson, said, a young man's fancy turns to love. But in Italy each spring the fancy of every young man, of every young woman as well as that of their parents, their *nonni*, (the grandparents), their *zii* (aunts and uncles), and possibly that of myriad *bambini* turns to something else, and that is to plans for the year's summer *vacanze* or vacation. Generally, sometime in May – but anytime after Easter will do – everyone you run into seemingly has begun their vacation planning, is keen to tell you about it, and above all wants to know what you've got lined up. "*Vacanze?*" they query with an odd intensity, making you feel obligated to come up with some kind of answer.

When I first came here to live, I found this terribly disconcerting. At home in the United States, once I'd gotten past the summer-camp stage that took me through my mid-teens, summers were primarily a time to get some kind of job that would put some money in my pockets and enable me to buy new sweaters or records without having to ask my parents to increase my allowance. The only time I got to travel during the summer was after spending my junior year in Florence when a jaunt around the "Old Continent" before heading home was an option not to be passed up. My then boyfriend, Hal, and I bought a scooter and drove 6,000 kilometers around Europe before returning to the United States. Otherwise, I thought of vacations as something I would have once I'd graduated and found a job, or possibly I didn't think about them at all. In any event, in my mind future vacations could be planned for any time of the year, depending on your job, on what exactly you wanted to do, where you wanted to go, and whom you could find to do it with, the latter a major priority.

In contrast, Italians are obsessed with vacation time and the importance they give to *le ferie,* the holidays – traditionally concentrated in the summer months – made me feel extremely vulnerable when I was unattached or unsure if I could find any friends with whom to organize a trip. During the ten years I had been involved with my divorced intellectual, we had always taken summer trips together to Greece, Turkey, Sardinia or North Africa. Now instead, I was back on my own and felt like cringing whenever someone asked me what I'd be doing that summer. I solved the problem by renting a beach house in Sabaudia, the resort town about an hour down the coast from Rome, with a girlfriend. "Oh, I'll be going to Sabaudia as usual," I would say, airily, whenever someone posed THE question. Nowadays, of course, this has become much less important to me. But I can see that others, younger than I, still find it oppressive to be forced to make a contribution to what is in effect a national game of show and tell.

The Sabaudia routine turned out to be a particularly effective gambit. Although I wasn't really aware of it at the time, it is a rather "in" place, and one that is all the more appealing because its "in"-ness is not particularly visible and the celebrities whom it has drawn over the years – poet and filmmaker Pier Paolo Pasolini, novelist Alberto Moravia, film director Bernardo Bertolucci, as well as a newer lot of singers, actors and actresses and TV personalities – are not of the real jet-set variety. They love being at the beach and inviting each other to dinner but they don't seem to give a hoot about a noticeably flamboyant lifestyle.

A particularly ugly town built in the "Fascist style" of the 1930s, Sabaudia does not have a port to attract flashy, look-at-me yachters and their guests. It has no historic castle to attract sightseers, and its coastline is too flat and regular to inspire billionaires to construct luxury hideaways with breathtaking views as in Portofino, on Tuscany's Argentario peninsula, on the Amalfi drive or even in nearby Circeo (named after Circe, the sorceress who sought – unsuccessfully – to lure Ulysses to his death). What it does have is kilometers of sandy beaches and dunes dotted with wild Mediterranean brush and a much welcome deficit of those *stabilimenti* or bathing establishments that most Italians appear to prefer.

A long, relatively narrow peninsula jutting into the Mediterranean, Adriatic and Ionian seas with nearly 7,500 kilometers of coastline, Italy is happily endowed with lots of beaches. But they are relatively narrow ones. And with 61 million-plus people inhabiting a relatively small country, much of which is hilly or mountainous, it sometimes can seem as if everyone is on the beach at exactly the same time. This sensation is heightened by the existence of the *stabilimenti,* an institution that allow Italians to go to the beach without forgoing the creature comforts to which they are often addicted. Rather than a bonafide picnic, where one runs the risk of getting sand in the *pasta fredda* or ants in the mozzarella, they want a place with a bar and a restaurant and, if possible, a swimming pool. Rather than a simple beach towel to lie on, they want a chair or a chaise longue and, if possible, a cabin in which to change – frequently – out of their wet suits into dry ones. And rather than solitude, they want plenty of people around to talk with – or about. Thus, most beaches end up being furnished with row upon row of chairs and umbrellas that, increasingly, are for rent at highly exorbitant prices.

The popularity of these *stabilimenti* is not all that surprising considering that Italians tend to do most things, including their beach-going, as a nation. Every year at the beginning of June, the lead story on most Friday night news programs (and again on Saturday at midday) is that of *l'esodo*, the exodus, in which the lead-in headline is usually a highly self-referential "Italians head for the sea" or "Italians leave on vacation", while the accompanying news clips (which always seem identical – and perhaps are – to those of preceding years) show cars with perspiring occupants lined up at turnpike pay booths or else beaches crowded with oiled, browning, semi-nude bodies.

One of the reasons the term "exodus" is used is because, although many of the people on the beach are just there for the day or for the weekend, many of the better-off leave town for the entire summer. A large number of Italian families owns vacation homes and in pre-recession days, many others could afford lengthy summer rentals. So as soon as school let out (generally in early June), many husbands packed up their wives and children and deposited them in their *seconda casa* for the duration. It should be noted, that his type of summer vacationing is not necessarily a boon for most Italian housewives; it often means simply a change of venue in which to do the same old chores. So those who can afford it, and of these there are still many, generally take their *colf* or *collaboratrice domestica* with them.

When I first came to Italy, these housekeeping jobs were occupied primarily by Italian women, often from the South or islands like Sicily and Sardinia or, in northern Italian cites, from the surrounding countryside. Today, instead, according to statistics compiled by Caritas, the charity organization set up by the Italian Episcopal Conference, almost 80% of registered domestics are foreigners with the major countries of provenance Romania (20%), Ukraine (13%), the Philippines (9%) and Moldavia (6%), followed by Peru, Ecuador, Poland and Sri Lanka. So the beaches are often dotted with darker-skinned or ethnically diverse people carrying beach umbrellas, coolers, inner tubes, spare diapers and, of course, sleeping or squalling infants.

Back in town, now populated largely by tourists, those who have yet to leave on a formal vacation and those who can't afford a proper vacation but can make daily treks to the nearest beach, everyone comments on everybody else's tan and exchanges tanning secrets *sotto voce*. It should be noted, however, that not all the tans are from the seaside. Yes, there are specific tanning salons or, these days, beauty salons where you can get yourself sprayed with a fake tan that will last you about a week. But among Italians there is a small though vocal minority of people who prefer the *montagna* to the *mare* on the grounds that the air is purer and the life-style healthier. In the end, it doesn't really matter: the important thing is that you go on vacation and have something to recount when you get that insistent query: "*E le vacanze?*"

One of the things I have always been struck by is that this endless summer life-style is enjoyed by the offspring of Italy's most well-off families to the same degree as their parents. High-school students telling you about their summer may relate that they have had two weeks in Morocco with friends, a few weeks in Sardinia with the family, and a three-week English course in the U.K. in August – naturally, all at Mom and Dad's expense. University students who have passed two or three exams successfully may be rewarded with a trip to Turkey in July and can spend August going to visit comfortably ensconced friends and relatives. (Speaking of university students, it is hard not to wonder whether the university system may not be a particularly telling gauge of the Italian national psyche. In most faculties, students can decide, on their own, which exams, and how many, they want to take each semester, meaning that some people take seven, eight or nine years to graduate. Furthermore, if they don't like their grade they can choose to reject it and re-take the exam at a later date. It's an astonishing victory for relativism and a negation of rigor and discipline, one that if we are going to be honest repeats itself in many aspects of Italian life.)

Getting back to vacations, August is still the month of choice for the overwhelming majority of Italians taking an annual holiday; although "choice" may not be the best word since traditionally, factories in Italy (and France) have always shut down in August, meaning most people were (and are) obligated to go on holiday at that time. Nowadays, thereis a somewhat greater degree of flexibility, and occasionally you'll run into someone who has chosen June or September rather than July or August to get out of town. It is becoming increasingly chic, for example, to stay in town during the month of August, enjoying the absence of traffic jams and lines at the post office and bank.

But there are also other times of the year in which it is *de rigueur* to take some vacation time. Anyone who can afford it also goes away for a week in late January, February or March, the so-called *settimana bianca* or "white week" when it is strangely acceptable to make up some excuse – generally illness related – to take your kids out of school for a week's skiing. In some schools classes have even been called off for a week because so many of the students are absent. Others Italians make sure to take off time at Easter, and some people go away at Christmas and New Year's, too. But by and large the old saying still stands, "Christmas with your family, Easter with whomever you please". In Italian – *Natale con i tuoi, Pasqua con chi vuoi* – it even rhymes.

And let's not forget the so-called *ponti* or "bridge" weekends when a holiday falls on a Tuesday, Wednesday or Thursday, enabling those who can to take extra time off to construct a very long weekend. The most important of these are April 25th (Liberation Day) and May 1, Labor Day for most of Europe (except for the U.K.); the two are so close together that some particularly creative vacationers even manage to eke out an ten-day holiday at this time of the year, even if it means taking the kids out of school and putting off things in the office. Not unexpectedly, not much gets done during these "bridges". "It's a problem because *i cervelli* (the brains) go on vacation even before *i corpi* (the bodies)," says Alex, the co-owner of a Rome garage who somehow grew up with a non-Roman work ethic. Recently, the government led by reform-minded economist, Mario Monti, floated a proposal to copy the U.S. and the U.K. and to move all such holidays to Mondays; not surprisingly there was no follow-through and every *ponte* continues to be a happily awaited event.

There have been other changes in holiday-going in Italy, changes that are making Italians more worldly and less provincial. In recent years, more and more people – particularly, but not only, the better-off and better-educated – have been opting for vacations abroad; the principal capitals of Europe are still high on the list of those with wanderlust. But the Maldives, Mauritania, Thailand, the Seychelles and Sharm el-Sheikh are ever bigger with those who can't wait until summer to renew their tans. Interestingly enough, many travelers to those seemingly exotic venues choose to stay at Italian-run resorts where pasta and Italian wines are mainstays on the menu.

As for the less wealthy, many have held on to old family homes or farmhouses in their native villages or regions, and naturally choose those locales for their vacations. But wherever the final destination, the fact is that vacations are sacred in Italy.

Indeed, Article 36 of the 1948 Italian Constitution states that "Workers are entitled to a weekly day of rest and to paid annual holidays, which they cannot refuse to take"! And a four-week vacation, long the norm here, is now law in the 28-member European Union. In Italy, as in France, the right to a lengthy period of annual time off is, in fact, one of those acquired social benefits for which the country's salaried workers would happily go to war.

Others are the so-called *tredicesima*, or 13th month of salary (some professions, such as journalists, get a 14th month of salary as well), pensions that for some (a minority) can even come close to 100% of salary, a system of near-permanent job tenure that only recently has crumbled (leading to widespread disillusionment among newcomers to the workforce), and a national health service that until recently came close to paying for every aspirin.

When I first arrived here, civil servants were even entitled to two extra weeks of yearly vacation for supposedly medicinal visits to hot springs, and when a more courageous-than-usual government finally did away with that, the *statali*, the civil servants, were furious. The first time cuts were made in the number of medicines paid for fully by the State, a great deal of grumbling ensued. And although economists have long been unanimous in insisting that pension reform (meaning, above all, a later retirement age) was unavoidable in a country with an aging population and a rock-bottom birth rate, this has long been one of the most hotly-contested issues here. The unions were so violently opposed (and some still are) that it wasn't until 2011 that the government introduced significant changes (women are now to retire at 62 and men at 65, with the retirement age being gradually increased over a ten-year period, and eventually made the same for both sexes). But no one has ever even raised the possibility of reducing vacation time.

Although it could be argued that long vacations create happy, well-rested workers with a significant commitment to work, it appears to many in Europe that vacations and greater leisure time long ago became more important than work and productivity.

The controversial French 35-hour work-week originally was designed to create more jobs for more people, but appears for the most part simply to have allowed people to work less and enjoy life more. Europeans, Italians in particular, often criticize Americans for being too hung up on work, and studies indicate that many Americans don't even take all the vacation time allotted to them, perhaps out of fear that they will lose business, or the esteem of their bosses. But despite the current recession, the fact remains that the U.S. economy is more thriving than that of the Old Continent. How many people know, for example, that the GNP of California is roughly the same size as that of all of France even though population of the former is far smaller?

And, on a lighter note, some people attribute to the more "relaxed" Italian attitude the fact that carpal tunnel syndrome never became as frequent as elsewhere. "It's simply that no one in Italy works that hard," quipped one long-time English resident of Rome. (Actually, I myself believe that a more likely explanation is that Italians are not subject to the same hysteria that sometimes motivates Americans to come down en masse with the same symptoms or, again en masse, to stop taking this or that medication or eating this or that food because of because of a clinical trial or FDA report. How else to explain the fact that Italian women seem to be in good health even though they never stopped using silicone implants for breast enhancement when U.S. medical authorities decided – incorrectly, it now appears – that they were intrinsically dangerous.)

Don't get me wrong. Obviously someone, somewhere, is working pretty hard, otherwise Italy would not have to its credit world-famous companies in sectors ranging from fashion to robotics. But there is a widespread commitment to relaxation, otherwise how can one explain the fact that in Rome a bit of sunlight is enough to get everyone out on the street, chatting in small groups and filling the cafés for a mid-afternoon or *caffè* or *prosecco?*

There is always time for a schmooze on the phone and, for just about everyone, weekends are sacred. This laid-back attitude must have something to do with the fact that Romans, when they're not complaining, always seem to be smiling. And doubtless it is the main reason why life is so pleasant in Italy and why so many foreigners, especially from more austere, northern countries, come here to visit and end up staying forever.

Chapter 14 – "*Puzzled And Dismayed*"
or, Life As a Stringer

T he day had started like any other. I had driven the moped down Via della Dataria, stopping only briefly to exchange pleasantries with Claudio, the stocky, uniformed *vigile* or traffic policeman who was on duty at the top of the hill in Piazza del Quirinale, his lackluster efforts part of the city's half-hearted and never totally successful attempt to keep unauthorized traffic out of the historic center. Augusto, the dark-haired, mustachioed receptionist on duty at the entrance desk of the *ANSA* building, waved me through with the same wink and a "*ciao*" as he did every day. (In "real life", Augusto was a *carrozziere,* or auto body shop owner, and would be the one to help me scrap my unregistered Volkswagen Beetle without my getting into trouble. But he had managed to fulfill the Italian's dream of *un posto fisso*, a steady job, and so for part of each day he was on duty at the ANSA building's entrance.) So, as I said, it was a day like every other day.

But when I got to my office on the mezzanine, something didn't look right. It took me a few minutes but I suddenly realized the brass sign saying *Newsweek*, the sign that I – a lowly stringer – had paid for out of my own pocket, had disappeared, leaving a faded, lighter tan square on the dark brown wooden door. That's really weird, I thought, walking down the hall to the *Reuters* office where Robin Lustig, one of my favorite colleagues and today only recently retired from the *BBC*, was writing a morning news story.

"You're not going to believe this," I said indignantly, hands on hips, and lapsing into Brit-talk, "but someone's nicked the *Newsweek* sign." Robin looked up at me with a sigh. "I probably shouldn't tell you this," he said, "but early this morning Loren Jenkins was in here and he was carrying a screwdriver". No, not possible. I thought. Could it be that Jenkins, a Pulitzer Prize-winning journalist who had recently been asked to re-open *Newsweek*'s long-closed Rome bureau, could feel so threatened, upset, annoyed by the fact that the magazine's stringer [ed. note: a stringer is a local-hire journalist who is relied on by a news organ that does not have a full-time correspondent in place, or else someone who helps out when the correspondent is away or has an overflow of stories to do] still had a *Newsweek* sign on her office door? So upset that he would walk six blocks to take it down, spirit it away and never mention it, ever? And, come to think of it, how did he even know the sign was still there? Spies? Night-time surveillance? To the extent that I can remember, at the time of the plaque's stealthy, forcible removal, Loren had indeed already asked me to take it down. But if I hadn't yet done so, it would only have been because I hadn't gotten around to it (no screwdriver, perhaps) and not because I thought it would do me any good to keep the sign in place. And yet, it appeared, he'd either gotten someone to tell him whether the sign was still there or he'd come skulking around, with a screwdriver in his pocket, just in case it was. "*Ammazza aò!*" as the Romans would say in the tone we'd use to say "Holy cow!"

Having met Jenkins several months earlier at a *Newsweek* meeting in Paris and having then found him, I'm embarrassed to say, both charming and attractive, I had been almost glad he was being sent to Rome. True, I would no longer be the magazine's only accredited correspondent, but I was supposed to be kept on as the new bureau chief's principal stringer. I'd been working for *Newsweek* for seven or eight years by then, and if I stayed on as a stringer it would be compatible with my main "string" which a few years before had become *The Washington Post*, like *Newsweek* then owned by the late Katherine Graham. And I actually thought, naïvely I now realize, that perhaps I might learn something from someone who had so much experience. Obviously I had no way of knowing that, after only a few months, Loren would replace me with one of his male buddies, a person I have always liked a lot but one so disliked by his colleagues that once, when he got into a car accident while under the influence, the only people willing to go pick him up at a local police precinct, take him home, and pour coffee into him were myself, an Australian freelance journalist named Kay Withers, and the *Chicago Tribune's* Phil Caputo, now a successful author.

And although the *Newsweek* developments hardly augured well, how could I have possibly imagined that several years later, Jenkins (until recently foreign editor of *National Public Radio*), would later move to the *Washington Post* and would return to Rome once again, this time to open a bureau for the *Post*, thereby doing me out of yet a second stringing job? My favorite "journalistic" memory of him from that second, unhappy but fortunately brief period, involved a breaking news story, I believe regarding Italian terrorism, while he was on vacation in Sardinia. He hadn't left me a phone number, so when the story broke I called the foreign desk at the *Washington Post*, a paper for which – after all – I'd been working for almost TEN years. When he got back to Rome he was furious and instructed (ordered?) me never to call the desk again if he were on Italian soil. "So let me get this straight," I said. "If you're somewhere in Italy, but unreachable, and the Pope dies, I'm not to call the desk?" "Correct," he answered, making it clear that his first priority involved safeguarding his own status and not making sure that the paper that paid his surely generous salary would be in a position to get the news.

As can be gleaned from the above story, being a stringer for a major American news organ can be fraught with risk. My dealings with Loren Jenkins may have involved a case of particularly bad chemistry, although given what several others who have worked with him have to say about him, I really don't think so. Perhaps he just found it hard to work with a woman; perhaps underneath all that bravado there was some kind of insecurity. Who knows? Who cares? But what happened also reflected the difficulties germane to being a stringer, particularly if your client was an important American news organ. In my experience, the more important the news organ, the worse they treat their stringers – and the less they would pay them. Although I must say that there were exceptions. The few times I filled in for a colleague at the *Financial Times*, I had excellent experiences. Once, for example, I made a mistake on a trade story for the *FT* and caught it only after it had already been published in the first edition. Trembling with embarrassment (I have always felt it's an essential part of my job to avoid putting mistakes into print), I called the trade editor, Andrew Something-or-other, to confess my sin, and guess what he said, and with real warmth, too? "Oh, thank you so much for letting me know." At the *Washington Post* they would have had me tarred and feathered.

From one point of view, there was a certain logic to the cold-heartedness of many American editors, especially if theirs was a major American news organ: their reasoning was that if they accredited you, you would enjoy a lot of derivative prestige that otherwise would be hard to come by. And this kind of prestige counts a great deal in a country like Italy where position is everything and where great importance is given to the opinions of foreigners with any kind of status even – it has to be said – if the latter may not really know what they are talking about.

Scene One: The roof terrace of Castel Sant'Angelo, the massive, circular, red-brick construction on the Tiber which has had many incarnations but which started life as the tomb built by the Roman Emperor Hadrian to house his mortal remains. It is darkest night but the monument's battlements and its terrace floor are ablaze with light from dozens of strategically placed, oil-burning saucer-lamps. A long, damask-covered table is set with the finest silver, china and glassware while waiters dressed in elegant livery hover, bringing, first, glasses of champagne and hors d'oeuvres, and later – at the table – serving wines to complement a six-course meal. For this is a state dinner given by Italian premier Giulio Andreotti for U.S. Vice President Nelson Rockefeller. And I, dressed in an inexpensive but passable black velveteen caftan that was the only full-length dress in my wardrobe, was there. Why? Because I was the accredited correspondent for the *Washington Post*.

Scene Two: U.S. Ambassador Richard Gardner, a Jimmy Carter appointee, is throwing a small dinner for former Secretary of State Henry Kissinger at the Ambassador's sprawling residence in Rome, the stunningly beautiful Villa Taverna. There are only two round tables and roughly 30 dinner guests. Danielle Gardner, the ambassador's Italian-born wife, had suggested on an earlier occasion when we met in the ladies' room that we wear "something really low-cut". But as her breasts were about three or four times the size of mine, I decided to pass and leave the honors to her. Also, I still didn't have any evening dresses and I believe I wore the same black caftan mentioned above. But, at least I was there, and why was that? Because I was the *Post*'s accredited correspondent.

Scene Three: About 100 well-dressed people – women in Valentino suits with Ferragamo shoes, freshly coiffed hairdos and lots of pearls and gold jewelry – are milling around in the magnificently appointed apartment in one of the buildings adjacent to the 16th century Quirinale Palace. It is 1982 and for the last four years, the apartment has been home to Antonio Maccanico, previously the chief of staff of the lower house of the Italian Parliament, the Chamber of Deputies, and subsequently appointed Secretary General of the Quirinale by the then President of the Republic, Sandro Pertini, the first Socialist ever to hold that post. I had met Maccanico years earlier when he was a high-placed member of the small but influential, pro-business Republican Party, but today I am here, why? Because I am the regularly accredited correspondent for the *Washington Post*. During the party I am introduced to Cesare Romiti, then CEO of the Italian automotive company, FIAT. The car company headed by patrician Gianni Agnelli has recently introduced a brand-new, mid-segment flagship car, the Fiat Uno, designated to be the 1980s' symbol of the company's renewed commitment to innovation. Romiti is aghast that I have not yet driven the Uno and insists he will send one over the next day (he does indeed) to be test-driven. I may be beautiful and charming, but he is doing this, why? Because I am the accredited correspondent for the *Washington Post*.

In other words, as the *Post*'s accredited representative I was more or less guaranteed access to everything and everyone. Any and all of Italy's political leaders were available to me. The editors of several of Italy's national papers or magazines were eager to have me write for them. I was invited to be on discussion panels and on several occasions hosted a morning call-in radio news program. And all this without actually drawing a salary or a retainer from the paper and while being paid very low, per-word newsprint rates! The people at the *Washington Post* clearly figured that such access and attention were worth their weight in *lire* so they didn't lose much sleep over what some might have considered exploitation. And for me it was a pretty valuable trade-off.

Ironically, my apparently happy situation in Rome also contrasted sharply with reality in another way. In 1979, Jim Hoagland, another Pulitzer Prize-winner and now a well-respected, conservative columnist for the *Post*, became the paper's foreign editor. Undoubtedly brilliant, he was, however, not easy to get along with and, even worse, took a sharp dislike to me. As far as I could tell, he thought I was too left-wing, by which I think he meant I gave too much importance to the doings of the PCI, the Italian Communist party, then the most powerful Marxist party in Europe, or he felt I wasn't objective enough in what I wrote. Or both. Even worse, I think he believed (although knowing myself I find it amazing) that I was a slacker. If something went wrong, he immediately assumed that I was just goofing off. And because there had been a couple of occasions when I (an unsalaried stringer, mind you) had missed a breaking (but not major) story because I'd been at a dinner or at the movies (remember, there were no cell phones then), he labeled me as someone who was lazy and unreliable. He was so sure of his diagnosis that he sent me a nasty message when I filed my story, one day late if you will, on General Dalla Chiesa's murder. Remember where I was when the government's special anti-Mafia czar and his wife were gunned down? Goofing off, as Hoagland seemed to think? No. It was simply the last day of my (unpaid) summer vacation and I was in the middle of the Mediterranean on a ferry, returning from Sardinia. I got off the ferry, drove in a rush to Rome, hurried to the office, and wrote a story immediately. But it was, unavoidably, a second-day story and was not enough to save me from Hoagland's wrath.

My theory, although naturally I could never prove it, is that Hoagland thought that anyone who was happy being a stringer in Rome (rather than in Cambodia or San Salvador) and anyone whose overriding ambition wasn't to get hired full-time by the *Washington Post* was not a serious person. As someone who throughout her life has cared about being good at what she did and indeed, with the exception of high-school physics, had always been good at what she did, working for a man who was so critical was a great source of anxiety and unhappiness. Once he sent me a telex which said: "Puzzled and dismayed by your failure to" I can't remember what. I was devastated and locked myself in the office I'd been given by the editor of the Rome daily, *Il Messaggero*. My good friend Marco Politi, who was then that paper's Vatican specialist and later wrote a book about Pope John Paul II with former *Washington Post* reporter Carl Bernstein, was aghast at the tone of the message. "*Incredibile, non è possible* – unbelievable, it's not possible," he kept saying, reading and rereading the telex. But in the end he made me laugh about it and for years afterwards when we'd meet, he'd raise his eyebrows and very somberly intone, "Puzzled and dismayed." No doubt I was too sensitive, but the situation cast a recurring pall over my professional conscience for years. My British friend, Kerin Hope, also a trained on the spot journalist, but in her case in Athens where she then worked for the *Associated Press* (today she covers Greece and the Balkans for the *Financial Times*) had this to say about my obsessiveness on the topic: "Your relationship with the *Washington Post* is sort of like the Cyprus issue; it lies dormant for months and then, every once in a while, it flares up and you are forced to take it out and worry about it again."

Chapter 15 – Paolo Versus the Pope

The relationship with Paolo had restored some serenity to my life, and I was enjoying myself, even if we couldn't see each other very often; after all, how many "estimates" can you need to deliver in the evenings, how many dinners with surveyors, contractors and architects can you be forced to arrange? How many evenings out with the boys are acceptable? And asking a friend, whose wife may know yours, to cover for you, is very risky.

It was a problem. But at one point my work schedule, too, became a major obstacle to our meetings. It was the spring of 1985 and Turkish terrorist Mehmet Ali Agca and Bulgarian airlines official Serghei Ivanov Antonov were on trial in Rome along with six other defendants for allegedly having conspired to murder the Pope four years earlier.

Agca, then 23, had been arrested in St. Peter's Square on May 13, 1981, literally with a smoking gun in his hand, and two months later he was sentenced to life imprisonment for trying to assassinate John Paul II as the latter drove through the crowded square in his large, open, white Popemobile. That trial, what the Italians call *un processo per direttissima,* a fast-track procedure resorted to in cases in which a criminal has been apprehended in the act of a crime, had lasted only three days, despite various outbursts by the tall, bearded Agca.

Now, four years later, the conspiracy trial, the really important part of the case, was about to begin. Agca and Antonov would be taking the stand along with a variegated cast of characters charged with involvement in what had been dubbed "the Bulgarian connection". These included Bulgarian officials and several alleged members of the Gray Wolves, the right-wing Turkish terrorist group to which Agca belonged and which was implicated in both drug and arms smuggling. "Trial of the century gets under way" screamed the Italian headlines, even though they had used the same phrase in countless other circumstances.

Nevertheless, were it to be proved that the Bulgarian secret services and, as suspected, the KGB had indeed been involved in an attempt to physically eliminate the Pope, thereby excising his influence from the potentially explosive Polish and Eastern European situation, we would indeed be talking the stuff of serious history.

Not surprisingly, given what appeared to be at stake, every newspaper and radio station in the West was interested in coverage, and I didn't have a free moment. On the morning of May 27, the "papal plot trial", which was to last ten months, finally got under way. But in the meantime things were complicated by a series of bureaucratic procedures which culminated in we journalists lining up early on the morning of May 27 to get accreditation and entry passes to the so-called *aula bunker*, the high-security courtroom that had been constructed for the first trial of Aldo Moro's assassins. The *Associated Press* beat us all to the punch by sending an intern over at 6 a.m. to get the first place in line; Phil Pullella, then covering the Vatican for *UPI*, showed up a bit later with a three-legged stool he later let me sit on because my back was hurting, and as time progressed we constituted a real mob. Italians, Americans, Europeans of all stripes, Japanese, Turks, Russians, Latin Americans, all armed variously with notebooks, cameras, lighting equipment and tape recorders, we rocked back and forth on our feet, told bad jokes, exchanged gossip and sweated while we waited to have our documents examined and to be let in. The late Claire Sterling, the American journalist who had launched the whole Bulgarian Connection, first in an article and then in a book, turned up last and yet managed to bluff her way in before anyone else, pissing off the entire press corps in one fell swoop.

The "bunker", a prefabricated, reinforced concrete building standing alone in the midst of one of the vast parking lots of the Olympic stadium sports complex on the northern side of the city, had been hyped as being ultra-modern, as well as terrorist-proof. But after waiting hours to get in, we discovered that the sound system was so bad that only the dozens of black-robed defense lawyers sitting in the first rows could really follow the proceedings. If you wanted to hear what was going on, you had to get there as early as possible and "capture" a seat near a loudspeaker, or at least duct-tape your tape recorder to it.

You couldn't see much, either, since people were always walking around, standing up, or reading (and rustling) newspapers. At one point, white-haired Judge Severino Santiapichi, his chiseled handsome features making him look like a judge supplied by central casting, got so fed up with the confusion that he jumped to his feet and informally called everyone to order, shouting "*Signori, abbiate pazienza, pazienza*

– Ladies and gentlemen, I beg of you, be patient!" But this only had the ludicrous effect of leading Agca, who had spent his years in jail learning Italian and carefully reading the Italian papers, to leap up, shouting "Yes! Pazienza! Francesco Pazienza, that's who," referring to a somewhat nefarious Italian wheeler-dealer whose last name means patience, and who had been named in a lot of dirty doings including the P-2 secret Masonic lodge, but not – as far as is known – in the attempt on John Paul's life.

As serious as the Bulgarian Connection might have been in terms of world politics (although to this day it is not clear just how real it was), the hearings and the preceding investigation had had some very ludicrous aspects. Given the importance of the story, there was considerable competition, particularly between the *New York Times*, which had signed up Claire Sterling to back up its regular correspondent, John Tagliabue, and the *Washington Post*, which had assigned to the case its young, dynamic Paris correspondent, Michael Dobbs, a former staffer in the Rome *Reuters* bureau. (As a stringer, I would never have been left in charge.) Seeking inside information regarding the two-year investigation, the indictment and the exact charges, the *Times* appeared to have successfully established a privileged relationship with Ilario Martella, the "courageous, independent investigating magistrate," as the journalistic rhetoric of the time had dubbed him, a man who in reality was so out of his depth that he soon suffered a nervous breakdown and was never heard of again.

But that was later. Now, with Martella out of bounds for us, it was up to me to protect the *Post* by getting chummy enough with other sources. One of these was Giuseppe Consolo, a right-wing sympathizer who was later elected to parliament, but then simply a very smooth, highly ambitious defense lawyer who as the lawyer for Antonov successfully used the limelight generated by the Bulgarian Connection case to become first, a TV personality, and later, through his then Christian-Democratic connections, president of a state-run bank. Spending too much time with Consolo, however, had its risks, since he was a womanizer. After one three-hour dinner during which he'd talked exclusively about himself, he'd turned to me (it was summer and I suppose his wife was out of town), and said, in excellent English "My place or yours?" (My answer? "Neither, I'm going back to my office.")

A second source of mine was a magistrate as highly placed as Martella but with a different role in the complex Italian judicial structure and who agreed to provide the *Post* with key court documents and to make himself available, off the record, to answer questions. To do this we resorted to an artfully staged felony. I showed up at his office one morning with an empty Land's End canvas briefcase in tow. And when he deliberately left the room, leaving the pre-trial documents, more than 1000 pages, on his desk, I "stole" them, barely managing to keep a straight face as I left the building with my bulging carryall. Following a lengthy photocopying session back at my office in Via della Dataria, there was a second encounter to return the papers, this time in a deserted parking lot. "I felt like I was in a movie," I told a girlfriend.

Also providing light relief was Agca's habit of periodically interrupting the proceedings by announcing he was the Son of God. "I am Jesus Christ, I bring a message regarding the end of the world," the tall Turk, his black hair cut close to the scalp, his dark eyes burning, would intone in accented and somewhat guttural Italian from the raised podium, the same one from which we also had heard (sort of) the testimony of a seemingly unending series of Italian hotel managers, Turkish smugglers, Bulgarian airline officials, arms experts, and so on. The prosecutors and the lawyers for the defense, almost indistinguishable one from the other in their long black robes, would grimace; Santiapichi would roll his eyes ceiling-ward and, after the first few outbursts, would hurriedly call for a recess mostly, we realized after the first few days, so he could go out and have a cigarette. And the press? We'd actually have to write down this drivel and report on it, an intellectual insult for anyone who believed journalism should deal with real information rather than mindless – and in this case, disruptive – "color".

In this situation, seeing Paolo was even harder than usual. Given the time difference with the U.S., we journalists could file our copy until as late as 11 p.m., and often did. So even had home-wrecking – never part of my agenda – been on my mind, it would have been hard to work up to a relationship with that fever pitch needed to convince an Italian man to leave wife and family. To be truthful, at one point, Paolo appeared to be getting close to wanting that. "I can't stand it, I want to be with you," he told me with tears in his eyes one evening after we'd returned to my apartment from a wonderful fish dinner at

Ostia, once ancient Rome's seaport. But by then it was clear to me that a full-time relationship between us would have been inappropriate. I really was in love with Paolo. I craved his company. I loved his touch. But in the long run, education and "culture" *do* count. It was true that if we went to a nearby hilltop town like Palestrina or Agnani there was a necessary division of labor; I filled him in on history, he examined the medieval structures and compared old building techniques with those of today. There was a lot to discuss about politics. Nevertheless, conversation did not always come easy.

Paolo's views on the woman's role in marriage were also light-years away from mine. He discouraged Annamaria from getting a job on the grounds that he would then either have to pay a housekeeper or suffer the consequences of an improperly run household. And since his wife didn't work outside the home, he didn't see why he should have to assume any responsibility whatsoever for the family *ménage* (sound familiar?). Taken to excess, this means that, while he'll complain if there is no bread in the house, it would never occur to him, even on his way home, to buy some. "I work hard every day, why should I have to work at home as well," he will say, even today, when challenged.

The beginning of the end came when I stupidly took Paolo with me on a three-day junket to Morocco, where I was to give a talk at a convention of Italian IBM employees. Things started off well enough, although it was clear to me during the plane trip (his first ever) that our expectations were different. Delighted to return to Morocco for the third time, I was dreaming of eating *p'stilla*, that wonderful Moroccan dish of sugary, baked pigeon, and of perhaps buying a couple of more kilims for my apartment. Paolo, on the other hand, was wondering whether he'd be able to smoke some good hash – and possibly smuggle some back in to Italy – the latter something to which I was resolutely opposed.

But these differences, it turned out, were not to represent the real pitfall; during our stay it became clear that Paolo felt totally ill-at-ease in my milieu, something we'd never experienced before since our meetings had always been largely private. At a tent dinner following a Berber "fantasia", where our dinner companions included one of Italy's premier economists, years later to be prime minister of Italy, Mario Monti, and his wife, he was clearly out of place. And the opulent Marrakesh Palace Hotel was just too rich for Paolo's blood. Its well-appointed salons and hushed dining rooms, its lavish buffets and urbane waiters, its luxurious swimming pool and solicitous attendants made him feel so uncomfortable that he did little else than smoke hash, becoming increasingly distant and removed.

Our last day brought peace between us. On one of his solitary walks, Paolo had made contact with a young Moroccan who invited us to his brother's shop for tea. It was a drum shop and the afternoon ended in a way that made Paolo particularly happy, an impromptu concert in what was little more than a market stall whose owners served *chai* (tea) but were also passing around a joint. So it all ended well, except for the Italian customs police cutting open Paolo's newly acquired drum to see if there was any hash in it. (There wasn't. Unbeknownst to me it was in his pocket.) But the trip made painfully clear the limited extent to which my life and Paolo's could ever be blended. So when I fell in love with someone else, the end came quickly. And painlessly, at least for me. Who knows how it affected Paolo? He must have realized something had happened when I stopped wanting to make love. But providing a real lesson in grace, he never commented, complained or even asked me any questions and today, after all these years, we are still friends.

Chapter 16 – The Judge (Part One)

The massive steel door to the office was forbiddingly shut, but after countless visits of this sort I knew the routine. You'd ring, be momentarily immortalized on a closed-circuit television screen hidden somewhere within, and wait for the tinny intercom voice to squeak: *"Chi e'?"* "Gilbert," I'd reply, using the soft "g" (as in George) because the correct pronunciation of my last name (which if pronounced correctly would be spelled "Ghilbert" in Italian) is incomprehensible to all but the relatively few Italians who understand English.

"I have an appointment with the Judge," I might add to give myself greater importance. After a few moments, the heavy door would click open onto a room in which every available surface appeared piled high with light blue or pink official folders, the ubiquitous *fascicoli* (pronounced fash-*ee*-coli) familiar to anyone who has come into contact with the Italian justice system. *"Buongiorno.* He's expecting you," would come the unsmiling greeting from a man in a checked jacket and no tie who might be a male secretary but, judging from the bulge under his arm, was just as likely to be a bodyguard. Ushered into a smaller but even more cluttered room, you'd perch on an empty chair waiting, sometimes at great length, for your presence to be acknowledged. More often than not the Judge (in Italian the word, *giudice*, pronounced *ju*-di-chay, is used interchangeably to mean prosecutors, investigating magistrates and sitting judges) would be talking on the phone or poring over papers and would barely look at you, even when finally getting around to asking what you'd come for. *"Dica.* Tell me." (In other words, what I can do for you), he'd query politely, even though we both knew that my questions regarding the latest terrorism or Mafia case would go largely unanswered.

The Judge, a much respected, highly controversial, and oft-feared prosecutor, was known to be a "hard" interview. In other words, unless you were one of the one or two male Italian journalists with whom he'd become close friends, he really wasn't likely to say anything other – if you were lucky – than confirm something you already knew. Often, in fact, you couldn't help but wonder if it was really worth the bother of fighting your way across town through the morning traffic and finding a parking space. It was less frustrating for Italian journalists who, as the judge well knew, were likely to write exactly what they'd planned to write no matter what the outcome of the interview. For us Americans, it was worse. Because our newspapers quite rightly demanded it, we had to worry about sourcing when we wrote about what was going on in the investigations into terrorism – right-wing, left-wing and Middle Eastern. But then, you could never tell, he might slip (or appear to slip) and tell you something really interesting, such as just where the Libyan terrorists had set up the bazooka they had planned to fire at the U.S. embassy, or why the bullets that finally killed three of the four Arab gunmen who turned their machine guns on innocent travelers at Rome's Fiumicino airport in December, 1985, came from Israeli and not Italian weapons. (Answer: Italian police at the airport had only automatic weapons and could not risk firing their own machine guns into the panic-stricken crowd. The terrorists, except for the one who survived, were killed by an El Al security agent with a handgun.)

Later, I often wondered why things had gone so differently that day. Perhaps it was because it was summer and his wife was at the seashore. Perhaps it was simply because I was late. I am *often* late, which means that right from the start I had no trouble fitting in to central and southern Italian time culture, according to which the exact hour of an appointment is merely indicative and anything up to 20 minutes delay is considered perfectly normal. But this time I was really late and knew that it was likely to be a problem.

There was a legitimate reason for my tardiness; I had not been dallying in bed, alone or otherwise. I had not, once again, misplaced my *motorino* keys or locked myself out of my apartment. And I had not been having an extra coffee at the bar. My appointment at what was often called "Judicial City" had been at 11 in the morning. But I'd been stuck in traffic along the Lungotevere highway that runs along the Tiber River and by the time I went through the metal detectors, had my purse searched (as usual, cursorily enough to miss the miniature mace canister an Italian secret services investigator had given me after the incident at my apartment with the young, would-be terrorist), and waited my turn to push into the tiny, overcrowded elevator in the four-story concrete monstrosity that houses the Procura of Rome, the equivalent of the district attorney's office, I was almost

45 minutes overdue. This meant that when I finally was admitted into the Judge's cluttered inner sanctum, he was on his feet making audible "I'm sorry, I've got to leave" noises; he simply couldn't miss his appointment – a commemoration service for a colleague gunned down at a bus stop a year earlier by left-wing terrorists. But his standing also meant that for once we were really face to face, looking into one another's eyes. But here, no doubt, I overestimate the impact of my allegedly hypnotic blue-green gaze. Perhaps his unusual affability would turn out to be due mostly to the fact that this time I had come for something slightly more entertaining than an update on the status of the Red Brigades or a rundown on the probable doings of Arab terrorist Abou Abbas, the man behind the Achille Lauro ship hijacking in November, 1985. "I'm to do a story for *Penthouse* magazine on Italy's courageous magistrates and I want to do a profile of you," I explained. He looked up from the file cabinet he was locking, smiled – in itself a small miracle, or so I thought at the time – and said, "Naked, I suppose."

There was a somewhat awkward pause, while we both chuckled in embarrassment. "An amusing idea, this article," the judge added, recovering his aplomb almost immediately, "but I'm afraid you'll have to come back another time." A burst of recklessness seized me and unexpectedly I could hear myself saying, "Look, why don't I buy you lunch?" And then, even more unexpectedly, all of a sudden he was nodding and accepting. "Yes, but *I* will buy *you* lunch. Be here at two o'clock. *Arrivederci.*"

I couldn't believe it. No one I knew among my foreign correspondent colleagues had ever gotten this far. In his late fifties, at the height of a career that had spanned three decades and had included more political scandals than most investigators would ever dream of, the Judge was thought to be a walking encyclopedia of everything, above-board and not, that had happened in Italy since the late sixties. "Guess who is taking me to lunch?" I blurted over the phone to my friend Victor, news editor (and subsequently, bureau chief) at the *Associated Press*, as I whiled away the time in the squalid, barely furnished Procura pressroom where someone had graciously left behind a couple of the day's papers. Having been the *Washington Post*'s correspondent (whoops, sorry, "stringer") for some time, I was pretty well connected, but nevertheless Victor's first three guesses were particularly flattering. "Andreotti? Craxi? Agnelli?" he asked quite seriously, naming the former Christian Democratic Prime Minister (subsequently charged with and acquitted of Mafia involvement), the then socialist Prime Minister (later charged and convicted in several cases of corruption and who would die several years later, in self-imposed exile in Tunisia) and the now-deceased, then silver-haired chairman of the Fiat Auto company, Italy's John D. Rockefeller. "Wrong," I said, "it's the Judge." "Wow!" said Victor in a hushed voice. "I can't wait to hear all about it." Next I phoned an Italian girlfriend at the Foreign Trade Ministry who loved hearing about my exploits. "What are you wearing?" she asked practically. "What difference does that make?" I retorted, bristling. "He's hardly someone I'd be interested in *that* way."

Or so I thought. Shortish, maybe a smidgen overweight, with a long somewhat Middle Eastern-looking face and an aquiline nose, the Judge was not a handsome man, although the dark but graying beard and brown, piercing eyes (not to mention his beautiful hands, but those I noticed later) did give him a certain panache. Since he was 58 (but looked older), I would in any event have considered him far too old for me. But, as I was to discover that day at lunch, he had other qualities; he was brilliant, mysterious and, most unexpectedly, excruciatingly funny, with a knack for accents of all sorts and, as I later learned, perfect musical pitch. He was also extremely courtly in a way that you could call either old-fashioned or typical of someone who was long out of practice.

"I've decided to take you to an outdoor place up on Monte Mario. The food is good and there's a nice view," he said politely but decisively when I returned upstairs at 1:55. "Fine with me," I said as we left the building, looking around vainly for the bodyguards and bulletproof sedan that by then were standard issue for a magistrate of his level. But he had already taken me by the elbow and was steering me towards the visitors' parking lot. "Let's take your car," he said. "*Cosa?* – What?" I gasped, thinking of the devastating effect terrorists' bullets would have on the flimsy bodywork of my dark gray Fiat Uno (purchased, with a journalists' discount, after the test drive organized for me by Romiti, the Fiat CEO). "*E' preoccupata?* Are you worried?" he asked gently, touching my arm. "Remember, the best security for someone like myself is to be unpredictable."

"Hmmmm." It was clear what he was saying. After all, predictability explained how the Red Brigades managed so easily to capture former Prime Minister Aldo Moro and kill his five bodyguards; prior to the ambush on Via Fani on March 16, 1978, the three-car motorcade alternated regularly between only two routes from Moro's home on Monte Mario to Palazzo Chigi, the seat of government in the heart of downtown Rome. And that, too, would be how the Mafia would eventually murder the Sicilian Judge Giovanni Falcone who, as prudent as he was, had never figured out a way to get into Palermo from the Punta Raisi airport without using the airport highway, which is where they placed the bomb that blew him, his wife Francesca and three of his five bodyguards to pieces, effectively depriving Italy of one its few real modern-day heroes. But in my head I was already imagining the hand-drawn sketch, typical in these cases, that the Rome daily, *Il Messaggero*, would print the next day to detail the manner of the attack: "American journalist's car", here, with a thick black arrow curving round to indicate the sketch of a car pock-marked with bullet holes; "restaurant" here, another arrow; "terrorists' position" here, another arrow, etc. "Oh, no, not at all," I replied airily in my best Intrepid Girl Reporter's voice.

There is something special about dining *al fresco*, especially when you have the impression that the food will not only be good but that there will also be a lot of it. The restaurant was one of those places that (no doubt after paying off the health inspector) display a vast smorgasbord of appetizers – five kinds each of zucchini and eggplant, pepperoni, mushrooms, pickled onions, stuffed tomatoes, baby mozzarella, lima beans and ham, calamari, seafood salad, cold pasta and pasta and *fagioli*, arranged enticingly on large, oval serving platters or bowls and generously garnished with olive oil and parsley – and the Judge set out to pamper me, repeatedly filling my plate with delicacies. "You must try this, and this, too," he said solicitously. He ordered different kinds of wine with every course. And then, amazingly from a person who in the past had said little more to me than *"Buongiorno," "Dica," "Grazie"* and *"Arrivederci,"* he wanted to know all about me, how and why I had come to Italy, where my family was from and what I thought about this and that. True, he was not very forthcoming about himself, something I would have to get used to, and that day I learned no secrets, reluctantly acknowledging to myself that Victor would be sorely disappointed. But unexpectedly there was a lot of laughing as we related anecdotes and exchanged gossip about his colleagues and mine. And then came the highpoint. "Shall we give each other the *tu?*" (the familiar form of address in Italian), he asked me timidly. "Oh yes," I said breathlessly. For by this point I was smitten, little realizing that the lunch would signal the start of yet another highly frustrating relationship.

What would happen next? Was this to be a one-time lunch or something more, I wondered as we left the restaurant? But I soon found out. This time he had decided to drive, taking my car along a circuitous, little-used route that brought us back behind the courthouse.

"Perhaps someday soon we could go together for a *grattachecca,*" he said, with a stiff little bow as he got out of the car near the courthouse. "Call me whenever you want," I said, wondering what a *grattachecca* was (it turned out it was only the old, Mulberry Street Italian ice, crushed ice with fruit syrup) and heading back downtown to my office at the Rome daily where, thanks to my role as the *Post*'s correspondent, I had been given hospitality.

Those days I was particularly busy. Along with my regular work, I still had to arrange my interview with Falcone, another of the three judges I had chosen for the article, and to write up the one I had already done with sitting Judge Severio Santiapichi, the man who a year earlier had presided over the Bulgarian Connection trial. It had taken some time to get hold of Santiapichi, but in the end I did get to interview him, he as usual smoking furiously, in the small, windowless office he was using in the "bunker" where the trial had been held.

But when it came to "my" Judge, I didn't have to wait long. Only two days after our lunch, he telephoned asking if he could stop by after lunch and take me out for a drink, an ice, an ice cream, *"quello che vuoi* – whatever you want"*, he added, thrilling me with his use, still somewhat embarrassing to me, of the intimate *tu* form. In Italy young people have always used *tu* with one another more or less immediately, although nowadays this probably applies to many people in their thirties as well. And colleagues in any profession – doctors, journalists, lawyers, magistrates, –generally tend to use the familiar form of address among themselves. But the Judge clearly belonged to that older generation that prefers the more formal *Lei* with anyone except really close friends, children, lovers and, naturally, colleagues. Indeed, one problem concerning early-stage relations between the sexes has always been the question of who makes the decision to move from the more formal *Lei* to the *tu*. Many men wait for the woman to suggest it. Others, like the Judge, plunge ahead and take the initiative.

When he called, I was sorry I hadn't worn a skirt and heels that day instead of my usual sandals and baggy summer slacks. I have a closet full of nice clothes, even some designer things thanks to contacts who have given me access to heavily-discounted factory salesrooms. But more often than not, somehow I always seem to opt for comfort, making me wonder whether I am, perhaps, less vain than I think I am. But I wasn't going to let a question of attire stop me. "I can take a break in about a half an hour," I told him, figuring that would give me more than enough time to finish the page I was working on, fluff up my mop of curly dark hair and put on a bit of eye makeup.

My rent-free office in the *Il Messaggero* building was located about midway between the Trevi Fountain and the Spanish Steps. I told the Judge I would wait for him in front of the newsstand on the corner of Via del Tritone, once again wondering how he would manage the meeting, since despite a decline in some forms of political violence, Italian and Middle Eastern terrorists were still plenty active in Italy. But there he was, alone, at the wheel of a large, beige Citroën sedan, with his *scorta*, or bodyguard, nowhere in sight. It wasn't very romantic, I admit, but the first words that came to my lips when I got into the car were: "Good Lord, how can you go around like this? Aren't you afraid for your life?" The Judge shrugged, one of those Mediterranean shrugs that can roughly be translated as "let God's will be done" and which, having grown up in what is substantially a Protestant culture where personal responsibility counts for more, I find infuriating.

Thinking back, I suppose that this was in part a show for my benefit. The Citroën, judging from the weight of its doors, clearly had been bulletproofed. There was (as I would discover later) a pistol in the glove compartment, and lying on the dashboard, I suppose as a concession to his official status, was one of those mini, red, lollypop stopsigns-on-a-stick that Italian police and *carabinieri* love to brandish at you from the windows of their cars as they careen by at breakneck speed, sirens wailing and blue roof-lights blinking wildly. Perhaps, I, too, would now finally get a chance to do that, I thought, briefly imagining myself cowing legions of reckless Roman drivers with a hand-held traffic sign. But still, the lack of security was mind-boggling. At that point in time, several dozen magistrates had already been assassinated in Rome, Palermo and elsewhere by terrorists or *mafiosi*. He could be next, I thought bleakly, and perhaps me with him.

"Where shall we go?" asked the Judge calmly. "*Dove vuoi tu* – wherever you want," I answered demurely, forcing myself into my feminine passive mode and savoring the intimate *tu* I had just pronounced. He put the car into gear without another word, a small smile of satisfaction playing about his lips. We drove through the tunnel under the Presidential palace, down Via Nazionale, along Via dei Fori Imperiali past the Roman Forum and around the Colosseum, continuing on past the Palatine Hill, where Roman emperors and their paramours once cavorted, and out onto the Old Appian Way. The umbrella pines were silhouetted against a blue, mid-afternoon sky, the birds were singing, and sprigs of grass struggled into the light from between the ancient, massive paving stones the Romans used over 2,000 years ago to build the bumpy but serviceable road that took their troops through southern Italy down to Brindisi, from where they would embark for Greece and beyond.

There are several nice restaurants on the first bit of the Via Appia Antica and a few cafés. But as we drove on it became clear that the Judge had something less structured in mind. More or less in the shadow of the massive, first-century B.C. tomb of Cecilia Metella, we stopped and parked the Citroën. We got out and walked, pausing here and there so the Judge could translate the ancient Latin inscriptions on the various small Roman tombstones into Italian for me. He never touched me. But whenever we came to a patch of particularly uneven Roman paving stones, he made a point of taking my arm, sending little bubbles of excitement fluttering through my innards.

This time it was I who tried to grill him about his background, his studies, his wife and children. For the most part his answers were laconic and sometimes ambiguous. And although it was only to be expected that he would be discreet about his investigations, I could see that he was also ill at ease when talking about himself or his emotions. But he exuded some kind of wordless need for affection. And was he funny!

When he was younger, he told me, he'd dealt with a lot of nitty-gritty stuff, like prosecuting petty criminals, particularly pickpockets. At some point, he recounted, he realized how well-known and effective he'd become. "One day I got on the 64 bus (a known favorite for pickpockets since it carries tourists from Termini, the central railroad station, across Rome to the Vatican)," he recalled," and about half the passengers got off." And then something happened which showed just how unflappable he was. As we paused by the side of the road to rest, sitting on a low stone wall and chatting, a solitary car slowed down and the driver, a middle-aged man with glasses, rolled down his window and said wryly, *"Buonasera, signor Giudice."* *"Sera,"* replied the Judge, matter-of-factly. "Who was that?" I asked, astonished; we were after all some 10 kilometers out of town. "I'm not sure," he answered carefully. "I think he's somebody I once arrested."

Part Four

On the Road

*O*ne of the other advantages of being a foreign correspondent
in Italy is that you get to travel a lot. By the mid-eighties, I
had seen a great deal of this country. I had been to Turin to
report on the Holy Shroud and on the Fiat car company's woes. I
had been to Venice to write about the flooding, the so-called acque
alte, the Biennale Arts Festival, the Venice Film Festival and later
the burning down of the Teatro Fenice. In Friuli and Campania, I
had covered the earthquakes that, in different years, devastated those
two regions and noted the disparity in the ways the inhabitants
reacted, the northerners actively and industriously, the southerners
passively waiting for state aid and outside help or intervention. I had
been to Milan for stories about Italian fashion or banking, to
Bologna for the bloody aftermath of the Italicus train bombing, and
to Genoa for the return to port of the unfortunate Achille Lauro
ocean liner, taken hostage by Palestinian terrorists who in the process
murdered a disabled American passenger. But at this point in time,
most of the traveling I will be doing is in and around the Italian
south or Mezzogiorno, largely because of the explosion of Mafia-
related crime. But I wasn't complaining. After all, even crime
reporters have to eat, and where better than in the Italian south?

Chapter 17 – Have Fork Will Travel

I hadn't had a plate of *rigatoni all'amatriciana* in almost a month, which explains why, at 11 p.m. on a Thursday evening, I am at the Tana de' Noantri, downstairs from my apartment, seated alone at one of the front-room tables where the waiters eat before the restaurant has opened, with an enormous dish of pasta in front of me.

The *'matriciana*, as many call it, is traditionally made with *guanciale*, *peperoncino,* white wine and tomatoes (when I make it myself I make it Roman style, putting in a bit of onion and using black pepper) and is one of my favorites. So having covered it with an extra couple of spoonfuls of grated cheese, *parmigiano* mixed with *pecorino.,* a cheese made from sheep's milk, I am enjoying every forkful. As soon as the limo that had picked me up at Fiumicino airport had deposited me in front of my building, I had made a bee-line for the restaurant just around the corner, without even going upstairs to leave my suitcase.

I say "alone" but in effect, I was busy – between mouthfuls – filling in Erminio, the gray-haired owner of the Tana de Noantri, on the details of my latest trip down South, which had culminated in an unplanned detour to Palermo.

I'd had to rush there from Calabria to cover the funeral of a well-known magistrate and his police escort, all of whom had been gunned down the week before by Mafia hit-men. Not surprisingly, given the Italians' penchant for style, the plethora of recent terrorist and Mafia killings had led authorities to perfect the art of staging public funeral arrangements. For the most part, the funeral rites in the city's imposing Norman cathedral had gone off as expected. But there had been one unforeseen development, the kind that most Italian journalists adore as it gives them ready-made headlines for several days on end: Rosanna Schifani, the young, raven-haired widow of a slain policeman had broken with tradition, making an impassioned speech that harshly criticized the government, whose top representatives were seated in the front pews. They, she cried, had failed to pursue the island's criminals with the requisite energy, and now her husband and several other brave men were dead and lying in their coffins.

Despite the unappy, occasion, I was as usual happy to go to Palermo, a city which despite the run-down aspect of some of its neighborhoods (unbelievably, there were still traces of World War II bombings there) nevertheless is one of Italy's most intriguing, with its fascinating mix of Arab, Byzantine, Norman and Italian cultural and culinary influences. Sicilian desserts are world famous; along with *cannoli* you could die for, *gelo di melone* and *cassata* (from the Arabic, *qas'at*), the ice cream is divine. And then, of course, there's what the Italians call *il salato,* all that is "savory" rather than sweet. Regular food, in other words. The best recipe I know for *aglio, olio e peperoncino,* the pasta of last resort for anyone who has nothing else in the *dispensa,* the pantry, but garlic, oil and chili peppers, came from a Palermo taxi driver. It differs from the Roman version because of the addition of parsley and, at the end, a sprinkling of breadcrumbs, which the driver called "the poor man's *parmigiano*".

Interestingly enough, while relatively few straight Italian men cook at home, an awful lot of them know exactly how to prepare food. I have gotten some of my best recipes from men. For example, years ago a telex operator at *Il Messaggero*, the Rome newspaper where I used to have my office, taught me how to make *spaghetti alla boscaiolo* (tomato, sausage, dried mushrooms, red wine, olive oil). Paolo, the contractor, clued me in on the ins and outs of making *fettuccine con funghi porcini.* And when I was at *Il Sole 24 Ore*, I was startled when, having casually mentioned to Aldo, the slender, highly-efficient bureau manager, that I had some swordfish at home but didn't know what I was going to do with it, I got an unexpected answer. "If you have *capperi* (capers), you could make it Sicilian style" (fresh tomato, capers, oregano, and parsley), he suggested. And so I did, throwing in some pitted black olives and a smidgen of anchovy paste just for fun.

But on most of my trips, I ate in restaurants. During the rush visit to Sicily, I had managed to arrange lunch with Milli, the wife of Palermo's then young, anti-Mafia mayor, Leoluca Orlando (almost a couple of decades later, and after several years as a member of parliament representing a succession of parties, he is in that role again). She took me to a small restaurant located in the heart of the Arab-style outdoor market known as the Vucciria (pronounced Voo-chi-*ree*-a). This was an eatery famous for Sicilian specialties such as pasta with sardines and *involtini* of swordfish, roulades of swordfish stuffed with *pinoli,* raisins and breadcrumbs. Everything was terrific, but I have to admit that over the years I had discovered that every restaurant in Palermo appeared to have its own version of these *involtini,* one better than the next. Another local delicacy that restaurants prepared in subtle variations were the fried patties of *neonata,* the tiny, just-born, just-fished, minnows that may taste particularly good to those who know that fishing them is illegal. And just about anywhere you went in the city you could eat a wonderful *caponata,* the local ratatouille with eggplant, capers and olives predominating. You could feast on *spaghetti alla Norma* (with eggplant). Or if you were a bit more adventurous, there was spaghetti with *bottarga* (tuna fish roe) or – in the right season – pasta made with the delicate orange pulp of sea urchins, *ricci.* Yum.

Restaurants apart, I always made a special trip to the Vucciria when I was in town if, for nothing else, than just to soak up the atmosphere. The cries of the fishermen are unintelligible but intriguing. The length of the pale green zucchini is amazing. And as I've already mentioned, it's one of the few places I know where you can buy freshly-made tomato paste concentrate by the *etto* (100 grams). Only a block or so away is the church of San Domenico, where back then you could still buy *cannoli* or, on special order, a pistachio and almond paste monster dessert called "the joy of the throat", unmistakably an Arab derivative, all homemade by cloistered nuns.

If visits to the Italian South, the *Mezzogiorno,* whether for work or not, were my favorites, this had a lot to do with the people, who are often warmer, more spontaneous and affectionate than their brethren in the north. But the food was no small attraction. In Calabria, where on more than one occasion I found myself following local elections and consequently interviewing politicians, pundits and university professors in places like Reggio Calabria, Lamezia Terme, Catanzaro, Crotone and Cosenza, I was repeatedly delighted by the local cuisine, a regal example of what the Italians call *cucina povera,* one in which basics available to even the poorest of peasants – including garden-grown vegetables and barnyard animals – are combined to form delicious meals. As in many poorer countries and warmer climes, there is much use of *peperoncino* (chili pepper).

There are many tasty meat and fish dishes in Calabria, but my favorites were always *i primi,* or first courses, especially when these were pasta dishes seasoned not with *parmigiano* but with the region's famous *ricotta salata,* which is made from sheep milk. And then there were dishes such as *pancotto,* really nothing more than day-old bread warmed up in a hot tomato broth and sprinkled amply with pecorino cheese. The *aglio-olio* is similar to the Sicilian version, except without the breadcrumbs. *Lagane* – fresh, broad noodles generally made the same morning – are cooked in milk. And Calabrian lasagna (in Italian it's plural, *lasagne*) is delicious, possibly because it is generally made with *ricotta* rather than mozzarella. Another popular pasta dish is spaghetti with the wild fennel that in spring can be picked by the side of the road. Calabrians make the most fantastic croquettes out of their luscious, purply *melanzane* (eggplant). And if you go to Reggio Calabria to visit the local museum and see the beautiful *Bronzi di Riaci* (two 2,500-year-old Greek warrior statues discovered in the nearby sea in 1972), you must stop for a meal and try the famous *tagliatelle alla reggina* (from Reggio Calabria), a dish that combines pasta with onions, zucchini and bell peppers,

Calabria is still one of Italy's poorest regions, a place where even today in the countryside you can still see a few old women dressed in black, elderly male peasants riding donkeys and, in small towns, piazzas where only men gather, their womenfolk no doubt at home shelling lima beans or rolling out fresh pasta. In the cities, of course, the young women seem like Italian girls anywhere, wearing low cut jeans to show their bellybuttons – even when their body types say they shouldn't – and scooting around town on mopeds or motorcycles. It is a place where organized crime, here called the *'Ndrangheta*, has managed to cause development to grind to a very slow trickle and has interfered with progress in more ways than one: work on the Salerno-Reggio highway, for example, has been going on for more than two decades because, experts say, subcontractors have been corrupted or threatened into giving kickbacks and then asking the State for upwardly revised costs and prices. But nature (where not ruined by runaway and largely illegal building construction) is gorgeous, the company is good, the wine is heady and the food is divine. Fish, shellfish and local meats like pork, rabbit and lamb are used artfully. And where else in Italy can you find desserts such as figs stuffed with a mix of walnuts, almonds, sugar and cinnamon and then baked in a warm oven?

I was introduced to a lot of these dishes later on by a young, right-of-center member of Parliament who was grateful to me because a piece I had written dramatized his situation: he had lost his first bid for the Chamber of Deputies by 300 votes and was demanding a recount (which subsequently turned out in his favor and sent him up to Parliament). I wasn't, of course, trying to do him a favor. I had come up with the idea of doing a series on constituencies where victories in the 1996 election had been razor-thin, and I had traveled to Sicily, Puglia, Sardinia, Calabria and a couple of places up North to do it. But he was grateful all the same. Pino Galati is the son of a local notary public (notaries, who have much more significant functions in Italy than in the U.S., are VIPs here, especially in smaller cities and towns, sharing the limelight with the mayor, the pharmacist and the captain of the *Carabinieri*), and had grown up Christian Democrat. I didn't find Pino at all attractive (in part because of a terrible hair implant which, pictures suggest, has now been corrected) but he was certainly kind and helpful. Furthermore, he had more old-style (read "Tammany Hall") political savvy in his little finger than others have in their entire bodies and was therefore interesting, and useful, to talk to.

The Christian Democrats had dominated much of the Italian South for decades after World War II, with the left's influence in the *Mezzogiorno* confined to major cities like Naples and Bari and the area's few industrial centers such as Taranto. After the party's collapse in the aftermath of the 1992 Clean Hands investigation, a plethora of Catholic parties had appeared. Pino had joined one which was first known as the Christian Democratic Center or CCD, but that later merged with another Catholic splinter party to form another right-of-center Catholic party (the UDC) that for a time allied itself to Berlusconi's party and then struck out on its own again. On one occasion, he took me to meet the other local politicians of Lamezia Terme, his hometown, and I had to laugh. There they were, the representatives of the local pro-Berlusconi coalition: the far-right Allianza Nazionale, Forza Italia, the CCD and its soon-to-be-partner, the CDU. And guess what all four had in common? Until two years before they had all, and I mean ALL been...... Christian Democrats!

Even more fun were my earlier trips, southeast, to Apulia (*Puglia*, in Italian, pronounced *pul*-i-ya), the largely flat, sparsely populated and hardy region located in the heel of Italian boot and which is often referred to as the California of Italy, since in terms of agriculture it is one of the country's most productive areas. Beautiful and earthy, it is an area where rugged natural splendor – miles and miles of ancient olive trees, rocky coasts and higher grassy plateaus – combines glorioiusly with dry-stone huts, white-walled Arab-like towns and powerful Norman and Baroque architecture. Historically, Puglia –

with its vast plains lands – has been known as the *tavoliere d'Italia*, the tableland, which freely translated might also mean "the breadbasket". First colonized by the Greeks, this area was where much of the Roman Empire's wheat and olive oil were produced. I confess I first fell in love with Puglia years before after seeing a really (really!) dumb movie about marauding Saracens called *Flavia, the Muslim Nun*, starring Brazilian actress Florinda Bolkan, who has long made Rome her home. However stupid the plot and bloodthirsty some of the scenes (Flavia was skinned alive by the invaders!), the movie was filmed in and around Trani, the ancient seaside city where a white, 11th century Romanesque cathedral stands out in magnificent contrast against the blue of the Adriatic sea, the kind of image that has always made me feel as if the Mediterranean were my ancestral home.

Also the most industrialized part of the Italian South, until recently when it became the first Italian region to be governed by an out-of-the closet homosexual, Puglia has not generally been in the news as often as the other parts of the *Meridione*, (yet another name for the Italian south). Nevertheless, for a time I was sent down there for work repeatedly, primarily to Bari, the region's "capital", or to the port of Brindisi, which for many years was the primary destination of Albanian people-smugglers and subsequently for the small boats launched from elsewhere to carry would-be immigrants to Italian and European shores. Most of the stories I worked on in and around Bari had to do with local elections or the economy, although one unforgettable saga involved the burning down in 1991 of the venerable Teatro Petruzzelli, a low, massive, red-brick domed building that together with those in Naples and Palermo had become one of the Italian South's three major opera houses.

Although it took about 15 years, today the theatre has been rebuilt but the fire, a result of arson, has remained a mystery. One of those originally accused was the theater's manager, Ferdinando Pinto, who was said to have done the deed to use the insurance policy to cover debts. Pinto, who always maintained his innocence, was convicted of the crime in two separate trials but acquitted by an appeals court in 2005, in other words 14 (sic!) years later. But the real saga of the Petruzzelli was another, one so complex that it was really difficult to explain to newspaper readers. In short, the theater, inaugurated in 1903, was privately owned but built on "public soil" and according to the original agreement between the city of Bari and the Petruzzelli family the property was to revert to the city in the event of destruction. But when that actually happened, almost 90 years later, the dispute between owners and the municipality was sharply bitter, complicated by disagreements among the Petruzzelli heirs, the Messeni Nemagna family. It was a real soap opera, Italian-style, and suffice it to say that, although an agreement between the parties was finally reached in 2003, the theater did not re-open to the public until October 2009.

Traveling around the area for work, I also had the chance to see some amazing archeological sites. Along with ruins of temples built by the early Greek colonizers (Puglia, Calabria and parts of Campania, the region around Naples, were all part of what was once called Magna Grecia, the area colonized by the ancient Greeks starting in the 7th century B.C.), the Archeological Museum of Taranto, is amazing. Once the biggest Greek city on the Italian mainland, Taranto boasts the *Ori di Taranto* collection, which includes some of the most magnificent ancient gold jewelry anywhere in the world. Puglia also offers wonderful examples of Norman and Swabian architecture, such as the imposingly octagonal Castel del Monte on the Murgia high plateau with its eight alabaster towers, which was built in the 13th century by the Holy Roman Emperor, Federico II. The 12th century cathedral in Otranto on the Adriatic is home to an incomparable Byzantine mosaic floor called the Tree of Life that has to be seen to be believed. Ostuni, on the same coast, is a starkly white, ancient town originally built by the Greeks and yet with a pronounced medieval character. Inland, visitors love Alberobello, with its picturesque *trulli*, those conical dry-stone dwellings that have their origin in prehistoric times but which mostly date from four or five hundred years ago.

On one of my first work trips to Puglia, someone gave me the phone number of Giacomo Principalli, a local intellectual and a leftist political activist who seemed to know everyone in town. An older man with a shock of white hair and a regularly rumpled look, he was also extremely generous with his home (I often used his spare bedroom), his time and his friends. Visiting Bari was thus particularly enjoyable because there were always dinners out or at someone's house, and I became friendly with several of Giacomo's close friends. The other thing I quickly discovered was that Giacomo is a wonderful cook. At his house in downtown Bari I got to sample many of Puglia's specialties, and he taught me to make *fave e cicoria*, a velvety puree of fava beans mixed with potato and eaten with steamed or sautéed chicory greens. The best known *pugliese* dish, of course, is *orecchiette con cime di rape*, pasta homemade with durum wheat flour and without eggs that with some able thumb work local women form into "little ears", and which is served with turnip tops and seasoned with garlic and, *a gusto*, more or less *peperoncino*.

But there are other dishes equally worthy of being tried. *Lampascioni*, a sort of bitter wild onion, baked in the oven, is another specialty of what is truly *una cucina povera*, a cuisine which makes do with the simplest ingredients, those available in the immediate surroundings. *Ciceri e tria*, downright delicious, are basically tagliatelle, fried and mixed with chick-peas. *Tiella*, in its classic mode – potatoes, rice, mussels and cherry tomatoes – is a masterpiece (variations include the addition of other vegetables or the replacement of the mussels with *baccalà*, dried cod). *Panzerotti* are mouthwatering crescents of dough with various fillings that are then baked or fried. I can't leave out that the *pugliese* mozzarella on Giacomo's table was succulent and juicy, and the *burrata*, a specialty from Andria and Martina Franca that is made with scraps of mozzarella mixed with heavy cream, was indescribably luscious. And there was no lack of good wine and of tangy, dark green oil, since the region is Italy's largest producer of both.

Sometimes of course we went out to eat, and once Giacomo decided to take me to a small restaurant in Bari Vecchia, a picturesque warren of alleys and low, white and light-colored buildings that grew up around the city's original port on a promontory jutting into the sea. "Don't bring your purse, it could be dangerous," said Giacomo, referring to the frequent purse-snatchings, or *scippi* (shee-pee), in the area. But I'd be darned if I were going to allow myself to be intimidated like that, so off I stupidly went, shoulder bag slung across my chest in my only concession to safety. When we came out of the restaurant we decided to go revisit the magnificent Basilica of San Nicola, the city's glowingly-white Norman cathedral, built in the 11th century to consecrate Bari's patron saint who, when he died, probably in 343 AD, was bishop of Myra, a glorious ancient site in what is modern-day Turkey. Every year, on the 8th of May, the city of Bari stages a re-enactment of the arrival by sea of the *barese* fleet, which after the Muslims conquered Myra had sailed to Asia Minor to bring back Nicola's body. Few of the locals, however, like to mention that part of the saint's remains are, instead, in Venice, Bari's traditional maritime rival. Apparently, Venice's own expedition to Myra in 1099, 12 years after the *baresi* went there, was successful in finding additional bone fragments that analyses have confirmed did in fact come from the same skeleton.

At some point, I became aware that two tough-looking young guys were following us, on foot. I said something to Giacomo but he, used to the scippo by *motorino*, pooh-poohed my concerns. When I slowed down to look in a shop, he paid no heed and disappeared out of sight, rounding the corner. The next thing I knew, one of the guys was tugging at my bag. I grabbed it with both hands and fell to the ground, fortunately with the bag under me, and my assailant on top. "*Stronzo, vattene!–* Get off me, you shit!" I screamed, and finally he got up and ran. It was a narrow, crowded street but amazingly no one, and I repeat, no one, stopped to help me; clearly, back then (things have reportedly improved greatly) they did not feel strongly about making their city safe for tourists. Attracted by the ruckus, Giacomo came running back with one of the *carabinieri* on guard outside the cathedral. But my attacker, luckily *sans* my bag, was nowhere to be seen.

Strangely enough, although my Rome neighborhood used to be one of the favorite terrains of local purse-snatchers, my only two experiences with this kind of crime both occurred in Puglia. The other time was even weirder. I was traveling in Puglia with my friend Theodora, also a native New Yorker, also a journalist who until shortly before had also lived in Rome, and we had decided to go to Taranto to visit that city's old town, its wonderful museum and the magnificent jewelry collection mentioned above. I was driving a four-door rental car and stupidly (my own car is a two-door) had left my purse – containing money, credit cards, passports and even our airline tickets – on the back seat. Unbeknownst to us, we had been targeted and were being followed. As we drove down Corso Umberto Primo, the narrow, one-way street cutting the old city in two, a man and a little girl on a motorbike came towards us, going the wrong way, forcing us to stop. At that moment, someone else opened the stupidly unlocked rear door and ran off with my purse. We were stunned. I recovered first, winding down the window and yelling "*Non finisce qui, siamo giornaliste* e *vedrai che cosa ti succede!* – This won't be the end of this, we're journalists and you'll be sorry!" Afterwards, however, I started shaking, thinking of all the important papers and documents that had been in my purse, but Theodora, now engulfed in her own burst of adrenalin, insisted we go back. We drove all the way around, retracing our route and guess what? When we got to the scene of the crime, they were waiting for us, with a plastic bag holding almost everything, airplane tickets included, except for the cash and my checkbook. They asked us to park and come have a Coke, claiming (yeah, sure!) that they had had nothing to do with the snatch and that the real culprits were members of another gang: Our guys simply had found the contents of my bag dumped nearby, they said. The scene was somewhat surreal, as we sat at a rickety wooden table in a mostly unfurnished room sipping Coke while a couple of local toughs busied themselves putting my credit cards and documents back into my now cashless wallet.

"But if you found my things, how come you didn't find my purse, too?" I asked at one point. "Shut up," Theodora hissed, kicking me under the table. I suppose I might have been looking a gift horse in the mouth but sometimes stupidity pays off. Ten minutes later, one of the boys walked into the room, smiled, and silently placed my empty shoulder bag on the table. I still have it and laugh every time I look at it.

Chapter 18 – Italian Heroes

The water was beautiful, clear and refreshing. Seen from the sea, the volcanic cliffs of western Sicily were striking. And the sky was so vibrant a blue that it was hard to believe that violent death might be lurking nearby. But it was. And I could not but be reminded of this when I came up for air. Above me the rotors of the hovering police helicopter whirred loudly and the silhouettes of several heavily armed men stood out against the classic Mediterranean backdrop of green and yellow prickly pear and purple bougainvillea. I was having a brief swim, alone (if you didn't count the armed guards), with Giovanni Falcone, the Palermo magistrate who throughout the 1980s was right in the forefront of the fight against the Mafia. We were taking a break from a meeting to discuss a book we planned to write together for the U.S. market and had changed into our swimsuits at the summer house that Falcone shared with his wife, Francesca Morvillo, also a magistrate, in the cliffside suburb of Addaura, about 15 minutes from the downtown area of the Sicilian capital.

I was no stranger to Palermo, having been sent there often when, starting in the late seventies, the Mafia began its "attack on the State", as Italian newspapers termed it, murdering policemen and magistrates. Apart from the bloodshed, it was a place I adored visiting; the traces of Arab and Byzantine domination are still evident in the architecture, the food is divine, the weather generally splendid. When I went to Palermo to write about the Mafia and the only partially successful attempts to limit its power, I generally stayed downtown at the sprawling Hotel delle Palme even though the scruffiness of the room furnishings and the threadbare carpeting in the corridors meant it was inexplicably run down. The Hotel Villa Igiea just outside the city on the coast was far more elegant and offered both a pool and the beach, albeit with a view of an oil refinery. And the Excelsior, off the more upscale Viale della Libertà, was also far more modern. But the Hotel delle Palme had that *je ne sais quoi* that made it a must for the in-the-know press. Above all, it had history. In fact, old-timers swear that in the fifties one of the rooms off the elegant lobby had been the site of a very important, high-level meeting among American and Sicilian Mafia families – Carlo Gambino and Alberto Anastasia were reportedly present – the one at which it was decided that the Sicilian Mafia would become the main conduit for the distribution of hard drugs. Its front desk staff was well organized and obliging and, then again, it had Toti, the hotel barman who was well-known to all the journalists, policemen and magistrates, Italian and foreign, who had transited there over the years.

Toti, the Sicilian nickname for Salvatore, was wonderful company. An ex-merchant mariner who was married to a Danish woman, he had lots of gossip and stories to tell and loved to pull out the collections of drawings he had cadged out of his most illustrious visitors. "I'm going to publish these one day," he used to say, while mixing me a Negroni and refilling the dish of peanuts that for me was often a substitute for dinner. In the evenings, a pianist was on hand to play in the bar, which was great, except when some tactless American, like the district attorney from Brooklyn whose name I shall withhold out of pure charity, would come along and ask the guy to play the theme song from *The Godfather*. After dinner we journalists would gather there to chat and more than likely, especially during the eighties, you'd find yourself conversing with some top-ranking national or local police investigator.

As I said, I had also gotten very friendly with Luca Orlando, the slightly overweight lawyer with straight black hair that fell into his eyes, who – unusually for a Sicilian – was fluent in both German and English. In 1985, Orlando would be elected mayor of Palermo for the first of what would be four terms, 1985 to 1990, the so-called "spring of Palermo", 1993 to 1997, 1997 to 2000, when he resigned to run – unsuccessfully – for president of the Sicilian Region, and again, starting in May, 2012 (in between, he was a member of the Sicilian Regional Assembly and, subsequently, of the Italian lower house, the Chamber of Deputies). But when we first met in 1980 he was simply an up-and-coming, 33-year-old Christian Democratic politician.

True, our first encounter had gotten off to a rough start when he kept me waiting, interminably it seemed, in an ante-chamber while he – as I could hear through the un-soundproofed door – made phone call after phone call. At one point, unable to contain my irritation, I threw open the communicating door. "Are we doing this interview or not?" I snarled. "If not, just say so and I'll leave now!" But we soon became good friends. Like most Sicilians, Orlando was extremely hospitable and would have me over for dinner or would take me around to visit Palermo's secret corners. Later, unfortunately, when he was mayor and started seeing himself as an "extremely important person", he began acting in a rather bizarre fashion. He'd schedule interviews at the most improbable times or hold them in the most unlikely places. Once I'd arranged a dinnertime interview for my friend John Wyles, then of the *Financial Times*, who was on his first visit to Sicily, and Orlando kept us waiting until midnight. Another time, in order to interview him I had to tag along on a bumpy ride down the coast to Trapani. And there wasn't even time to sample that city's fabulous fish couscous!

Despite its run-down aspect, Palermo has some marvelous monuments, which make it a must for anyone interested in Italy and its variegated history. First of all, there is the Palazzo dei Normanni, today the seat of the Sicilian Regional Assembly, which houses the magnificent Cappella Palatina with its stupendous Byzantine frescoes. The Zisa fortress, the name of which in Arabic – *al-aziz* – means "splendid", is imposing. The complex surrounding Santa Maria dello Spasimo, today deconsecrated and a center for the fine arts, stands in an area which was once an Arab neighborhood. And churches such as the Martorana, in Norman-Arab-style, are decidedly Middle Eastern in appearance, not surprising at all when you consider that the Arab domination of Sicily lasted until late into the ninth century. Furthermore, only a taxi ride away is the cathedral of Monreale, in the suburb of the same name, where breathtaking mosaics on a gold background recount the stories of both the Old and New Testaments across more than 60,000 square feet of wall space.

The city had also given me a new and precious friendship that, alas, was to be all too short-lived. The first time I was sent to Palermo to do some reporting, I did what many journalists do when they arrive in a place for the first time: I searched out a local colleague to clue me in and point me in the right direction. Although Italian journalism can leave a lot to be desired, as colleagues Italian newspeople are generally superb, always willing to give a foreign colleague a hand and brief him or her on the situation. On that occasion, my lucky choice was Giacomo Galante, well-known editor and reporter for the now defunct, then crusading left-wing tabloid, *L'Ora di Palermo,* who quickly lived up to his reputation for being both friendly and well-connected. With his kinky brown hair, ready smile and warm, brown-eyed gaze, Giacomo turned out to be, quite simply, one of the nicest human beings I had ever met. Smart, impassioned and principled, he always had time for me and was eager to be good friends. He knew all the players in Palermo, in politics and in the justice system, and was happy to share. Soon we became quite close and I felt that he could have been a brother. As far as I could tell, Giacomo was a man who did not lie, steal or cheat on his wife, a locally well-known psychotherapist with whom he was deeply in love.

But fate has little respect for goodness. In the summer of 1988, they took their two children on a trip to Cuba, traditionally a favored destination for Italian left-wingers. On their way back, after a take-off inexplicably attempted in the midst of a violent storm, their chartered flight crashed and burned, killing everyone on board. I saw the report while I was reading the news wires at the *Messaggero* and could not believe my eyes. Giacomo left his elderly mother, his sister (who was his wife's best friend), his brother-in-law, who had been his best male friend, his niece and nephew, more or less the same ages as his own children, and the family dog. I didn't know them, but desperate for someone with whom to grieve, I telephoned and accepted an invitation to spend a weekend together in Trapani, Giacomo's hometown, where we wept together at his grave.

For years, however, I associated Palermo primarily with the late, Giovanni Falcone, probably one of the truest heroes current-day Italy has known. Ever since his 1979 transfer from Trapani to the Palermo *ufficio istruzione* (the Palermo district attorney's judicial investigation office), Falcone had been in the front line of the fight against the Mafia. And a veritable war was indeed being waged. The government appeared incapable of protecting even its most faithful servants: that year, Judge Cesare Terranova was murdered, and a year later, prosecutor Gaetano Costa and Carabiniere Captain Emanuele Basile were killed in two separate assassinations. In 1982, it was the turn of General Dalla Chiesa and his wife. The following year, Falcone's highly respected boss, Rocco Chinnici, was assassinated. And in July of 1985, the two police officers with whom Falcone worked most closely, Giuseppe Montana and Ninnì Cassarà, were mowed down in two separate shootings. Only a few days before his death, Cassarà had summed up the atmosphere in which this entire group of heroes, probably modern Italy's finest men, was living. "We've got to accept the fact that we are *cadaveri ambulanti*, dead men walking," he presciently told Falcone's best friend and close colleague, Paolo

Borsellino (who would be blown to bits himself together with his five bodyguards in the fall of 1992). Indeed, things had gotten so bad that when summer came around that year, the police insisted that Falcone and Borsellino take their families to the isolated island called Asinara where they could be well protected. Falcone and Borsellino, though politically on different wavelengths, adored one another. A well-known, much beloved photo shows the two with their heads together while participating in some kind of panel discussion, smiling and probably giggling.

Starting in the early eighties, Falcone's name was the one most heard when it came to the repeated attempts to bridle organized crime. In 1984, it was he who succeeded in convincing the influential, second-tier Mafia boss, Don Masino (Tommaso) Buscetta, to turn state's evidence after he'd been extradited from Brazil. And after Rocco Chinnici's murder, it was he who became the prime mover in the so-called anti-Mafia pool, which was set up when it became clear that, for reasons of security as well as personal survival, no magistrate in Palermo could afford any longer to work alone. Together with several others, in fact, Falcone was instrumental in building the case against 474 alleged Mafia members who went to trial in 1986 and became known as the *maxi-processo*. So if you were writing about the Mafia, which I did regularly for the *Washington Post* and others, you had to have contact with him.

Interviewing Falcone, a shortish, slightly stocky man with dark hair and a moustache who always reminded me of a 1940s matinee idol, was exhilarating. As in the case of my Rome judge, the security procedures you had to go through to get to him were mind-blowing. But once you got into the inner sanctum and got him talking in his delightful Sicilian accent, you knew you were in the presence of a top-class intellect who was also imbued with the determination to do his best, and fully aware – given the precedents – that he was risking his life. He was also funny. "Isn't he dead? – *Ma non è morto?*" I once asked him about a Mafia bad guy; "*Sì, mortissimo* – yes, very, very dead," he answered, deadpan. And another time when, while feasting on *spaghetti alla Norma* at lunch at the downtown Hotel Patria restaurant with him and some of his colleagues, he had another *bon mot* for us all. I was passionately expounding on the AIDs problem in Italy, saying that in contrast with the United States, where at that time the largest proportion of the disease's victims were homosexuals, in

Italy there seemed to be a really high risk of heterosexual contagion. "The problem is," I said forcefully, "that *i tossicodipendenti italiani* (Italian drug addicts) screw a lot." Falcone looked at me, paused for a moment between two sips of hearty red wine and then, deadpan, drawled in his thick Palermo accent. *"Anche gli tossico-INDIPENDENTI italiani–* The same goes for Italian non-addicts."

Falcone knew that he was a marked man. When I visited him and Francesca in Addaura, that awareness was more acute than ever. A year before, a gym bag containing an unexploded bomb had been found outside his summer house and for a while Falcone had stopped going there. He was convinced, he told me, pointing out where the bag had been left, that it had been more than just an *avvertimento*, a warning. "Clearly, someone wants to kill me," he said, insisting that the bomb truly had been meant to go off and had been put there by enemies who were not necessarily the usual Mafia suspects. He may have become somewhat paranoid for, in describing his enemies, he used that old term, "dark forces", *forze oscure*, a phrase that crops up repeatedly in statements by certain Italian politicians or activists who feel the country is in danger and which to me has always smacked somewhat of over-dramatization.

But who was I to judge? If Falcone was right, there was even more reason to be alarmed than one would have thought. The Mafia's rampant use of violence against "the State" indicated that the criminal organization was determined to hold on to its increasing wealth and power. But if others were involved in what he termed a plot, then it meant that criminals had infiltrated the government or had corrupted some of its highest-ranking representatives. In any event, Falcone was not the only one targeted. Can it possibly have been mere coincidence that the bomb had been found on the same day he had scheduled a meeting in Addaura with Carla Del Ponte, later head of the International War Crimes Tribunal but then Switzerland's most prestigious anti-Mafia investigator, and herself deeply involved in trying to track down the origins and final destination of billions of dollars of dirty drug money?

I can't remember now how I myself got out to the Addaura house on the day of the interview; it may be that Falcone himself picked me up at the airport, or perhaps he'd just sent a car. In any event, at lunch there were to be just the three of us, Falcone, Francesca and I. Bodyguards and driver had been temporarily banished to somewhere out of doors, and Francesca busied herself preparing a lunch of cold pasta while Falcone and I took to the sea in a vain attempt to gain some respite from the ferocious Sicilian summer heat. I was feeling a bit uncomfortable being with the two of them but not (surprise!) because I was having an affair with Falcone; he had never made any kind of a pass at me, although I did know of at least two other women journalists, both Italian, who had been involved or were then involved with him.

There was nothing between him and me except for friendship and, on my part, immeasurable respect, as this was a man who was truly putting his life on the line. But there was something about the way he kept snapping at the woman who some years later was to die at his side that kind of turned me off. It's true that he was living under a death sentence, and knew it. And this no doubt was putting enormous pressure on their relationship. But no woman likes to be treated with disdain, especially in front of female members of the press with whom, it could always be feared, her much admired husband might be having some kind of dalliance.

Given all the mythology that has grown up over the last ten years about Falcone, and consequently about Falcone and Francesca, people in the know didn't like to talk publicly about whatever personal problems the pair might have had. But it appears the relationship was going through a very difficult patch. A few years later, in 1991, when his chances of becoming a member of the country's Supreme Judicial Council, the governing body of the Italian magistracy, were dashed by petty jealousies and who knows what else, Falcone accepted an offer by the Minister of Justice to come to Rome to head up the Penal Affairs Division, and Francesca – fearful that the geographical distance would be fatal to their relationship – decided to follow him, a decision which, in effect, made her death inevitable.

From without, however, Giovanni and Francesca seemed to be the perfect match, and their courtship several years earlier had left *le tout-Palerme* agog. It was not a question of anything scandalous; they were both legally separated or divorced from earlier partners and they would marry in 1990 when Falcone's divorce became final. But many in the city were rather nonplussed. In the first place, people felt inconvenienced by the traffic jams caused by the "mating" of the two magistrates' respective armed escorts. Falcone alone had a permanent police escort that was almost a small war machine: four cars whose drivers would resort to sounding sirens and blazing headlights even in the daytime, and a helicopter circling above. Police in bulletproof vests and carrying both side-arms and machine guns operated the vehicles. When he got into an elevator, three heavily armed police officers got in with him while the others fanned out on the stairs. This meant that when Falcone and Francesca went to a restaurant, their respective bodyguards occupied all the surrounding tables. When they went to the movies, police would spread out through the adjacent rows. Result? They were obliged to cut their private and social life down to the minimum, while Falcone, who cared about staying in shape, was forced to limit his physical activity to only one type of regular exercise, swimming, and to do this had to get up at dawn to use the city swimming pool at a time when he would be totally alone. These precautions, which inevitably resulted in a progressive curtailment of the couple's life-style, reflected Falcone's concern for the dangers to which ordinary people could be exposed because of the threat he lived under. But well aware of the risks he and his colleagues accepted in the name of some higher good, he nevertheless was embittered by the frequent complaints of his fellow *palermitani.*

I was terribly disappointed when Falcone wrote to me to say he was pulling out of our book project, particularly because he didn't give me a real reason, and because shortly thereafter he did do a book – albeit a much, much smaller one than we had contemplated – with another journalist, a highly respected French colleague, Marcelle Padovani, whom I had known for years. But whatever his defects, he was a man one could only admire. Bright, analytical, funny and above all brave, he was also far more playful than the average Italian could ever have imagined, given the solemn press coverage he received for his investigative breakthroughs. For example, driving through Palermo with Falcone at the wheel was an experience one was eager to forget, except for the fact that he allowed me to activate the siren, something everyone's inner child has always dreamed of doing. No doubt frustrated by a life-style that was increasingly hampered by security measures, any thrill was welcome and he often bullied his bodyguards into relinquishing the wheel to him. But he was not a very good driver, and certainly not good enough to manage adroitly the police-prescribed, bumper-to-bumper escort formation in downtown Palermo traffic jams.

Indeed, his insistence on driving was an obsession that probably cost him his life. Falcone was in the driver's seat when returning from

Rome to Palermo on May 23, 1992, when a car bomb hidden along the highway connecting the Punta Raisi airport to Palermo exploded, killing him, Francesca, and the three bodyguards traveling in the car in front. His driver, who was riding in Falcone's place in the back seat, survived.

Chapter 19 – The Judge (Part Two)

I may have been busy with visits to Palermo, where I was writing about Falcone and the other courageous investigators who were doing their best to bring organized crime to its knees. But back in Rome, I was concentrating on my own magistrate and wondering where this relationship would go, if anywhere. It was not long after our walk along the Old Appian Way that the Judge called again and proposed "*un drink*" at a tree-shaded café above the Spanish Steps, where instead we ate ice cream, discussed current events and flirted in a subtle but exciting way.

In the 1980s, Italians had still not fully embarked on the cellular phone spree that was to turn most restaurants into giant phone booths, consigning the Italian pay phone to an early obsolescence. However, because of his investigations – many of which had international ramifications – not to mention a passion for technological hardware, the Judge was ahead of his time. Halfway through his *gelato* the *telefonino* in his briefcase rang. "Oh phooey," I thought, imagining a summons from the *Procuratore Generale*, the district attorney. But fortunately it was only a colleague of his, a fellow magistrate with whom he shared several cases. "I'm having an aperitif with the correspondent of the *Washington Post*," he said with, it seemed to me, a smidgen of pride. "Why don't you join us?" So before long there were three of us at the tiny table, the two of them first bantering away and then, in a more serious vein, discussing the latest developments in terrorist bombing techniques, including an explosive which, they said, looked enough like a piece of fabric to be stuck without detection to an airplane seat and exploded remotely days later. It was fascinating – and chilling.

I was actually well acquainted with the new arrival, a shortish, unprepossessing man with a round face and a reputation for being a dogged and incorruptible investigator. I knew him well in part because he was an expert on the Red Brigades as well as on Arab terrorism, and partly because once, during a late-evening briefing in a dusk-darkened room brightened by a glass of whisky, we'd had a "close encounter". That is, he had unexpectedly dashed around his desk and thrust his tongue into my mouth. On reflection, I decided that the misunderstanding was in part my fault; without really wanting to, I'd allowed a business atmosphere to degenerate, to assume the appearance of something different. But we had managed to remain friendly. On this occasion, however, I could see that he was puzzled – and intrigued – by the precise nature of my relationship with the Judge. And so was I, as later, his colleague having been picked up by his limo, the Judge insisted on accompanying me back to the *Messaggero*, which meant holding my hand all the way down elegant Via Sistina and onto bustling Via del Tritone. Isn't he worried that someone will see us, I asked myself? I certainly was (although not enough to withdraw my hand).

The next week, the Judge invited me to dinner, taking me to a small *trattoria* known for its artichokes that is situated right off the Lungotevere, the broad, leafy road that runs along both sides of the Tiber. Afterwards, parked fittingly enough in the shadow of a courthouse, a squat Fascist-era building not far from Castel Sant'Angelo that Roman prosecutors call the *Casa Madre*, he gave me a chaste good-night kiss. A few days later, when I returned to Rome after a reporting trip to Greece for the *Herald Tribune*, he insisted on coming to pick me up at the airport, meeting me out on the tarmac in the company of a uniformed police officer (but as usual without his bodyguards). "I wonder who they think you are," he mused aloud. "Perhaps a witness in an important case?" I offered slyly. He smiled and took me home, with only a brief stop for an *aperitivo* at a bar near my house where at least three people nodded or said hello to him.

At this point, however, I was beginning to get worried. The Judge had done nothing more than give me an occasional peck on the cheek and in all these weeks had made no serious passes. I didn't know why and, even worse, I wasn't sure what I wanted to do about it. The turning point came on a Tuesday in late July. In the morning the Judge had telephoned to ask if I was free in the afternoon. "I thought we could go to the lake," he said, meaning Lago di Bracciano, about 25 miles northeast of Rome. We agreed to meet in front of the fountain at Piazza Trilussa in Trastevere, near my home. The piazza – really only a tiny open-ended square between the Lungotevere and the fountain itself – was only two blocks from my apartment. But the Judge was worried that he might get lost in the maze of narrow, winding streets with which he was unfamiliar. This time, although we were only going out into the country, I had decided to dress better than usual and for the occasion had put on well-fitting, white cotton slacks and a white and tan short-sleeved cotton knit sweater with brown beads around the neckline, an outfit that would be fine if the afternoon were to turn into evening and we would end up going out to dinner. And I put a folded-up silk shawl into my handbag in case it got chilly. But I wasn't certainly wasn't prepared for the Judge's new look.

Waiting there to greet me was an almost totally different person. The Santa Claus beard was now trimmed to flat, youthful proportions. Gone was the elegant, well-cut sober suit and starched and monogrammed white or light blue shirt that had seemed a sort of uniform. The Judge was wearing blue jeans and with them brown moccasins without socks, a striped blue and white shirt with the sleeves rolled up and the top three buttons undone to reveal a gold chain, from which some religious medallions were hanging, and a seriously hairy chest. He seemed ten years younger and appeared happy, smiling, relaxed, seductive... and VERY affectionate. We drove by the courthouse so he could leave off some papers and then took the Aurelia highway out of Rome, stopping off in the miniature, old hilltop village of Ceri for a coffee and a quick look around and then continuing on to Bracciano.

It was mid-afternoon and by then we were holding hands continuously while he piloted the massive Citroen with one hand. We strolled along the shores of the lake arm in arm, enjoying the summer colors, watching the fishermen and, at intervals, kissing chastely. We had yet another coffee, this time at a café on the lakefront and read the papers. And when, at dusk, we drove around again to enjoy the sight of the castle which, like most Italian monuments, is beautifully illuminated, I was practically sitting in his lap. So when, after dinner at Trevignano (pasta with *funghi porcini* followed by delicious roast eel) we returned to Rome, I had a feeling things would be different. "Would you like to meet my cats?" I asked shyly. He would, he said, so shortly after introductions were completed we found our way into the bedroom and then, after a moment of awkwardness (he was worried I might find him too hairy) things got serious. Remember the beach scene in *From Here to Eternity*? It came into my mind as we rolled passionately across my bed.

For me that day was a watershed. I was in love and so, I believe, was he. (Actually, I know he *thought* he was in love because some time later a colleague of his, unaware of my identity, told me that the Judge had confided in him that he was in love with an American journalist and happier than he'd been in years.) As usual, I don't think I had any particular expectations. I knew seeing each other often was unlikely because of his job. And it was obvious to me that an Italian male of his age with two grown children was hardly about to leave his family and move in with an independent, unwifely journalist. But it was August, when everything, including some kinds of crime, comes to a halt in Italy, and I was delighted when he said he'd be taking some time off. I was moving myself and the cats, Cleopatra, Topaz and Duchess, 100 kilometers down the coast to Sabaudia. "When are you coming to visit?" I asked. The answer was gratifying: in a day or two. "Just let me organize myself," he pleaded.

Every day the Judge would phone me, generally between one and two p.m. Since the beach-house I was renting didn't have a phone, this meant waiting for long, sweaty minutes at the custodian's cottage until the telephone would ring. "I think I can take a few days off at the end of the month. Do you want to go north or south?" he asked. "South," I said, really excited at the idea of a vacation together. But in the meantime, when was he coming to Sabaudia? "Tomorrow afternoon, but I'll confirm tomorrow," was the reply. And tomorrow and tomorrow and tomorrow. The Judge somehow never found the time to come to Sabaudia, and the idea of a vacation in the Italian South, for a few days a cheering chimera, vanished altogether when he announced he had to make a trip abroad to complete an investigation.

I was disappointed and confused, but things were only to get worse. When the judge returned to Rome at the end of the month, he called me and we met for dinner at Cucurucù, an outdoor restaurant on the river not far from the Olympic Stadium. We'd been given a quiet table on the outer edge of the patio. The Judge held my hand, smiled into my eyes and then said he had to go home, pleading tiredness. So we weren't even going to make love! I couldn't believe it. "What's going on here?" I bleated. "You didn't come to Sabaudia, you didn't have time for a vacation with me, and now you don't even want to make love?" Didn't he realize, I asked him, how many expectations he'd created? *Sono molto delusa* – I am really disappointed," I said sadly.

I didn't hear from the Judge after that for more than two months, and I probably should simply have chalked the whole business up to experience, realizing that the man probably had serious problems, emotional and possibly sexual. A machine answered the few times I tried to call and there was never any response to my messages. Then one day as I was sitting in my office, now in a side street behind the *Messaggero*, the downstairs door buzzer sounded. "It's you!" I exclaimed joyfully as we awkwardly embraced. "Why did you disappear like that?" "Oh," he said, not meeting my eyes, "I guess I was a bit *esaurito,* a catch-all Italian word which literally means exhausted but which is often used to signify a sort of mild nervous breakdown. By this time I ought to have learned my lesson, right? There were myriad signals advertising loudly and clearly that the Judge was obviously not interested in (or not capable of) a sustained romantic relationship with an available woman. But I was "in love". And back then when I was "in love" I couldn't recognize a signal even if, like this one, it was bleeping loudly on and off in my face.

So we started up again, if that's the appropriate term. The Judge called me several times a day, from his car, from his office, on his cellular phone, from home. "I'm at Rebibbia (a prison), I just interviewed so and so"; "I'm at the courthouse, I've got to gear up for an interrogation"; "I'm at home now. I've got a dinner but I'll call you later"; "I'm calling to say *buona notte.*" We spent hours on the phone, days, possibly weeks. Sometimes, late at night (where were his wife and *figli,* I wondered?), he'd regale me with music, since he played both piano and the electric organ by ear. Alternatively he would get me laughing uproariously with funny stories related in a perfect Russian or Arab accent. For my part I would leave musical messages – from Whitney Houston's *All at Once* to Puccini's *Nessun Dorma* – on his answering machine. It was romantic bliss – but at a distance. Quite a distance.

I won't say we never made love again, although I have to admit that there was never again a real replay of *From Here to Eternity*. Sometimes he would organize a small, *intimo* dinner in the tiny, rooftop apartment he owned in a *vicolo* behind Piazza Navona. And once or twice a month we'd meet for lunch at a Chinese restaurant not far from the Trevi fountain and then spend the rest of the lunch-hour break at my place for what turned out to be primarily oral sex. By this, of course, I mean fellatio since, as I've already explained, most Italian men – although this is a well-kept secret – do not seem to be keen on cunnilingus. In fact, this is a sex act that doesn't get talked about much, even by women. Some men will do it once or twice at the beginning, perhaps to show how generous they are, sometimes never.

But with one notable example, the Italian men I have known are just as happy never to do it at all. One American woman friend of mine went down south in Italy to spend a few days with a man, a waiter, she'd met on a previous trip and to whom she'd felt attracted. He'd been very nice, taking her around Sicily to show her examples of Baroque architecture in which she was very interested. But when they made love things were not so great. "He had an orgasm before I did, so I asked him to go down on me," she told me when she returned to Rome. "And you'll never guess what he said," she added. But since I know my chickens I had no doubt. "I bet he said no," I proffered, "and I'm not at all surprised."

Fellatio, now, that's another story. You, the woman, are supposed to want to do that all the time while all the time telling the man how *bello, grande, duro, fantastico* or *enorme* his *cazzo* (prick) is. *Cazzo*, by the way, now appears to be the single most frequently used word in the Italian dictionary, much as "fuck" or "fucking" is for some less-refined speakers of our own English language. Walk down any street in Rome and keep your ears open and "*cazzo*" will resound from every side. "*Non me ne frego un cazzo!*" (I don't give a fuck!), "*Ma che cazzo vuoi?*" (What the fuck do you want?), "*Non mi rompete il cazzo*" (Don't break my balls!), which has to be said with a real snarl, or just plain "*Cazzo!*" (fuck!) when you stub your toe or discover your TV satellite picture has once again gone on the blink.

In part, the Judge's predilection, along with an interest in pornography, may have had its roots in nature. He was, after all, not a young man. And because of health problems he was forced to take medicine for hypertension, which, as I later learned from a newspaper article (God forbid he should have mentioned it to me himself!), can create erection problems. But be that as it may, the younger, jeans-clad, open-shirted romantic male that took me to Bracciano was never to make a second appearance.

The romance, then, was predominantly verbal and the phone calls, as much as I liked them, indeed loved them, indeed had come to count on them, even to organize my life around them, were – I well knew – a poor substitute for a real relationship. It was ridiculous and frustrating, and I was starting to get depressed. "I've got to find a way to break out of this," I'd say to myself over and over, and I began working in earnest on detaching myself from what I well knew was a psychological mess, although it came complete with what seemed like

169

heartache. Then, one day, help arrived, from none other than the Judge himself. One morning I told him – naturally over the phone – that I would be checking into a clinic for an operation; it was nothing to worry about, I explained, but I had to do it. "An operation," he repeated, sounding alarmed. "Okay, I'll call you," he said, and that was that. Once again I didn't hear from him for two months, and this time I was really turned off and determined to keep my distance. The funny thing was that when we did finally speak (I called him for work reasons), he laid the blame on a new promotion. "Please forgive me," he said. "You see, I am now simply just too busy to carry on a relationship."

Chapter 20 – Fernando. Another Man With a Gun

*M*afia. For any correspondent working in Italy this is one of the key trigger words for journalistic coverage – along with Vatican, Pope, neo-Fascists, *communisti* and, increasingly as time went on, terrorism. Good law and order sources are therefore essential if you don't want to end up being a hack who simply rewrites the wires.

So when Fernando showed up at the side of a magistrate I was meeting for dinner at the Hotel Forum's delightful roof garden, with its splendid view of the Roman Forum, the latter's alabaster columns and marble arches artfully illuminated against the darkening sky, I immediately made a mental note that he could turn out to be an extremely useful contact. He certainly wasn't the first police detective I had met, and possibly not the highest ranking. But he was decidedly different from the rank and file. I already knew his reputation as a skilled investigator. Never having met him, I was pleasantly surprised – by his linguistic skills, by his sophistication, by his youth and, I have to admit, by his good looks. "Hmmmm", I remember saying to myself, characteristically ignoring the thin gold band he wore on his left ring finger.

Given the well-known Italian inclination towards pleasure, which quite naturally includes *bonhomie*, even the highest placed sources are quick to relax if the ambience is right. And in terms of access, being an attractive woman is hardly a disadvantage, especially if you: a) write for an important paper and/or b) have shown by your questioning, perseverance, and published articles that you are a serious reporter and not a lightweight.

So Fernando's unplanned presence that evening, although not immediately productive in journalistic terms, was a stroke of real luck. And gratifying. I was with two attractive and intelligent men with good senses of humor, who laughingly related stories regarding their American counterparts, like the U.S. district attorney who during a visit to Palermo went white every time he was driven somewhere in the city by a police car, which in true Sicilian fashion would, with roof lights flashing, siren blaring and speed limits disregarded, career wildly down – for the most part – the wrong side of the road.

That evening, as usual in Italy, we ate well: *fettuccine* with *porcini* mushrooms, *straccetti* (pan-fried paper-thin slices of beef) for them, a poached sea bass for me, as I am constantly fighting to keep my weight under 130 pounds. And although they weren't exactly flirting, it was clear to me that they approved of my appearance. That evening, just to remind everyone, myself included, that I do have legs, I had replaced my almost ever-present pants with a two-piece Basile black summer suit which had a short skirt and a flowered jacket with a plunging neckline. Maybe I ought to dress like this more often, I considered, as my dinner companions continued to eye me more or less unobtrusively. After coffee and several grappas it was alas, time to go home. I had come by cab; my car was at the shop and my skirt was too tight to use the *motorino*. So I was only too pleased when they offered to drive me home. Fernando had brought his office car – an armored, blue Fiat sedan that actually had small gun portals low down on the passenger's door. The judge had come by foot; when he came to Rome he felt freer than he did on his home turf in the Italian South and like my Judge was convinced that a varied and unpredictable schedule was the best defense against assassination. So there I was in a car, albeit armored, together with two of the highest targets on the Italian underworld's hate list. Yikes!

The next day I got Fernando's number from an Italian crime reporter and telephoned him. A male voice with a heavy Roman inflection answered politely enough, but said, bluntly, and with no real attempt at cooperation: *il Dottore è fuori* – the boss is out. (In Italy, *dottore* means doctor but it also is the title given to any male with a university degree, and is frequently used in this sense, particularly by people from Southern Italy.) "No, I don't know when he'll be back," he added, brusquely. This, I was later to find out, was typical of Fernando's staff of bodyguards, a group he privately referred to as *gli animali*, "the animals". Given the obviously low cultural level of my interlocutor, I wasn't sure if it was worthwhile to leave a message, but what could I lose? I left my name and number but was not particularly hopeful for a quick reply.

To find an Italian government employee (or a politician) at his or her desk on a first try is always a miracle; if they're high-placed enough to have a private secretary you can at least hope for a call back. But otherwise it's try and try again until you get lucky. And although more recently things have been tightened up, for decades many lower-level civil servants got away with a lot of malingering: coffee breaks were rife and many *statali* would even leave the premises for a bit of shopping during what were supposed to be office-hours; generally from 8:30 a.m. to 2 p.m. In some ministries – for example, the sprawling Treasury-Budget complex – you didn't even have to leave the building to go shopping: salesmen were somehow allowed in to "work" the various floors, selling everything from jewelry and watches to sunglasses, underwear and makeup.

In Fernando's case, however, it didn't even cross my mind that he might be engaged in any of this unproductive behavior. A glance at the daily papers was sufficient to imagine just how busy he or any of his associates might be. A few weeks earlier, kidnappers had seized a young child and were holding him for ransom, probably somewhere in Tuscany. The infamous *Banda della Magliana*, the gang that had long been terrorizing the Roman neighborhood of the same name with robberies and armed assaults, was back in business. And investigators had reached the conclusion that a joint venture between organized crime and right-wing terrorists had been responsible for a recent train bombing.

So the *forze d'ordine*, police and *carabinieri*, were up to their necks in crime busting. Instead, surprise! Only two hours later the phone rang and it was Fernando returning my call on a cell phone from who knows where. I said that I had enjoyed meeting him and hoped we could keep in touch. He was friendly (not flirtatious), expressed similar sentiments, and told me to call him whenever I needed anything. We would, we decided, have dinner together at some unspecified future date.

This was early 1986, and the Mafia was on my mind for professional reasons as well. After four years of investigation by the pool of dedicated Sicilian magistrates led by Falcone and Borsellino, the so-called *maxi-processo* or maxi-trial had opened in Palermo to consider the indictments on charges of Mafia involvement made against 474 defendants charged with some 90 murders and a variety of other crimes ranging from drug trafficking and kidnapping to robbery and extortion. Most of these crimes had been committed during a previous four-year wave of gang violence caused by an all-out war among rival groups competing for drug proceeds (the *narco-lire,* as Italian investigators and journalists then liked to call the illicit earnings from a vast international network of narcotics smuggling). Some 450 people had died. Most of these were *mafiosi* belonging to a variety of *famiglie,* or clans. But there were also the *morti eccellenti,* high-ranking magistrates, politicians and policemen who had been killed, people such as Piersanti Mattarella, the young, Christian Democratic president of the Sicilian regional government, Pio La Torre, the head of the Sicilian branch of the Communist party, and cops such as Giuseppe Montana and Ninni Cassarà with whom Fernando had worked closely.

I flew down to Sicily for the opening of the trial along with dozens of other wisecracking Italian journalists and Rome-based foreign reporters. We stood on line for what seemed like hours to get accreditation, and after a long, boring and inexplicable wait we were all finally admitted to the high-security modern courtroom that in unintended (but unavoidable) contrast had been built in reinforced concrete onto a wing of the Ucciardone prison, a looming, gloomy, dark gray structure with a distinctively dungeon-y look, built by the Bourbon monarchs back in the 18th century.

The situation in the "bunker" (as, once again, the Italian press dubbed the courthouse) was tense, but the tension appeared somewhat artificial since it was clear that no one in his or her right mind would have contemplated any violence. Outside, at least 500 police stood guard with machine guns and armored vehicles. Inside, scores of *carabinieri*, the black of their uniforms relieved by the red stripe down the leg, formed a human barrier separating us from the 30-odd, barred cages built for the 250 defendants. The rest of the room was occupied largely by some 200 defense lawyers, defendants out of jail on their own recognizance and relatives of Mafia victims.

We journalists – whether *palermitani* or *romani* – were upstairs in a balcony along with the public where, as we waited for the proceedings to get under way, the principal pastime was greeting old friends and colleagues, the usual sort of journalists' old home week and, oh yes, planning where, after filing our stories, we would go to dinner. (After long discussions among those who knew Palermo best, it was decided to spend the evening at the Mondello beach resort where, given the season, the restaurants would be likely to have *ricci,* sea urchins, which despite their gooey orange appearance are a real delicacy.)

Meanwhile, there was drama enough in the courtroom to keep us busy until dinnertime. In one of the cells down below sat the biggest boss then in custody, 61-year old Luciano Liggio, at the time reputed to be, as one investigator put it, "the uncontested boss of *Cosa Nostra*" and who started off the proceedings by firing his lawyers. Actually, Liggio had already been in jail for years. He'd been captured some 15 years earlier when a chic wine shop he'd been running as a front had been – unfortunately for him.– written up, with photos, in the some newspaper or magazine, and it was doubtful he was still running the Mafia from "inside". But it was a catchy thing to write about. The star witness of the trial, but whose testimony was not scheduled for that day, was to be Tommaso Buscetta (pronounced Bush-*ett*-a), a former second-rank boss, who had been captured in Brazil two years earlier and whose disclosures were said to be giving Falcone and his colleagues in the "anti-mafia pool" invaluable corroborating details of Mafia activities and of the organization's structure, then estimated to stand at between 3,000 and 6,000 foot-soldiers controlled and manipulated by a governing body known as the "*Cupola*", the Dome.

Although it was to take 350 court sessions and 1,314 witnesses, eventually 342 of the suspects on trial would be sentenced. But on that first day pessimism was running high. Investigators were worried that the complicated proceedings and the myriad defendants would lead politicians to lose interest. Both Falcone and Borsellino, the island's two top investigators, had warned repeatedly that despite some apparent success, police activity had failed to keep pace with the growth in the Mafia's activity and structure. And, they reminded us frequently, the Mafia's leaders were experts at adapting to changed conditions. The tradition of secrecy, or *omertà,* was so effective that authorities were usually two years behind in learning what was going on in the underworld. Even the current lull in gang wars was not encouraging. The decline of internecine-shoot-outs only meant the hundreds of arrests had put the Mafia on the defensive; there was greater unity among the bosses and therefore heightened control.

All this concentration on organized crime meant Fernando was rarely far from my mind. And once back in Rome, we were again in touch. Despite his hectic schedule (a series of trips to the Abruzzi region, a dash to Catania in Sicily, a meeting in Paris) and my own unpredictable schedule as correspondent for three American dailies, a Canadian newsweekly and *CBS* radio, we managed to chat on the phone several times. I had yet to see him again since that first dinner with the magistrate, but anytime I phoned him I could be sure that within a day or two at most he'd get back to me. Living alone, as I did,

I could take calls at any hour and sometimes he would call close to midnight, occasionally just to say hello. Was this courtesy, a currying of journalistic favor, or something else. Who knew? Who cared? It was fun.

Came the day, however, when finally we managed to set a date for dinner. Could he meet me near my gym, off via Veneto, perhaps outside of Harry's Bar? He could. We had a drink and from there went on foot (amazingly enough, there were – once again – no bodyguards in sight) to a nearby Sicilian restaurant where he was well known. I let him order for me and we feasted on *pasta alla Norma,* that is, with eggplant, and then grilled swordfish. But to be truthful I really wasn't paying that much attention to the food. After years in the police, Fernando was clearly used to keeping his mouth shut. But that evening, perhaps because he had such an attentive audience, perhaps because of the wine, he responded generously to my gentle prodding, which by the way had no ulterior motive than to gather background and satisfy my curiosity. I have always been fascinated by detective work and was dying to know what I had missed by choosing journalism instead. Clearly, some aspects of his profession were – to say the least – unpleasant, for example killing people. In uniform only briefly at the very outset of his career, Fernando had once been forced to kill an armed terrorist, who had taken hostages at a foreign embassy. Since that time he'd been gun-shy, and generally kept his Beretta in the car. By the time he reached his forties he had, instead, become well schooled in undercover work. He'd posed as a potential drug buyer in a variety of sting operations. He'd traveled to the Far East on the heels of a heroin smuggler. And he had done countless *pedinamenti,* or shadowing, of suspects. One time he'd been sent to keep an eye on a second-level *mafioso* who was believed to be in contact with a major boss wanted for a series of kidnappings and murder. Using a fleet of second-hand cars supplied when necessary by his department, Fernando tracked the guy down to Sicily and back through Italy to Padua. At one point he needed to get a closer look to see with whom the fellow was meeting. So he parked and went into the café into which the *mafioso* had disappeared and ended up playing cards only two tables away from him.

Some years earlier I'd come to the conclusion that despite all my liberal credos (I am passionately in favor of gun control), I had a definite weakness for law and order types; it is, after all, rather significant that over a period of 15 years I have had love stories or flings with at least five men who carried guns. Be that as it may, by the end of the evening I was totally enthralled. By the time we got to his blue bulletproof sedan, again the one with the secret gun barrel holes (in case of an ambush, he explained), I was having trouble breathing. This man was clearly no longer just a potential source. "*O Dio*, I wonder if he, too, is feeling attracted," I asked myself. Fernando had been friendly and outgoing, and after all had invited me to dinner. But so far there had been no outward sign that he was feeling anything more than curiosity or friendship.

In these situations I often become what George Sanders once referred to (in Roberto Rossellini's unmemorable "*Viaggio in Italia*) as a "shameless, brazen hussy". Sometimes, I simply can't stand to wait to see what will happen and prefer to force the issue. So, with my heart in my mouth I decided to make a move, albeit a small one, and reach for Fernando's hand. "What will he do, will he pull his hand away?" I agonized. The incident with Alberto, the Milanese headhunter had been terribly embarrassing and I wasn't eager to have it repeated. Fernando, however, didn't pull away. He squeezed my hand back, then brought it to his lips and kissed it, then continued to hold it, atop the gear shift, as he set the car in motion and headed towards my part of town.

In an earlier conversation Fernando had made clear his attitude towards his wife, whom he'd married years ago when the two of them graduated from university. "You may not get all of the interest, but you need never worry about losing the capital," he said he'd told her. So I knew the score. I wasn't dealing with a totally faithful husband, but neither was this a man who was fed up with his wife and inclined to leave her. Perfect for me! At the same time I didn't know exactly what to expect. Did this happen to him often? Was he blasé about it? And above all did he expect an immediate "payoff"? For all my apparent boldness, as I've said before I really am too shy to jump into bed with someone on the "first date". This is, I suppose, a paradoxical aspect of my personality, and I really don't know how to explain it. Perhaps it's simply that I find sex so intimate that it is difficult for me to overcome the initial psychological barriers. This may also explain why, unlike some of my girlfriends, I find it difficult, if not impossible, to go to bed with someone just out of camaraderie or in a "why not?" frame of mind. And when I have, it generally has been a disaster. I need to feel strong sexual passion or attraction to get over my shyness.

Well, there was no need to worry. When we got to my piazza, Fernando parked the car and for a while we sat there silently, holding hands, in the dark. Then, we kissed, and kissed and kissed and kissed some more. I can still remember those kisses, possibly the most wonderful of my life, so sensual, so personal, so passionate and so totally involving. For me, it was a perfect start. I hate it when a man sticks his tongue down my throat when we've barely met. I find it offensive. But with Fernando there was none of that. His way of kissing was tailor-made for me. At first he just brushed my lips with his. Then after a while our lips parted, but he still didn't try and use his tongue. That came quite a bit later. And by then I was as ready for deep kissing as I've ever been. (Usually, I have to see a guy several times before I feel ready. I actually find deep-kissing more intimate than intercourse!) And as he kissed me Fernando caressed my face and my hair, whispering my name repeatedly. "Fernando," I whispered back, wondering what was happening. I was so glad that he hadn't done anything but kiss me, hadn't used his hands and, when I finally broke away, mumbling something about it being late, hadn't even asked if he could come up.

The next day I was to learn that at exactly the time Fernando and I had been sitting in the car, kissing, there had been a small earthquake in Rome, and we hadn't noticed a thing! No wonder, I guess. For when I got out of the car my head was reeling and my legs were so wobbly I could hardly get up the steep, 17th-century stairs to my apartment. This was not what I had expected. Nor did I expect it when the phone rang almost immediately and I heard Fernando's baritone voice saying, "I'm heading home but I just wanted to say *buona notte.*" The next day at 8:00 a.m., while I was having my bi-weekly massage, he called again, once more phoning from his car as he drove to work in the modern EUR section of Rome, to say hello and tell me that he'd be back in touch soon. "Who was that?" asked Tommaso, my masseur, busily trying to get the kinks out of my back, when I finally hung up. An avid newspaper reader, he recognized the name straight off. "You're going out with *him*?" he exclaimed. "It looks like it," I said, somewhat dazed.

I had learned from my relationship with the Judge that getting together with a committed law-and-order, married workaholic is not easy. So I wasn't at all surprised when a few weeks went by before I saw Fernando again. And in the meantime (again, shades of the Judge), I did get a lot of phone calls – from Rome, Milan, Palermo and even from Washington. Fernando's style on the phone was conversational but fairly impersonal, so when – finally – the day of our next "date" arrived, it all seemed somewhat anticlimactic. He was to pick me up around the corner from my office, which was then about two blocks down busy Via del Tritone from the *Messaggero*. But although I'd dressed with care – an Armani jacket, a short skirt and a silk striped shirt I'd recently bought in Milan – I felt a bit detached. "I'm mostly kind of curious," I confessed on the phone to a girlfriend who works for the *Los Angeles Times*. "Probably, I won't even like him any more."

Sure. At 9:00 p.m. sharp I closed up the office, took the creaky wooden elevator downstairs, and pushed open the heavy, paneled door to the street. Fernando's car was parked at the intersection with Piazza Poli and he, dressed in a blue blazer and charcoal pants, was striding towards me. I swear I almost fainted. I took one look at the man and my knees went weak. "You look a bit strange," he said when we were in the car. "Oh, it's nothing," I lied. "I think I have a cold coming on." We went to the same restaurant on the Lungotevere the Judge had taken me to, the one that specialized in artichokes – Roman style, Jewish style, fried, baked, whatever – but I didn't really enjoy myself. One difficulty was the acoustics; the noise from the other tables was almost deafening. But the real problem was me; by this time I was so consumed with desire that it was hard for me to speak.

The meal seemed interminable. At a table to our right, two women, a daughter and her mother, were carrying on noisily about the complexities of Italian taxation. Almost everyone in the restaurant was smoking, (something that fortunately since 2001 is no longer possible). And a television in the kitchen was broadcasting a soccer match. I couldn't wait to leave and was happy when, finally, we left and headed towards my home. This time, I felt sure, he'd definitely want to come upstairs and I was terribly excited. But instead there was almost a repeat performance of our previous encounter, except that somehow (it was barely perceptible) he was both less gentle and more detached. And so, after some 45 minutes of kissing, I asked, timidly, whether he would like to come up. "No, *cara,*" he said. It was late, he said, he'd just flown in from Geneva that day and hadn't yet been home. Why didn't I invite him for dinner one of these days? He walked me to the door of the building, looked into my eyes, and whispered "*Ti telefono domani*– I'll call you tomorrow." I smiled and said good night but inside I was aching with disappointment – and worried. I was so turned on that I felt as if I were in danger. "What am I going to do?" I remember wondering. "If I'm not careful I could end up being this man's sex slave." On the other hand, wasn't his reluctance to come upstairs a worrisome sign?

I needn't have worried, because Fernando never called and if it hadn't been for a series of coincidences I might not ever have seen him again. Which probably would have been better, given the way things went. When I phoned him a few days after our date, he wasn't in, and although I left a message he never called back. I tried a few more times, and then gave up. I felt desperate. By now my crush had ballooned into a real infatuation, or perhaps obsession would be a better word. His behavior was so peculiar, so unsettling, that I spent entire days wondering why, why, why? Later, looking back, it seems to me now that the answer was obvious. Fernando either was worried about any further involvement or perhaps had some sexual issues, enough at any rate to worry about his performance. And this, as would become clear during our next – and final – encounter seemed to be the most likely explanation.

About a month after he had faded from sight, I was talking on the phone to our mutual friend, the magistrate. I needed some facts for something I was writing, the magistrate was going out of town and didn't have much time, and he suggested I talk to Fernando instead as he was very much up on the subject in question. "I'll tell him you'll be calling," he said. My deadline was nearing and I did need the information, but I have to admit that the main reason for my decision to call Fernando was because I wanted terribly to see him again.

"I can come over tonight about nine-thirty," said Fernando, when we finally spoke. He was calling me from his office, a few days after I had phoned to say I needed his help on my project. When the downstairs doorbell rang I was nervous. I hadn't wanted to overdress, since this was supposed to be a working session, so I had settled on a black but sober Mila Shoen at-home outfit that I rarely got to wear with, underneath, some very sexy, just-in-case Victoria's Secret underwear. We had a drink (I had made sure I had some of his favorite malt whisky on hand) and chatted, until he said, "I don't feel like working," and took my hand. So perhaps it was going to be all right after all, I thought. True, I was by no means as excited as on the previous occasions, but I figured it wouldn't take all that long before I was. We started kissing, and then I made what in retrospect may have been a terrible error. Instead of letting things take their natural course, I suggested we adjourn to the bedroom, a big mistake. In general, this may be something you can only do with a man who is genuinely sexually self-confident. But in retrospect I have to say that every time I have taken the initiative with an Italian, it has totally backfired.

Later I thought that if I hadn't done that with Fernando, things might have gone differently. Maybe not. Who can tell? As it was, it turned out to be one of the most disappointing sexual experiences of my life. Fernando made love to me hurriedly, clumsily, with a total lack of either eroticism or affection. He did a bit of this and a bit of that, pulling me first into one position, then into another. Penetration (if it actually took place) was brief and totally unsatisfying. And most inexplicably, afterwards he acted as if everything were completely normal.

I was stunned. How could someone who kissed like he did make love so badly? I felt totally let down but, I thought, perhaps he was just nervous and the second time things would go better. But there was to be no second time, then or ever. While getting dressed Fernando started to talk to me about the information he was supposed to have given me. Before I knew it, we were arguing. That is, *he* was arguing, shouting that he wasn't the magistrate's gofer and accusing me of using him. "Fernando," I cried, almost on the brink of tears, "we've just made love. Why are you talking to me like this?" By now Fernando was knotting his tie, and slipping into his jacket. "*Sì.* We've just made love," he answered, as if he were making some kind of point. He leaned over me on the bed and kissed me perfunctorily on the cheek. Then before I knew it he was out the door. I never saw or heard from him again.

Part Five

I know my chickens

*A*s we move into the nineties, free-lancing is becoming a bit of a strain so when I'm offered a job working – full-time – for an Italian newspaper, I jump at the chance of having a steady job and, for the first time here in Italy…a regular paycheck. However, it makes some things more complicated. On the one hand, the new job means getting used to a different kind of journalism than that which I'm used to. On the other, it requires other bureaucratic adjustments such as going back to driving school to get an Italian driver's license, nationalizing my car so it will have Italian tags and becoming, finally, a bonafide resident of Rome. At the end of all this, I will truly have become an old hand at dealing with the various aspects of Italian bureaucracy, but could it be precisely because of these changes that I am starting to feel the first stirrings of dissatisfaction and intolerance? I'm still enjoying life in my neighborhood, which I consider a veritable anchor for my day-to-day happiness. But other things are really starting to bug me. There are great problems of substance: what kind of a country is it that cannot protect its best and bravest, I wail, when in May, 1992 Giovanni Falcone and his wife and bodyguards are blown to bits? Laws are made and then not enforced. Much needed infrastructures get talked about, incessantly, but never get built. Civil court cases are postponed again and again. Ethics are generally relegated to the back burner. And, furthermore, does daily life really have to be so convoluted? It would appear that the gene for organization and precision is truly missing from the Italian DNA. Some people find this charming but I, increasingly, do not.

Chapter 21 – Career Changes. I Become (Or Do I?) An Italian Journalist

As you can well imagine, being a freelance reporter or writer is not always easy. Unless you are Seymour Hersh or the late Christopher Hitchens, you are not well paid. If you write for magazines, you spend a lot of time trying to *get* paid, or to solicit promptness on payments that you desperately need in order to cover your rent. If you work as a radio stringer, you are paid a pittance. And if you write for a daily newspaper, you are definitely not going to get rich; the last time I checked, the *Washington Post* was still paying only about $150 for a feature. And then, too, although most reporters work really hard, a freelance *really* has to hustle. In my case, since I was operating as a full-time foreign correspondent, certain daily news stories had to be covered so, unlike others, I was generally kept pretty busy. But for the duller, no-news periods, one had to constantly come up with ideas for features, travel stories and profiles to guarantee yourself at least the semblance of a regular income.

As I've already explained, if you work abroad, even as a freelancer, the perks can counterbalance many of the frustrations of freelance work. But still, it does get wearing. So in 1991 when John Wyles decided to leave his post as Rome correspondent for the *Financial Times* and become Deputy Editor of a new Italian daily, *L'Indipendente*, I was happy to join him. As correspondent for the *Washington Post* in a country that is extremely concerned about what others think of them, I had automatically gotten a bit of media attention and had made a sort of name for myself. Now, I thought – wrongly, it turned out – I could really go places as an *Italian* journalist. With a chance to write, at length, about subjects that interested me, I might even become something of a local pundit with invitations to talk shows and the like.

Italian dailies have generally been – and are – wordier than ours are, and this may be in part because the financial support they receive from the state (mostly for newsprint) means they don't have to rely as heavily on advertising as ours do. Furthermore, a long-standing tradition, for example the idea of the so-called *terza pagina* (the third page) begun back in 1901 by a now defunct but once famous daily called *Il Giornale d'Italia*, has traditionally given journalists with literary pretensions – along with writers, historians and other analysts – the chance to air at great length their views about cultural and literary subjects.

For the rest of us, the *inchiesta*, or investigation, was the best shot at journalistic satisfaction. Although it sounds like a vehicle for true investigative reporting, it was generally mostly an opportunity for a good reporter to do a thorough, in-depth reportage on a particular subject, often in more than one installment. This is what I like to do and am good at: getting lots of facts onto a page in a fairly readable fashion. "*Accidenti*! – Wow!" There's so much information in this article!" an Italian colleague from the Pescara edition of the *Messaggero*, once said, admiringly, when I'd asked him to vet a story on politics in his city for Italian spelling or grammar mistakes. Italian journalists, too, love to write in depth, but tend to favor the evocation of mood or the expression of opinion over hard information. They often consider themselves to be writers more than mere reporters.

Nowadays, Italian papers rarely do *inchieste*, preferring interviews with people that count (although they rarely are subjected to hard and relentless questioning) and innumerable sidebars and pages on a single political subject that more often than not appear (and are) written for perusal primarily by politicians and other journalists. Frequently, papers here will dedicate pages and pages (five, six, seven) to one political story, stories to which the *New York Times* might dedicate only one long story and perhaps an accompanying news analysis.

This loquacious tendency has gotten worse in recent years, something that is hard to understand since fewer and fewer people seem to get their news from print sources rather than TV, and to counteract this you would expect newspapers to become simpler rather than more complex. Nevertheless, back in the early 1990s, there still seemed to be occasions for real, in-depth reporting and I was looking forward to my new position. Even more exciting was the fact that the launching of *L'Indipendente* in the fall of 1991 had been eagerly anticipated by the Italian intelligentsia. Hundreds of *soi-disant* intellectuals and normal, well-informed people turned out for a pre-publication presentation at the Rome Campidoglio listen to Riccardo Franco Levi, the paper's founder, describe what kind of paper he wanted the new, Milan-based *Indipendente* to be. Ricky, who was said to have put most of his own personal fortune into this burgeoning editorial venture, believed that Italian readers really wanted a newspaper like Britain's *Independent*: concise, sober – that is, with no screaming headlines, no hearsay and, above all, no political ties.

But was that really what they wanted? Polls and market research replied in the affirmative but after a few days of thrillingly sky-high sales, skepticism began to set in and readers, many of who probably only imagined they wanted newspapers with less melodrama and more commitment to cold analysis, dropped in droves by the wayside. Levi, a former journalist, probably wasn't really cut out to be a newspaper editor. Too kind, too gentle, too concerned about what others said and thought. But in any event, he should have been given the time to find his way and, if possible, make the paper economically feasible. Instead, almost before you could say *"L'Indipendente"*, his shareholders, for the most part smaller, Northern industrialists, were threatening to sell out. Only three months into our new venture, Levi was gone and we had a new editor, Vittorio Feltri, a *simpatico*, brilliant and caustic muckraker whose concept of journalism was (and is) anything but Anglo-Saxon.

Even before Levi left, and before John Wyles also decided to cut his *Indipendente* adventure short and move to Brussels to set up a consulting business, I could see that professionally I was not going to have the status I had hoped for. People with better political connections were given more space and better stories. My articles were thought to be too long and were cut. And I seemed to be on a different political and journalistic wavelength from many of my colleagues.

On the other hand, I really can't complain about this experience. Most of the journalists in the Rome bureau were young and committed, and a strong *esprit de corps* developed almost immediately. I had been given an excellent salary and a fairly high rank *(capo servizio)* that in the future would serve me well. And – miracle of miracles for a dyed-in-the-wool freelancer – I was now paid regularly and the *azienda*, the company, made regular payments for me into INPGI, the national journalists' pension fund, which meant that if I worked for Italian papers long enough I would end up with some kind of pension! Yippee!

As far as I can tell, Italian journalists (like members of the Italian parliament) are among the best paid in the world. In the first place, you negotiate your salary on a before-taxes basis, meaning the amount you will pay in annual taxes gets added onto your pay packet only after your salary has been decided on. The basic part of your salary is based on the journalists' national contract, the rest on your paper's pay scale and its in-house contract, the so-called *contratto integrativo.* By law, all journalists get not only the extra 13th month bonus in December, but a 14th month paycheck in June.

When you just start out, you nevertheless get 26 vacation days a year, which given the journalists' six-day work week adds up to over four weeks annual vacation, plus five days personal leave. After five years, your annual vacation days increase to 30 plus five days, and after 15 years to 35 days (plus five). And if you work for a lifetime, which means 35 years of social security contributions to INPGI, you'll end up with a pension that is pretty close to your final year's salary. The journalists' health-insurance plan, Casagit, which is not optional and costs a significant percentage of your salary, nevertheless gives very good medical and dental coverage. And some newspapers provide additional perks such as free foreign language lessons, a leased company car, a cell phone with at-will use, a home laptop, and – where there is no caféteria – lunch vouchers, which can also be used in supermarkets.

To be fair, many Italian journalists work hard, averaging about ten hours a day. But they are still viewed as a rather privileged category. True, they no longer can ride buses free or go to the movies for free as was the case in Mussolini's day. But they can still get into most museums or exhibitions without paying. If you're a smooth operator you can get complimentary tickets for shows or the opera. Until recently, you could get a 30% discount on all domestic flights (now it's 15%). And if you have trouble with any of your utilities, the utility company's press office will be glad to give you a hand in working things out. In addition, since many Italian journalists have a different sense of what constitutes a conflict of interest from what we do in the United States, they often accept any manner of gifts or paid vacations from companies they regularly cover. No wonder, therefore, that it was Italy that allowed Silvio Berlusconi to become prime minister without divesting himself of his TV and newspaper holdings.

I've never worked inside a U.S. paper, nor did I go to journalism school, but I grew up an avid reader of the *New York Times*, which I still consider the best newspaper in the world (although *Le Monde* runs a close second), and I learned an awful lot from the correspondents and editors of the various papers I worked for in Rome. So while I know that American journalism certainly has its defects, and indeed there have been too cases of U.S. reporters for major newspapers inventing material and going undetected for months or, more occasionally, of reporters who let their political views or affiliations color their coverage, or of editors who apply self-censorship to avoid angering the government, it certainly is a whole lot more accurate than the Italian variety.

In Italian papers, rumor often takes the place of fact. Unconfirmed and overblown stories are often printed as fact – one trick is the frequent use of the conditional verb tense which translates into English as "is said to", as in "Prime Minister Silvio Berlusconi *avrebbe mangiato quattro bambini*", is said to have eaten four babies". Interviews are far too frequent, and often seem little more than an offer of free space for this or that politician or public figure. Headlines rarely reflect the speculative or tentative nature of the accompanying story, and there is no respect for privacy in the sense that even Italy's top newspapers think nothing of reprinting wiretapping transcripts or confidential judicial papers, although they must know that the people who leaked them almost certainly had an axe to grind.

Sources often go unnamed in journalism, everybody knows that, but for this to work, the newspaper must have significant credibility. In the 1980s, when the *Washington Post* or the *New York Times* attributed this or that to "a senior administration figure", most readers probably didn't know that this was the codeword for Secretary of State Henry Kissinger, but they had a reasonable amount of faith in the reporters writing the stories. In Italy, stories are rarely sourced and you don't even find disclaimers such as "several phone calls to Signor X's office went unreturned". A corrections box such as that which appears in many top U.S. or British papers to rectify misspellings, mistaken dates, faulty identifications and so forth, is generally unheard of here, as are Ombudsmen and Readers' Representatives.

Once I pointed out to a *Messaggero* night editor that the first edition he was putting out had misspelled the name of a town where the U.S. president was holding a summit. "Oh, no one will notice," he shrugged, rather than change it.

And even the best Italian papers are guilty of overkill; they repeatedly write stories about things – for example laws or changes in taxation – that they know well may never happen. And those six or seven pages on a single topic are far too many articles for any normal person to read and digest. Increasingly, headlines consist of quotes by this or that political or economic player, which means there has been no real attempt by the newspaper itself at analysis. Sometimes, in fact – and I've heard others say the same thing – I have to read a story about developments in Italy in the foreign press to get a good, quick overall view of what is going on. And this is particularly true if you have been away and missed the first few days of coverage; Italian news stories never give you any background. So no wonder average daily Italian newspaper sales – at 3,990,000 in 2012– and which have never been very high, have been shrinking steadily and are down 41% since 1990.

As time went on, my position at the *Indipendente* became increasingly untenable. The new management was eager to get rid of the higher-paid journalists hired by Levi, of whom I was one, and since anyone in Italy with a *contratto a tempo indeterminato*, a permanent contract which amounts to a sort of tenure, cannot be fired, what they do is kind of freeze you out or offer you money to go quietly.

Fortunately, the *Indipendente* opted for the second option, and as by this time I had totally lost my taste for being a freelance, I started looking around. It all worked out well. A year and a half after being hired by the *Indipendente*, I received a nice little goodbye check and also landed another job, this time at the prestigious *Il Sole 24 Ore,* the economic and financial daily owned by Confindustria, the equivalent of our National Manufacturers' Association.

I was hired by the *Sole* at the same salary that I'd had at the *Indipendente* primarily because a friend of mine who was the head of the Rome bureau thought my hiring would be a grand idea, and convinced the paper's then editor that I would be a real asset to the paper. My brief was to be to travel around Italy and cover it with the eyes of an American, or rather a non-Italian, writing stories on this or that. And I would also be asked to write editorials. What could be better? Finally, I would have my place in the sun. Or maybe not.

Chapter 22 – "Guasto!" (Broken!)

Guasto. If you had come to Rome to live in the sixties or seventies without knowing any Italian, *guasto* would surely have been one of the first words you would have been forced to learn in order to survive. One of the best novels written about postwar Italy, now out of print, was *The Salamander* by Morris West. West's story of a young *Carabiniere* officer who discovers, and seeks to dismantle, a shadowy, subversive group headed by a charismatic wealthy potentate not only seemed to foreshadow the P2 scandal of the Italian 1980s, but miraculously got almost all the details right about this complex country. In fact, my friend Janet and I, who were then together running the small *Newsweek* office as freelances, found only one error: What was it? At one point, West's hero, Colonel Dante Alighieri Matucci, sends his associate, Stefanelli, out to make photocopies at a coin-operated machine at the Stazione Termini, and I can assure you there weren't any such machines in the city then and, as far as I know, to this date there still aren't. Furthermore, said Janet, in her understated British way, if there had been one it would have had a sign on it reading "*guasto* – broken".

Photocopy machines, toilets, elevators, vending machines, public pay phones, ticket-punching machines on buses, air conditioners, heating units and even highway tollbooths were often found bearing signs reading "*guasto*". And this discouraging message was almost always scrawled, crookedly, by hand, on a piece of dirty scrap paper. Clearly, there was a widespread maintenance problem which, after a while, one came to accept as normal. The first few times you were unable to do something you'd planned to do because this or that was *guasto* or *chiuso*, closed, you were furious. Then, after a while, you became like the Italians, shrugged and tried to find another solution. "Why don't people react more?" an English friend asked in amazement some years ago when I told her about some of the difficulties one found in daily life here. The answer? Italians have no, or few, expectations. Or, if they do react, they do so with and a good deal of profanity. But when I first arrived here, and for years afterwards, their anger was rarely channeled where it would do some good. And this because until recently Italian institutions were totally unresponsive to consumer needs and concerns, something most people knew, or sensed. Hence their passivity.

Nowadays, fewer things seem to be *guasti* than in the past, but a lot of things that are supposed to work, don't. A company prints an e-mail address on the package its product comes in, but it either doesn't work or no one ever answers you. ("Oh, we never look at our e-mail," a woman from one company told me airily when I finally resorted to the telephone.) Or the Rome city government sends out a letter to all homeowners about a planned change in the parameters for real estate taxes and give you an 800 (toll-free) number to call which no one ever answers. And physical maintenance is still a big problem. Take ACEA, the electricity company that is responsible for public lighting here in Rome and which likes to boast about the excellent job it does illuminating Rome's many glorious monuments. In truth, the Italians are masters at lighting up their monuments and ACEA does a brilliant job with "dressing" the city's architectural masterpieces in light. But how about the city streets? Although lately things seemed to have improved, the number of streets that on any one night may be shrouded in darkness is startling.

To be honest, I had never been in a city in which so many streetlights were out so often; indeed, sometimes entire streets could be without light for nights on end. Obviously, there is some kind of problem with the equipment, and perhaps with the organization needed to get things fixed. And problems of this kind are aggravated by the fact that few Romans rarely play the good citizen, which in this case would mean calling the company to tell them that this or that streetlight is out.

Given today's technology, I was sure the electricity company had a master board of the city that would tell them, at a glance, which streetlights were out of order, *guasti*. But apparently not. They don't seem to have regular inspections, either, possibly because night work means paying overtime, and therefore must depend on Rome's inhabitants to report the breakdowns. Sometimes I think I may be the only one who does call. Once when all ten streetlights on the Garibaldi Bridge had been out for 17 days (sic) in a row, I finally called in and reported the breakdown and the lights were back on in 48 hours. They had no idea – or so they said – that the lights were out. Another time, I phoned in about two of four streetlights that were out in Via della Paglia, a narrow cobblestoned street I walk down every evening when I come home from my garage and which, without light, is pitch black. Two weeks later they were still out and ever since, just in case, I carry a small flashlight in my purse.

Possibly because of their Catholic faith, which often seems to stress acceptance or resignation rather than personal responsibility, many Italians seem to feel that taking action is not up to them. The attitude seems to be almost a Middle Eastern one as in "God will provide" and if not, "*pazienza*", one must have patience. In the apartment building I now live in, where all the other occupants but one are Italian, and all but me are European, no one other than myself would make a move if, in between our bi-weekly cleanings, the stairwell gets littered, or someone breaks a bottle of milk or, even worse, drips olive oil on the steps. If a dog gets into our courtyard and does his thing there, no one (including the people whose apartments give out onto the courtyard) would ever think of cleaning it up. And if a light bulb blows in the hall, or if the intercom and door buzzer stop working, no one but me calls the building administrator.

Foreign residents in all countries share some salient characteristics. You may love the place you're living in, you may have put down roots, and you may have even made plans to stay on, possibly forever. But it doesn't generally take too much to bring out the "them-us" syndrome, although the causes no doubt differ from place to place. In Italy, for most foreigners from "northern countries", that is from northern Europe and North America, this spark is fired primarily by a the vagaries of an unresponsive and Byzantine bureaucracy, and – on the other hand – by the seemingly widespread conviction of many ordinary Italians that polite behavior such as standing in line is either a Nazi characteristic or a British folly, one that in any event has no real application to this country. Indeed, although things are now gradually changing, left to themselves many Italians appear constitutionally unable to stand in line. "Where do you think you are, in Bulgaria?" a well-dressed man once snarled at me when I protested that he had pushed ahead of me on the cashier's line at a downtown café. It is true that the cashier's desk was built to encourage this kind of impolite behavior, in the sense that the cashier sat behind a semi-circular mahogany counter that could accommodate several people, all in front-line position. Trained from birth to wait my turn, I had taken up a position behind someone who was paying for his *cappuccino* when the man I argued with, clearly middle-class in provenance and who, one would have thought, could have been expected to know better, walked right by me and up to the counter.

I've already mentioned that because of the waiting-in-line problem, for decades the post office was the *bête noire* of many foreign residents from countries where good manners get a better deal. Back in those days, there were no "external aids" for line formation: no lines painted on the ground, no railings or cords indicating that a queue was to be formed, no numbers distributed and certainly no employees telling people that they should form a line. The result was that instead of a line, there'd be a sort of huddle of humans surrounding a teller or ticket window, with all the consequent arguing about who was next.

It may well be that Italians enjoy mêlées, or at the very least the competition involved in trying to be first in line; it is probably significant, in fact, that Italy was the last major Western European country to introduce reserved seating on its national airline flights. In the late 70s, long after just about everyone else was giving out seat assignments, if you flew Alitalia you'd be bussed out to the airplane and then it was every Italian for himself (or herself) as people dashed, pushing and shoving, to the airplane to try and grab the best seat. And even nowadays if you fly a low-cost European airline that does not give seat assignment out of Italy, be prepared for would-be tramplers. It's as if people, especially in Rome and points south, simply aren't aware that being orderly can be, no, *is*, advantageous for all. Or else they just need direction.

Back in the 70s, when Rome's Leonardo da Vinci airport at Fiumicino was terribly disorganized (today it's excellent, except for periodic baggage problems), there was what I thought was a telling incident. Passengers in need of one of the all-too-few luggage carts being pushed in dribs and drabs into the baggage pick-up area were practically brawling when, losing it totally, a woman shouted out something like "*Fate la fila, per Dio!* – Form a line, for God's sake!" and, miraculously, found herself being obeyed. Although I'm sure the organization she inspired lasted only so long as the original participants in the mob had gotten their trolleys and trotted off.

The numbers system now in use in most post offices and banks has helped. But some stores, although they have installed a numbers system, and sorely need one, don't seem to use it. Every time I go to the popular bakery in cobble-stoned Via del Moro near my house – luscious, hot *pizza rossa* at all hours of the day –and try to take a number, I find that the panel is more often than not turned off or – surprise! – *guasto*.

At Volpetti, a very crowded and much quoted delicatessen in Testaccio, a numbers system would really make things easier for customers. *"Ma no, Signora, non è per noi,"* one of the owners disdainfully told me, as if their products would lose value if a customer didn't have to worry about getting the attention of a *commesso*, a salesperson, or making sure that the person who came in after you isn't getting served first. Today, many stores and agencies have wised up. But when safeguards aren't in place, there are still plenty of *furbi* around. A *furbo* is a cunning, wily or crafty person who knows all the angles, and there are many of them in Rome, not least among older people. A while back I was in the *farmacia* to pick up some medicine and, as a polite person, I was waiting my turn behind a "give 'em privacy" yellow line painted on the floor about three feet back from the counter. (A sign explaining the line's purpose was right in front of me.) An old woman I know by sight from the neighborhood who is either half-cracked or pretends to be such walked right by me and up to the counter. *"Mi scusi"* I said, using the sarcastic New Yorker "I beg your pardon" tone I learned at my mother's knee. "Oh", she said, in the classic *furba's* all-innocence response: "Oh. Sorry. I didn't see you. Are you perhaps waiting?"

Preferring confusion to order is not limited to waiting lines but spills over into other sectors of life, at least in Rome and other more southern regions of the country. One of these is driving, an area where stereotypes about Italians, or at least about Romans, tend to be confirmed. Gridlock, here caused by a willful invasion of the intersection, is a daily occurrence. Red lights and stop signs often are viewed as optional. Using *la freccia* (directional lights) to signal an intention to turn right or left is infrequent, to say the least, or else left to the last minute, that is when the driver has already begun his turn, frequently from the farthest lane on the opposite side of the roadway. And pedestrians are not much better. They cross when the light is red, neglect the zebra stripes to cross instead wherever they want, and often just don't look to see if any cars or buses are coming.

By the way, let me take this occasion to explain the zebra stripes. Italian city administrations have confused foreigners by using the stripes in two different ways, one as a path marker, if you like, at intersections manned by traffic lights, the other to designate non-traffic light crossings where pedestrians should be given precedence. Here's the rule. Where there are traffic lights, these must be obeyed. You, the pedestrian, have precedence only at a crossing where there is no traffic light, only the stripes. But it is suggested that you nevertheless exercise caution. I notice that nowadays few drivers in Rome automatically stop for you unless you have the courage to stride forward, arm outstretched, palm up in a dorky "stop-right-now" gesture.

Another Roman habit that takes getting used to is that in many areas of town, such as Trastevere where I live, people seem to prefer walking in the street even when sidewalks, however narrow, exist. They seem convinced they are invincible and often don't even look before crossing the street.

But things in Rome are certainly better than points farther south. Naples is famous for the degree to which drivers ignore stop signs and red lights. I have been driving in Italy for 30 years and have had only one, minor accident, but I would never drive in Naples: I'd be too frightened. My friend Mimmo, who owns three men's shops in Rome but who comes from Naples where his father was in the same business, says that nowadays, after two days in Naples, he can't wait to leave again. "Life in Rome is not easy, but at least there are some certainties. In Naples, forget it. The only thing that counts there is *prepotenza*," roughly, bullying or arrogance.

Understandably, the indiscipline described above takes a lot of getting used to, as does the *maleducazione* – incivility – that unfortunately characterizes much of Roman life and which is described elsewhere in this book. But there are dozens of other ways in which daily life was, and is, complicated not by ordinary Italians but by the powers that be. I sometimes imagine that behind the scenes there is a committee of evil, gray-bearded old codgers who sit around a bare, wooden refectory-type table in a large, unheated, tapestry-hung room with exposed beams and a mammoth stone fireplace, naturally unlit, rubbing their hands together, speaking Latin and thinking up ways to make everyday life unbearable for the average Italian.

Lost your driver's license? Until just a couple of years ago, it could take up to a year to get a new one and in the meantime you'd have to drive around with a copy of your application for a replacement, a piece of paper that got increasingly ragged as time went on. The same thing applied to car registration documents, and at one point I myself was seriously considering artfully "losing" my car's registration papers and applying for a new set. Why? When I bought a red Opel Astra 16-valve sports model – a demo car – from General Motors in the summer of 1994, the *Motorizzazione,* the motor vehicle bureau, was still a few months away from instituting the current, more rational system in which the new owner of a used car would simply be sent an adhesive name-and-address label to stick on to the old registration booklet. At the time I completed my car property-transfer transaction with GM, however, the old rules were still in effect and the *libretto,* or registration booklet, had to remain in the name of General Motors. I was given a *foglio rosa*, a pink, A4 form which is generally used for new car registrations and which expires after a certain amount of time. In very small print on the bottom of the paper, however, there was an asterisk explaining that in a case like mine, the *foglio rosa* could also be used as a (non-expiring) adjunct to the original *libretto*. The problem was that every time I got stopped at one of those roadblocks set up to randomly check out this country's residents, the policemen or *carabinieri* I encountered were unaware of this, refused to believe me and gave me either a ticket or a long lecture on why I shouldn't be going around with an expired *foglio rosa.*

The fact that the policemen didn't know their stuff didn't really surprise me. Not long before, I had asked three different Rome traffic policemen, or *vigili,* how old a child had to be before being able to ride in the front passenger seat of a car and had gotten three totally different answers. Not so hard to understand, I guess for two reasons. First, if you get your job through pull and not merit then you don't really need to get good grades on a qualifying exam and, second, if Parliament changes the law every few years it is understandably difficult to keep up.

Getting back to the *libretto,* had I pretended to have lost it, the first thing I'd have had to do before doing anything else would have been to *fare una denuncia*, report the loss to the police or *carabinieri* and get a document testifying that I had indeed lost it. And this is hardly unique. Every time you lose something in Italy, be it your car insurance stub that goes on the windshield, or the car registration tax stub (the so-called *bollo,* which also needed to go on the windshield but now has been turned into a property tax and can be kept inside the car), or your passport, your identity card, your credit card, your cell phone, your wallet, etc. the first thing you have to do is to go to the police or the *carabinieri* station and file a report. If these were thefts, this might be understandable. But the fact that law enforcement officers have to waste time filling out lost property forms seems quite a waste of time and resources.

In general, there seems to be a penchant for creating complications. As a journalist, I sometimes had to go to the Chamber of Deputies to interview a Member of Parliament. Entrance was controlled by the Association of Parliamentary Journalists, colleagues who consider themselves to be a superior breed of *giornalisti,* and they'd worked out a rather complicated system for access by others. This involved bringing a letter from your bureau chief, getting a pass (blue) from the guard at the front door, walking down several really long corridors to the press room where reporters were working, getting your letter stamped by the day's prefect (a fellow journalist but one belonging to the Parliamentary Journalists' Association), retracing your steps back to the entrance, turning your badge in for one of a different color (yellow), and then walking all the way back to the press room through which you could (finally!) enter the so-called lengthy Transatlantico (so-called because it is believed to resemble the large salon on an ocean liner), the main corridor of the Chamber where deputies mill around, exchange views, or gossip, and wait until they are called back in to vote again. Whew!

Or what about when Parliament introduced a points system for driving licenses and then decided that they had to give millions of points back to all the people who had lost points without being properly identified by a traffic policeman (which means everyone who lost some then had to file an application to get them back). Or when it was decided from one day to the next that the license plate for the 50cc moped (the kind with the least powerful engine) had been redesigned and everyone had to go out and get a replacement. Help!

Also adding spice to daily life are the annual or bi-annual aggravations that pile up alongside income, real estate, garbage and VAT (value added) taxes, the latter being the closest thing Europe has to a sales tax, almost all of which had to be paid at the post office. Until a few years ago, once a year every Italian or resident with a driver's license also had to remember to go to the *tabaccheria* to buy a stamp costing the equivalent of $40 that had to be pasted onto his or her license and – if you were an Italian citizen – a different one to stick onto your passport. The problem here was that more often than not, the *tabaccheria* would have run out of these stamps and you had to dash around the city to find one that still had them in stock.

Some of the *tabaccherie* also sell *carta bollata*, the official, lined paper with a watermark or the *marche*, tax stamps, needed for applications for many of the official documents issued by the *Anagrafe*, the massive central Registry Office on the Lungotevere opposite Tiber Island and a stone's throw – in the other direction – from the Campidoglio. This is the records office that provides all inhabitants of the *centro storico* with residence permits, birth certificates, marriage licenses and the like. If you had forgotten to buy this paper or stamps, or were unaware that you needed them, you had to go back outside the building and hope that the closest *tabaccheria* had them. One would think that these things could have been purchased right *inside* the *Anagrafe*, which after all had a cashier's window on the premises for other kinds of payments. But no, that would have been too easy. The only *in situ* solution came, unofficially, from the retired *Anagrafe* employees who skulked around the front door and sold them at a somewhat inflated price. And all this was made even more difficult by the *Anagrafe*'s hours which until recently were only from 9:00 to 12 in the mornings only three days a week. There were huge lines, and invariably you had to go back several times in order to get things done. Today, things at the *Anagrafe* have somewhat improved: they have a numbers system, are open two afternoons a week and also have a home delivery service for documents, although I've yet to try it. But they still don't sell the *marche* or the *carta bollata*.

As I've already said, I avoided the *Anagrafe* for as long as it was possible. I felt on solid ground since I had my *permesso di soggiorno* and because, after only a few years of delinquency, by the early 1980s I was also paying Italian income taxes regularly. And remember that for many years I had those special export license plates on my car, enabling me to drive with my U.S. license. But for most people, the only way to get an Italian driving license is to be an official resident in an Italian town or city. As I've already mentioned, Italy – like most continental European countries – requires everyone to register as a resident in the city in which he or she lives. Not everyone does this. Because of local patriotism, or perhaps in order to take advantage of lower property or vehicle insurance rates, many Italians prefer to pretend they are still residents back in their native town or village, even though this means making the often long train journey back home when it comes time to vote. But wherever you are registered, you will end up with a *carta d'identità,* which, if you are an Italian citizen, can also now be used for travel within the European Community and which, if you're not, is still a valid and increasingly necessary identification document.

Here in Italy, people have always been required to carry I.D. with them at all times and today, given the direction the world is now moving in, it will increasingly be the case in other countries, too. Even in the pre-terrorism days, you couldn't book a plane ticket in another name or check into a hotel with an assumed name, because a copy of your identity document had to be sent off to the police. And this could have collateral damage. More often than not, you couldn't even invite someone up to your hotel room – unless they left their documents downstairs with the concierge. And let me ask you, how many married men want to do that?

Chapter 23 – La Farmacia (Part One)

Whenever I walk into the pharmacy, I can tell immediately whether Franco has been smoking. A nice-looking man of medium height, with wavy gray hair that not all that long ago was *castano*, medium brown, Franco has a passion for those smelly Italian cigars called Toscanelli, and although he often limits himself to clenching an unlighted one between his teeth, he also doesn't seem to think there's anything odd about smoking in a place where medicines are sold and also prepared.

When I complain, he ignores me, which isn't all that surprising. Until the beginning of 2003, Italians smoked everywhere and considered it quite normal; they lit up inside stores, including those which sell fabric or paper goods, in the airport, ignoring repeated loudspeaker announcements that no smoking was allowed, at the greengrocers where cigarette ash dangled perilously over the *zucchini* and the cherry tomatoes, and even in hospitals, although from time to time crack Italian *Carabinieri* units called the NAS, set up to enforce health standards, would appear, unannounced, and hand out hefty fines to all the doctors and nurses they found *in flagrante*. Once I even had blood taken by two white-coated doctors who took my vital fluid with cigarettes dangling from their lips, an open window their only concession to my passive smoke concerns.

Today, this is no longer the case. Amazingly – one of the few modern miracles I am aware of – as of January 16, 2003 an overwhelming majority of Italians have accepted and obey the legislation that bans smoking inside all bars, restaurants, stores, ministries and other offices. This has made life so much more pleasant for non-smokers like myself and is probably the most significant change I have witnessed here in decades. The new law was a godsend also because many Italians, including – I have noticed – intelligent, left-wing feminists over 50 (the kind of people that in the U.S. would have stopped smoking ages ago), are still puffing away, something that can make dinner at a friend's less than pleasant, forcing you to ask to sit at the other end of the table or, at times, even to turn down an invitation.

Back in 1977 when Franco's parents, both pharmacists in the family's native Foggia in the southern Italian region of Apulia, realized that Franco and his younger brother, Enzo, had settled irrevocably in Rome, they decided to buy the Antica Farmacia della Scala from the Carmelite monks who still live upstairs and who had run it for centuries, preparing medicines for pilgrims and popes alike. Decorated with paintings of different medicinal plants (another wall bears a painting of the fathers of modern pharmaceutical science, Louis Pasteur, Robert Koch and Alexander Fleming), it is nevertheless less ornate than the original herbalists' shop upstairs, which dates back to 1670 and which these days unfortunately you can get to see only with the special guided tour held once a year on FAI days *(Fondo per L'Ambiente Italiano)* when many monuments around the country are open, free, to the public. The monastery is connected to the small baroque church next door, Santa Maria della Scala, which is open only in the afternoons and doesn't seem to be doing much business. The last time I went in there, Mass was being celebrated by an Asian priest – the number of Italian vocations has been dwindling – and there was exactly one worshiper, an elderly woman. I thought that in those conditions it would be *maleducata* to walk out so I sat through the Mass, grateful that my Jewish grandmother, who once almost fainted when I came home singing "Away in a manger, no crib for a bed", had long since passed away. Over the years, for one reason or another, I have often found myself attending Mass, and generally my thoughts go not to grandma Becky but to all those Jews in the Rome ghetto who were forced in centuries past to go to Mass by the Pope's soldiers, and generally coped by putting wax in their ears to avoid listening to what for them was blasphemy.

The Pizzi pharmacy is not the only pharmacy in the area, but for years (although no longer) it was my default drugstore. First of all, my health service doctor, Riccardo, has his office right in one of the pharmacy's anterooms, and if you phoned him he would leave a prescription – or a sick-day absence certificate – at the counter, something quite unusual in Italy where doctors cannot phone in prescriptions. Secondly, Franco's wife Paola was a whiz at preparing the paperwork for my prescriptions in the right way for submission to the journalists' insurance plan, Casagit. To get reimbursed, the sales slip and the prescription are not enough; you have to cut a little cardboard square called a *fustella* out of the box and attach it or paste on the removable stickers most pharmaceutical boxes now sport. Franco hated doing this stuff and when he sees me come in, he usually bellowed, "Paola, *la Sari* needs you!!" and runs off to do something else. Enzo, a smiling, slightly overweight man in his forties with curly dark hair and a hairline that is starting to recede, is somewhat better at this than his brother, but I saw him less often as he generally works afternoons when I am downtown at my job.

Go to any small Italian town or village and you will find that the *farmacista* is always considered one of the local notables; he may be one of the few university graduates in town and will take his place at local ceremonies and events along with the *sindaco*, or mayor, the town *avvocato*, or lawyer, the *notaio*, or notary public, the *maestro*, the school teacher, or the *preside*, the school principal. But even in a big Italian city, the *farmacia* is a pretty important place. The pharmacist is often considered to be a surrogate doctor, who will take your blood pressure, suggest medications when you haven't yet had time to go to a doctor, and in some specialized pharmacies will mix up more or less traditional concoctions as well. Italians are very concerned with their health and this syndrome has no doubt been fanned by the exaggerated generosity in past years of Italy's national health system, the *Sistema Sanitaria Nazionale* or SSN, which despite repeated attempts at reform, still provides so many medications at near zero cost that many people take home an inordinate number of pharmaceuticals, things that they probably don't really need and which may well expire, soundlessly, on their medicine cabinet shelves.

When I first arrived here, I had the feeling Italians were rather physically "delicate"; they seemed to fear illness would be lurking around every corner, although this didn't (and doesn't) stop a lot of them from smoking. Fortunately, they no longer attribute every ailment to the *fegato*, the liver. Like most Americans, I was almost unaware that I had a liver and at first was mystified by how often Italians would talk about theirs and tell you how it was doing. This liver-consciousness has diminished, but other old-fashioned attitudes have not: parents here still tell their kids they can't swim for at least three hours after a meal, even if the meal was only a small sandwich, and have them change their suits frequently. My friend and former colleague, Gerardo, was clearly brought up this way by his mother, and even though he is now well over 50, he still changes his bathing suit every time he comes out of the water.

As any foreigner who speaks Italian will quickly notice, Italians attribute many digestive problems to "having caught cold on the tummy", although I'm still not sure what exactly that means. They tell you frequently that something they have eaten "has remained on the stomach". And as they still seem unaware that most colds are transmitted by hands touching mouths and noses, and then other hands that will touch other mouths and noses, they remain convinced the major health peril is a draught, by which they mean what I myself would often describe as "cross ventilation". Indeed, don't be surprised to find yourself in a taxi in which the right-side window doesn't work or is missing its wind-down handle. The driver has done this deliberately to keep himself from getting a draft on his neck that will give him problems *al cervicale,* the cervical spine. He is also likely to eschew air conditioning on the grounds that it will give him pneumonia.

As a sufferer from slight claustrophobia, I find this more than annoying: on more than one occasion I have been known to get out of a cab once I have noticed the window crank is missing and that the A/C is off (or is, he claims, *guasto.*) On the other hand, Italian taxi drivers are normally great to chat with (in contrast to many of the surly Middle Easterners who drive cabs in New York these days) and, furthermore, they don't expect tips. I generally round off the fare, but if you don't have any extra change or are in a hurry you don't have to worry about being assaulted – verbally or physically – if you neglect to tip.

Not surprisingly, given this hypochondriac bent, expenditures by Italy's 20 regions for the nation's socialized health system (something that is common to most of Europe) weigh enormously on Italy's finances. Various efforts have been made to rectify some of the system's distortions.

Medications have been divided into two groups: category A, those paid for entirely by the state, in other words supplied free to everyone, no matter his or her income, and those, category C, which you have to pay for yourself or get underwritten by your insurance company, if you have one. Italy's 20 regional governments can now decide on their own if they want to impose a surcharge, for some incomprehensible reason known as *il ticket,* on the 670-odd pharmaceuticals the government has decreed can be provided without cost to Italian residents.

But these regulations change frequently and differ drastically from one region to another or can be modified by successive regional governments. At present, five of Italy's 20 regions (Friuli, Marche, Sardegna, Trento and Val d'Aosta) have no tickets. In Lazio, the region surrounding Rome, and where I live, residents now pay an average "ticket" of €4 for any pharmaceutical that costs over €5 (less if you buy the generic) and €2.50 for those costing under €5. Five years ago, Lazio residents paid nothing for the cheaper medicines and €1.50 for the more costly ones, but the budget deficit is such that regional lawmakers here realized they had to make a change. Despite the hullabaloo about health costs, Italy is only 11th among European countries in terms of overall health system expenditures (€112 billion) and annual per capita outlays, €1,842 euros or $2,359. You also pay *il ticket* on certain diagnostic procedures – generally with a maximum of 36 euros – and nowadays if you go to see a doctor who works in a public hospital, there is a ten percent surcharge that goes straight into regional coffers.

Indeed, another problem, and one which accounts for a high percentage of the losses by the SSN, is that a large number of people are cheating. How? By making false declarations about their allegedly low yearly incomes or by getting unscrupulous doctors to say they are suffering from any one of a number of rare or particularly serious diseases. People with very low incomes, especially those over 65, and those suffering from certain pathologies are exempt from the surcharges. Some calculate that this kind of tax evasion may cause Italy's 20 regions – altogether – more than €1 billion a year. But the authorities rarely double-check, and there is little doubt that many members of Italy's army of *furbi* may well be getting free medication without being eligible.

Minor surgical procedures and diagnostic tests can be done either at the government health clinics scattered through the city, the *Aziende Sanitarie Locali* or ASLs, or at the myriad diagnostic centers that operate both privately or on the basis of *convenzioni* (agreements) negotiated with the governing region. If, however, you are in a hurry, and if you have private insurance that will cover it, you are best off having your diagnostic procedures, and your surgical procedures, done privately, even if that means you have to pay for them. According to a 2012 report by the Paris-based OECD (the Organization for Economic Cooperation and Development) on health-system delays in 13 developed countries, in Italy waiting times for doctors' appointments, diagnostic tests and certain procedures can be extremely long, although the situation varies considerably from region to region. Average waiting times mentioned in the report were: x-rays in a public hospital, 61 days; sonograms in a health service clinic, 66 days; and any kind of endoscopic exam, up to 78 days. Efforts are underway to deal with these delays – for example, many hospitals now use centralized reservation systems to set up appointments – but in recent years the situation in some areas has been near tragic.

According to a study done in 2011 by the welfare department of the CISL trade union, in the three-year period from 2006 to 2008 it could take as long as 540 days to have a mammogram scheduled (Puglia), 90 days to get a bone-density scan done (Veneto) and 74 days to see a geriatrics specialist in the generally well-organized Tuscany region. I myself know someone who had to wait seven months to get a heart bypass, and one of my next-door neighbors here in Rome waited almost a year for a hip replacement.

Of course, this is not unusual for a country with national health; all the Brits I know decry their own system violently and even in Sweden, once a model for such things, there is considerable disorganization. The fact remains that the Italian national health system is often more virtual than real, forcing people who can afford it to look for an alternative solution. On the other hand, it does exist, the doctors are generally excellent and I am sure the millions of Americans who are without health insurance would be very happy to have something like it.

As a pharmacist, Franco is very popular because he takes time with you if you have a problem and because he is very good at diagnosing minor ailments and suggesting effective remedies. He does a brisk trade in skin creams and potions of various sorts, which he makes up according to doctors' prescriptions or according to older, herbalist formulas.

For example, for water retention he will make you a concoction of *pilosella*, *betulla* and *centelle*, and he has several formulas for curing a skin fungus. He is always ready to take your blood pressure for you if you're feeling faint and – although this is irrelevant to his profession – he is a skilled amateur magician; if you bring a child by and he has the time, he will amaze everyone with card and coin tricks. He is also pretty free with the compliments. "*Che bella faccia che hai oggi*– how good you look today," he'll say to me quite frequently. "Your eyes are an incredible color today," he'll say another time, although the best –

though unintended – compliment for someone who prides herself on looking younger than her age, was the time I mentioned I had temporarily stopped my pill (I was on hormone replacement therapy) and he, thinking I meant "the pill" said "Oh, *cara*, be careful, you might get pregnant!"

Chapter 24 – "It's The Law, Stupidino"

It is late afternoon and the daily, or nightly, game of cat and mouse between Rome's *vigili urbani*, or traffic police, and the unlicensed street peddlers who set up their portable tables and lamps in Piazza Sant'Egidio where I live, or nearby, is about to start. And, as usual, the mice will win. Not because they are smarter but simply because they care more about breaking the law than the authorities care about enforcing it.

Piazza Sant'Egidio is a longish, somewhat trapezoidal, cobble-stoned piazza that runs from the back end of the Basilica of Santa Maria in Trastevere to Vicolo del Cinque and Via della Scala. On one side there are several residential buildings, including a Renaissance palace called Palazzo Velli, and a couple of smaller 16th- and 17th-century apartment buildings, including the one I live in. There is also a very popular café named *Ombre Rosse* after the John Ford classic, *Stagecoach*, which in Italian was called *"Red Shadows"*. When I was young, back in the pre-political correctness era, we used to call Native Americans "redskins", and that's how the Italians still refer to them, *i pellerossi*.

That row of buildings is, you might say, the "lay" or secular side of the piazza. But as a whole the piazza is dominated by things of and related to the Catholic Church. The Museum of Rome originally was a Carmelite convent and shares its side of the square with the small and rarely used church of Sant'Egidio. In between there is a small building which houses part of the headquarters of the *Comunità di Sant'Egidio*, a grassroots Roman Catholic organization founded by a group of students in 1968 that is socially active at home and politically active abroad. A police car (which of late has morphed into an Army jeep) has been stationed permanently in the piazza for years because of threats engendered in the past by the *Comunità's* peacemaking role in conflict situations in places such as Lebanon, Mozambique, Bosnia, and Palestine. The *Comunità* also owns the restaurant at the short end of the square and the squat Renaissance building on the other end which was once the rectory of the Basilica of Santa Maria di Trastevere, and which now houses some offices and, on the ground floor, a restaurant. They also own a lot of other real estate in the neighborhood, including the large block-long building around the corner from the pub in Via della Paglia where they hold meetings and where support groups meet. When the *Comunità* holds major get-togethers, its members, who all seem to be more or less identically dressed, pour into the square and clog it so that cars or bikes, and even pedestrians, find it hard going. This, added to the fact that events involving the *Comunità* sometimes lead police to shut the piazza to all other traffic, can be annoying to us non-Catholics. But they are good people, committed to volunteer work with the poor, the elderly and Italy's growing immigrant population, and are seemingly very different from all those young Italians who appear to care more about consumer goods and physical appearance than anything else.

I'd once contemplated having an affair with someone of standing in the *Comunità*; I'd met him at a dinner party where the candlelight made him look very good (me too, no doubt) and the wine gave us both ideas and apparently made him forget his marriage vows. Unfortunately for me, they must have meant more to him than he knew because when we finally got together he was, shall we say, absolutely non-operational. But the person I know best in the organization is Claudio Betti, one of its founders and today the *Comunità's* vice-president as well as the man in charge of international relations. Unlike most Italians, he speaks fluent English as well as French. A bulky man with a rough complexion, a booming voice and a ready smile, he is funny and cheery, despite the fact that a few years ago at Christmas with no warning he had a massive heart attack and almost died.

What Claudio and I have in common is that we both think that laws on the books should be observed ("it's the law, *stupidino!*"). He was therefore – at least in principle – an ally in the battle against the peddlers who, starting in the nineties, began occupying our piazza, increasingly a pedestrian thoroughfare for the hordes of evening visitors to Trastevere, an area celebrated for its restaurants and, more lately, for its pubs and *boîtes*. "What would happen if an ambulance had to get through here?" Claudio mutters on the way back from the bar where we've just had yet another espresso. And there are security questions as well. What's the point of stationing a police car here if the peddlers are allowed to bring all sorts of un-searched bags and suitcases into the piazza? But in line with the Italian penchant for tolerance, Claudio was reluctant to have the *Comunità* take a public stance on an issue which, albeit peripherally, involved jobs, even if the latter were off-the-books employment. "Someone might throw a bomb at us, or beat me up," he'd say, half-jokingly. I thought that was somewhat odd. After all, the *Comunità* had been active in so many trouble spots where danger was truly rife, and now they were worried about a bunch of bearded jewelry makers and bad artists? More likely, it was simply the tradition of Italian *buonismo* (knee-jerk niceness) kicking in, a reluctance to play the bad guy. After all, one of the Italian left's historical slogans was: "*E' proibito proibire* – It is prohibited to prohibit". So, not suprisingly, on one occasion when the street vendors or *ambulanti* were (temporarily) evicted from the piazza and staged a protest in nearby Santa Maria square with the help of a leftist party, the slogan resurrected for the occasion was "*Vietato vietare! –* It is forbidden to forbid!"

Originally the peddlers were for the most part Italian, younger, hippie types who sold jewelry or other handicrafts. More recently, Asian and African faces have made their appearance. But whatever the peddlers' provenance, their interest is identical: sell their wares on the street because, understandably enough, they can't afford to open a shop. One by one, perhaps through word of mouth, they had found their way to Sant'Egidio and for a while, at least, they reportedly were taking advantage of a cockeyed municipal ruling designed to help young artisans make a living by allowing them to act as unlicensed street vendors – as long as they didn't stay in any one place for more than an hour. Sure. As if anyone among Italy's lazy and possibily understaffed *vigili,* a city police corps, the members of which often seems to do nothing except stand at intersections and chat (to one another or on their cell phones), was really going to enforce that!

Since any licensed peddler in Rome, or any other Italian city, has to pay an annual fee for the "occupation of public soil", and since restaurants with outdoor seating also pay for the square meters of sidewalk they use to put tables at, one would think that it would have been easy to get rid of the peddlers who were not paying fees or taxes to anyone. Erminio, for example, once got fined because his tables were occupying a half a square meter of space more than he'd been allotted. And Alessandro, at the Bar dei Parenti, was told in no uncertain terms that he'd be fined if he were to add a third table to the two he was authorized to keep on the street. So wouldn't you think that the peddlers would simply be told to get lost? Sure. But not in a country where generally it has been deemed more important to *pass* laws than to actually enforce them.

So, gradually, the *ambulanti* had turned the southern half of the square – the fairly small area, some 50 by 70 yards, right in front of my building and *Ombre Rosse* – into a sort of permanent market. They set up their stalls – on more than one occasion I counted as many as 40 different ones – in the late morning and remained there until the wee hours, clearly doing a thriving business. Many were innocuous, hard working, at times talented and often pleasant, but – as was to become clear – a few of them were toughs with criminal records. Furthermore, they made the piazza dirtier, noisier and more cluttered. Their presence, narrowing the space for cars and ambulances, appeared also to be a real security consideration. And – but this seemed to count less – they were there illegally.

The police car that was stationed almost permanently in the square to protect the *Comunità* was surely useful as a general deterrent against purse-snatchers, drug peddlers and apartment robbers. But its presence did nothing to deter the peddlers. "We are not allowed to neglect our *obiettivo*, our target," one policeman told me sternly when I pointed out that one of the street peddlers had set up his stand smack in front of our doorway. Furthermore, with the exception of the young officer who rushed to ring my bell when he saw smoke coming from the window (I was merely frying bacon for a Sunday brunch!), the young men and women on guard duty do not seem very interested in law enforcement. Like most young Italians, however, they seem to spend much of their time (even when on duty) smoking, talking on their cell phones, having a coffee at the bar, and occasionally themselves purchasing some trinket from one of the unlicensed peddlers or even a pirated CD from the Nigerian street sellers who, dressed like American rapsters, sometimes set up shop on a blanket spread out on the cobblestones. To be fair, the one time we had a serious crime in the piazza, a fatal knifing, they were on hand, not to prevent the bloodshed but at least to apprehend the murderer and call an ambulance.

The victim, a thickset, pony-tailed Sicilian named Claudio, was rushed to the hospital where, unfortunately, he died. I was out of town and heard about it on TV, knowing even before the reporter finished the story that Claudio would be the victim. A talented leather craftsman who generally arrived at the piazza by driving his large, white camper with Trapani plates the wrong way down a one-way street (another sign of what happens in a city where law enforcers don't do their job), he had angered the other vendors by insisting that the best spot on the corner, the one right by my front door, belonged to him. These turf wars were not new; a year earlier Mario, a gentle painter-sculptor who was one of the regulars, was beaten up by one of the tougher guys, whose punishment was banishment from the square for six months. How, you might well ask, can a magistrate banish an illegal street vendor from a piazza in which he has no right to be in the first place? But this is Italy.

Everyone was very shaken by the murder and felt terrible for Claudio's wife, Grazia. This kind of violence fortunately is rather rare in Rome and therefore was particularly shocking. The only "good" thing that came out of it was that the *vigili* were ordered to set up their own surveillance, stationing a patrol car in the piazza and keeping the peddlers away. Unfortunately, here in Italy consistency is not the order of the day, and such diligence was not to last. First, the schedule was cut to weekends only. Then for a while, the *vigili* disappeared totally, with the result that the peddlers soon were back in force. Whenever anyone with pull stepped into the fray – for example, an MP living around the corner – there'd be a few weeks of vigilance. One year, there seemed to be a tacit agreement that the vendors could hang out in the piazza during the day, but had to clear out in the evenings. Other times they'd be banned full-time. And then, once again, the *vigili,* the cats, would stop paying attention. The news would go out on the vendors' cell phone tom-tom, and the mice would return, more or less stealthily, to their posts, betting that for a while, at least, the coast would be clear and that when controls did resume, the dear, kind policemen would simply warn them off without resorting to the more extreme, but perfectly legal, measure of confiscating their goods.

Another tactic used by the peddlers – then as now – was to fold up their tables, pack up their merchandise and run around the corner until the *vigili* left, knowing they probably wouldn't be back, at least for 24 hours. The *vigili* know this but appear not to care. And neither, apparently, do their superiors. Once, in an attempt to clear up the matter and find out what one could legitimately do to stop the "invaders" – who were blocking doorways, cluttering the piazza with plastic bags, and restricting the space for traffic, public and private – I went to the Trastevere *commando* of the *polizia municipale* (the *vigili*) and was told by the chief honcho for this sector that the peddlers were totally *abusivi*, illegal. "So why are they still there," I asked? "*Ah, Signora, la coperta è troppo corta* – The blanket is simply too short, he replied.*" And while it is true that the *polizia municipale* of Rome is severely understaffed, it is also true that the *vigili*, probably the most hated *categoria* in Rome, are largely unprofessional and do not – as a group – come near to fulfilling their obligations to the community. Romans say that most *vigili* are on the take, but I have never seen or heard anything, first-hand, to back that up. What instead can be seen by the naked eye is that as a group they don't have a sense of duty. If they did, maybe life could be made far more livable in a city afflicted by severe traffic problems, uncontrolled double-parking and general confusion. Instead, they more often tend to be totally passive, unless they are in a bad mood or have some kind of ticket quota to fill. Me, I would frequently get ticketed for leaving my moped outside my house, which is on a street where parking is supposed to be prohibited. But what about Attilio, the greengrocer who until a few years ago had a shop in my piazza? He was often seen chatting with one of the local *vigili* but seemingly was never told either to stop smoking in his store or to correctly label his fruits and vegetables, as required by law, with the prices and origins of his produce.

A persistent stereotype about Italians and their well-known lack of discipline is the one that describes them as extreme individualists who because of their verve and intelligence simply can't bear to be bound by the constraints of law that other, ordinary mortals are forced to accept. But the explanation may be a lot simpler, and much less flattering. For historical reasons – centuries spent as the subjects of warring city-states with the rule of law often taking a back seat to power politics and family loyalties – many Italians, especially those from points south, have little respect for the law and, seemingly, little understanding of its purpose, which is that of setting the boundaries for civil cohabitation. And there may be some connection, too, with the Roman Catholic Church's somewhat flexible attitude towards sin and thus, in general, towards wrongdoing. Otherwise, how to explain that 137 years after Italy became a modern nation-state, so many people still choose simply to ignore laws they don't like. Maybe other nationalities would be the same if in their countries, too, law enforcement were considered an optional, even by the people charged with that task. In other words, who knows to what degree people obey a law primarily because they know that if they don't, they will get into trouble. In Rome, instead, it is clear: people know that most of the time they can get away, not with murder, of course, but with many other misdemeanors. The result? Ignoring the rules has become a quasi national habit.

My friends Daniela and Victor Simpson like to tell about the time they visited a château somewhere in France, parking their car – as required – in the lot and, like almost everyone else, walking up the road to the entrance despite a steady rain. "Only one car ignored the signs and drove straight up to the front door," Victor likes to recount. "And guess what plates it had? *Roma*," he adds, laughing. But because of the implications, it really isn't all that funny.

And consider the argument I once had with an Italian of UPS. "I am very disillusioned, *molto deluso*, with the United States," he told me as I was filling out the label on an envelope I was mailing to Washington, D.C. "I grew up thinking the United States was a democratic country," he continued, "and instead I was wrong." Uh oh, I thought, another opponent of our oft-mistaken foreign policy. But, no. The man was outraged because a *prosciutto* he tried to ship to his cousin in Milwaukee had been confiscated. I could not convince him that laws governing the entry into the U.S. of agricultural products (Italy doesn't seem to have any) were designed to protect the general good and were hardly undemocratic. He didn't seem to be able to grasp the difference.

In Italy, most laws are honored more in the breach than the observance. *"Fatta la legge, trovato l'inganno"*, goes one saying that means, "pass a law and we'll find a way to get around it". You don't have to spend much time in Rome to realize that stop signs, and even red lights, are often disregarded, as are those reading "no parking or standing", and even "one way". When, not long ago, the city government installed new cameras to catch drivers who illegally use the lanes reserved for buses and taxis, on the very first day spy cameras photographed some 6,000 unauthorized vehicles! Many Romans think nothing of getting on a bus even if they don't have a ticket and travelling free, and would probably complain in the event an inspector caught them. Absenteeism runs rife, with too many unethical doctors willing to supply fake illness certificates. Though present in most countries, tax evasion is endemic here among the non-salaried, and although estimates differ, most recently has been said to account for between 18 and 21 per cent of GDP, an increase of almost 200 per cent over the last 30 years that makes it the "leader" in percentage terms in Europe. Studies indicate lost revenue amounts to at least 120 billion euros a year; in other words, if tax evasion were to be eliminated, the massive Italian public debt, which last year almost led the country into bankruptcy, could be wiped out in 15 years. The major culprits are said to be industrialists, banks and insurance companies, storekeepers and artisans, in that order, with some categories not declaring as much as 80 per cent of their income.

Just about every year, newspapers here publish an analysis of the tax declarations filed by the self-employed and remark that the low level of reported incomes would suggest that most Italians are living in dire poverty. Although prior to the current recession, appearances have always suggested that Italy has one of the highest standards of living in Europe, only 0.14% of the population declares an annual income of over 200,000 euros ($250,000) and thousands claim not to earn more than $7,500. Furthermore, the results of surprise raids by the finance police during the course of 2012 and 2013 year indicate that as many as two-thirds of Rome's cafés, bars and restaurants don't give official cash register receipts to customers. People are reportedly pretty scared of the *Guardie di Finanza*, also known as the *Fiamme Gialle,* from the yellow flames on their insignia. But they themselves are not always above cutting corners. My dentist was flummoxed when he was asked by a *Finanza* major to provide his wife with a (false) certificate claiming he'd been performing oral surgery on her on a day she had skipped work. But he did it. "What else could I do? I mean, I might need the guy for a favor sometime."

Problems on the enforcement side clearly have something to do with this widespread "lawlessness", especially where the traffic police are concerned. In short, the cops just ain't doing their jobs. According to one survey carried out in 2005 in six Italian cities and involving 72,000 people, only 1.3 out of 10,000 people using their cell phone while driving were actually fined for this behavior and only 4.6 out of 10,000 recalcitrant motorcyclists got into trouble for not wearing a helmet. The survey also reported that one out of four Italians didn't use his or her safety belt but only one out of 10,000 got a ticket. And although seat belts have been mandatory since 1988, compliance only improved following the introduction of a driving license points system in July, 2003.

Think about what happened in 1988. At the start, police, *carabinieri* and *vigili* enforced the new law. But such vigilance lasted only for about a month. After a few weeks of giving out tickets, it was as if an order from on high had arrived, and things changed. Since it is hard to imagine some high-ranking policeman actually giving an order, saying, "Okay guys, give it a rest, who cares if they don't buckle up," one can only surmise that centuries-old, highly homogeneous cultural attitudes had prevailed. *Come un suol uomo* – as if they were all the same man – Italian traffic cops simply stopped paying attention and for ten years more, beltless driving was once again the order of the day. Now most Italians use them, at least as far as I can tell.

When law enforcement is so sporadic – or arbitrary – it is counterproductive. People feel not that they have broken the law and are being punished, but that they are being picked on or singled out. At the same time, the laxness probably also explains why most Romans don't seem to be afraid of the police. When I ride my moped home in the evenings, I am always surprised that other motorcyclists think nothing of driving up the main street of Via del Corso on the other side of the white line, even though at Piazza Venezia there are at least two *vigili* on duty. And just the other day I watched, amazed, as a woman in a small "city car" backed into two spaces reserved for motorbikes, and this right in front of a police station in central Piazza del Collegio Romano. The Romans, too, "know their chickens". The irony is that reportedly there are more laws on the books here than anywhere else in Europe. But the heritage of Roman Law and, much later, the influence of the Napoleonic Code, appears to be largely academic, much appreciated only by some members of Parliament and a relatively small number of theoreticians.

Given all this, one of the miracles of recent Italian history is the unexpected way most Italians have been observing the new, anti-smoking law that went into effect here on January 16, 2003, making Italy the third country in Europe – after Ireland and Norway – to ban smoking in all workplaces, trains and buses, stores, restaurants and bars unless new, powerful and expensive ventilation systems were installed. Italians now toss their cigarettes before entering a café, leave the restaurant between courses if they must smoke, and wouldn't think of lighting up inside a store. There are some problems in offices and, believe it or not, inside the Chamber of Deputies and the Senate, but basically it's a miracle. My theory? It's one of the few laws that even the most recalcitrant know in their heart of hearts to be just. All the rest – except of course for really serious things like murder, rape and robbery – are considered annoying impositions from on high.

In case anyone was wondering, this negative assessment is not simply the opinion of one expatriate crank. Not long ago I was at my weekend apartment at Lake Bolsena, and as there was unacceptable carousing going on after midnight at the restaurant downstairs, I decided to dial 112, the emergency number (Bolsena, population 4,000, does not have active *vigili* or *carabinieri* on night duty except in July and August). The operator switched me to the *Carabinieri* headquarters at Montefiascone, around 20 minutes away. After listening to the carousing through my cell phone, the officer who had answered the call – clearly having picked up on my accent – asked me where I was from. And after learning I was American, he went on. "Tell me, why is it so many of you foreigners come here? Can't you see this is a country where there are no real values and where no one respects the law?" Then, apologizing, he said he didn't have a car to send over to stop the noise. Are you sure? I asked again. "Yes. It's a particularly bad day for us. The mayor, the city director, and the public works commissioner have all been arrested".

Chapter 25 – Romans, Yesterday And Today

In Italy, Romans are viewed ambivalently by their fellow citizens. They have a reputation for *simpatia*, generosity, good humor, sarcasm and skill at sparkling repartee. I mean, I ask you! In what other city would an eleven-year-old boy whom you have almost hit with your scooter after he darts out from between two parked cars, turn to you with that well-known Italian gesture (the hand, palm facing inward and fingers and thumb bunched together, is slowly shaken back and forth) and say, "Aò! (a typical, Roman exclamation, generally voiced in loud and possibly aggressive tones) Who do you think you are? Herod?"

But they also are known for their slyness (*furbizia*), for general, all-around overbearingness (*prepotenza*), for boisterousness and for vulgarity. Indeed, Italians from elsewhere in the country like to say that the initials once written on the standards of the Roman legions, S.P.Q.R. *Senatus Popolusque Romanus* (and today for the most part on sewer covers and other official Roman signs) actually translate to "*Sono Porci Quei Romani* – Those Romans are pigs". So it is not surprising that to a foreigner, or at least to an Anglo-Saxon foreigner, Romans often appear just plain rude. True, some of the behavior that could be classified as Roman rudeness is simply the fruit of cultural differences that one just has to learn to accept.

But Roman arrogance and bravado can at times be most annoying. This behavior can be divided into several categories. The first comes from never having been taught that which elsewhere is known as the Golden Rule, the "do unto others...." maxim that encourages us to put ourselves in the shoes of another, *anonymous* human being. Romans rarely seem to take the time to say to themselves: "I won't do this because I wouldn't like it if someone did it to me". Consequently, their lexicon of bad manners includes:

- Not slowing down the car to avoid splashing passers-by when driving through the puddles left by a torrential Roman rain;
- Leaving the motor of a car or motorbike running under someone else's window at two o'clock in the morning while saying unending goodnights to a friend or friends;
- Talking in loud voices after midnight in the halls of an apartment building;

- Allowing one's children to scream and run around restaurants while other people are trying to eat;
- Allowing your children to run up and down the stairs, screaming, in an apartment building after Sunday lunch without ever thinking of saying, "Shhhh, people may be resting"; stopping your car in the middle of a narrow Roman street to chat to a friend on foot even though there are people in cars behind you presumably with some place to go;
- Double-parking directly opposite a car that is already double-parked on the *other* side of the street, thereby narrowing the roadway even more than necessary;
- Parking a car in an area like Trastevere, where there are few sidewalks, in such a way as to block a doorway;
- Talking during a movie and getting irritated when asked them to stop;
- Not looking behind you when you open a heavy door to make sure it doesn't slam in someone else's face, something even the supposedly rude Parisians and New Yorkers do when they exit a building or the subway;
- Not apologizing when you inadvertently dial a wrong number, but simply hanging up;
- Not saying "*mi scusi* – excuse me", before you reach across the counter – and someone else's coffee or orange juice – for a packet of sugar or sweetener;
- Not saying "excuse me" when you inadvertently knock into someone on the street or in a shop;
- Not saying "excuse me" if you are trying to see something in a shop window and someone else is also standing there, as opposed to pushing by in front of them without a word.

We Americans have lots of faults but some really nice qualities as well. During a four-day, pre-Christmas visit to Disney World in Orlando, Florida, a few years ago, I was stunned, but gratified, by the frequency with which people said "excuse me" or "pardon" or "I'm sorry" and, in general, how friendly, and kind – as in, "can you see okay?" or "let me make room for you" – the average Disney visitor was to his fellow "mouseketeers".

What I gradually came to realize was that some of this behavior simply reflects the fact that Mediterranean peoples generally do not have the same conception of personal space of Anglo-Saxons, or perhaps the dimensions of their personal space are simply quite a bit smaller; in general, Mediterranean peoples don't take the same care we do in not "invading" the personal space of another. But there is more to it than that.

Despite the importance of Christianity, the ethics of which are well known, and perhaps because of their country's tormented history of invasions by marauding enemies, few Italians – Romans at the fore – seem to automatically harbor sympathy, love or solidarity with their fellow human beings, that is with people one doesn't actually know. Instead, they appear to be have been brought up being told they should be nice only to people they *do* know, family in the first instance, next, friends and third, acquaintances. So that if they don't know you, by which I mean that they have had no previous contact with you, you don't exist and, face it, are to them more or less invisible, not even a blip on their radar. This is clearly a cultural difference and, let's be honest, not a terribly admirable one. If they don't know you, you can be pretty sure that unless it's an emergency – for example, you've collapsed on the street from a heart attack or been hit by a car, cases in which the Golden Rule kicks in even here – they simply don't "see" you. A prime example is their behavior when they get behind the wheel of a car, but there are many others as the reader can see from the list a few paragraphs back.

But there is a saving grace. If they *do* know you, Romans are warm, delightful, amusing and often thoughtful people. If I had to make a list of the incredibly generous favors that the Romans I know have done for me, it would probably be endless. And to be fair, it doesn't take much to move you from the category of stranger to that of acquaintance; even a brief but pleasant exchange will do the trick, as anyone who has ever asked a Roman for directions will know. I remember my friend Mary Suro once complaining that when she was pushing her baby's carriage around Rome, no one ever offered to help her navigate Rome's sidewalk curbs (curb cuts are still infrequent here and until only recently were unknown in this city). "But you have to ask," I told her, and in fact that's the secret. When asked for help, no one here will ever turn you down, and is usually more than gracious. I know this, because I drive a moped that is really too heavy for a woman with an unpredictable back, and I often ask for help maneuvering it out of a tight parking space. (On the other hand, it is also true that the only man who ever stopped *spontaneously* to offer me help – without my asking – when he saw I was having trouble with the bike, was a Dutch tourist.)

This lack of unprompted concern for others in Rome is most visible, unfortunately, when people get behind the wheel. Once someone of this ilk gets into the driver's seat of a car (or on the front seat of a two-wheeled vehicle), he or she can act in ways that are, at best, disconcerting and at worst dangerous. I have been driving a moped or a scooter for three decades now, and have had only one small accident in all that time. But as far as I'm concerned it's a miracle that I am still alive. Other riders constantly cut in front of you, as do the drivers of many cars. Although driving manners on the open highway have somewhat improved, there are still innumerable drivers (practically all male, I may add) whose technique for passing or getting you out of the way when you are both in the fast lane, is to come up right behind you (no more than a couple of meters behind) with flashing headlights, and bully you to over to the right. And almost no one on in this part of the peninsula, except the occasional woman or older man, will ever slow down or stop to let you make a U-turn or pull out of a driveway.

Fact is, the years spent here have left me with the impression that most Romans, and many non-Roman Italians as well, really act as if they were the only people on the face of the earth. Not long ago I was in Stockholm and as I was walking along a fairly narrow footpath I could see, ahead of me, a family with bikes who were standing still and totally blocking the way. "I bet they're Italian," I said to myself. And I was right. And don't laugh, but the same thing happened, even more recently, when I was touring the African country of Namibia. My group was struggling up a sandy path to the top of a promontory from which you had an excellent view of a *pan* studded with dramatically picturesque trees. But at the very top, the path was blocked by another group of tourists. "I bet they're Italian," I said to myself and since, as they say here, "I know my chickens," you guessed it, I was right.

Part Six

Sex and the (Eternal) City

*T*he Italians have a saying: *"Meglio soli che mal accompagnati – Better unattached than badly matched" – and as the millennium approaches, I am still single and in terms of relationships with the opposite sex appear to have chosen a life-style that leads me into one dangerous alliance after another, if "dangerous" is the right word to use for an obvious predilection for relationships with married men. I often wondered what it was that led me to this kind of behavior: possibly the fact that I was the offspring of a very unhappy marriage and therefore shied away from commitment. Or was it simply a preference for drama over daily routine? Who knows? Married men were quite available, so from that point of view there was no problem. But as I matured, and as I became increasingly frustrated at work, these kinds of love affairs – although initially exciting – became harder to bear and far less satisfying. Fortunately, I have a sense of humor and, as a full-time journalist with a generally exciting life and lots of interesting contacts, I was able to put my peccadilloes, and those of others, into a social and political context which taught me even more about my adopted country.*

Chapter 26 – "Frutto Proibito, Frutto Saporito"
(Forbidden Fruit Is The Tastiest)

Giacomo was a high-powered bureaucrat whose life-style incorporated a considerable amount of traveling and evening entertaining. "Tonight I have to see the damn Japanese," he would grumble to his wife, secretly having already planned only a brief *aperitivo* with the foreign businessmen, after which he'd have his chauffeur drop him off a block from his mistress's apartment in the colorful Trastevere district. Given his life-style, he had lots of opportunities to cheat on his wife. But even the more "ordinary" nine-to-fiver with a roving eye quickly learns how to arrange his life to accommodate transgression.

Simona, a single woman who works in a travel agency, has been having an affair with a married man who works for his wife's family's furniture company. From early on in his marriage, and with his wife's consent, Michele reserved two evenings a week for going to the gym and a third for playing *calcetto* (five-a-side soccer). Now, unbeknownst to his spouse, he goes to the gym at lunchtime and spends those two evenings with Simona. On soccer night, instead, which he wouldn't give up for anyone, he has already made sure that he and Simona have spent their lunch break together.

In a sense, this is hardly surprising. Although it sounds like a cliché, and though of course there are exceptions, narcissism and disregard for others could not be but "normal" traits among men in a country in which male children are pampered from birth and told constantly by the *mamma*, the *nonna*, the *sorella*, and the *zia*, how wonderful they are.

In some ways, Latin males may have been the victims of an exaggeratedly hostile press: to their credit, it must be said, in their mating habits they tend to be warm, affectionate, seductive, protective, fairly secure in their masculinity, uninhibited and, with some areas of exception that I mentioned in an earlier chapter, sexually generous. But there is no doubt that the lack of responsibility fostered by family traditions has left many of them emotionally immature and, not surprisingly, preoccupied primarily with their own gratification.

Most middle-class Italian adolescent boys are rarely if ever asked to do household chores. They don't learn how to cook or clean, and if their families are well-off, they get generous allowances, usually do not work in the summers but are instead allowed and encouraged to travel, at Mamma and Babbo's expense. They are given cars or expensive motorbikes without having to work for them, and often can count on being given an apartment once they get married. Until then, unless they have a girlfriend with an apartment or if they go off to work in another city, Italian men generally live at home, allowing *mamma*, or *la governante,* the housekeeper, to prepare their meals or do their laundry. *Bamboccioni*, overgrown babies, is the term used by the late Tommaso Padua-Schioppa, a well-known economist who served as Treasury Minister in the nineties, to refer these young Italian adults who don't cut the apron strings. It is now an accepted word in the Italian language.

Granted, this reluctance to leave the nest reflects, in part, the soaring rate of youth unemployment combined with the high rents that keep many singles and young married couples from getting mortgages and then setting up house. But there is a general attitude of indulgence towards offspring that considers it only just and right that the latter be handed the world on a platter. "If a family can afford it, they should give their children everything," insists a 66-year old *paterfamilias* with whom I had a ferocious argument about bringing up children. The quarrel started when he expressed his anger at a next-door neighbor, a Swiss, who had given his son permission to use the family car but only if he would pay for the gas. "But isn't that the way it should be?" I offered. "No, it's really selfish," retorted my interlocutor, whose own son was regularly given gas money along with the car.

Other Italian fathers (and mothers) realize they are spoiling their children, male and female alike, but don't quite know how to cope in a world in which children, all of whom want to keep up with the Joneses (we say the Rossis here in Italy), seem to be calling the shots. Teenagers increasingly are allowed to go out late on school nights to meet friends at discothèques, and at 18 or 19 they frequently go away for weekends. And it's hard to be a stern parent when even your country's jurisprudence is against you. Not so long ago, in two separate judicial sentences, the Italian Supreme Court, *la Corte di Cassazione,* ruled that an Italian parent must support his child until he or she finds a job that is consonant with his or her educational training, even if this doesn't happen until they are in their 30s. This is like saying, "Kids, don't bother trying to find odd jobs to support yourself or contribute to the household: your parents will support you almost as long as you want, that is until you finally find yourselves". Add to this the fact that university students are allowed to take years and years to complete all their course work (and can even "reject" a professor's grade if they find it unfair or exceedingly harsh), and it becomes clear that the entire concept of personal responsibility has taken second place to other concerns. It is my opinion that this has a particular effect on young men, especially those from economically-advantaged backgrounds. From the time a male is born, personal satisfaction – i.e. pleasure – seems to be given first place. And although pleasure is by no means limited to sex (food, sun, fast cars, travel and parties also have high standing), it gets high priority. "It is better to have remorse than regret," was the way Giacomo put it when he revealed to me, with a total absence of embarrassment, that his first major extramarital affair had been with his wife's then best friend.

As every single woman who has been around the block knows, a relationship with a married man is inherently frustrating; in any country: weekends are almost always out; considerable, sometimes exhausting, planning is involved to spend an entire night together; holidays are taboo, in that they belong, automatically, to the wife. And, although today's young adults sometimes appear to be catching up to the rhythms of our disposable world, leaving their wives and husbands at the drop of a hat, even if one or two *bimbi* have already been born, the older generation of Italian males has always been highly unwilling, and thus unlikely, to break up a marriage unless they were totally miserable… or unless the wives leave them. And what makes it even more curious is that in Italy, where divorce was first introduced in December 1970 (and reconfirmed, despite ferocious Church opposition, in a bitterly contested 1974 referendum) relatively few people actually cut the knot. The number of divorces is increasing, but it is astounding how many people one meets who have never gone further than a legal separation.

This can give rise to some really ludicrous situations. When, Giovanni, the live-in lover of a Swedish colleague died (he was considerably older than she), the church where the funeral service was held was divided in two, both literally and figuratively. Dark-haired

227

people largely occupied the pews on the right: Giovanni's wife, grown children, brothers, sisters, cousins and friends, etc. Whereas most of those seated in the left-hand pews were instead blonds: my colleague, her children, relatives who had arrived from Stockholm for the funeral and friends, mostly from the foreign press. In fact, Italian men may set up house with a second (or a third) woman but they don't seem to ever get around to re-marrying, preferring a legal separation to an actual divorce. Often, too, perhaps because it's hard to shake off the Catholic upbringing most people here receive, they will still refer to their former spouses as "my husband" or "my wife"". As for a divorced woman collecting alimony, she too is unlikely to remarry; she will just live "in sin" with number two – in order not to lose her *alimenti* (alimony) check.

So if what you want is marriage, avoid Italy's *uomini sposati*. On the other hand, there is little here to convince men (or women) to say "no" to extramarital sex. This is, after all, a society in which pleasure comes first and where high-content sexual messages are constantly being beamed.

In recent years, young and very young women more or less everywhere – and perhaps even more so here in Rome (as opposed to Milan), where vulgarity is often the rule – have increasingly been dressing in a progressively more provocative fashion. This is true in other parts of the world as well. But in Italy it has been "institutionalized" in the sense that prime-time TV variety programs featuring scantily-clad damsels have long been an unshakable element of everyday life, as are mainstream news weeklies with naked women on the cover. Advertisements – on billboards and TV alike – continue to use female nudity to sell products like cars or stereos. And lest the reader think I am exaggerating, I call attention to a July 2007 article by Adrian Michaels, the Milan correspondent of the *Financial Times,* expressing astonishment not only at the degree to which female nudity is used here by TV and advertisers, but at the extent to which Italians accept this as normal, indeed don't even notice it. Women accept it, even deliberately choose it, because they feel it is a primary part of their essence to be beautiful and seductive. And men, well they are encouraged to believe they live in the midst of a luxuriant orchard with lots of fruit just ripe for the picking.

And what about Roman Catholicism, with its emphasis on the straight and narrow? The number of regular churchgoers started declining sharply in Italy quite a while ago and although attendance is still high at gala performances by the Pope (at papal elections and funerals), there is no indication that the trend is likely to be reversed. Surveys have repeatedly shown that a majority of Italians now reject interference by the Catholic Church in their sexual lives. In fact, an astonishing number of young Italian couples, most of whom are baptized Roman Catholics, now forgo marriage when they first decide to cohabit and with no apparent qualms at all have children out of wedlock. And the Church itself could easily be accused of hypocrisy. Take Pier Ferdinando Casini, the handsome, 57-year old leader of the UDC, a small Catholic political party that started out as an ally of Silvio Berlusconi and then opposed him by joining forces with several other centrist parties. Casini, who presents himself as an heir to Italy's Christian Democratic tradition, constantly speaks of family values and has regularly opposed everything from euthanasia and abortion to civil unions and gay marriage. Nevertheless, in 1998, he left his wife Roberta for Azzurra Caltagirone, a woman 20 years younger than he and the daughter of one of Italy's richest men, publisher Francesco Caltagirone, and whom he married in a civil ceremony in the fall of 2007. What happens when Casini goes to church, many people have long wondered. Does he take (or is he given) communion, to which, at least by pre-Francis Church rules, he should not be entitled?

Chapter 27 – Carlo And His (Un)Clean Hands

The situation was both touching and ludicrous. Here I was, certainly no longer a *spreeeng cheeckeen* – as my Italian doctor had recently pointed out in his charmingly accented English – perched on a parapet atop Rome's *Gianicolo*, the Janiculum Hill, waving (I hoped) at my current Italian lover, imprisoned somewhere inside the 18th-century Regina Coeli jail down below. Carlo, until recently a powerful state bureaucrat, had been caught in the net of the magistrates running the 1992 "Clean Hands" investigation. In an undoubtedly commendable effort to wipe out the rampant (and largely tolerated) corruption that had plagued Italy for decades, the judges seemed at times to be throwing judicial caution to the winds. To the overwhelming satisfaction of many on the far left, they were arresting almost anyone – politicians, businessmen, bureaucrats – they could get their hands on.

For the last two months, therefore, my tall, elegant and once high-living lover had been held in preventive detention in a twenty-yard long holding pen together with a variety of accused drug pushers, robbers and pimps. His delightful sense of humor, plus his somewhat dubious protestations of innocence – and probably the weekly visits from his wife (not even in Italy do mistresses qualify for visitation rights) – seemed to be keeping him sane. But, he wrote in one of his letters, it was the view of the Janiculum Hill's statue of 19th-century hero Giuseppe Garibaldi that made him feel closest to his loved ones, including me.

During those hours in which the cell doors were left open so that the detainees could socialize, he could see the statue from a window at the top of a certain staircase somewhere in Block 4. So, he suggested in one of his missives, why didn't I go up there? That way he could at least catch a glimpse of me. Okay, I answered, speeding my reply for a mere 12,000 lire (then about $8.00) through the postal service's first attempt at 48-hour *posta veloce*, or fast mail. Our long-distance visual assignation was set for the following Tuesday between 11 a.m. and noon or, should it rain, on Thursday at the same time. "I'll wear a pink T-shirt so you can identify me," I specified in my answering note.

It was a lovely early summer day, so clear that from the lookout points on the hill you could see the domes and *campaniles* of all of old

Rome's magnificent churches as well as the hills beyond. This being a weekday, the Janiculum park was almost deserted; the Commedia dell'Arte puppet theater was closed, the children's ponies stabled somewhere out of sight, and only a handful of American tourists were taking in the view. Happily, I noticed in a burst of national pride, they were ignoring the tourist junk – plaster of Paris statuettes, pennants, rosaries, postcards – sold by a solitary, bearded peddler, one of those cunning, "I've-seen-it-all" Romans whose gold neck chains often have a crucifix at one end and a Jewish star on the other, just in case the group passing through comes from Brooklyn rather than Cedar Rapids.

I had arrived on my ancient green Peugeot moped, the same one I had bought shortly after arriving in Rome some twenty years before and used over the years for personal transport, work and sentimental spying ("So the bastard isn't in his office, after all!"), as well as for journalistic endeavors, such as coming within several yards of the red Renault 4 that cradled the bullet-ridden body of former prime minister Aldo Moro, or slipping through police roadblocks to get to St. Peter's square on the day that the mad Turk, Ali Agca, tried to assassinate Pope John Paul II.

It was immediately clear to me that the logistics were such that from RC, as the inmates refer to their prison, Carlo wouldn't possibly be able to see me if I stood at the base of the statue. Upon friendly interrogation, facilitated by my ability to do a rapid switch into a now perfected, "helpless but *simpatica*" mode that seems to appeal to Italian men, the peddler pointed out a much better lookout point some hundred yards away. So it was there, in this secondary *piazzuola* that I settled down to wait and wave. There were two other people sunning themselves there, a long-haired female art student and a slightly disheveled-looking man. Both were wearing pink T-shirts.

From my new perch I could see below me the rear portion of the Botanical Garden, the heavy stone walls of the prison barracks, and the tree-lined Lungotevere river road beyond. Perhaps this was the place, immortalized in dozens of postwar Italian films, from which inmates' friends and family screamed messages at night to their loved ones, the so-called *telefono*, as in "*Marioooooooo. Tuaaa sorellaaa siiii è sposaaataa* – Mario, your sister has gotten married". Who knew? The real question was whether or not Carlo could see me. I didn't have the vaguest idea from which window he might be looking and I confess I felt rather ridiculous. So it was only every once and a while, when my two neighbors, one sketching, the other dozing, appeared not to be looking, that I would furtively sneak a wave. Then, suddenly (or was it there all along?), a white cloth appeared from one window. My heart leapt: Carlo! Since neither of my companions seemed to be paying any attention, for a while I excitedly waved the beige linen Annie Hall hat I had recently ordered from the Tweeds catalogue.

I couldn't stay there indefinitely, of course, since my new job at an Italian national newspaper awaited me and it was time to get back to the office. Several months earlier, I had landed a job with a new Italian paper that was promising to adhere to an "Anglo-Saxon" style, format and standards, but wasn't doing so at all. That was a disappointment in itself, but the *delusione* was made even harder to bear since, after years of free-lancer freedom, I now had to get used to dealing with an on-the premises boss and having to show up in an office on a more or less specific time-table. Fortunately, the boss – at least at the outset – was the man who had gotten me the job, John Wyles, a Brit who had left his post as the Rome correspondent of the *Financial Times* to join the *Indipendente* as its deputy editor and Rome bureau chief.

A few days after my expedition to the Gianicolo, Carlo's next "express" letter came revealing, to my acute but fortunately unwitnessed embarrassment, that I'd been waving at someone else or possibly at no one at all. Carlo had seen me "only with the eyes of my heart," he wrote disappointedly in his excellent English, the deliberate upslant of the slats on the prison windows making the lookout point invisible. But never mind, he said. It made him happy to know that I was thinking of him as much as he was thinking of me. Probably, confined to his cell for over eight weeks, Carlo was indeed thinking about me more than he had ever done before. After all, what else did he have to do? The main thing on his mind, though, was whether the magistrates investigating his case would find enough evidence to convict him of bribery. And he was close to panic about what was going to happen to his job (and his generous salary) when he got out and, in the meantime, about the effect his imprisonment was having on his wife and children.

He, of course, was not the only one to be facing such problems. At times it seemed that Italy's entire establishment – politicians, bureaucrats, bankers, managers or financial officers of state-owned companies, industrialists, judges – was under investigation, or even indictment, for taking, giving, or extorting bribes or kickbacks. In some ways, therefore, Italy was in the throes of a bloodless revolution. Only this time a band of crusading, seemingly disinterested (or, in the conservative view, communist-sympathizing) magistrates was playing the part of the political radicals that elsewhere have assumed the role of, or passed themselves off as, the midwives of history. In any event, after years of widespread corruption, pork-barreling, vote-trading and general sleaze, it seemed – briefly at least – that Italy's postwar political parties were finally getting their comeuppance.

But there was a nasty, Jacobin side to the figurative bloodletting. Many cooler heads were shocked by the unchecked use the magistrates were making of a law that legalized preventive detention in the cases of those alleged likely to flee the country or muddy the evidence. The threat of jail was used, in many cases successfully, to extort confessions or testimony regarding the suspected offences of friends and colleagues.

One man in his late sixties, until then the president of the country's largest state-owned holding company, was dragged out of bed before dawn and transported across the country in an uncomfortable Black Maria. The 64-year old wife of a bureaucrat who allegedly had amassed a fortune while director general of the Health Ministry, spent more than six months in prison, her weight dropping to 39 kilograms, and this despite the fact that she was the principal caregiver of her paraplegic son. (Years later, both she and her husband would be acquitted.) An out-of-office Sicilian Christian Democrat politician, disgraced by the accusations and suffering from stomach cancer, was nevertheless jailed for several months before being released. A well-connected CPA was kept in solitary for two weeks and then sent home because of lack of evidence. The former chief of the Italian state energy corporation, Gabriele Cagliari, widely believed to be guilty of the embezzlement and corruption charges filed against him, but months, if not years, away from trial, suffocated himself with a plastic bag after four months (and a day) of imprisonment, during which he'd never even been formally questioned.

In these circumstances, the house arrest accorded to some began to take on the aura of a summer vacation. But even here, families were divided, children traumatized, and lovers separated. One woman I knew found herself suddenly single. She had been living for years with a man who, like many separated husbands here, had never bothered to get a divorce, and when a magistrate released him from jail in favor of house arrest, he sent him back to his estranged wife.

Inside, Carlo recounted, the sole pastime, other than masturbation, was chitchat with other prisoners and, in the afternoons when the cell doors were opened, he would invite another fallen bureaucrat and a former ambassador to tea! The worst thing, he said, was the constant blaring of the television, with the channels permanently set to soccer or to mindless TV programs like "*La Ruota della Fortuna*" – "Wheel of Fortune" – or soppy South American soap operas. Inside Regina Coeli, he wrote, there was no library, no way to get exercise except by pacing up and down in the corridors, no type of organized activity, and when in one letter I asked him about the caféteria, he wrote back: "*Cara*, I know you are picturing the caféteria in *Escape from Alcatraz*, but don't. There is no caféteria." In fact, at Regina Coeli, food was dished out from large black *pentole* brought in at mealtimes to a central station on each cellblock, setting off a mad dash generally won by the youngest, fastest and toughest detainees. And it was lousy. Anyone who could afford it, therefore, preferred to eat the food his or her family would supply. In Carlo's cell (a rectangular room which included a rudimentary toilet stall as well as a hot plate), the cooking was done by a small-time accused drug trafficker named Rocco. His best dish, Carlo wrote, was *pasta al tonno*, a relatively simple dish made with onion, tuna fish and tomato sauce. "We have been eating a lot of *pasta al tonno*," he wrote.

So the fact that his mind was on me, with whom he'd shared great sex, great conversation, great food and wine, was normal. The main problem was the amount of time that I was spending in thinking and worrying about him, assembling and delivering care packages – a robe and slippers, shorts and a T-shirt since it was now summer – and talking to his lawyer, whom I knew from news stories I had covered. All this, I knew, was a mistake. Time and again, Carlo had succeeded in disappointing me, but not because he'd promised he'd leave his wife, and then hadn't. In the first place, that wasn't his style. And secondly, I myself was hardly sure I wanted a full-time relationship with him or, for that matter, with anyone else. But I still felt disappointment over his apparent lack of commitment, his unexplained disappearances for several days, his inability – and this he *had* promised – to find any significant chunks of time to spend together. The usual story. Almost.

The extra twist here was that I had apparently been going out with a man who, along with being married (a liar, therefore, at least where his wife was concerned) had also been on the take. It soon became clear that, unlike some of the others arrested during the Clean Hands crackdown, Carlo was almost certainly guilty. Apparently, he had been accepting bribes in return for making sure that certain contracts were awarded to the "right" people. The problem, as became evident when I was to see him again after he was released, was that he didn't feel guilty, only unlucky. "I didn't do anything different from what everyone else was doing. I simply got caught," he insisted, gradually convincing himself that he was a victim rather than a crook.

After he had spent several months in jail awaiting trial, the magistrates in charge of his case allowed him to return home under house arrest and then released him on his own recognizance, confiscating his passport and requiring him to report regularly to the local police station. Eventually, like many others, he was allowed to plead guilty and to *patteggiare*, that is, to negotiate a fine in place of doing any more jail time. Naturally, he never got his job back and, bitter and still convinced of his innocence, has gone into private business. I saw him a few times after his release: you can't leave your friends in the lurch, after all. But my heart was no longer in it, especially after I realized, with a sinking feeling, that the man's gold and steel Cartier watch he had given me was almost certainly a piece of payola.

Chapter 28 – Deadlines And Deadbeats

Another day had passed and the deadline for turning in copy was approaching. Outside, the shadows were lengthening: the Piazza Adriana park looked deserted, apparently empty except for the darkly handsome lawyer from downstairs who was walking his large black dog, and a taxi driver, his yellow cab idling at the curb while, or so it appeared from above, he relieved himself in the overgrown grass on the park's outskirts. The massive outline of Castel Sant'Angelo (we English speakers call it Hadrian's Tomb) stood out against a whitened, early-evening sky, as did the looming Baroque cupolas of historic Rome which, from my vantage point on the Vatican side of the Tiber, seemed aligned one alongside the other.

In the newspaper's bureau, on the fourth floor of the six-floor, 19th-century building we had moved into several months earlier, a few colleagues still sat hunched over their computers, hastily winding up their breathless stories on Italy's latest political drama. What I was doing, having long ago concluded 15 minutes of intense primping, was waiting for Daniele. And I'm ashamed to admit that I spent a lot more time anxiously peering out the window of my office, incidentally the only non-smoking room on the premises, than I did putting the finishing touches on the AIDS "package" that was supposed to run that weekend but probably wouldn't.

I had done a lot of work on the series, talking to government officials at the Health Ministry, seeking out social workers in the bare-walled, linoleum-floored prefabs that make up much of the rambling *Istituto Superiore della Sanità,* the Higher Institute of Health, that occupies several acres not far from the Policlinico Hospital which, just in case, is fairly convenient to the sprawling Verano Cemetery. I had even sat in at the Institute's AIDS *linea verde* or "green line" (the equivalent of a hot-line number) to hear how the experts were handling the calls. "Get tested!" they kept telling the callers, largely youngsters who had had condomless sexual encounters with people they would never see again, mostly – it seemed – after drunken or drug-spiced evenings at the local discothèque. The whole thing kind of made me nervous, and I found myself confiding to the doctor on duty that I myself had recently been incautious, having made love with a

26-year old Argentinian hunk without insisting he wear a condom. "Don't panic. Ask him if he's ever been tested (yeah, sure!), and in six months time, get tested yourself," was his advice.

In any event, compared to what was going on in the U.S. prior to the advent of protease inhibitors, the AIDS emergency in Italy seemed tame, and subsequent governments were soon to discontinue the public advertisements that at the time were being aired regularly by both private and state-run networks. By the end of 1993, fewer than 2,000 people reportedly had died from AIDS and only about 100,000 people in Italy's population of 58 million were believed to be infected with the HIV virus. Nevertheless, the illness was spreading rapidly, gradually moving out of the major high-risk group of intravenous drug users (not homosexuals as was originally the case in the U.S.) to affect gays and heterosexuals.

I felt pretty worked up about the topic because of the deaths of several friends and acquaintances in the U.S. as well as of Bruce, an engaging young American who had worked at the Rome CBS bureau in the eighties and, one year later, of his handsome artist companion, Mauro. In addition, as an unattached, single woman, I had been repeatedly shocked and upset by the refusal or reluctance of many men, particularly in my own somewhat-over-40 group, to use condoms, in short to take the danger seriously. Take the vet with whom I almost went to bed when he made a "house call" to remove the stitches out of my three, newly sterilized female cats.

This guy was so good-looking people would stop on the street to gawk at him, thinking he was perhaps an actor or some other kind of celebrity. But as I realized later, he nevertheless needed constant confirmation. We had mutual friends and used the *tu* form of address. But I had nevertheless been surprised one day on a visit to his office to find myself in his arms while my cat, Cleopatra, fretted in her travel cage.

I blush to admit that at first I actually believed he felt a particular attraction for me; it was only later that I realized he did this with a lot of his patients' human owners, the female ones at least. Anyway, he suggested coming over to my place to take the cats' stitches out, and since I'd enjoyed kissing him I thought, "Why not?" Almost as soon as he walked in the door, he got down to business, picking me up in his arms and carrying me into the bedroom. It was all going a bit fast for me, since the vet did not seem to go in for foreplay. And what about protection from AIDS?

Broaching this subject was not easy back then for a woman in any country, but it may have been even harder in a place like Italy where most men are not keen on condoms and generally make sure you know it. One male friend confided he didn't use condoms, because "We all have to die some time!" And a researcher I interviewed who was working with a group of Brazilian transvestites in Rome said many of his subjects told him that clients often paid double or triple to be allowed to penetrate "bareback", without protection. In the case of the vet, I kept making hesitating sounds and gestures, hoping he would pick up on it. But all he said was "Don't worry about getting pregnant, I'll be careful". Finally I had to make it clear that it was not pregnancy that was worrying me. "*Dio mio*, how stupid of me, you'd never believe I was a doctor," he said when he finally got the message. After which he lost his erection, took out the cat's stitches – the putative reason for his visit – and soon after took his doctor's bag and left.

My articles on AIDS were to end up being published, but in shorter versions than I had envisaged. But at that moment I was not thinking about my articles. I was thinking about Daniele the *carabiniere* and reaching the increasingly obvious conclusion that he wasn't going to show up. Fortunately for my sense of pride, I hadn't told anyone in the office I was expecting him so I was spared the public embarrassment of being stood up.

But I was disappointed. In the first place, Daniele's visit would also have been the first time since the paper's founding six months earlier that my co-workers at the *Indipendente* would have actually seen me with a man. Flavia, a trainee, had her Carlo pick her up every evening. Giulio (unaware that he was being cuckolded) could be relied on to take Laura, a secretary and the paper's translator, home. Elisa, an economics reporter, was married to a well-known reporter at *ANSA*, the national news agency.

Natalia, who wrote about television, was pregnant so Pietro, her live-in companion, was often on the premises. And me? The secretaries by now were quite familiar with the last names of the various men who phoned me regularly ("Tosatti, Frezza, Tavani," Antonia, the head honcho, would bellow at me when I returned from lunch or a dash to the gym). But no one had ever seen me *in compania*, which wasn't all that hard to understand seeing as I was going through one of my periods of *magra*, or famine – months and months without a real relationship – and was still feeling a lingering regret for that *dolce* crook, Carlo.

I am all too familiar with such periods of "famine." In fact, I secretly believe they recur to punish me for an earlier "feast"; a five-year stretch, probably the most satisfying of my life, in which I'd had two important love stories running at the same time and guiltlessly had enjoyed every minute. But Daniele's failure to show also made it clear that my stop-gap relationship with this young *carabiniere* captain was doomed. One should never put up with that kind of behavior. But when you're not even really in love, it is – or should be – simply intolerable.

The main problem appeared to be sexual. Although he was a northerner whose father was a university professor, Daniele seemed to have real problems responding to a sexually liberated woman. And the immediate cause of his defection was almost certainly my suggestive comment over the phone the previous day regarding what I felt like doing to him, or rather to a certain part of his anatomy. This is not what you expected from a 32-year-old, healthy Italian male in the final decade of the 20th century, an era in which 15-year-olds of either sex are rarely virgins, bared bosoms are on every beach and magazine cover, and regardless of AIDS, sexual encounters appear to be the stuff of everyday life. "If you'd said that to me I'd have dropped everything and rushed over to your place," insisted Tommaso, at the time my masseur and confidant. But I'm not so sure I believe him. As I said before, Italian men seem to want you first to love them, and then desire them. If it's only the latter, it seems to upset them. And then, despite his youth and beautiful body, Daniele was so sexually insecure that, excuse the pun, further intercourse had become impossible.

I'd met him by chance. Arlene, a girlfriend visiting from New York, had been given his number by someone back home and when she phoned him he'd volunteered to take her sightseeing. "I'm going out with a policeman. Do you want to come, too?" she'd generously offered, thinking it might be a treat for me as well. God forbid, I had thought, sniffing disdainfully to myself at the idea of spending an afternoon with some "ordinary" cop, I who had known and "loved" at least one top investigator and had interviewed and dined with many others. Arlene, of course, was also unaware of the existence here of different police forces: there are seven in total, the best known of which are the *Polizia di Stato*, the state police (light blue cars);

Guardia di Finanza, the treasury police, (grey uniforms, green berets and grey or blue and yellow cars); *Polizia Municipale* or *Vigili Urbani,* the city and traffic police, and the, *Carabinieri* (dark blue cars), the military corps under the aegis of the Defense Ministry but which is organized territorially and therefore also acts as the primary police force in most smaller Italian towns and villages. But had I known Daniele was a *carabiniere* it would have made little difference. What did change my snobby mind was my discovery, when I went to pick her up outside his office, not only that he was an officer and a plainclothesman – definitely a plus – but, most intriguing, he belonged to the Italian special task force set up to track down Italy's thousands of stolen art works. Now that's interesting, I mused, already imagining an unbeatable scoop after the next museum break-in.

Ever since I first arrived in Italy, the papers had been full of stories about thieves waltzing in and out of museums and churches more or less at will, with booty estimated at billions of dollars. One of the first stories I did was based on an interview with an Etruscan-tomb robber named "Umberto *er Tolfetano*" (Umberto from Tolfa, in Lazio dialect). A short, balding man who made a living as a *tombarolo*, someone who sneaks into ancient burial places and empties them out before archeologists or police arrive on the scene, Umberto was the kind of character that makes a news feature come alive. But he was just a small-time antiquities robber. There is much, much worse. And if such thefts are by no means limited to Italy, they are a significant problem in a country known to possess an enormous proportion of the world's art treasures. The special *Carabinieri* art works corps has succeeded over the years in effecting considerable redress, and indeed, like the *Carabinieri*'s special anti-food and drink adulteration corps, the NAS, has always had a splendid reputation. But let's face it, there was more on my mind. The lad was undeniably charming and I was sadly bereft of amorous entanglements.

About five foot nine, slim and dark-haired, Daniele was not really good-looking but full of enthusiasm and *joie de vivre.* As soon as I found a suitable excuse I phoned him and not long afterwards he asked me out. He was delightfully unconventional for a military man and I found his stories amusing. He had shocked his superiors by requesting a six-month leave to sail across the Atlantic, a trip he'd already made once before prior to enrolling in the *Arma,* as the *Carabinieri* corps is often referred to. He had used his skills as a diver to recover a stolen urn from a Venice canal. And he loved undercover work. Visiting antique shops suspected of fencing, he'd play the part of a researcher while his graying *maresciallo*, or sergeant, would pose as a university professor. Daniele loved to talk. He told me about his sisters and his mother, about his friends who lived on the Côte d'Azur, about his partners in the sailing enterprise, his silly commanding officer, and about his subordinates, whom he often referred to as "the beasts". What he didn't tell me was that he had a girlfriend and, indeed, was more or less engaged to be married. True, at 32, he was too young for me. But still, it's a glaring omission when you've just gone to bed with someone or are about to do so.

Although I liked Daniele, at the start I really hadn't felt attracted to him; I don't know why, something about his lips or the way he kissed. Then, boom. One mild, summer evening I found myself feeling turned on. "Do you want to come up for a drink?" I asked him after dinner, thinking that eleven months of celibacy were really quite enough. We sat on the sofa and started kissing and I thought, "What the hell!" even though I find making love the first time terribly difficult. Daniele took me into my bedroom, undressed me, and didn't complain about using a condom, immediately impressing me with his sophistication. As usual, it being the first time, I felt kind of paralyzed and nervous. But I enjoyed the lovemaking and his display of affection afterwards. He, however, appeared very worried. As we lay in the darkened bedroom, listening to the dialogue from the English-language movie house down below where the roof had been opened to let in a bit of fresh evening air, he started fretting. "You didn't like it," he kept insisting, ignoring all my reassurances, so that in the end I felt depressed rather than elated.

As shy as I am at the outset, I have enough experience not to have exaggerated expectations the first time I make love with a man; I enjoyed being with Daniele but assumed that the lovemaking would get better when we got to know one another. But it didn't work out that way. The next time I saw him, wrongly assuming he wanted genuinely to please and excite me, I decided perhaps he'd like a little "help". This involved my slightly shifting (we're talking centimeters here) the hand he had placed between my legs. Mistake! Daniele stiffened, pulled his hand back as if he'd been burned, then lost his erection. "I know what to do," he snarled, retreating to the other side of the bed. "But *tesoro*," I said trying to soothe him, "I only wanted to show you what I like, just like you do when you put my hand on your penis." But it was useless. "I can figure out what you like by myself," he snapped. "And by the way," he said abruptly after a brief pause, "I'm engaged."

I wasn't totally surprised, but the entire exchange was irritating. Like the totally innocent (or the completely selfish), Daniele was soon fast asleep. I, on the other hand, felt frustrated, annoyed, and rejected. So when sleep wouldn't come I took a blanket into the living room, curled up on the couch and watched a late night re-run of *Lou Grant*, in Italian of course. I must have dozed off when I felt a warm body slip in behind mine and heard Daniele saying, "*Che c'è?* – What's wrong? Please come back to bed. I'm sorry." And like the softhearted fool I am, I did.

The next time I saw Daniele things went fractionally better. He came clean about his girlfriend – a cellist from Venice – and about his confusion over what to do next: already miffed because she'd discovered he'd been to bed with a friend of hers, she was upset by the idea of his being away for six months on a sailing trip. He didn't want to lose her, he said. "On the other hand," he pointed out sadly, "this is almost certainly my last chance to make this crossing."

Naturally, after all this verbal intimacy, we ended up in bed and I guess you could call it a success. This time I was largely passive; I refrained from making any explicit sexual demands, did without an orgasm, and got my kicks from the sheer pleasure of looking at and touching his wonderfully beautiful body. He was passionate, and so I was pleased, although a bit startled, when at breakfast Daniele said he wanted to see me again that night. "I'm afraid I'm busy," I said truthfully. "*Cerca di liberarti* – try to get out of it, he begged. "Remember, I'll be leaving soon." So what happened? You can guess. I changed my plans, he never called, and when I phoned him it appeared that he had no intention of taking my call. "*Il capitano non è disponibile* – the captain is not available", intoned a polite, but distant, adjutant.

"What a jerk," I thought, although not, I must confess, without a bit of pain. But that was it. I certainly wasn't going to see or talk to him ever again. Then, one day several months later, the phone rang. "*Sono Daniele*, I'm back in Italy. When can I see you?" he said as if nothing had happened. And in his mind I guess nothing had. Once again, I gave in and agreed to see him. We went out a couple of times, made love in a way that I found pleasant, considering I was reluctant to make my needs known, but which nevertheless seemed to leave him vaguely dissatisfied with his performance. "We still have to get to know one another," he'd whisper afterwards, although it was evident that greater intimacy was clearly just what he didn't want.

That night, as I waited in vain at Piazza Adriana, I found myself wondering if my sexual boldness over the phone had been designed, unconsciously, to force some kind of a turning point. Whether or not it was that which caused him not to show, I would never know. But I was furious, and I couldn't resist sending him a "big sister" letter warning that if he didn't shape up where women were concerned he was likely to end up a married man with a frustrated and, possibly, wandering wife. In other words, that he was likely to end up as a bona fide *cornuto*. So that was that, or so I thought. But, surprise! A year and a half later he telephoned to say he wanted to apologize. He said nothing about the letter and seemed somewhat nonplussed, almost disappointed, when I assured him I wasn't at all angry. "Shall we get together?" he asked timidly. "Okay," I laughed, knowing that was what he wanted to hear. If he liked, I'd see him the following week, I said, assuming he'd never call. And, once again, since I know my chickens, I turned out to be right. He never called.

Chapter 29 – Under the Roman "Sole"

I probably should have taken it as a sign. A bad one. Before I even reported to work at *Il Sole 24 Ore* at the end of the summer of 1993, the paper's editor had left. Gianni Locatelli, the man who had made *Il Sole* into what it had become (the country's most prestigious economic and financial daily) and who, incidentally, had recently hired me, had been offered the post of director general of *RAI*, the Italian state broadcaster, which must have seemed like an offer he couldn't refuse. This meant that I had a job at the salary and rank we had decided on the previous April. But I would also have a new editor who might not be as keen as Locatelli on having me fulfill my pre-arranged brief, which was to travel throughout Italy writing about situations that intrigued me (or my editors) but doing it from the vantage point of a non-Italian. And I would also be asked to do editorial commentaries, he had said.

Make no mistake. I had been delighted to go to *Il Sole 24 Ore* which, along with *Corriere della Sera*, is one of Italy's few real quality newspapers, basically non-ideological and capable of limiting to a minimum interference from the entrepreneurs or economic groups that own it. It is the property of Confindustria, the Italian National Manufacturers Association, and working for the newspaper was definitely a step upwards for me. Often described as the *Financial Times* of Italy – in recent years it has generally been Italy's fourth or fifth best-selling paper after *Corriere*, the much more left-wing *La Repubblica,* the Fiat-owned *La Stampa* and Rome's *Il Messaggero* – under the guidance of Locatelli first, and others afterwards, it had turned itself into a real "niche" daily. With its in-depth reporting on all aspects of the economy, as well as its one-step-ahead coverage of *norme e tribute* (regulations and taxes), it is a "must" buy for anyone in Italy involved in finance or economics, including Italy's tens of thousands of tax accountants and investment consultants. Confindustria clearly has a viewpoint (although this can change depending on who is at the association's helm), and it would probably not hire an editor with a diametrically opposing outlook. Nevertheless, on a day-to-day basis there didn't seem to be any blatant interference with what one wrote, or at least I myself never encountered any. The country's manufacturers clearly believe it is in their own interest to own a newspaper that is highly credible and therefore has a strong influence on both government and public opinion.

The first time I set foot in the *redazione romana* (the Rome bureau) of *Il Sole 24 Ore* (the paper was founded in 1965 when the venerable *Il Sole* merged with the post-war *24 Ore*) it seemed like a morgue. At *L'Indipendente*, there had always been noise, laughter or yelling of some sort. But at *Il Sole*'s then bureau on downtown Via del Corso, only a block from Palazzo Chigi, the late-Renaissance building that since 1961 has housed the Prime Minister's office, everyone seemed busy at his or her desk and very, very serious. It was a bit intimidating, although once I would get to know everyone, the reality, thankfully, turned out to be somewhat different. Fortunately, I had one friend there from my pre-*Sole* days, special correspondent Gerardo Pelosi who, although we often argued about air conditioning and his habit of throwing the newspapers he had read on the floor, was supportive from the start.

The new job meant I was back in the same neighborhood where I had spent most of my time as the *Washington Post*'s correspondent. The building where *Il Sole*'s bureau was then located, a squat, block-square edifice owned by the Italian insurance company, RAS, had an atrium café that was handy for conducting less formal interviews as well as for pleasant coffee breaks. At the rear of the building was Piazza San Silvestro, the *piazza* that hosts the main branch of the Italian post office, a taxi stand, a newsstand and bus stops for numerous city bus lines. Right downstairs on Via del Corso was Spizzico, a sort of Italian fast food take-out and caféteria which had started life decades before as Alemagna, an elegant café and pastry shop where, back then, the well-dressed *le tout Rome* would go for a coffee or for afternoon tea and *pasticcini*. Clothing and shoe stores abounded. My bank was a mere two-block walk, and an extensive choice of restaurants and cafés was within walking distance. And, of course, Parliament was almost right across the street. In other words, it was a great place to be based, both for work and for one's personal and social needs.

Of course, starting a new job can always be daunting. And things were not helped along by the fact that when I first began work at *Il Sole* in September 1993, I encountered significant hostility from some of the journalists who were worried I might encroach on their beats or simply couldn't understand what an American was doing on their turf.

The first time I attended an *assemblea*, or union meeting, one veteran journalist, Franco Colasanti, caused me great embarrassment by saying, without even looking at me, "And another thing we have to discuss today is who is this Sari Gilbert and what is she doing here?"

For more than five years, Colasanti, a veteran political reporter whose experience could have been very helpful to me, refused to speak to me unless I asked him a direct question, at which point he was generally brusque and unpleasant. He eventually ended this cold freeze. But I suspect that this came about only when he realized that I was not having an easy time at the paper and could no longer be considered any kind of a threat. His behavior, in any case, was extreme. Most of my other colleagues got over their collective miff fairly quickly. "We're sorry, but no one told us you were coming aboard," that year's union representative told me when he (finally) apologized for the general, though not unanimous, cold shoulder. For there were others who right from the beginning were far above the skirmish: colleagues like Dino Pesole, who had left *L'Indipendente* before me to become a *Sole* contributor and whose full-time hiring, I later discovered, was delayed by my arrival. Or Luigi Lazzi Gazzini, who also had seen his scheduled promotion pushed back because of my arrival. But, gentlemen to the core, they both welcomed me with maximum kindness.

From a professional point of view, despite my lame duck status as Locatelli's last hire, things didn't seem too bad. The new editor was Salvatore Carrubba, more of a scholarly type with less of a journalistic reputation than Locatelli, but who was competent and, not a small thing, *un vero signore*, a real gentleman. He allowed me to do some of the things I had expected I'd be doing – in-depth reports on subjects such as immigration, home health care and the plunging Italian birth rate – and for a time, too, I was also kept quite busy by daily political coverage, since the then day editor, Franco Locatelli (no relation to Gianni), kept me busy following the birth of Silvio Berlusconi's *Forza Italia* and the arrival on the political scene of the *Lega Nord*, the Northern League, the somewhat xenophobic and autonomist political party. Frequently, I covered local elections in places as distant from one another as Milan and Palermo; I did many features on the integration of the newly-arriving foreigners, something that to me was one of the most significant social changes underway in Italy. And for a time happenstance also turned me into the in-house expert on party finances, which in Italy come primarily from the public sector.

But things quickly got confusing. My direct boss, bureau chief Aldo Carboni, the man who had engineered my hiring, didn't think I should be doing daily political coverage but rather should be concentrating on in-depth stories, where my "American eye" might provide a different focus. But at the same time, he seemed very distracted and didn't give me much support when it came to actually getting these broader pieces into the paper or getting new assignments. The paper's editor, who had since changed yet again, didn't seem much interested in me either. Ernesto Auci, who had started out as a real journalist at *Il Sole* and *Il Mattino* of Naples, but then became chief spokesman first for Fiat, the car company, and later for Confindustria, had become editor in 1996. This might seem strange to Americans since in our country you generally do either journalism or PR, not both. But in Italy the roles of journalists and company or political party spokesmen are considered almost interchangeable, and most news people see no professional conflict in going to work for a business entity he or she had previously covered and might be covering again in the future.

Shortly after his appointment, I asked for a meeting with Auci to introduce myself, present a summary of my experience and capabilities, and recount my vicissitudes at the paper so far. These latter he seemed to find amusing, but after that he more or less ignored my existence until one day in the spring of 2000 he asked me if I'd be interested in working on an English-language version of our then new website. I said yes, and that was what I did for a year and a half until one day, despite all their earlier investment and market research, the powers that be in Milan decided an English-language website didn't make economic sense after all (now they've got one again) and – literally from one day to the next – cancelled it, throwing out pages and pages of biographies and regional studies we had produced or translated into English.

The next editor, a grumpy-looking man named Guido Gentili, who took over in July 2001, also showed little interest in me, as did the new Rome bureau chief, Roberto Napoletano, a *simpatico* but rather frenetic editor who somehow never seemed to consider me a real resource. This meant that for almost a year after the termination of the English-language website, I wrote no articles at all until finally (and after I had threatened to take advantage of the significant protection Italian labor law gives a worker), Gentili agreed to my proposal for a column: I called it *Visitors*, and in it published interviews and profiles of non-Italians who had a special relationship with Italy. After almost a year, in September, 2003, that column, too, was abruptly terminated, leading to another year of near inactivity, absurd given my more-than-decent salary. Finally, the paper accepted an idea I had for another column, this one called *Stranitalia*, one which would compare things in Italy – traffic problems, laws, women's rights, adoption – with things as they are done in other countries. *Stranitalia* (now the name of an internet news blog I publish) ran for almost two years, giving me a fair amount of positive feedback from readers. Following a reorganization of the Monday edition, where my column appeared, *Stranitalia* started appearing more and more infrequently and eventually it, too, was discontinued. And in any event, even while I was doing it, there was no getting away from the fact that it was not what I had been hired to do.

I was still drawing a very respectable salary and enjoying all the company perks: a company-paid leased car, a free-use cell phone and a small home computer. But I was significantly under-utilized, doing much less work than most of my colleagues, and feeling pretty bad about all this. The thing that most rankled was the fact that when I started work at *Il Sole*, I was somewhat well-known in Italy as a journalist; when I left in December, 2007, I had no "name" at all and would occasionally bump into colleagues who upon seeing me would say, "You're still here? I was sure you'd gone back to the States." In the end, once I left the paper in December, 2007, I decided to sue on the grounds that I had been effectively downgraded in rank and was suffering from a consequent decline in my professional standing. I won the case and was awarded some damages but I subsequently lost an appeal that my lawyer and I filed because the first judge had awarded me only about a third of the amount we had requested.

My feelings about *Il Sole* were irrevocably tarnished when I discovered that their defense, backed up by not a single piece of paper but by a couple of lying colleagues, was that they had stopped giving me work because at a certain point (after about eight years) they had discovered my written Italian was sub-standard but did not have the heart to fire me. This is not true; of course my written Italian is not 100% perfect, but it is darn good and in any event, says Stefano, my lawyer, they didn't hire me because I was Dante but because I was a very good journalist with a lot of experience.

Sometimes people ask me what *Il Sole* had against me but honestly I don't think this was deliberately planned at all. I suspect that it was more a combination of a lack of imagination on the part of my post-1996 bosses, and perhaps an unconscious preference for dealing with younger and possibly more malleable journalists. Probably, if I had been more aggressive, more driven and more profoundly ambitious I would have been making a real pain of myself until I got what I wanted. But I just couldn't fathom the situation. "Since I'm no longer a freelancer, why should I have to fight to get assignments?" I would ask myself. And how was it, I would wonder, that a company would pay someone such a good salary and not want to get its money's worth? With 30 years of journalistic experience, I surely could have been useful. Who knows? But I never got an answer to the $64,000 "why" question and, in the end, I more or less stopped caring.

Chapter 30 – It Had To Happen

I suppose it had to happen. Looking back, it was probably inevitable that sooner or later I would have had an affair with someone in the neighborhood. But who would have thought it would have been he? Physical attraction is a funny thing. It can, of course, be purely physical, although even there we may have been unconsciously imprinted, early on, to respond to a particular type. But often it is "mental", in the sense that one can respond, physically, to an idea of a person rather than his reality. For example, I had found Luca, the television programmer, extremely attractive, but in addition to that that there was something about him that reminded me of all the rich, dashing fraternity boys at college, the ones who drove sports cars and got all the girls but hardly ever looked at me. And we women are particularly good at transforming a frog into a prince and then convincing ourselves that we must have that prince, which almost always leads us to jump into bed with them. Luca was certainly no frog. Far from it. But the degree of my passion for him clearly meant that there had been something else going on there.

Other times, of course, attraction depends on where you are in your life at the time you meet someone. But exactly why it happened this time was hard to say. I was definitely eager for a sexual relationship with someone I liked, trusted and would see more than once (one-night stands have never interested me). I didn't have a steady boyfriend. My last experience had been with the Catholic journalist (American readers should be aware that although almost all Italians are baptized, only a portion of them actually would define themselves as Catholic) who didn't want to take his underpants off. And, although I blush to admit it – "Yes, Virginia, size does matter" – I was hoping to have a sexual relationship with someone who not only was sure of himself sexually but also had a penis of respectable dimensions.

I was in a nearby café late one evening, having stopped after a late night at the paper for a "baby" – a small whisky or bourbon. I don't drink a lot but I do like hard liquor, probably more than many women. And after a bit of aimless chitchat with the barman, Stefano, someone I'd known for ages, I saw that all of a sudden he was looking at me in a new and different way. "Why don't you come with me for a pizza after I close?" he said, surprising me greatly. To be honest, up until then I had never given him a second thought, at least of that type.

We often chatted or joked, or talked about books, but that was that. And this was not just because he was younger than I (when we first met he was only a few years out of university) but because he was, I thought, kind of funny-looking, someone who had always reminded me of Howdy Doody, the TV marionette we baby-boomers grew up with. He has very crooked teeth that his parents never thought to get fixed, and which don't seem to bother him. And he almost always looked like his dark brown hair had forgotten what a comb looked like. And yet, that day, after his invitation, he started to look a bit different to me, and when he gave me my change and our hands touched I felt a real jolt. "Hmmm," I said to myself as I put the lira coins away in my change purse. "Hmmm," I thought again as I crossed the piazza on my way home.

Stefano, on the other hand, – or so he later said – had been curious about me for some time. So when I turned down the pizza invitation, he had somewhat shyly asked me if we could do it some other time. It was obvious that what he had in mind was more than company for a late-night snack and I had made it clear I was not sure. "*Ti faccio sapere* – I'll let you know," I had said, while sipping the last of my Jack Daniels. But soon after, however, I found myself feeling unexpectedly turned on. Well not turned on, exactly, but *incuriosita,* intrigued, wondering if I should immediately take him up on an invitation to *fare sesso* – have sex – not that he had used those words. The alternative was to mark time, possibly arranging some other kind of first meeting, on safer ground than my apartment.

As I've said, I am always nervous and uneasy about making love with someone for the first time. But beyond that, I had little "moral" compunction. After all, I was a warm-blooded, unattached, adult woman with a healthy desire for sexual contact, and who knew when I would next have a real love relationship that would, naturally, include sex? So after a few days of mental to-ing and fro-ing, I decided to take the plunge. After all, if I decided I wasn't really attracted to him, I could always back out. So I phoned Stefano and told him I'd decided that the answer was "yes", but rather than a pizza at two a.m., the bar's closing time, why didn't he simply come over for a drink.

In all this, I have forgotten to mention that Stefano, naturally, was married, with a young and musically talented daughter. He'd talked frequently about his wife, an economist with a very good job at a government research institute, and to whom he clearly was quite attached. But his feelings for her, and for his daughter, for him evidently did not mean sexual fidelity.

Indeed, there was a soon-to-be divorced Frenchwoman living in my very own building who had had a stormy – and for her, at least, a passionate – affair with him. I had suspected this ever since the time I had seen them in the doorway, arguing, she crying. And then, during one of our late night bar chats, Stefano had confirmed the relationship saying that he had had to end it once she had taken to phoning him at his home.

But although I was concerned that the Frenchwoman might be upset if she saw us together, his marital status really didn't bother me. At the time, I didn't know his wife. And at the risk of sounding callous and unfeeling, when I was younger I never felt it was my responsibility to worry about the wife of a cheating husband. Furthermore, it was clear to me from the start that Stefano could never be someone in whom I'd be seriously interested.

First, he was too laid back, not enough of an achiever for me. Secondly, he was excessively narcissistic, and at work he was always sneaking looks at himself in the mirror on the wall facing the bar's counter. Although I have to admit I did feel a sneaking admiration for someone who could be so content with his looks despite what most Americans would consider a serious defect, teeth that were clean but which really could have used years of attention from a good orthodontist.

Then, there was the fact that he slept around. This concerned me because Italy was then in the midst of the AIDS scare, although quite frankly no one but me seemed worried. I was pretty sure, knowing him, that if I insisted he would agree to be tested, especially if I were to present the idea of testing as an alternative to using a condom. Despite Ministry of Health TV messages about the need for protection, Italian men seemed as reluctant as ever to use condoms. I suppose one can't really blame them. Who likes condoms? They will only use them if they are 100% sure that they don't want to run the risk of a woman's getting pregnant; when they are less than 100% sure, they prefer *coitus interruptus*.

I don't remember all that much about Stefano's first visit, that is, other than my surprise and satisfaction upon discovering that despite his relatively small frame, this was a man with a very large penis and a hard erection that lasted quite a long time. "*Che sia duro e che duri –* may it be hard and last a long time," as the Italians say. Not only that but he was imaginative, responsive, sensual in his kissing and, furthermore, one of the few Italian men I've met who really seem to like cunnilingus. Well, I thought, isn't this a happy surprise!

Once I started making love with Stefano, I naturally became a bit more curious about him. His father had been a jeweler, his mother, a stay-at-home *mamma*, and he also had an older sister to whom, for some reason, he rarely spoke. Having lost my only brother, whom I adored, I am always somewhat upset when siblings fall out. Perhaps because Italians have all this hype about the family (many accuse Americans of not caring about kin, not realizing that caring has little to do with living next door, or even in the same town), this kind of intra-familial estrangement has always struck me as odd in Italy. There's no reason, of course, why Italian families should be different from any others, but the platitudes Italians mouth about families are so persistent, and so pervasive, that one comes to believe them and is then surprised when they turn out not to be true. I had a very difficult relationship with my mother but rarely found a sympathetic ear here. "*La mamma è sempre la mamma,*" people from various walks of life would prattle at me.

But, of course, there are many Italian family relationships that have gone sour. Fabio, the politician, had two brothers but hated one of them and didn't seem to care at all when the latter fell in the bathroom, hit his head and died. My friend Silvia recently admitted she can't stand to go home to visit her family in the Veneto region because her mother is a kind of religious freak who thinks her daughter is living a life of sin in the big city. Elisabetta, a woman my age who became a psychotherapist, still resents her mother, now deceased: *la Signora* (she was unbendingly formal) had always kept her daughter at arm's length and Elisabetta felt unloved. Nevertheless, unlike her brothers, she stepped up when her mother got Alzheimer's, only to discover when the latter died that she had made a special bequest of an apartment she owned to Elisabetta's younger brother and left nothing special to her. Miriam's mother and father have hardly spoken to her since she left her alcoholic husband and set up house with a charming man whose only faults appear to be that he has no money and that he is 9 years younger than she is.

Furthermore, divorce and the financial problems that accompany it, also create stress, just like anywhere else. Tommaso, a physical therapist who for years came to my home to give me massages, doesn't speak to his father not only because he left Tommaso's mother for another woman but because he managed to leave her with very little to live on. Claudio and Sergio, brothers who run a jewellery store across the street from my apartment, also don't speak to the father with whom they began their working life. Not only did he, too, leave their mother for another woman, but at some point they discovered he was trying to squirrel away some of the jewels and ornaments that made up the shop's capital to help him set up house with his new *innamorata*. Claudio and Sergio went to court to stop him, since under Italian law a parent cannot disinherit a child. As in many American states, if an Italian *capofamiglia* dies without a will, his estate will be divided in strictly regulated parts among his legitimate heirs, according to the degree of relationship. But in Italy a wife and children are always guaranteed a part of a man's assets, even when a will says the contrary. So the judge ruled that Claudio and Sergio's father, Giuliano, could not deplete the estate, even while he was still alive.

In Bolsena, the small lake town where I have a weekend apartment, there are similar stories. For example, I was bemused to learn that Vincenzo, the owner of a *trattoria* where I often eat, was totally estranged from his mother and one sister because of an argument over the ownership of a warehouse. At one point the mother even went to the local police to file *una denuncia,* a complaint, against her son claiming that he had hit her. "*Completamente falso,*" says Vincenzo, a smiling, mild-mannered man who is amazingly open about the several operations he has had on his testicles to correct a problem that has been keeping him and his wife, Rossella, from conceiving. His mother simply tripped while they were in the midst of an argument and, in fact, she subsequently withdrew the complaint, although he says he'll never forgive her for lodging it. Vincenzo gets along fine with his other sister, who runs a *trattoria-pizzeria* at the other end of the Corso and who also is estranged from Mamma and the remaining sister. Only two blocks away in the town's main piazza, Giulio, the butcher, and his mother, Maria, haven't spoken to his sister, Concetta, for years. Why? Because she married a man of whom they didn't approve.

When I met him, Stefano and his wife lived in the same building as her mother, a widow, and only a couple of blocks away from his mother, also a widow, and they all seemed to get along fine. Like many Italian men, Stefano has always seemed devoted to his mother, and he tried to see her every day. The problem was that he didn't see his wife all that much. After discovering that one of his employees at the bar was dipping his hand into the till, he took on a cashier during the day and decided that he himself ought to work nights, which was in fact the time when the café made the most money. With his wife busy during the day and generally asleep when he gets home in the wee hours, the result was that he spent more time with his mother and his daughter, whom he picked up each day from school, than with her.

The other thing that makes one wonder about the Italians' long-touted passion for family life is the country's negative birth rate. For more than two decades now, Italy has boasted one of the lowest birth rates in the Western world. At present it is up slightly to 9.2 births for 1,000 people, but the population is actually shrinking. (In 2011, 556,000 children were born in Italy, but in the same year, 592,000 people died, which means the population was deceasing rather than increasing.) In addition, the only reason that the average number of children per woman has risen to its current level of 1.42 (a decade ago it was as low as 1.1) is because immigrant woman are reproducing at a greater rate than ethnic Italians. Something like 25 percent of Italian women are now childless and another 25 percent will never have more than one baby.

Although the one-child syndrome is even more pronounced in the more developed Italian North, where a higher percentage of women have joined the workforce, Stefano and his wife were nevertheless a fairly typical example of the trend. As a working woman with fairly high-powered job, Stefano's wife didn't want to be slowed up by a second pregnancy, nor did she feel the family would be able to dedicate enough of its resources to a second child (sports, music, schooling etc.) without – and this is a key point for many young couples – affecting the couple's overall life-style.

Poorer families have similar concerns, especially because the services and incentives offered by the government are insufficient, and, in fact, significantly lower than those offered in nearby France. Although many Italian families can still count on the traditional assistance of one or both grandmothers, nowadays more people than before have left their native cities to work elsewhere, even if this means doing without the family support system. And seeking help elsewhere is expensive. Free daycare is available in many regions for children as young as six months, but low-income families with working mothers get precedence. The people who are above the cut-off point, but who are by no means rich, often have to bear the burden of pre-school child care alone and nowadays think twice before doing it more than once. Or even just once, since the rock-bottom Italian birth rate also means that an increasing number of Italian couples aren't having any children at all. I once asked Stefano's 11-year old, Marzia, how she felt about not having brothers and sisters ("fine") and what kind of a family she thought she might want to have. She didn't seem to think it mattered all that much. "My aunt and uncle have no children," she said, "and they are very happy. My parents have just me and they're very happy, too." Out of the mouths of *bimbi*.

But were they? Happy, I mean? A couple of years later when Stefano and I were no longer seeing one another, but had remained friends, he told me that he and his wife had called it quits. What had happened was that one evening when they were talking, Stefano, for reasons known only to him or to the psychiatrist he later saw for a while, confessed that ever since they had married he had always had other sexual relationships on the side. She was stunned, and that was the beginning of the end. They have a good relationship for separated spouses (in their case, too, there is still no talk of divorce), but she is now with another man, and Stefano is on the most recent of his relationships with younger, foreign women, most recently an adorable-looking Japanese shop girl at Gucci's who – and I am not joking! – I recently saw walking down the street, several paces behind him.

As for me, my sexual relationship with Stefano lasted for a couple of years and then petered out. The principal problem is that he rarely could come over until two o'clock in the morning, something that I was willing, even eager, to do as our "little passion" was at its height. After that, I would find that I just couldn't keep my eyes open so instead of asking him to come over I just preferred to go to sleep.

Chapter 31 – The 4th of July
(Or the 12th of Never)

For twenty years, I never missed the annual Fourth of July party thrown by the U.S. Ambassador in the extensive gardens of Villa Taverna, the imposing American ambassador's residence in Rome's high-income, residential Parioli district. On these occasions, about a thousand people – mostly Italian VIPs, foreign diplomats, American businessmen and a variety of journalists – stand in line to shake hands with the big man of the moment and his wife, if he has one, and then wander around checking out each other and networking like crazy.

The Italians – politicians, industrialists and managers, high-level bureaucrats and military officers – crowd around the refreshment tables, deigning even to stand in line (a most un-Italian thing) and trying to pretend they like hot dogs, chili con carne or fried chicken wings and prefer beer or Coke to Gavi de' Gavi or Montepulciano. Me, I went in order to remind the political and diplomatic big shots I saw only rarely of my existence, and then to drink bourbon with the people I genuinely admire but also didn't get to see very often. For many years, that is until his brutal murder in 1992, this group included Palermo investigating magistrate Giovanni Falcone, along with other magistrates and police investigators like Nicola Calipari, the intelligence officer later killed by an American soldier in Iraq while he was spiriting a released Italian hostage to safety.

These Italians were – and are – special: courageous men and women involved in the struggle against terrorists (both international and domestic) and organized crime and consequently much more interesting than the old-family nobles American ambassadors to Italy always seem to be palsy-walsy with. And although no doubt dealing with bloodshed and horror on a daily basis turns some people into gloomy depressives, on others it has the opposite effect, creating a deep and joyous attachment to life and, in some cases, such as Falcone's, an irrepressible sense of humor. Gianni De Gennaro, until 2007 Italy's chief of police but before then a "simple" anti-Mafia investigator, had a quick temper but also a quick tongue. Prosecutor Domenico Sica, who to many was a solemn and forbidding figure, was another example. Caught up in the most important domestic and international terrorist murder cases, he and investigating magistrate Rosario Priore developed their own comedy act, addressing each other as "Abu Sica" and "Abu Priore", and frequently taking time off for bicycling in the Villa Borghese park. It was the only way they could recuperate a bit from the heart-rending cases they were involved with: colleagues murdered by the Red Brigades and innocent civilians killed by other kinds of terrorists.

Sica had been particularly shaken by the death of 11-year-old Natasha Simpson during the 1985 Fiumicino airport massacre, a tragedy which for me was much closer to home. Daniela and Victor Simpson, two American journalists who are long-time friends, were at Fiumicino airport on December 27th, 1985, waiting to check in for a flight to New York. Daniela was outside, alone, walking the family dog for the last time before boarding, when five Palestinian terrorists standing outside the El Al counter pulled machine guns out of bags and started spraying the place with bullets. Victor, waiting inside with the couple's two children, heard the shooting and pushed the children down on the ground. But Natasha, whom I'd known from her birth, was hit by a bullet that entered near the hip and traveled upwards inside her body, killing her. Nine-year old Michael also was wounded, and Victor himself was shot in the hand. Several other people died before Israeli agents at the El Al desk, armed with handguns, were able to kill four of the terrorists. In the meantime, Italian police had locked all the doors to the airport which meant that hours went by until Daniela found out what had happened to her family, two of whom she eventually located in the hospital, the other – Natasha – in a morgue in the seaside town of Fiumicino. It was a tragedy for the Simpson family. But they deserve immeasurable credit. For all these many years they never became bitter or filled with hatred, and this even though Victor is Jewish.

If we somehow had fallen out of touch, I could always be sure that I would run into Daniela and Victor at the Fourth of July party. Victor was chief news editor (later he became bureau chief) at the Associated Press and understandably has excellent contacts with the embassy. As long as I was writing for American papers, I, too, had excellent contacts and in the 1970s, in particular, there was a group of really intelligent, experienced, highly professional and humanly delightful career officers at the U.S. diplomatic mission in Rome, people like Jock Shirley, then the USIA chief, and his wife Kathy, a political officer, Deputy Chief of Mission Alan Holmes, political officers Martin Wenick, Roland Kuchel and Fred Spotts, and press officer Chuck Loveridge. We didn't always share the same views on politics but they were all helpful, insightful, professional and fun to be with.

Attending the party was also a way to check out just whom the Embassy thought – or had been instructed by Washington to think – were the "in" people in Rome, and conversely, who were the pariahs. Back in the 1970s and the early 1980s when the PCI, then the largest Communist party in Western Europe, appeared to be on the verge of entering the Italian government, its leaders were nevertheless termed *persona non grata*. True, starting in the mid-to late seventies, there had been, we knew, secret, low-level contacts with the Communists, but no party official was ever invited to the July 4th shindig. Members of the far-right MSI were also kept at arm's length while, in contrast, the guest list was strong on Christian Democrats, Socialists, Liberals and Republicans. Italian military officers and foreign diplomats were always heavily represented, as were the aging Roman nobles mentioned before who, except for those who are heirs to major art collections, play no significant role whatsoever in modern-day Italy. Indeed, the 1948 Constitution does not recognize noble titles which, in effect, have no legal value whatsoever. You may be a count but that title won't show up on any legal document.

The Clean Hands investigation of the early nineties radically changed the Italian political scene, making it inevitable that the Embassy invitation lists would have to be revised. The Christian Democrat and Socialist parties had disappeared off the political map, with some members accused of corruption (their names being duly purged from the invitation lists) and others being absorbed into *Forza Italia*, the new center-right party founded and led by TV magnate Silvio Berlusconi). Forza Italia later jouned with the rightwing Alleanza Nazionale to form the Popolo della Libertà, the PdL. But this grouping was dissolved in November, 2013 when the 77-year old Berlusconi, recently convicted of tax fraud, decided to bring back Forza Italia, presumably in the hopes of reviving his followers' political fortunes. The Communists, in the meantime, had morphed into a largely social democratic formation called the Democratic Party of the

Left, the PDS: subsequently they changed their name to DS and then, after a merger with progressive Catholic groups, to the PD, the *Partito Democratico*, the Democratic Party.

Back then, other "new" faces at the annual party included Gianfranco Fini, once a member of the MSI, then founder and leader of the more mainstream respectable *Alleanza Nazionale*, which subsequently merged with Berlusconi's *Forza Italia* and has then split into several smaller pieces. To show how significant the United States' point of view was back then (today it is very reduced), headlines here trumpeted Fini's first appearance at Villa Taverna in the late nineties, as they did that of Fausto Bertinotti, then leader of *Rifondazione communista*, a far left communist party that had broken away from the PDS and which today no longer counts for anything.

The Embassy's Fourth of July party of necessity has to reflect the degree to which Italian politics had evolved during the last quarter of the 20th century. Since that time, a former communist, Massimo D'Alema, has served as Prime Minister and subsequently Minister of Foreign Affairs. Another former Communist, Walter Veltroni, has been deputy prime minister and mayor of Rome. Bertinotti, known for his friendship with Fidel Castro, for a time was Speaker of the lower House. And former Marxist Giorgio Napolitano, now 87, has just begun an unprecedented second seven-year term as Italy's President and, judging from the standing ovation I witnessed when he attended a symphony concert I was at, is widely loved and admired. Fini, the former post-Fascist party leader, for a time was both Deputy Prime Minister (under Berlusconi) and Speaker of the lower House. And until being caught up in a distasteful situation involving an apartment in Nice that had belonged to Alleanza Nazionale but somehow ended up being lived in by his current girlfriend's brother, he was being touted as a likely prime minister. Today, therefore, the presence at the Fourth of July party of these and other former "pariahs" is now only a run-of-the-mill event.

But on this occasion (it was July, 1991), rather than just concentrating on my networking abilities, I was holding my breath in lovesick fear. I knew that Maurizio, very much in the Embassy's "in" category, would be there and I wondered what would happen if we ran into one another. I had met Maurizio during an interview in his sprawling office overlooking the red and ocher rooftops of central Rome. The subject was something economic and terribly boring, so when I was ushered into his office I was delighted to find myself sitting across a gleaming walnut desk from so attractive a man. True, he wasn't really my type (in men I prefer the short, dark Al Pacino type), but since until recently most of the men in Italian public life looked either like 16th-century Jesuits, *mafiosi* or second-rate Mediterranean tycoons, this slim, good-looking, gray-haired man was a pleasant surprise. And then, too, I was mesmerized by his hands. Slim and smooth, with long tapering fingers, the kind you long to be caressed by. Flirting shamelessly (I get this way sometimes), I couldn't resist interrupting him as he expounded at length on a discussion of trade policy. "Are you aware that your hands are exceptionally beautiful?" I asked. The response was unforgettable. In the first place, he blushed. And then, looking into my eyes, he replied "*Ma Lei è bella tutta* – You, however, are beautiful all over." I was in love.

So there I went again, falling for an Italian man who was married and, as it soon became clear, a habitual adulterer, and, once again, without really asking myself why I was doing this. Despite years of experience that should have given me at least a *soupçon* of wisdom and a modicum of cynicism, I still saw Maurizio as someone pretty special. Reserved, bespectacled, his rampant sexuality concealed behind a misleadingly mild exterior, he was hardly the typical ladies' man. Our first "date" was a lunch at which he graciously reviewed the technical accuracy of my foreign trade piece, barely hinting that one day he would love to take me to New York, and giving up after only one attempt at a chaste, post-prandial kiss. For the second encounter, he'd picked me up with his motorcycle in Via Veneto near my gym and whisked me off to a restaurant in the country where he somehow managed to let it drop that for him foreplay was the most enjoyable part of lovemaking. And during our third rendezvous he'd demonstrated amazing patience when a bout of shyness led me to interrupt what would have been our first time in bed. "That was the day I realized it was something serious," he said sometime later, fortunately not on the same occasion on which he announced triumphantly that I was almost certainly his third (or was it his fourth?) "great love," that is, after his wife and two other sentimentally significant *amanti*.

Maurizio's account of how his infidelities began was hardly unique. He and his wife met at the university, fell in love, got married and spent about a year happily "fucking like rabbits". Then, however, he told me, his wife got pregnant and, giving the most radical interpretation to her doctor's warnings about intercourse (it was a difficult pregnancy), swore off all forms of sex for the duration. Although it would be interesting to hear her side of the story, Maurizio claims that after giving birth she lost interest in lovemaking. So did they discuss the problem, see a counselor, do some reading? Not in Italy, and certainly not in the sixties. Maurizio's solution was simply to look elsewhere. "What else could I do?" he asks innocently. "My wife has a very low sex drive. She rarely wants to make love more than once a month, after her period, whereas I want sex much more frequently."

Nevertheless, he wouldn't think of breaking up the family. Only once, during the "reign" of my immediate predecessor, he says, had he thought seriously of leaving his wife and starting over. Caterina, for that was the name of his earlier mistress, was herself married, though childless. But just give her the word, she had told Maurizio, and she would to leave her own husband. Maurizio professed not to understand his own behavior, but interestingly enough it was not his extramarital affairs that he thought odd but rather his inability to leave his wife. "I don't understand why I have this morbid attachment to my family," he confided one evening, genuinely bewildered. Instead, it is a fairly common syndrome. Most Italian males live at home until they get married. Not only are they generally not autonomous (one economist friend who did cut the "umbilical cord" of marriage expressed astonishment at all the things one had to do to run a household, such as paying phone, water and electricity bills, which until recently in Italy had to be done in person) but in such a climate, it is easy to see how the wife quickly becomes a second mother.

I knew all this but somehow couldn't keep it in focus. The fact is that sex with Maurizio turned out to be wonderfully gratifying. His dedication to foreplay may perhaps have been greater than his overall stamina. But he was one of those rare men who like giving pleasure as much as they crave getting it. "How shall I touch you, *amore*, like this? Like that? Here? Or here?" he would ask in a whisper, watching my face for changes in expression. Like many of his countrymen, he was also terribly, and consistently, affectionate, so that one of us had to learn to hold a fork in the left hand so we could hold hands even as we ate. A sensualist who delighted in fine wines and food, and who had the money to take me to the best places, Maurizio also seemed just as happy to sit in his underwear at the huge marble table in my kitchen drinking beer and eating pizza. He was funny, attentive, intense and generous. In short, with the innate talent of the true lover, he made me feel that I was the only woman on earth. And I believe I was that for him, that is for as long as it lasted.

Which was, after all, not to be all that long. In the first place, I was getting frustrated. Despite Maurizio's promises that we would have ample time together ("I know I'm married but, you'll see, I can organize things so we'll be able to be together a lot"), in the end we only had one real, long weekend together. And that turned out to be less than idyllic. Actually, we did have wonderful, somewhat kinky sex and some great meals in the tiny, Southern fishing village of Maratea, where blue sky, rocky cliffs and cascades of blazingly scarlet bougainvillea flowers make you feel like beauty is reaching out and grabbing you by the throat. But no one had thought to warn us that the beach should be avoided for swimming (there was also a pool) if we wanted to avoid the seasonal scourge of sand fleas. I ended up with over 50 bites – on each ankle, and he wasn't much better off. Later we made a lengthy detour to revisit the ancient Roman ruins at Paestum, below Naples, only to discover that entrance to the site is allowed only until the official sunset time, which on that day had taken place three minutes prior to our arrival. And things were also not helped by the fact that, upon our return, Maurizio found his wife on the warpath. His excuse for his absence was a trip to Paris to negotiate a minor trade contract. But his lie had been exposed when his boss, with whom he was supposed to have made the trip, unexpectedly called his home over the weekend. There was a fight, a spate of recriminations and the consequent guilt feelings, which meant that for a few weeks – that is, until desire once again reared its unrepentant head – Maurizio was pretty much *uccel di bosco*, a forest bird, that is, one you rarely get a glimpse of.

The Italians have a saying, "to take a step longer than one's leg". This, in fact, is what Maurizio, like many Italian married men, had done. He had been carried away by his own enthusiasm, and made promises he couldn't, or didn't want to, keep. "You misrepresented yourself," I told him gently at one point when it became clear that the relationship was to have much less continuity (and content) than I had imagined. "I guess so," he said, coloring and looking a bit surprised. "I'm sorry." The affair, intense, passionate and highly sexual, ended quite suddenly when, citing an alleged depression brought on by political infighting at work, Maurizio disappeared from my life as quickly as he'd entered it eight months earlier. I tried calling a few times but he was distant. "I'm in a meeting. I'll call you back," he said, more than once, but he never returned my call. And when once I met him on the street (my office was around the corner from his), he was cold and distant, leaving me desperately hurt, and also bewildered.

So at that year's Embassy blow I was somewhat out of it. Suddenly, as I was walking along, glass in hand, towards a cluster of colleagues, someone touched my arm. It was Maurizio. "*Come stai?*" he asked, his dark eyes peering into mine. "I was hoping you'd be here." And then, all at once, in words no doubt repeated through the ages by thousands of adulterers, I was finally hearing an explanation of his behavior of the year before; our *storia,* or love affair, had gotten too intense (or so he said). He had been worried it would reach a fever pitch similar to that of his previous extramarital relationship, when he'd almost gotten to the point of choosing between *moglie* and *amante*, and in the process put his wife, his lover and himself through hell. In other words, at 50 he'd discovered himself just too old to risk hearth and home. "Why couldn't you simply tell me," I asked, "instead of disappearing like that?" "Oh," he said, as if surprised by the question, "*pensavo l'avresti capito da sola* – I thought you'd have figured it out for yourself."

Part Seven

Through a looking glass, darkly

*I*t started out as an adventure but at some point my life in Italy became the stuff of an everyday existence, although not necessarily that which I had imagined when I was younger or that which others, who live elsewhere, envisage when they dream of the boot-shaped peninsula that calls itself Il Bel Paese, the beautiful country. From afar it seemed to be a land of mystery and magic, but the texture of daily life has turned out to be different, fraught sometimes with high drama but generally with an ordinariness that at times is sweet and energizing and other times incomprehensible, frustrating and ambiguous. Examples: As a group, Italian women often seem caught in a time-warp in which sexiness wins out over autonomy; There is a flip-side to the highly generous (on paper) Italian national health system that is dark and, far too often, slipshod, with people forced to pay for private health because of delays and inefficiencies. The justice system is, if not broken, then seriously warped, with some 5.3 million civil cases currently pending because of understaffing and poor organization. The crime rate here is still far lower than in many countries but Italians are as fascinated with crime and bloodshed as people elsewhere. Italian politicians seem generally unresponsive to the needs of their electors. And, as we all know, Italian food is wonderfully rich and healthy. But even here there is a side to it that is conventional, prosaic, and even uncompromising and obdurate. And, increasingly, as the social fabric of the country changes, your waiter is as likely to be from Bangladesh as from Abruzzo.

Chapter 32 – "A Tavola Non Si Invecchia"
(Eating Keeps You Young)

Marco is on the phone talking to Caterina, his *fidanzata*, the word most Italians now use when they want to say girlfriend or boyfriend (in which case, *fidanzato*), although literally it means fiancé or fiancée. Actually, Caterina now really *is* Marco's *fidanzata* as the two, who are already living together, have decided to get married and are looking for an apartment, not an easy task these days given Italy's high real estate prices. But at the moment they are discussing dinner. Marco, who is 40 and from Puglia in the Italian South, is explaining over the phone to Caterina, who was born in Rome of North American parents, the best way to cook asparagus. He also tells her he has left the *sugo* he has made (his mother's recipe) for tonight's pasta dish on the stove, adding as an afterthought that they must absolutely finish the buffalo mozzarella they bought the day before as putting it in the refrigerator will ruin it (there are two schools of thought on storing unused mozzarella, but the non-refrigerator camp, to which I am a fairly recent convert, feels extremely strongly about this). Furthermore, although we are now in the 21st century, he still conforms to the old Italian habit of telephoning her before leaving the office to say *"butta giù la pasta* – throw in the pasta" (that is, into the boiling water). He doesn't actually say those words, but he does phone her when he leaves the newspaper so that, if they are having pasta, she can boil the water, heat the *sugo* – of whatever variety – and time the cooking of the pasta to coincide with his arrival at home. Other times, they have long discussions about how this or that should be prepared.

A rather small, dark-haired man with a well-trimmed moustache and goatee, Marco started out in journalism as an expert on schools and education but, increasingly, has been writing about anti-terrorism and other police-related issues. This, along with classical music, has become his real passion and he has been busy building up sources among the country's various police forces and secret services, using a mixture of flattery and self-promotion on the phone that I often find excessive. Yet he always takes a quick break to discuss dinner with

Caterina, and often spends time polling colleagues about the best place to eat out, be it for fish, Sicilian food or steak.

In this he is not very different from some of the New York "foodies" I know, except perhaps without the edge of fanaticism that many big-city Americans display about food and wine these days, especially – it seems – Italian food. I keep meeting Americans who have purchased pasta makers so that they can make pasta from scratch, although nowadays almost no one here – except someone's grandmother and a few devotees with not much else to do –would bother to make fresh pasta.

True, this is also because there's almost always a shop around the corner that sells fresh pasta. But most people here simply no longer have the time to make their own pasta and, after all, there are so many types of dried pasta available you could select a different shape or length every day for a month, or possibly two months, without repeating yourself.

Romans, in particular, have an unparalleled knack of being both passionate and laid back about things at the same time. They love wine but don't generally obsess about it. And they adore food but with some exceptions tend to focus more on the ingredients and less on the suppliers. Last June an Eataly food mall opened up in Rome (this was the 15th, the first was in Turin, the second in New York), but before that there was no place in Rome even remotely comparable to New York's Dean and DeLuca, Zabar's and The Garden of Eden, or even the Whole Foods Market. Nothing like the food department in Harrod's in London or that of Berlin's KDW, Fauchon in Paris, or the Söderhallarna in Stockholm, the places where many people in those cities feel they absolutely *have* to shop. Nothing even like the warren of small but high-end food emporia just off Piazza Maggiore in food-struck Bologna. True, if you live in Testaccio or nearby in Trastevere and were having company you might zip over to Volpetti on Via Marmorata for any of their specialties: *torte rustiche* (the Italian version of a quiche), salamis, sausages and all kinds of olives, cheeses and the sweet condiments you serve them with, fried zucchini flowers or *supplì* (rice and mozzarella croquettes), and *ciambelloni*, whether *dolci* or *salati*, sweet or savory.

Anyone with sophisticated food tastes who lives in Monti, the wonderful central-city area between the Roman Forum and Santa Maria Maggiore, will no doubt make regular excursions to the giant, once outdoor, now indoor, market at Piazza Vittorio that to serve the city's ethnic groups makes sure that there are foods and spices from all over the world. If you live smack in the center of Rome, in the *centro storico*, there are some well-known but small food shops around Campo de' Fiori or in Via della Croce near Piazza di Spagna. All sorts of people are likely to make a pilgrimage to the bakery in the Jewish ghetto that is renowned for its breads and its chocolate or sour black cherry ricotta cheesecake. And if your apartment is in Prati, you probably would make a point of stopping by Franchi in Via Cola di Rienzo for great specialty take-out or cheeses from anywhere from France to Calabria, although as an Anglo-Saxon who from time to time suffers nostalgia attacks, I find myself more likely to go next door to Castroni, where I can get chutneys, the best English teas and crackers, basmati rice, Norwegian or Scottish smoked salmon, Swedish herring, sour cream, peanut butter and, at Thanksgiving, pecan nuts, canned pumpkin and cranberry sauce.

The people at Castroni have really gotten into the spirit of things foreign. One recent November, I was there to pick up some American-style ground coffee for visiting friends and I noticed they were really low on pecans. "Are these the only pecans left?" I asked, worry clearly creeping into my voice as I thought of of an American friend who was planning to make a pecan pie for the holiday. The clerk looked at me indignantly and snapped: "Of course not, Signora, we are well aware that it's only a few weeks until T'anksgiving!" (the *th* sound is very hard for Italians).

But the fact remains that, Eataly or not, most Romans seem happy to do most of their shopping *sotto casa,* in their own neighborhoods, and small wonder. In the first place, practically any decent grocery store here will have a good selection of prosciuttos, sausages, salamis and cheeses. And, not surprisingly, Italian supermarkets themselves generally have an excellent, well-stocked *bancone* where the countermen make a point of trying to be as friendly as your local grocer. Furthermore, just about every neighborhood has its outdoor or indoor *mercato rionale,* or district market, where you will find a variety of fruit and vegetable stands to wander among until you see the reddest *pomodori*, the juiciest blood oranges, the greenest, pointiest, *broccoli romani,* or the most wonderfully varied mix of freshly-prepared *minestrone.* There will be several fishmongers and butchers to choose among. And if you need something special, say a 15-pound turkey, a bunch of cilantro, limes, some sweet potatoes, pink grapefruit, or a particular kind of sausage, just ask the butcher or the greengrocer if he can order it at the wholesale market, *i mercati generali,* and if at all possible he'll be happy to oblige.

But to say the average Italian is not hysterical when it comes to food – other than what is, to my mind, an unreasonable fear of OGM (genetically-modified organisms) that they share with most of Europe – does not mean that Italians don't love their *cibo.* "*A tavola!* – To the table," your hostess sings out to summon her guests to the dinner table. "*Si mangia!*" her husband echoes – Time to eat! "*Buon appetito,*" your dinner partners chorus as they are about to tuck in, all making it clear that they consider food and the processes of preparing and consuming it a central and irreplaceable part of life and, possibly, its principal pleasure. The degree to which food is a major concern for Italians is impossible to convey. Perhaps the full extent of this will only start to become clear to you once you've 1) shared a great meal with people who spend the better part of the time at the table talking about something special they had eaten the week before or plan to eat the following week, or 2) been, as I have, in a beach-house kitchen with six people arguing about the best way to prepare the clams they had just dug up: *in bianco,* that is with garlic, parsley and a bit of white wine, *in rosso,* with a tomato sauce, *in bianco* with *peperoncino, in rosso* with *peperoncino,* sautéed in garlic and oil, etc. etc. etc. (Actually, the clams, which were outside soaking in a pail of salt water, never got cooked at all because while the group was arguing about what to do with them someone ran off with the bucket!) You'll also get an idea of the prevailing food ethos if you are present in a get-together when pasta is being cooked, that is, when there will probably be at least three people in the kitchen sampling a spaghetti strand and saying things like "another 45 seconds" or "15 seconds more, please!" In fact, for Italians it may well be that the *way* you cook something is even more important than the ingredients.

"When you cook *cozze* (mussels), do you let them steam open in the *padella* (pan) or do you open them beforehand with a knife, like you do with oysters?" Marco asked me out of the blue one day, peering around his monitor to establish eye contact in our small, two-desk office. "*Come?* – What?" I answered, rather startled, peering mirror-wise around mine. Now, I confess I don't cook mussels very often, but when I do, after cleaning them I put them in a deep *pentola* in which I've heated some oil, with a bit of garlic and *peperoncino*, add a bit of wine and/or water, cover and cook over a medium flame until they are steamed open. It turns out that in Puglia where fewer women are employed outside the home and therefore have more time (and this was definitely truer in the past, for example when Marco was growing up), you open the mussels first, one by one, with a knife as you might do with American clams, which are bigger than Italian ones, and quite a bit bigger than *cozze* as well. But that's the way they did it while he was growing up and, by God, Caterina was just going to have to learn to adapt.

Italian food is today recognized as one of the world's major cuisines, possibly now considered superior to French cooking and in many parts of the world probably even more popular than Chinese. There is little doubt that many of the millions of foreigners who visit Italy each year are as much interested in eating Italian as they are in the country's artistic heritage. However, these visitors probably are not aware first, that some Italian eating habits have changed drastically from when I first came here and, second, that not all is always perfect in the world of Italian food.

As far as the changes go, in general Italians today eat smaller meals; just like Americans, many have quick stand-up (or sit-down) lunches when they're in a hurry, have become used to caférias, which here are called "self-service" (self-sairrrrvysse"), and eat ice cream or other snacks on the street, something that in the old days was an out-and-out no-no. Supermarkets increasingly prepare "heat and eat" portions of pasta, vegetables and meat for Italy's growing number of singles or, during the summer months, for husbands who have remained in town while their families frolic at the sea. Furthermore, to make foreign visitors happy, in some areas of cities such as Florence, Venice and, of course, Rome, restaurants now open for business at noon and stay open all day, as opposed to those traditional places that continue to close at around 3:30 p.m. and then re-open around 7:30 or 8:00p.m. This is convenient for tourists, but be aware that if you lunch before one p.m. or dine at six or seven, there will not be an Italian among your *commensali,* your fellow diners.

Another anomaly is a certain mental rigidity in some selected areas that contrasts with the flexibility that generally makes dining in an Italian restaurant so delightful. Remember that wonderful scene in *Five Easy Pieces* in which Bobby (Jack Nicholson) tries unsuccessfuly to convince the inflexible waitress to bring him toast with his breakfast even though for some odd reason side-orders of toast are not on the menu? Well, normally, the experience of eating out in Italy is the exact opposite of this. You're not hungry, or you have a bad tummy, whatever. You simply say to the waiter, could you bring me a plain poached sea bass and some spinach cooked without salt, no oil on anything and some lemon on the side, and whether it's on the menu or not, that's what you will get. So it's surprising that at times in the food sphere a wall of incomprehension descends between customer and provider.

I have already mentioned my dislike for the *fettina,* but fortunately some Italian beef, especially the well-known *razza chianina* from Tuscany, can be fantastic, especially in its best-known form – the famed *fiorentina,* or T-bone steak. Unfortunately, from my point of view, Italians have some very rigid ideas about how to grill beef; they insist that beef on the bone – and filet mignon, too – should be downright bloody, and not simply rare or medium rare, which is the way I, personally, like it. Knowing nothing about barbecue, they also insist that charring meat on the outside is a no-no and that it should never be turned more than once. And on this they often refuse to budge.

The result is that I have had repeated arguments in restaurants and once even got up and walked out of a *trattoria* when the chef refused to make my *fiorentina* as I wanted it. What happened to that old adage, the customer is always right? His only solution was to slice the meat open and cook it further (this happens sometimes when I order filet mignon as well). But that means you end up with well-done meat, which is not what I want. On these occasions, I've tried to explain that we Americans know a lot about grilling and barbecuing and that it is indeed possible to grill a steak so that it ends up pink inside without being too burned outside to eat. Occasionally, I've even found a restaurant where the chef is obliging. But so often does it become a problem that for the most part, when I want beef I order *tagliata,* sliced steak, generally served with either *rosmarino* and truffles or with balsamic vinegar and *rucola,* and which is usually delicious. If I want a "real" steak, I buy it from the butcher and then take it home and grill it myself.

This kind of mental rigidity in a country that prides itself on its creativity is surprising, but the *fiorentina* is not the only example. At my gym, one of the city's best, the caféteria is inexpensive and the food, for the most part, is not bad, except for the cooked vegetables. It would appear that many Italians still don't know that the best way to cook vegetables is to steam them and that vitamin-wise, the less they are cooked the better, and the Italians working in the gym's kitchen can be counted among them. It would appear that they leave brussel sprouts or broccoli boiling on the stove until someone remembers that they are there, and which, consequently are served limp and mushy. And there is no getting them to change. "*Piacciono così* – People like them this way," is what I'm told.

Once I asked the owner of the well-known Trastevere bakery, Valzani, which specializes in Sachertorte, if she could make me a Sacher with chocolate between the layers rather than jam. "*Impossibile!*" she barked. "*La Sacher è così e basta* – Impossible! The Sacher can only be made like this, that's all there is to it." And more recently, I asked a butcher where I often shop if he would make me some *spiedini* (kebabs) without any pork. He absolutely refused. If I wanted the *spiedini* without the pieces of red pepper he generally includes he would do that, but I couldn't ask him to *fare una cosa che non aveva senso* – do something that made no sense. Um. Er.

I thought I'd mention that in Turkey, Morocco, Tunisia and so forth where Moslems don't eat pork, no kebabs have pork. But there was nothing to be done. "*Non sono musulmano,*" he insisted – "I am not Moslem." So I went to the *ferramenta* – the hardware store – bought the wood sticks one uses for *spiedini*, went to another butcher, bought the meat and made them myself.

But if the newly modern Italian life-style means that for many people here great food and long-lasting meals have been relegated more to evenings, holidays and Sunday lunches, they still remain a very central concern for the average Roman, and this is something that anyone who knows Italy is well aware of.

Take that humorous, comparative ranking of capitalist systems that some time ago appeared on the Internet in the form of the "you have two cows" jokes that parody introductory economics courses. For Japan, the joke runs: "You have two cows. You redesign them so they are one-tenth the size and produce 20 times the milk. Most are at the top of their class at cow school." What do American with two cows do? "You sell one cow, lease it back to yourself, and do an IPO on the second. You force the two cows to produce the milk of four. You are surprised when one cow drops dead. You spin an announcement to the analysts that you have downsized to reduce expenses. Your stock goes up." And what about Italy? The jokesters were not far off the mark when they put the pleasure principle first. "You have two cows, but you don't know where they are. While ambling around, you see a beautiful woman. You break for lunch. Life is good." And indeed it is.

Chapter 33 – Farmacia (Part Two)

The entire team at the *farmacia* was a likable bunch. But if Franco, Enzo and Paola were all quite *simpatici,* I have to admit I have always had a particularly fondness for Riccardo, the SSN doctor, even now that I've given up all thoughts of trying to seduce him.

When I first got myself put on Riccardo's list, transferring from another, older Health Service doctor located near Piazza Navona who lost my custom after suggesting a vacation in the mountains as a cure for an attack of hives, I found him very attractive. About 5'7" – my favorite height in a man – and with cropped, pepper-and-salt hair that made me think of a shorter, Italian George Clooney, Riccardo was a type that really appealed to me. But once a couple of subtle come-hither comments on my part fell loudly into the void, I put the idea out of my mind. Riccardo may well be one of those Italians who does not cheat on his wife. Possibly he has an ethical sense that would preclude him from getting involved with a patient. Or maybe I simply don't appeal to him.

A *calabrese* who is one of six children, Riccardo moved to Rome years ago and restricts most of his visits to his native region to Christmas, Easter and summer vacations. As a *medico di famiglia,* a family doctor, he has office hours three mornings and two afternoons a week. There is no system of making appointments and the wait can be long, although eventually he did introduce a new system to speed things up. This allows people who have merely come for a prescription renewal, or for a sickness certificate to justify having missed one day (or in a journalist's case, two days) of work, to sneak in between two patients needing a real examination. And pharmaceuticals salesmen must wait until two patients have been seen before they get their turn.

Generally, however, I go armed with copious reading matter or, these days, with my iPad on which I've installed Sudoku and a variety of solitaire games. But more often than not, I find myself listening to the chitchat, or even joining in, for there is no doubt that the small waiting room is really an excellent venue for a slice of *la vita trasteverina* and for Italian life in general.

The majority of the people who crowd Riccardo's waiting room seem to be seniors who are clearly not among Italy's most prosperous citizens. The Italian health system offers substantially (although not totally) free health care for everyone, including the likes of Silvio Berlusconi, Italy's second or third richest man, although I highly doubt he has ever (at least since he became rich) availed himself of it. Some people – those who can afford it or who have private insurance – prefer to get treated privately and others (like myself) kind of mix the two. If I can get what I need quickly – say, a bone-density test, a flu shot or a sonogram – I might do it with the health service, the SSN. If it is something that will take longer but that I want to do quickly, like an MRI, I will do it with the excellent journalists' health insurance policy I have paid for over the years. But even where that policy is concerned, some visits to Riccardo are a necessity. The policy, understandably so, will not reimburse me for any pharmaceutical that the SSN distributes gratuitously or almost gratuitously, and to get any such medicine the prescription has to be written on the special SSN prescription pad that all SSN doctors have. But he will also write me other prescriptions on a plain white doctor's pad if I tell him that I spoke to my gynecologist on the phone and she told me to buy this or that. And then, too, since he happens to be a good doctor, I go to him if I am simply sick.

In Riccardo's waiting area – a small rectangular room with wooden benches along both of the longer walls – conversations generally hinge on health-related questions, including the dysfunctions of the national health system, other bureaucratic tangles, or on important neighborhood events, like the time a group of residents from nearby Via Garibaldi managed to win the "Enalotto" biweekly lottery with a numbers system they'd been playing for years. Each one walked away with about $200,000 except for the *carabiniere* who just that week had decided not to participate and was consequently grinding his teeth in despair. But any important news event can get great attention – as long as it's not related to politics.

Murders, particularly unsolved ones, get a lot of attention. Not so long ago one of the most impassioned topics in the waiting room, as well as in bars, trains and buses, was the debate raging between *innocentisti* and *colpevolisti* – those who supported the innocence and those who assumed the guilt of – Annamaria Franzoni, a young mother from Cogne, a tiny northern Italian mountain hamlet, accused and then convicted of the bludgeoning to death on January 30, 2002, of her younger son, a three-year old *bambino* named Samuele, or

Sammy. Her story was that she found the boy dying when she returned to the house after a ten-minute absence to walk her older son, Davide, to the school bus stop on the road. Arrested shortly after the crime, but almost immediately released from jail by a judicial review panel, in July 2004 Franzoni was convicted of murder and sentenced to 30 years in jail, which on appeal in April 2007 was reduced to 16 years. In 2008 the sentence was reconfirmed by the court of last resort, the *Corte di Cassazione* but she has never admitted her guilt.

"It's a tiny, out-of-the-way village where an outsider would have been noticed immediately. It must have been her. Who else could or would have done it?" insisted Signora Maitani, a sixtyish Trastevere *casalinga*, or houswewife, who was sitting across from me one day when the entire neighborhood seemed to have the flu. Like the majority of Italians, she is convinced that Annamaria is guilty and may have even blocked out her memory of the murder. "Obviously, something in her mind snapped," she added. "But there's no real proof!" retorted Signora Lamberti, a heavy-set woman with huge, swollen legs. "It could very well have been a passing vagabond, or a madman, or maybe even a jealous neighbor," she said heatedly.

With fewer than 600 homicides a year, Italy is non-violent enough for murders, especially unsolved ones, to have the same kind of national impact that the O.J. Simpson trial or the murder of JonBenet Ramsey had in the United States. Furthermore, with few exceptions – one being the so-called "Monster of Florence" who between 1968 and 1985 committed eight double murders, the victims of which were primarily couples parked in lovers' lanes – there have been few serial killers here, no Sons of Sam, Ted Bundys or Jeffrey Dahmers, not to mention the all-too-common horrors wrought by American snipers, rapists and gun-toting American high school students. So today in Italy some people still talk about the hideous kidnapping and sexual torturing of Donatella Colasanti and Rosaria Lopez (the latter murdered) in October, 1975. Older folk in Rome still shake their heads over the 1958 murder by strangulation of Maria Montanari by electrician Raoul Ghiani, who had been hired by the woman's husband, Giovanni Fenaroli, to kill her so he could benefit from a life insurance policy he had taken out on her. And the entire country goes through a trauma – and verbalizes about it – when a child is involved, for example when, early in 2006, Tommy, the two-year old son of a post office manager in Northern Italy, was kidnapped and inexplicably murdered.

Ghiani and Fenaroli were captured and sentenced to life, but normally in Italy the wheels of Justice turn very slowly – and creakily – providing an abundance of grist for the conversation (and speculation) mill. In Rome, although it seems hard to believe, an Italian court recently exonerated the fourth suspect charged with the August, 1990 murder of 21-year old secretary, Simonetta Cesarini, in her office in downtown Via Poma. It took 20 years for her Filipino houseboy to confess (in 2011) to the killing of Contessa Alberica Filo della Torre, strangled in July 10, 1991 in the bedroom of her luxurious villa in Olgiata, the prosperous, gated-suburb outside of Rome. And prior to little Sammy's murder, there were two other serious post-2000 crimes which captured the "popular" imagination in Italy and which led to *tante chiacchiere* – much chatter – in Riccardo's waiting room. One was the mysterious death in January 2001 of Contessa Francesca Vacca Agusta, an aging and imperious beauty, widow of a wealthy Italian arms manufacturer. Until her death, the Contessa lived in a cliffside mansion not far from Portofino in Liguria with her former, younger lover, Maurizio Raggio, her latest (and, as it turned out, last) lover, a Mexican playboy who inherited most of her wealth, and a young woman whom she had taken under her wing. When she disappeared people immediately decided it was foul play. Instead, after her body washed up in France several weeks later, it was ruled that it had been an accidental death; she apparently fell off the cliff after some heavy drinking or dope-taking.

Next came the brutal murder on February 21, 2001 of Susy Cassini De Nardo, a 40-ish northern Italian mother, by her teenage daughter, Erika, and the latter's would-be boy friend, Omar. The fact that the pair not only knifed Signora De Nardo to death with something like 120 stab wounds, but also killed Erika's 12-year old brother, Gianluca, by drowning him in the bathtub, shocked people profoundly, as so it should have. But those crimes, as publicized as they were, received less media attention than Sammy's murder because a mother being murdered is never quite as bad as a mother being a murderer

In contrast to the near furor, and biting anti-Italian reactions that it inspired back home, the murder of Amanda Knox's roommate, Meredith Kercher, did not really stir Italian passions. This may be because most of the people involved, except for Amanda's then boyfriend, Raffaele Sollecito who was acquitted with her in October, 2011, and like her is now to stand trial once again, were foreigners and mostly students whose lifestyles were very different from those of the average Italian. The Meredith Kercher murder has put the Italian justice system itself on trial. First, Amanda and Raffaele were convicted and sentenced to 25 and 26 years in jail. Then on October, 2011, they were acquitted on appeal. The appeals trial then was annulled and in January 2014 the two were reconvicted although Raffaele is free on his own recognizance until a third-stage appeals trial before the Italian supreme court is held and Amanda, as most Americans know, is already back in the U.S. and it is unclear, should the conviction be upheld, whether or not Italy would try to extradite her. What a mess

When Riccardo is not at Piazza della Scala, he is busy doing house calls for the very sick, another service provided almost free of cost (depending on one's income) to every Italian resident. I've only had to call Riccardo to come see me at home twice in the last ten years, but both times I felt uncomfortable about not paying, since indeed I could afford it. According to the current regulations, the *medico di base,* another name for the family doctor, is now allowed to have at least 1,500 patients on his or her list, for each of whom he is paid roughly 85 euros a year depending on the region. Additional payments, for certain kinds of medical certificates, can bring a health system doctor's income up further. But this is all before taxes, and before expenses, which include equipment and paying for a substitute for holidays. "It's a salary, although not a particularly good one," shrugs Riccardo. However, he does work only as a family doctor, whereas others I have known have multiple specialties and therefore earn even more. My friend Raffaele holds office hours five times a week for SSN patients but also functions as a vascular specialist, a rheumatologist, a nutritionist, and a psychological counselor, having taken extra courses to qualify in each of these specializations. Can he possibly keep up in all of these *materie,* I wonder? Sandro, an orthopedist I go to who is a whiz at treating certain kinds of back pain with *mesoterapia*, local injections done with tiny, tiny needles, has a private orthopedic practice but three mornings a week and two afternoons also operates as a *medico di famiglia.* I recently sent my friend Ron to him for an excruciatingly bad case of hemorrhoids. "I was kind of surprised when he didn't even examine me," Ron recounted later. "But he did give me the right medication and a few days later I was fine."

Signing up on Riccardo's list was not hard, but it did get me involved in yet another bureaucratic tangle. As a foreigner – but this was before I got a full-time job with an Italian newspaper – I had to go to a special office to sign up for the SSN and, despite the fact that I then had a four-year *soggiorno,* or Italian residence permit, I nevertheless was required to renew my SSN enrollment card or *tessera* every January, which meant bucking huge crowds of other people in the same situation. I got around this by making sure I didn't get sick in January and putting off the renewal process until sometime in February, but it was annoying.

Then the office got a new director who was – *rara avis* – an efficiency-minded Roman. This man, let's call him Piero Bianchi, and who has now retired, came up with a simple but, for Italy, revolutionary idea. Why not stagger the renewals, he said, asking me if I would mind having only a ten-month card for the first year so that it would expire in late October rather than on December 1st. "*Per niente,*" I replied, "Not at all" being only too glad to avoid the renewal hassle. For that matter, meeting Bianchi was an eye opener.

Most of my Italian friends are left-wing and back then probably would have refused to even speak with Bianchi since he was, as he told me up front when we struck up the first of our many conversations, a card-carrying member of *Alleanza Nazionale.* (AN, which subsequently merged with Silvio Berlusconi's *Forza Italia* to form the PdL, the People of Freedom party, was the more acceptable, post-1994 version of the *Movimento Sociale Italiano*, the post-World War II remnant of Mussolini's Fascist party.) Although there were a few diehard pro-Mussolini nuts in the party, most of AN's members appeared to be committed democrats to whom one ought no longer refer to as "*i fascisti*". One wing of the party was particularly committed to dealing with social issues and Piero belonged to this group and seemed passionately dedicated to getting a better deal for the country's growing numbers of Third World immigrants. "Can't you get your paper to do a story on their housing problems?" he'd ask. "Or can you suggest whom I can write to about immigrant hospitalizations?" he'd query. Before retiring he made me an exceptional gift, a non-expiring *tessera* to go with my new permanent *permesso di soggiorno,* a sort of green card you can now get after having been here legally for six years.

A *medico di famiglia*'s chief function is to diagnose what ails you and then prescribe medications, diagnostic tests or visits to a specialist. As I said, unlike some of his colleagues, when you are sick Riccardo will actually examine you. But he is also unusually conscientious and sticks to the rules, which means he won't prescribe anything for someone he doesn't know and won't give you a medication he doesn't think you really need. This sounds good but can backfire. An Italian colleague who also lives in the neighborhood had a problem. An immunologist she consulted about her recurring genital herpes prescribed a medication originally prescribed only for herpes zoster (St. Anthony's fire), saying he'd had good results when it was taken every day as a prophylactic. The medication is expensive and the journalists' health insurance refused to pay for it because it would be free if prescribed by a health system doctor. But Riccardo wouldn't prescribe more than two boxes because the Ministry of Health had labeled it only for the treatment of shingles, which often after an initial bout generally does not return. My friend thus had to pay for the medicine herself. In the end, she wrote to the Health Ministry and, although it might have been a coincidence, only a couple of weeks later the drug was reclassified so it could also be used for the treatment and prophylaxis of herpes simplex. She was annoyed with Riccardo because of all the money he had caused her to spend during the preceding year. But I told her we owed Riccardo a lot. To save money, and rightly so, the journalists' insurance plan refuses to reimburse us for class A medicines (those paid for by the state). This means that if a specialist prescribed us a class A pharmaceutical, we have to go to Riccardo and ask him to rewrite the specialists' prescription on the SSN's special red and white prescription forms. Riccardo finds this extremely irritating, but does it. Which is why I always give him a gift at Christmas, be it wine, *prosecco*, some newly pressed olive oil or French cheeses that I have brought back from Paris.

On the other hand, Riccardo does not do things like bandage cuts or put in stitches, things for which you have to go to the *pronto soccorso*, the emergency room, of the nearest hospital. Most family doctors don't have enough insurance for any kind of emergency treatment and, furthermore, many don't want to spend the money for such things as sterilization equipment. Riccardo also does not give shots, which in Italy are, along with suppositories, often used in preference to pills on the grounds that this way the pharmaceuticals do not pass through the stomach. If you need a shot, you either have to find someone in the neighborhood who gives them as a way of making money (your neighborhood pharmacy generally has some names) or –

since lots of ordinary Italians know how to give shots – you can ask one of your friends.

I periodically suffer from back pain, and when I have an episode, I use a "cocktail" of anti-inflammatory and muscle relaxants to unblock me. When that happens, I have a choice. For years I relied on my physical therapist-masseur, Tommaso, who in that period came twice a week anyway, to give me the shot. Or I can call on Cristina, another physical therapist in the neighborhood with whom I am friendly. Marco, one of my close journalist friends, in a pinch will bicycle over on his way to the Vatican which he covers for a major Italian daily. Once, the men's locker-room attendant at my gym, a guy named Wilmer who also suffered from back pain and knows what it means, drove across town at 10 p.m. to give me a shot. I could also ask for help from Claudio, a jeweler down the block. And Daniela, who runs the *edicola*, the newsstand, at Bolsena, has a magic touch, unfortunately learned because of the long-drawn out illness, in the end fatal, or her husband, one of the town's most-loved *vigili*. Once in an emergency I turned to my long-time friend, Minni. But she was so bad at it, I immediately crossed her off my list. Tommaso says I should learn to give myself shots, but that is something I just don't think I could manage.

Chapter 34 – Pretty (i.e. Sexy) Is As Pretty (i.e. Sexy) Does

It is August 22, 1994, and I have just returned from a vacation on a Greek island with some Italian friends, which was enjoyable except for the fact that my fellow travelers seemed unable to unplug from the gossip of Italian journalism and the intricacies of Italian politics. I had taken a new translation of the *Iliad* with me, thinking that it might be a good idea to re-read it *in loco*. Unfortunately, I kept getting caught up in discussions about who was likely to be the next editor of *Corriere della Sera*, the country's major newspaper, about whether or not former prime minister Giulio Andreotti, now deceased, had indeed kissed a Mafia chieftain on the cheek, and if former Socialist prime minister Bettino Craxi, who had fled to Tunisia (where he later died) to avoid prosecution on corruption charges was, in fact, guilty. "Might as well have stayed at home," I had more than once found myself thinking. But, oh, was the swimming great! It's been decades since, with the exception perhaps of Sardinia and smaller offshore islands such as Sicily's Aeolian Isles, Italy could offer a holiday-goer seawater as clean and clear as that in Croatia, Egypt, Greece or Turkey where many Italian vacationers now head.

Back in Rome, wandering around my largely shuttered neighborhood, it becomes clear that the old rituals still hold. "*Ben tornata* – welcome back," the postman says to me, and I have to reply "*Ben trovato* – good to see you." Then it's *ben tornata* and *ben trovati* with Goffredo, my former, now retired plumber, and his wife Pinuccia, *ben trovata* and *ben trovato* with Gianni, the caretaker at the museum in the piazza and again with Laura, who owns the shop called *La Ciliega* where (before it closed and was turned into a café) I often went to buy a T-shirt or scarf or just simply for a chat. I know this will go on for weeks, as I will continue to bump into people I haven't seen since before the summer vacation. However even now, a week after the *Ferragosto* holiday (August 15th), the city still seems pretty much bemired in its summer doldrums, a product of the long-standing Italian tradition of shutting down all factories in August and thus encouraging myriad suppliers and other businesses to follow suit. A few days earlier the Metro section of the Rome newspaper, *Il Messaggero,* had trumpeted "*I romani sono rientrati*! – The Romans are back home!"

In Trastevere, however, the majority of shops – food and otherwise – are still shut and I have to walk several blocks under a hot sun to find a bar where I can get my morning coffee. My hairdresser is closed, as is the hardware store, the upholsterer, the picture framer and the dry cleaner. Even the neighborhood's only laundromat is shut, probably because the maintenance people are out of town. Need a plumber? Forget it, he is almost certainly *in vacanza*. Need to get your driver's license renewed? Better to wait until September when the motor vehicle bureau will be fully staffed. Want to get the kitchen ceiling painted? Well, maybe, if you can find a Romanian or Egyptian immigrant who really needs the money and can't afford (yet) to think about vacations. And if you are renovating a house or an apartment, take care to start *i lavori* way before the summer holidays or to hold off until afterwards. Because if you need to order fixtures or furniture and you try to do it in June (or, for that matter, in late November, when Christmas is nearing) you will be told that the usual 60-day waiting period (sixty days!) will now be extended to ninety.

On the upside, I find that downtown in Via del Corso where the bureau of my former newspaper was then located, there are scads of places to park my moped, another unusual luxury. Furthermore, the newspaper's fourth-floor offices are largely deserted, a skeleton summer staff having been supplemented by a group of journalism-school interns who don't seem to have much else to do but rewrite the agency wires. I was looking forward to getting through some of the backlog I had left on my desk before leaving for vacation, but, alas, I had forgotten that Carlotta, a sometimes friend who worked for a news agency in the same building, was also back from her vacation and, as she was quick to tell me when we met in the elevator, was deeply in the doldrums.

Carlotta and I had once socialized, but by then, except for idle chat on beauty treatments and fashion house sales, we didn't have much to say to one another. Intelligent and hard working, Carlotta, 45, is also a top-class Italian social climber, although one of her redeeming qualities is that she is perfectly frank about this. Another is that she is admirable in the depth of her determination. Journalism, she told me once, was for her above all a ladder to social advancement, and she frequently telephones the potentates she has interviewed (nowadays, Italian journalism seems to consist primarily of interviews) to find out if he or she liked the way she has used their quotes. "Did you read me today?" she'll purr. "Did you see what great exposure I gave you?" she'll bubble. When she published her first book, a modest collection of essays, it was, she confided, primarily "a calling card" and every time I stopped by her office for a chat, I was forced to overhear countless telephone conversations about the cocktail parties, TV appearances and round tables she'd successfully engineered for herself. The most important thing, she once told me, harshly critical of my having resigned myself to the backseat position to which the new editor of my paper had relegated me, was visibility, visibility, and more visibility. And when I told her I really didn't care about visibility, I could see her regard for me drop sharply.

A tall, thin brunette whose father was a respected high school principal in a small, provincial city, Carlotta's bad mood had been caused by the fact that after taking her sailing for a week in the Aegean (in a manned, 18-meter ketch rented for the occasion for a hefty $25,000), her married lover – an older, extremely wealthy, top state manager from the North – had artfully disappeared for 36 hours and had spent the time, she soon discovered, closeted in a provincial hotel with a 35-year old art gallery owner. Having an affair with a married man is always difficult, and Carlotta was doubly hurt: she thought she'd pulled off a real coup by getting her lover to leave his wife behind for part of August, and now she finds that he was two-timing her as well as his spouse.

The summer's misadventure had left Carlotta extremely worked up and though, normally, she doesn't bother even to ask me how I am, this time there was no one else to talk to about her desperate plight. So I listened, and listened and listened, reminding myself that it was sociologically interesting to meet in the flesh one of those women one reads about who grow up convinced that position – and money – are the only things worth caring about. Not surprisingly then, these have been the most important qualities in her choice of men. Divorced from her builder husband whom she married because she mistakenly judged him a real mover and shaker, and whom in the end she had nudged to the altar only by getting pregnant, of late she had been extremely absorbed with her current, semi-clandestine affair. Mr. X,

20 years her senior, is extremely rich and clearly fond of her. But he has made it clear he is never going to break entirely with his wife, and therefore does not like to be seen publicly with Carlotta. However, since he was extremely generous with his money – for a while he put a monthly amount into her bank account, bought her a car, and paid for part of the apartment she recently bought as a long-term investment – she seemed willing to grit her teeth. Her only complaint in the economic realm, she said, was that he had never spent more than the equivalent of five thousand dollars on a present for her! Wow!

Since Carlotta is also very serious about her job, her attitudes belie a sort of female schizophrenia. This is not all that surprising since there is still a lot of confusion in today's Italy about what it means to be a woman. Today, Italian women make love when and where they want to, have abortions (too many) and, increasingly, live with their boyfriends and have babies without even getting married. They now work in almost every sector; they drive buses, fly planes, clean the streets, direct traffic, carry guns if they are soldiers or police, run businesses and, though to a much lesser degree, are surgeons and even more occasionally police chiefs, bankers and top-ranking newspaper editors. Nevertheless, according to OECD, in 2011 only 46.5% of Italian women were working, either full time or part-time. And if that percentage is significantly lower than most other developed countries including the U.S. (62%), France (59.7%), the U.K (65.3%). or Germany (67.7%), this is only in part because of an absence of adequate social support structures that make a woman feel she has to choose between being a mother or holding down a job.

The fact is that to a degree many Italian women still seem somewhat reluctant to leave behind their past and assume a full role in modern society. Until the elections of February 2013, when the percentage rose to slightly over 30 percent, there were fewer women in the Italian parliament than in any other major European country. In general, Italian women's salaries lag further behind men's than elsewhere. And on TV, as I have already mentioned, although there are many female newscasters, women appear mostly as entertainers and their image is based on sex, beauty and youth.

There are sexpots in every country, of course. Aren't we Americans the purveyors of the wet T-shirt contest, lap dances and pole dancing? But in Italy these admirable areas of human endeavor appear almost to have made their way onto prime-time TV: few evening programs forgo the ample cleavages and puffy lips of the so-called *veline* or showgirls who generally play second fiddle to a *simpatico* but not very attractive male host. And I wonder what other Western country had one porn star in Parliament and gave prime-time coverage to an interview with another porn star, the late Moana Pozzi (beautiful and intelligent she reportedly died of Hepatitis C, which is after all a sexually transmitted disease)? What about Berlusconi, who just recently was convicted of having sex with Ruby, an underage prostitute, and for using his influence as premier to get her released after an arrest on robbery charges? Aside from his by now notorious parties with bevvies of beauties, the former Italian prime minister repeatedly has made beauty and sex appeal requisites for women chosen as candidates for his party. Some of those turned out to be women of quality. Others less so.

One example of the latter group is Nicole Minetti, a former dental hygienist with other ambitions whom Berlusconi managed to get elected as a well-paid councilor in the Lombardy regional assembly in 2010, when she was only 25 and was totally without political experience of any kind. Minetti, who looks as if she had most parts of her redone, in July 2013 was convicted in the Ruby trial of aiding and abetting prostitution. Not only was she the person who, in October 2010, on Berlusconi's bidding, went to to take charge of Ruby when she was released from prison, but the court held that she had been involved in organizing Berlusconi's meetings with the underage prostitute. In March 2013, a Sicilian regional minister lost his job after saying that in recent years, the Italian parliament had been filled with "whores". But it is generally believed that at least some of the women Berlusconi had gotten elected (remember, in the current Italian parliamentary election system, being put high up on a party's list more or less guarantees you an MP's position) had, indeed, slept their way to election.

The fact is, although of course this is a generalization, a large percentage of attractive Italian women seem more inclined to want to grow up to be sex objects than anything else. And often their families seem to approve. When Berlusconi was casting around for young women to attend his parties, some of which ended with some of the women spending the night and possibly sharing his bed (the details were rarely clear), it was startling to learn that some were encouraged by their mothers. If they got close to Berlusconi, even if it meant spending a night with him, wouldn't it be worth it if along with the presents he regularly distributed, they might get help in finding a good job, or even getting into television? Oh boy!

By the way, in Italy there is also, apparently, a widespread conviction that blondes do have more fun, otherwise one cannot explain the seemingly inordinate number of Italian women, compared even to neighboring France, who dye their hair blond or even platinum blond. Although the last two Miss Italias have been brunettes, as are most of the country's male soccer stars, the overwhelming majority of TV announcers are blond, blonder and blondest – at least from the neck up.

Since his wife continues to live in their Northern Italian home, Mr. X does manage to spend quite a bit of time with Carlotta, and although she chafes at the limitations on their social life, most of the time the situation is bearable. And why shouldn't it be? In many ways, Carlotta has it made. She and her former husband, who have two daughters, still share the same apartment, which allows her to take advantage of his hands-on fathering, not to mention the live-in baby sitter and the family chauffeur. But from time to time things become difficult because, despite his age, 69, her paramour is clearly still prone to periodic sexual cheating. Furthermore, by raiding his cell phone and address book while he was asleep or in the shower, she was able to keep track of Signor X's escapades. At one point she even had him followed by a private detective. "He'd kill you if he knew," I tell her. But she is defiant. Her snooping is legitimate, she says, because, "I need to know with whom I am dealing" and because, she says, after seven years she believes her rights are the same as a wife. I think this is nonsense and tell her so. But the real problem is his having all that money, which clearly has a lot to do with her willingness to continue in the same diminished role. Evidently, she can't decide between whether she wants to be a journalist or a kept woman. Probably, she wants to be both.

Chapter 35 – Beauty is as Beauty Does (Or Perhaps Not)

*B*ella, bello, bellissimo, bellissima, belloccio, bellona, bellezza. Barring certain curse words, the word *bello*, or its derivations, may well be the most frequently utilized word in Italian.

"*Ciao bello*," you say to your pal when you phone him. "*Ciao, bellissima*," you say to your girlfriend when you bump into her on the street. "*Che bello!*" you say when your friend says he is going to the Seychelles for a month-long vacation. "*Che bello!*" you repeat when the waiter brings you a heaping plate of rigatoni. The castle, cathedral or panorama *è bellissimo*. The waiter who has been working out, and it shows, is *belloccio*. The sexpot across the hall is a real *bellona*. "*Buongiorno, bellezza*," you might say to your little girl when you wake her up in the morning. Or if you are a man courting a woman you might well tell her that she is *una vera bellezza*, that her eyes are *bellissimi*, her mouth is *bellissima*, that she has *un bel corpo* and *un bel sorriso*.

In Italy, in fact, Italian women, or shall we say a large proportion of them, are indeed beautiful, or at least extremely good at making themselves appear as such. This is not, of course, because they drink Acqua Rocchetta mineral water, although that company would like you to think it is.

The company's slogan is "Puliti dentro, belli fuori – clean inside, beautiful outside", and one of their recent newspaper ads ran: "We are a people of beautiful women: 15% are blond, 82% are dark, 10% are tall, 31% have light eyes, 69% dark eyes," and claimed that its product, endorsed by Cristina Chiabotto, a former Miss Italia and by the now-retired Juventus soccer hero, Alessandro Del Piero, is *molto utile per la tua bellezza* – very useful for your beauty. Italian women are beautiful in part because centuries of the cross-breeding among various branches of Indo-European peoples has had undeniably fortunate results. But also because from the time they start walking, or perhaps even before that, they are told how important it is to be beautiful and consequently spend a lot of time and energy cultivating that aspect of their being. And this is reinforced by the role given to women by the advertisers and the media.

I have already mentioned the way in which female beauty – and female nudity – is used in Italian advertising, even though much of Western Europe and North America got over it some time ago. In a story from a few years back, *Financial Times* reporter Adrian Michaels related how passengers getting off planes from Milan were greeted by an enormous poster of a woman's cleavage to advertise the business products of Telecom Italia, and how both Rome and Milan were plastered with billboards of three scantily glad computer-generated damsels advertising the cell phone provider named "3". As for Italian television, semi-nude dancers or nearly naked show hostesses are the rule and have been for the last 20 years. No quiz show or variety show is without its *vallette* (think Playboy bunnies without the tails and ears) and even Striscia la Notizia, an extremely clever evening news spoof, dotes on its two wiggling, pom-pom girls, one brunette and one blonde. Not surprisingly, every season thousands of young Italian girls show up to try out for the two Striscia La Notizia parts, roles that would guarantee them, at the very least, a future on the pages of Italy's gossip magazines. What are the prerequisites? Charm, an ability to gyrate gracefully and, of course, beauty. No, not just beauty, rather perfection or something close to it. In Italy the emphasis on beauty (real or artfully obtained) is such that one often hears men term as "brutta" – ugly – women who are just plain, or even normal. And as for older women, forget it. We are simply off the radar screen. Men, too, have not escaped the beauty trap and like males elsewhere are increasingly resorting to a variety of beauty treatments to make themselves more appealing. But as we all know, a male's attractiveness to women, or at least to many women, often depends more on his wealth, fame and influence, otherwise there'd be no explanation for the success of some men, especially of the older variety – like Berlusconi – with the opposite sex.

Beauty is generally theorized as having something to do with proportions. The Greek philosopher Pythagoras spoke of objects proportioned according to what he termed a Golden Ratio, and in subsequent centuries ancient Greek architecture sought to follow rules of symmetry and harmony, as did the later Greek and Roman artists, defining the standards for Western male beauty as later Renaissance artists did for female beauty. Obviously, over time these standards have somewhat changed. But in recent centuries they have been fairly consistent, the difference between Italy and other countries, at least to my mind, being that here many people define beauty in terms of flawlessness.

It is probably axiomatic that a surfeit of emphasis on superficial beauty can undermine the development of the inner person and lead to the neglect of what most of us would term more important values. Early on in my life in Italy it therefore occurred to me that if an excessive concentration on beauty, and therefore on appearance, can negatively affect the individual personality, couldn't it have the same effect on an entire people? For me, personally, this represents a veritable paradox because what I truly loved about Italy during the first years I lived here was precisely the importance given to beauty in the broad sense. Compared to the United States, where ugly seems to be the guiding light for many towns and where linoleum, garish store signs and luncheonettes with plastic counter stools caused me near physical pain, Italy offered nearly unadulterated beauty. People's physical attributes were only part of it; the rest involved clothing and accessories, art and architecture, *oggettistica* or objects, food (and the context in which you ate and enjoyed it), and of course the country's natural beauty, which for most of us does not just mean its hills, shores, woods and mountains, but the juxtaposition of all of those against the architecture of the past.

Many of us Italy freaks are almost likely to swoon with joy when we round a curve in the road and see a small, stone hill town perched on the next sloping rise. Think of all those Florentine and Umbrian painters who rarely neglected to include a skyline or sketch of this or that city against the panoramic background of their Annunciation or *Madonna e Bambino*. Sure, this was in part to point out the difference between the spiritual and the temporal spheres of human life, or to do honor to the birthplace of this or that patron. But even then it must have been obvious to anyone with some sensitivity that, in those days at least, there was a strict relationship between the kind of architecture you chose for your palaces and public buildings and one's natural surroundings. Villages and towns were built with local stone and clay, thereby assuming the colors of the environs. For strategic reasons these towns were generally built on a hill or promontory and therefore appeared to be a natural emanation of the latter rather than something superimposed on them by calculating contractors. Add to this the fact that in much of Italy – excluding the Alps and some other parts of the North – the climate has been temperate with lots of sunshine during the day and cool breezes in the evening and the pleasure (beauty) factor is complete.

So what happens to a people who for centuries devote maximum time and attention to enjoying the benefits of "beautiful" surroundings? I exaggerate, of course, because we all know that throughout Italian history and even during the effervescent Renaissance years, many people here were peasants, workmen or soldiers too poor, and far too weary, to pay attention to cool breezes and glorious sunrises and the tang of a special sauce or the spicy *ripieno* (stuffing) of a lovingly roasted bird. But their masters and rulers certainly did pay attention. And since those are always the people who create the values of a civilization, they were inevitably passed on down to the next generations. It wasn't just simple materialism; that is a condition that touches many people, especially when they become affluent. But if beauty and pleasure come first for an entire people, if that's where they place their greatest energies, wouldn't it be easy for them to be lulled into a state of inactivity or at least dullness when it comes to resolving boring, practical difficulties? Who can say? But if that were the case this would, indeed, be a paradox. The cultivation of beauty and pleasure – the thing that makes Italy so appealing to us foreigners – may prove to have made them less capable than others of efficiently managing the needs of a modern society. If you concentrate on immediate pleasure, how well equipped are you for thinking about the future? In fact, although often brilliant, sometimes imaginative, and definitely amusing, as a people Italians are not known for their organizational skills. So while other countries are building bridges and tunnels, Italy is talking about it and doing next to nothing. While some 15 years ago, France managed to turn strike-ridden, inefficient Air France into Europe's most profitable major airline, in Italy Alitalia was, and still is, trembling on the brink of bankruptcy. And let's face it, even creativity has suffered. With World War II and the postwar years of defeat, destruction and poverty now oh, so far behind them, Italians of late have produced very little of distinction in art, literature and film.

It's hard not to reach this dire conclusion after years and years of seeing problems go unresolved and at times totally unaddressed. For decades now the Italian newspapers have been writing about the crowded, dangerous and unfinished Salerno-Reggio Calabria *autostrada*, and despite repeated promises by one government after another, so far the situation remains unchanged. The disastrous situation of garbage disposal in Naples and the surrounding area has been broadcast repeatedly throughout the world and yet no permanent solution has been found. Every summer, and I mean *every* summer, Italy is plagued by forest fires deliberately set by arsonists, and yet the country's authorities do not seem to have developed the databanks and intelligence that would help them put people behind bars or work preventively to avoid a new outbreak. Venice is still cursed with the high waters that every winter threaten hygienic conditions and make life there difficult, and a new threat has emerged with the increasingly frequent port stops of mammoth tour ships that cannot but damage the lagoon. And closer to home, local administrations, for example right here in Rome, appear totally unequipped (or unwilling) to clear the sidewalks of Trastevere, Piazza Navona and even those adjacent to St. Peter's of the hordes of illegal vendors selling counterfeit items or, let's face it, just plain junk.

Obviously, the beauty (pleasure) factor is not the only thing that explains the absence of effective government action, or the impression one often has that many in Italy seem to confuse talking about an issue with actually getting down to resolving it. But a case can be made for saying that, as a people, Italians are distracted from concentrating on everyday affairs by the importance given to pleasurable pursuits, be that planning for and going on vacations, shopping, decorating their homes, buying new cars and driving them (too fast), and, in general, having fun. Foreigners are always saying things such as "Ah yes, the Italians, they really know how to live." One hears this all the time. But is that really the case? I mean, in the end, if you can have a great lunch but you don't know where your two cows are, how long-lasting is that happiness going to be?

Chapter 36 – The Republic of Unshared Pears

"**I** would really like a pear, but they are too big. Will someone split one with me?" This, in 1949, was Luigi Einaudi, the second President of the new, postwar Republic of Italy, when, at a lunch he was hosting for journalists and intellectuals at the majestic Quirinale Palace, the major-domo arrived bearing a silver tray laden with luscious-looking fruit. The anecdote, originally related by the man who volunteered to split the pear with the President, the late writer Ennio Flaiano, is quoted in the runaway 2007 political bestseller, *La Casta* – The Caste – to dramatize the difference between Italy's political leaders in the immediate postwar period and those who followed.

Einaudi, a well-known economist and journalist who in 1945 had also been head of the Bank of Italy, was then 74 and came from a generation of Italians horrified by the twenty years of Fascism and for whom public service had been a noble tradition. Clearly, he had also been deeply affected, at least intellectually, by the poverty of the war years, poverty that was so extreme that when, in 1947, Prime Minister Alcide De Gasperi travelled to Washington D.C. for the first time, he was forced to borrow an overcoat from a fellow Christian Democrat, Attilio Piccioni. Against his principles, De Gasperi also agreed to accept the gift of two valises from a luggage company so as not to arrive in the American capital looking like a poverty-stricken immigrant. (Flaiano, by the way, ended his original account with these words: "A few years later, the Presidency passed to another and the rest is history. For Italy it was the beginning of the Republic of Unshared Pears.")

The authors of *La Casta (Rizzoli, 2007)*, Gian Antonio La Stella and Sergio Rizzo, two highly respected journalists from *Corriere della Sera*, are clearly not happy with Italy's current leaders; the book's subtitle is "*How Italian Politicians became Untouchables*", and the near-record sales in a country where books generally sell fewer than 20,000 copies showed that hundreds of thousands of Italians agreed with them even before the startling election results of February, 2013 when a new party, the Five Star Movement, ran away with 25% of the vote.

We all know that corruption, abuse of power and selfishness exist in every country and, unfortunately, that politics often attracts people who share those defects in the extreme. But in Italy, a Western European country in the Greco-Roman tradition where, especially given the presence of the Roman Catholic Church, one might have expected certain values to have taken deeper root, the situation appears acute.

The country's leaders have not known how, or wanted to know how, to channel resources into productive action that would benefit the common good. Rather, they have repeatedly directed them to unproductive activities such as subsidies to political parties, fancy cars for high-level bureaucrats, consultancies for so-called free-lance experts, armed escorts for hundreds of politicians even though terrorism here is, if not dead, then at least dormant.

Extremely depressing reading for anyone who had hopes for this country, the 250-page volume makes it clear that along with the distracting obsession with beauty and pleasure, current-day Italy is badly governed because of the untrammeled greed of its so-called ruling class – the authors call it "collegial bulimia" – intent primarily on preserving its own privileges and, secondly, on creating more of them.

These privileges, as well as the prestige of being a party leader, also explain in part the broad opposition among politicians here to any change in the current electoral law which would, by setting higher election thresholds, reduce the number of political parties (at the moment 16 are represented in parliament). For years now there has been talk, but no action, about reducing the 945 members of parliament (deputies and senators combined), and of changing the structure and responsibilities of the two houses so they are no longer mirror images of one another. Furthermore, well into 2013, Italy continues to be afflicted by a severe case of ideology-itis, another major stumbling block to any country intent on dealing with and resolving practical problems.

Here are some of the more shocking pieces of information and situations revealed in the book, some of which have been published and confirmed elsewhere. As for the others, I am assuming that the two reporters, who are considered among the best in the country, have checked their facts, but of course I can't swear to it.

Unlike the U.K. where any citizen can consult the Civil List to learn the expenditures of the royal family, the Quirinale Palace, the residence and seat of operations of the Italian Republic's President, does not detail its expenses for the perusal of Italy's citizens. Furthermore, at the time the book was written, the Qurinale's budget (subsequently reduced by President Napolitano) was 224,000,000 euros ($305.5 million) more or less four times that designed to support the residence of Queen of England. If you exclude military personnel, slightly more than 1,000 people work for the Quirinale, including (in 2001) 45 chauffeurs, 59 artisans (the Queen apparently has 15), and 115 gardeners. In contrast, the West German Bundestag has 160 full-time employees, Buckingham Palace 433, and the French Elysée, again excluding military personnel, 535. The annual gross cost for a Quirinale employee is 74,500 euros; in Britain the comparable figure is 38,850 euros.

Italy has more members of Parliament, 952 if you include the small number of appointed Senators for life, than any other European country. This works out to one MP for every 60,371 Italians, (the corresponding number for France is 66,554, for Germany, 112,502, and 91,824 for the U.K.). Even more startling, and this is a figure that makes it clear why many are asking for change, the total number of elected officials in Italy – considering all levels of government: national, regional, provincial, municipal and city districts – is mind - boggling: 179,485. The salaries and perks enjoyed by parliamentarians also are reportedly unparalleled in Western Europe. Italian MPs take home something like 15,706 euros a month (as a point of comparison, my last year at *Il Sole 24 Ore* my excellent salary was roughly 4,000 euros a month, which was about twice as much as a well-paid company employee and two and a half times that of a factory worker.

But this is not all. Italian MPs also get an incredible number of special privileges including an additional 4,000 euros a month to pay their assistants. Despite calls for reform, many of these elected officials keep the money for themselves and do without an assistant, unofficially referred to as a *portaborsa,* a bag-carrier, or use it to pay these generally young gofers a smaller fee under the table, keeping the rest for themselves, even though this is patently illegal. Another 3,100 euros a year is theirs for trips abroad. They also travel free on toll highways, trains, planes and ferries and do not have to pay for movie or theater tickets. Their bank accounts accrue no charges, unlike the ones most Italians have, and pay higher interest rates. And for those who are not re-elected to a second term, it is no doubt comforting to know that when they reach the right age they will nevertheless qualify for a very generous life-time pension (more or less equal to their salary). Furthermore, despite their high salaries, they pay less to eat at the Parliament's in-house restaurants than, say, street sweepers in Venice pay at their company's caféteria. Again at the time of the book's publication, at the Chamber of Deputies, a portion of *lasagne* went for 1.59 euros, a main fish dish, 3.53 euros, a portion of bread, 52 cents. And to make the disparities with the common man even more blatant, public agencies that own real estate continue to sell apartments to politicians and other dignitaries at cut-rate prices that they would never offer to any of us.

Non-elected parliamentary personnel are also raking it in – relates the book – being paid according to a pay scale that would make most Italians green with envy. The barber at the Italian Senate, the book says, earns 130,000 euros a year to cut – free of charge – the hair of all male senators (women senators get a special hairdresser allowance!). The Chamber of Deputies' three doctors were earning 250,000 euros a year apiece. After an economy move in 2006, two were convinced to leave, each of the two reportedly receiving severance pay of 1.25 million euros. And not to be outdone, the Italian MPs in the European Parliament are also the highest paid, with a base annual salary (not including perks, travel, assistants etc.) of 149,215 euros. The next highest paid in 2006 were the Austrians with 105,527 euros and the Germans with 84,108 euros.

Incidentally, another perk enjoyed by MPs and other government officials here, and one which costs the Italian Treasury millions, is their armed escorts. Clearly, police escorts, sometimes two to four policemen or *carabinieri*, other times more, were first assigned for good reason during the 1980s when "red" terrorism reared its ugly head here, taking at least 430 lives. And Mafia violence has destroyed countless other lives. But the issue of the *scorte* has since taken on a life of its own and turned into a major status symbol. More than a decade ago in 2001, Berlusconi's Interior Minister decried the fact that over 6,000 men and women were being used to escort politicians and other dignitaries for a total outlay of 1,100 billion lire, three times that spent by Spain and the U.K. which had their own terrorism problems. From time to time, cuts have been made, but in January 2007, 654 people (including 84 politicians) were still accompanied by full-time armed police.

When Silvio Berlusconi was prime minister in the early part of this millennium, he had 81 bodyguards on his detail, about the same number as the Israeli secret service needed in 1976 to free the hostages held at Entebbe in Uganda by Palestinian and German terrorists. And was there any good reason, the book's authors ask, why in the summer of 1999 the then Interior Minister, Communist Oliviero Diliberto, had to take two bodyguards with him when he and his wife enjoyed a six-day vacation in the Seychelles? True, Diliberto paid for his own vacation, but the state had to pick up the tab for room, board and who knows what else for the two policemen, leading critics to wonder why the minister hadn't picked a place close to home where local police could have done the same job.

Another ongoing issue concerns the state-owned limos, called *auto blu* because of their dark blue color, a real status symbol in Italy, and something just about anyone who is anyone in public life will demand and get. It is not uncommon for it to be revealed that such cars have been used inappropriately for travel or for shopping excursions by wives and daughters rather than for real office needs. But aside from this, these powerful, chauffeur-driven cars are extremely costly for the public administration. After cuts in 2010, in early 2012, there were still 64,524 in circulation. At that time, the Quirinale palace, the Supreme Court and the two hourses of Parliament had 37 at their disposal, and thousands and thousands are owned or leased by regional, provincial and city governments and by every type of public or semi-public utility or company, even the most obscure such as the National Institute for the Protection of Wild Fauna and the Higher Institute for Olive Oil Production. It should be noted than many Italian bigwigs, say Supreme Court justices or former prime ministers, are allowed to keep their *auto blu* for the rest of their lives.

One incredible episode recounted in the book involves Giancarlo Galan, then the president of the Veneto Region and a man I knew well when he first arrived in Rome in the early nineties as one of the team engaged by Silvio Berlusconi to devise a structure for the new party that was to call itself *Forza Italia*. To me he seemed like a decent, principled guy. But if the story Stella and Rizzo tell is true, power and privilege surely went to his head. According to the book, in January 2007, Galan and his 12 regional commissioners decided to scrap the Region's former cars and lease an entire new fleet, the principal requisites – spelled out in a the official offer – being that all the cars have diesel motors of 3,000 ccs, a width of 180 cm, a length of 480 cm, leather seats, satellite navigators, four-wheel drive, automatic air conditioning units, parking sensors and, among other things, back seat cigarette lighters. This meant that the only makes possible were Alfas, Audis, Mercedes and BMWs, all capable of doing 300 km an hour in a country where the maximum speed limit happens to be 130 kph. When the region's executive council's decision became known, there was widespread criticism including from three of the Veneto region's highest-ranking prelates, whose comments received ample space in local newspapers. Galan's reaction was to threaten that he would respond with a cost-cutting campaign the first victim of which would be the social programs so dear to the Catholic Church. Later he denied having been serious and as a concession agreed to cut the number of *auto blu* – from 13 to 12. But the entire episode was definitely what in Italy one would call *una brutta figura*, something you do of which you should be ashamed or embarrassed.

Many Americans dislike the fact that the US has, and has had, political dynasties such as the Kennedys, the Bushes and, perhaps, the Clintons. But here, too, Italy is not to be outdone, with scores of MPs (not to mention university professors and even low-level bureaucrats) stepping aside for their offspring, siblings or other relatives. And for those of us back home who decry junkets, what to say about the 1986 visit to China by the late Socialist prime minister Bettino Craxi in which he was accompanied by over 100 people, or the time a 120-person delegation of the Sicilian Region travelled to Oslo to learn how to organize a cycling championship? The Campania Region once took 160 people to New York to the annual Columbus Day parade.

In one year, 2005, the two houses of parliament together spent over 20 million euros in air travel (twice what Italy gave that year to counter hunger in the world). And then there are the planes bought by the government itself. Since 2000, Palazzo Chigi has owned four A319 Airbuses, planes that when used commercially have a range of almost 7,000 km and can carry 124 passengers. Its fleet also includes seven Falcons, two helicopters and another three Falcons assigned to the secret service. The cost of all these planes was 65 million euros. And yet, notwithstanding this, in the last year that Silvio Berlusconi was prime minister his government managed to spend 180,000 euros a day in official flights and 65 million euros to rent additional planes. It would appear that Italian cabinet ministers and other dignitaries believe that traveling first or business class on commercial flights is somehow beneath them. And all this in a country where infrastructures are decaying, recession is at the door, and many normal people, thanks in part to the price hikes that followed the introduction of the euro, are having trouble making ends meet.

In April, 1993, Italians went to the polls in a referendum to decide whether the country's system of public financing for its political parties ought to be continued or abolished. The result was overwhelming: 90.3% of those who voted wanted to eliminate the subsidies that the parties had been receiving for decades and wanted them to finance themselves. What happened? Since putting an end to the state subsidies would have caused many political parties to go bankrupt, opposing ideologies were brushed aside and, as soon as passions died down and it was decided that the *vox popoli* could be safely ignored, parliament came up with a variety of ways to get around the referendum's result. They came up with a system of *rimborsi elettorali*, that provides the parties with "reimbursements" that are far, far superior to the money that the parties actually spend during election campaigns. For a couple of years while I was working for *Il Sole*, I covered this issue and was almost convinced by party treasurers that some sort of public subsidy was the only way to make sure that political parties could be protected from having to rely on lobbyists, good and evil (read organized crime). But the current situation is ridiculous, since despite the referendum, the parties now have more public money than they ever had before and which far exceeds their actual expenditures.

Five years ago, when they wrote their volume, Stella and Rizzo estimated that since 1976, taxpayers had paid a total of 3.5 billion euros into party coffers. More recently, and specifically following the Five Star Movement's success at the polls, a new government moved to modify the election subsidies mechanism, but it is too soon to say if any real changes will result. But this is only part of the story. Every year some 60 million euros are given to Italy's party newspapers, even though the genuine party papers are read by practically no one and even though many of those receiving the subsidies are merely publications set up by faux political movements of one kind or another precisely for the purpose of qualifying for the funding. Not surprisingly, the country's lawmakers have also passed other laws helping their parties to survive and in turn to help themselves: the government pays the social charges and pensions of employees of private and *public* agencies who are given leave to work for a political party; parties can set up foundations to which people and businesses can leave money or make donations and, the biggest *beffa* or hoax of them all, an Italian who gives money to a political party gets a bigger tax break than one who give donates funds to charity.

Italy's politicians have also closed ranks, repeatedly, every time someone lucid proposes that the country's 109 provinces be abolished, since these administrative structures have very few important, substantive functions and those they do have, like overseeing high-school construction, could easily be taken over by the 20 Italian regions or the nation's 8,000-odd *comuni* or municipalities. In 2013, Prime Minister Enrico Letta issued a decree-law (an act subsequently to be approved by parliament) abolishing the provinces only to be told by a high court that to do so he would, first, have to change the Constitution. But the provinces do have a purpose, that of providing the parties (these figures are from 2007 but are unlikely to have changed much) with some 4,200 high-paying high-level positions – presidents, vice-presidents, commissioners and assemblymen – to distribute among friends, supporters and acolytes, as well as jobs for about 57,000 employees who, supported by taxpayer money, have very little to do of any great importance.

Another way of winning friends and influencing people is that of the famous *consulenze*, thousands of well-paid special consulting assignments handed out, despite the fact that the number of people employed by the Italian civil service, nationwide, was already a staggering 3,350,000, of whom 57,000 work for the provinces, 81,536 for the Regions and the remainder for municipalities and ministries. A report published by *Il Sole* revealed that 900 million euros were spent annually in *consulenze,* while many full-time government workers sit twiddling their thumbs, faking medical certificates so they can stay home "sick", or asking friends to punch in and out for them.

This litany could go on forever, but at the risk of boring the reader even further, I would limit myself to only one additional item. *La Casta* opens with a truly incredible piece of evidence of ruling-class shenanigans. There is a law in Italy that offers special subsidies to what are called *comunità montane*, mountain towns that suffer economically from depopulation, geographical isolation and poor infrastructure. Much of Italy is mountainous so this makes sense, but what about Palagiano on the Taranto plain in Puglia? It is exactly 39 meters above sea level and has absolutely nothing mountainous about it, and yet thanks to a 1999 boondoggle by the Puglia Region ruling that towns *near* some kind of a hill can be classified as *comunità montane* and therefore can qualify for certain kinds of assistance and the right to set up an office, get a budget and give one or more people some kind of job. But then again, the authors point out, to create benefits – and more jobs to distribute – local administrators in Calabria once invented a lake at Piano di Lacina and a vast plantation of centuries-old olive trees underwater in the port of Gioia Tauro.

Chapter 37 – Divided We Stand (Still)

United we stand, divided we fall. The slogan (as we Americans should know) is a great one, but one which here appears to fall on deaf ears. Ever since the decline of the Roman Empire (and indeed even before the Empire's founding, when battling tribes warred over its fertile lands), Italy has always been a bitterly divided country. Thousands of years later, the only major difference is that – normally – blood does not flow in the streets; instead, it is verbal venom and ideological intolerance that run wild, interfering with the thoughtful decision-making that should be at the basis of good government.

Ancient Rome conquered the world but at home, peace lasted only a few centuries. First, there was the division between the Western Roman Empire, itself gradually split asunder among the so-called barbarian tribes, and the Eastern Roman Empire. Then Sicily and the Italian South were tormented by Muslim invaders first and Saricens later, and then invaded by Franks and Carolingians, whose successors established the Holy Roman Empire which had its own designs on Italy.

At the start of the 11th century, ruling monarchs in France, England, and Spain began to consolidate their national power, setting up institutions to help them govern. In Italy, however, the papacy stood in the way of such a development, and the country was divided, on the one hand into a series of city-states, dukedoms, principalities and maritime republics that fought and made peace at regular intervals and – on the other hand – the papacy.

Starting in the 12th and 13th centuries, much of the country was divided between Guelphs and Ghibellines, factions supporting, respectively, the Pope and the Holy Roman Empire, a protracted conflict that over time also involved France, Austria, Spain and Germany and which culminated in the 1527 Sack of Rome. Warfare – on land and on sea – was almost constant and in the decades (and centuries) following, there was more internecine fighting, followed or accompanied by foreign invasions. These curtailed or ended the independence of many of the peninsula's once-powerful city-states so it is fair to say that up until the Congress of Vienna in 1815 (and also for a while after that), the history of Italy was characterized by foreign domination.

Violence and conflict – from within and without – were also recurring themes of the 19th century, largely revolving around the gradual but inexorable move towards Italian unification that culminated in the capture of papal Rome in 1870 and the establishment of an almost united Italy under the aegis of the Piedmont-based House of Savoy. But unification was not to bring social peace. Along with the breakdown in relations with the Vatican state, or what remained of it – a conflict healed only by the 1929 Concordat between Church and State – the first part of the 20th century brought to the fore new differences regarding both Italy's international standing, that is in its relations with its allies, and the social and political structure of the country.

Despite having fought on the "right" side in the First World War, the country paid a huge price for its participation in that conflict – more than 600,000 dead and significant economic consequences. And the widespread dissatisfaction that resulted from a post-war settlement seen as the consequence of scandalously bad treatment by Italy's allies is recognized as having played an important role in dictator Benito Mussolini's rise to power. The installation of the Fascist regime consequently took place against a background of social unrest that saw the haves and the have-nots increasingly on opposite sides and the political representatives of these two groups increasingly at odds with one another. And this situation could not but be exacerbated by World War Two, the downfall of Nazi-Fascism and the onset – and prolongation – of the Cold War.

Why this brief summary of Italian history? Italy is surely not the only country where political divisions have been harsh and invasive. During the 20th century, similar situations existed in many other European countries. And in our own country, red and blue contrasts are often sharp enough to make polite political discourse something to be longed for. But in the case of Italy, we are speaking of centuries rather than of decades of conflict and hatreds. And if the lines of division are not the same as in the past, today they remain sharp enough to make government extremely difficult; it is often as if the country's principal political groups had totally lost sight of the common good and are not happy unless they have someone not simply to compete with electorally, but to downright hate and despise.

When I first came to Italy to live, the major line of division was between Communists and non-Communists. The Left was substantially Marxist in orientation and the Right was dominated by pro-Western forces such as the Christian Democrats and some smaller non-Catholic formations, with a rump version of the Fascist party on hand to make just about everybody furious. The Cold War was in full swing and the United States therefore helped in keeping this Right-Left animosity alive: it effectively vetoed any idea of the Communists as a legitimate political party long beyond the time in which it was clear that no matter what financing that party was receiving, or had received, from the Soviet Union, it was not a subversive force and had (long before) accepted Italy's multi-party democratic system as well as its membership in NATO. At that time, the animosity between Right and Left was such that most of my left-wing friends would not even speak to a right-winger, and even if they did, you could be sure they did not count any among their close personal friends, a sectarian context that may have contributed to the years of terrorism that today most Italians appear, shamefully, to have forgotten. Today, the contours of the "battlefield" have changed despite the fact that until only recently right-of-center politician Silvio Berlusconi was still wont to carry on about *i comunisti,* the communists, even though no one under the age of 25 could even possibly know what he was talking about, the once-powerful Italian Communist Party having long since morphed into a rather amorphous left-of-center political organization.

For the last 15 years at least, "combat" has been waged primarily between the "Berlusconiani", who claim there is a conspiracy headed by left-leaning magistrates to make sure Berlusconi ends up in jail (and there is indeed little doubt that a hefty number of Italian magistrates have forgotten that their job is to enforce the law, not to make it), and the huge swath of Italians who despise Berlusconi and who think he is either a crook, a sleaze or a threat to Italian democracy, or all three.

Why does this matter? As I write there is a government in power that one would call a Grand Coalition, in that it includes parties that normally are opponents. To ward off a period of unprecedented political instability after a national election resulted in a stalemate among three political groups, the PdL, Berlusconi's party, and the PD, the biggest left-of-center group, agreed to govern together, even though they are generally archenemies who spend their time insulting one another. There is no way of knowing how long the government will last, but it is fair to say – despite a lot of talk about "pacification" – that the outlook in the long term is not promising. So far not a day has gone by in which representatives of one or the other side has not failed to criticize or insult his or her counterparts. True, politics is often largely the stuff of argument: watch the British Prime Minister addressing the House of Commons or tune in to C-Span to watch a session of the U.S. Congress and this becomes obvious. But often it is mostly posturing. In Italy, after centuries of practice, it really seems more like unadulterated hatred. Which means that lawmaking and overall government frequently end up on the back burner.

Chapter 38 – Little Yellow One

"**C**iao Biondo – Hi Blondie," says Giancarlo to the client who has just walked into the bar and ordered an espresso. But there's really nothing at all blond about Kader, who is a very dark-skinned Tuareg from Algeria and the owner of a small shop that sells North African imports about half-way down Vicolo del Cinque. Now a naturalized Italian, Kader is only one of a number of foreigners from third-world countries who have set up businesses or are working here in Trastevere, as well as elsewhere in Rome or in Italy at large.

Farther down Vicolo del Cinque there are the two restaurants owned by Tony (for the vital statistics office, Moanm Hammad), an Egyptian who came to Rome 30 years ago as an illegal immigrant, washed dishes in a downtown restaurant and for a while shared a miserable apartment with eight countrymen. Around the corner in Via della Scala until just recently there was a jewelry store, featuring mostly silver and semi-precious stones, owned by another Egyptian, Walid, 30, and his uncle. At the pizzeria next door, during the day the take-out slices are made by Ali (yet another Egyptian). Until two yeaers ago when the pizzeria changed hands, sales were handled by Fadel, a Jordanian Palestinian who has been here 18 years and who, like Tony and Kader, is married to a Roman woman. Once I asked him if his wife had converted to Islam and he laughed and said, "Don't be silly, she's more Christian than you are."

"You can be sure of that," I replied rather cryptically, since because of his outspoken hatred of Israel, I'd always avoided telling him and Ali that I was Jewish. (Eventually, I did so and now when I wish them Happy Ramadan they offer Rosh Hashanah or Sukkot greetings in return.)

Fadel and Ali taught me to say *sabah el cher* (good morning, in Arabic) to which one is supposed to reply *sabah al noor*. But Fadel preferred to greet me every morning with a rousing "Ciao, Brooklyn," which, try as I might, I could not get him to change into "Ciao, Manhattan," since that is where I am from. When he does, it comes out "mon-HAA-tan" but he puts a lot of energy into it. Fadel says he would like to move to Australia because he thinks it's a place where there'd be a lot of opportunity. But it's hard to imagine his wife, Luisa, and two sons being very keen on leaving their home.

Other third-world foreigners in the neighborhood don't seem anxious to go anywhere. About 100 meters away in Vicolo del Cedro is a small antique instruments shop run by Mosen, an Iranian who came to Italy as a refugee after the Shah's overthrow and who seems unlikely to go anywhere except, perhaps, back to Iran if the regime there should ever disintegrate. And just 100 or so yards away at the *Tana de' Noantri* on the corner of Piazza San Egidio and Via della Paglia, the cooks turning out the restaurant's delicious *rigatoni all'amatriciana* and its *carciofi alla romana* are two Egyptian brothers, Mustafa and Ahmed, who have been in Italy since the late eighties. Hired in the early nineties by the restaurant's owner, Erminio Salviati, when the old Roman chef left, they are now a fixture in the restaurant and have learned to cook most local dishes as well as any Roman. The one exception, to my mind, is *carciofi alla giudea,* artichokes, Judean style, although I don't believe this is even remotely political in nature.

Since *La Tana* is located on the ground floor of the building in which I lived for 30 years, it is not surprising that Erminio and I go back a long way. Once stocky and smiling, he is now thinner and grayer, having suffered two heart attacks and, apparently, a great deal of stress from running this restaurant which until recently had a staff of 17 full-time workers, and this in a country where there are so many laws and by-laws that it's amazing any businessman can keep his sanity. When I first started eating there, Erminio had a partner, a congenial younger cousin named Mimmo. At some point and for reasons I have never been privy to, Mimmo left and opened a bar near the Pantheon and then, unexpectedly, died. Today, Erminio's right-hand men are his two sons-in-law, Maurizio and Mauro. Also on staff are Maurizio's younger brother, Roberto, who makes no secret of the fact that the younger generation is dying to take over (but for that to happen, Erminio will, literally, have to die) and Cristina, Erminio's daughter, who works in the evenings as the cashier.

In Italian *tana* means a den where an animal would take refuge and in Roman dialect, *La Tana de Noantri* means literally "our den" or, more liberally translated, "our cozy place" or "our hangout". From my personal point of view, this could not have been more appropriate. For this large, spacious *trattoria* that is neither cheap nor expensive and has a long and varied menu featuring good solid Italian food, with a few

Roman specialties thrown in, is where I've eaten countless dinners with friends and boyfriends, shared meals with any number of visiting journalists or other American visitors, and where, after a trip away from Rome, I inevitably rush on my first night back to eat a giant plate of *rigatoni all'Amatriciana*. It is also the place where I once roasted my Thanksgiving turkey when, having confused kilograms and pounds (I was then newly arrived), I ended up with a humongous bird that simply wouldn't fit into my oven.

Not surprisingly, I have long been on a first name basis with all the waiters at the Tana. But most amazingly, over the years Erminio himself has done me more favors than I can count. As Giancarlo would do years later, Erminio always kept a set of my spare keys hidden in his cash drawer, an essential for a person such as me who has a bad habit of locking herself out of the house. And for someone who has always hated going to an Italian bank, it was great to have Erminio downstairs to cash a check or, if necessary, to lend me some money. Then, too, whenever I didn't have time to cook, which was often, I could stop by the restaurant and Erminio would fix me a plate of cold hors d'oeuvres and vegetables to take upstairs. And he has been an invaluable friend in whatever emergency, for example whenever my back has gone out and I have been housebound. "Erminio, can you make me some pasta?" I would ask over the telephone. And up the stairs would come Loreto, the slight, gray-haired, wisecracking waiter who until his retirement was my favorite, or chubby, smiling Massimo, or tall, skinny, balding Gino, with a steaming plate of *spaghetti aglio, olio, peperoncino* or some other kind of Italian comfort food. Another time, two of the Tana's waiters carried a chair bearing my elderly mother, who was visiting from New York, up two flights of the building's very steep stairs to my apartment. Once Roberto, then only 19, came upstairs to kill an enormous insect that I found quite frightening. And if I needed a drop-off point for packages – or traffic tickets (which, unbelievably, are often delivered by hand) – there was never any problem.

At the *Tana*, one of the most interesting recent developments was Erminio's decision to move Mainul, a Bangladeshi who started out as a *mozzo*, a vegetable chopper, from the kitchen to the *sala*. The main reason for his promotion to waiter, which Mainul has been managing brilliantly thanks to his growing command of Italian, was, says Erminio, "because you can no longer find young Italians who want to

309

learn this trade." But it was also a coming to terms – like it or not, and many Italians do not – with this country's new reality: that Italy, like other European countries, is gradually becoming multicultural and multiethnic.

There is nothing new about foreigners in Trastevere, or for that matter in the rest of Italy. In ancient Roman times, for example, this area – the so-called Trans Tiberium (the area "across", that is, on the other side of the Tiber River) – was the place where foreigners settled, foreigners in those days being mostly Jews from Palestine (there were reportedly dozens of synagogues here), Syrians, as Arabs were then referred to, and early Christians who for the most part were simply Jews who had converted. Much more recently, artists, writers and expats from Northern countries settled here. But this is nothing surprising since from the days of the European Grand Tour, Italy as a whole, and Rome in particular, has always been a Mecca for upper and middle-class non-Italians, whether they be aesthetes, sensualists or downright sybarites.

Today's phenomenon is totally different. Over the last three decades, immigrants from Latin America, Asia, North Africa and Africa have been pouring into Italy in the hopes of finding a better life, or at least a way to make money to send home to their needy relatives. This is, of course, a European-wide phenomenon, but it is particularly striking in a place like Italy where for centuries the population has been extremely homogeneous, even stiflingly so.

Unlike countries like Britain, France, Belgium and even Holland, where the colonial empires of the not-so-distant past had brought the native population into frequent contact with peoples of other hues, Italy – despite its early 20th century incursions into Somalia and Ethiopia – had remained nearly "intact". When I first arrived in Rome in the early 70s, nearly everyone you saw on the street – on buses, in cafés – was white, and almost certainly a baptized Catholic (Jews and Protestants amount to fewer than 100,000 people in a country of over 57 million): quite boring really and a huge change from my home town of New York, where rainbow diversity has long been the order of the day.

Today, things are radically different. In 1970, two years before I arrived, there were only 144,000 legal immigrants in Italy, fewer than the number of Italians who went abroad that same year to seek work. Today, slightly over five percent of the Italian population, and that is some 3.03 million people, are legal immigrants and this number is expected to double over the next ten years. So if Italy still lags behind Germany and France in the number of its legal immigrant population (no one is quite sure how many illegal immigrants there are), and if it ranks behind the U.K. and Belgium in the proportion of the population that is foreign-born, the social fabric of the country nevertheless is in enormous flux. The numbers regarding schools – close to over 500,000 immigrant children, representing four percent of the school population – give an idea of the magnitude of the change; a genuine cultural shock for a people who say they're not racists but who are nevertheless having trouble absorbing the newcomers, the overwhelming majority of whom have arrived uninvited and have been legalized thanks to Italy's generous history of repeated amnesties. Too generous, say some, convinced that such a policy may well have contributed to encouraging ongoing illegal immigration.

This illegal immigration question is most noticeable – and most irritating to public opinion – during the summer months, when good weather and calm seas allow countless boats with their desperate human cargo to land in places like Sicily or the islands of Lampedusa or Pantelleria, filling shelters to the maximum and creating all sorts of sanitary and legal problems.

The law requires forced repatriation in most cases, but that is more easily said than done since many of the immigrants arrive, probably deliberately, without identification. But here, too, things have been changing. In the nineties, the biggest influx by sea was from nearby Albania but subsequent bilateral agreements between the two countries have significantly reduced that traffic. Now, as has also been happening in Spain, most new (and uninvited) arrivals come from Africa, and there is no respite in sight. As it is, *clandestini* are believed to amount to several hundred thousand, but a firm figure would be difficult to come by.

At the moment, the "new Italians", those who are here legally, can be divided roughly into two categories: those whose main goal seems to be spending enough years here to make enough money to eventually go home and set up a small business, possibly with the help of a small Italian pension, and those – a far smaller group but one which is growing – who seem to be truly interested in becoming Italians. But whatever their goals on arrival, in the long run their presence here is bound to have a profound effect on this society.

Whatever Italians might prefer – and many are ambivalent – one day, and not so far in the future, there will be more than a few Asian bus drivers and coffee-colored policemen and women. The government formed in the spring of 2013 boasted the first black cabinet minister, a naturalized woman doctor originally from the Congo, who, it must be said, has had to endure insults from several politicians and a good number of "normal" citizens alike. Unlike elsewhere in Europe, however, well over half of the immigrants are Christian in origin – Filipinos, Latin Americans, Poles, Rumanians, Ukrainians and Croats – meaning this latter-day wave of immigration may (may!) turn out to be less traumatic than elsewhere where the proportion of Muslims is significantly higher.

But turning Italy into a country which appreciates its growing rainbow characteristics has been slow going, especially since upward social mobility is going to take much longer here than it has in places like the United States, a young country built by immigrants, or Canada, which is actively seeking recruits for citizenship. In the first place, as a group Italians seem to have lost all collective memory of their own immigrant past, decades in which they braved unbelievable hardships, poverty, language difficulties and discrimination in order to settle in countries as far away as the United States, Latin America, and Australia and consequently tend to be startlingly intolerant of the new foreigners' linguistic shortcomings or cultural differences. Some years ago, I overheard Emilio, now deceased but then 72, who ran a grocery with three of his five brothers and sisters, cursing under his breath because the soda truck delivery guys, Sri Lankans I believe, spoke such poor Italian. *"Non capiscono niente,"* he was grumbling – "They understand nothing." When I piped up saying, "Ah yes, and just think that's exactly what they said about the Italians some 80 years ago in New York," he stared at me and then, visibly chastened, added in embarrassment *"Ha ragione, Signorina, ha ragione* – You're right, Signorina, you're right."

This attitude can be explained in part by the fact that, although many of the immigrants who have come to Italy in the last couple of decades have had some higher education or indeed are college graduates (12 percent as opposed to a seven percent, overall, of Italians), so far most have been channeled into those menial, low-skill or heavy-duty jobs that Italians no longer want. Whatever their education levels, they are for the most part factory workers, house cleaners, domestics and, increasingly, *badanti* or eldercare workers. Filipinos, Sri Lankans, Cape Verdians, Latin Americans and Poles tend to specialize in those household jobs. Egyptians and Bangladeshis are cooks, dishwashers, and gas station attendants. North Africans, Rumanians and, again, Poles, are housepainters and construction workers. In the South, the immigrants, sometimes illegal, sometimes here on seasonal contracts, work as migrant farm workers, tomato canners and fishermen. In the Italian North, thousands of foreign laborers, including many Africans, work in factories and, according to industrialists in some areas like the Italian Northeast, the presence of the newcomers has now become essential to ongoing production. Given the sharply low Italian birthrate, without the immigrants, who now account for 9.4 percent of live births, there simply aren't – and won't be – any people to take those jobs.

In the United States, our regrettable history of racism and discrimination has led us to become so aware of ethnic differences that most of us generally bend over backwards not to risk offending someone. In Italy, this is not the case, and since political correctness has yet to take root here, you still find newspaper headlines saying "Moroccan rapes woman" or "Croat runs over child". Although in France it is no longer considered acceptable to order a coffee by asking for *un petit noir*, a small black, in Italy a coffee with milk and chocolate is still called *un marocchino* – a Moroccan. Not all that long ago, a sports broadcaster covering gymnastics referred to an Asian woman contestant as *la giallina*, the little yellow one. And some many years ago I was inspired to write an irate letter to *Corriere della Sera* to complain about a headline that read, literally, "Mark Spitz, the Jew, wins Olympic Gold", rather than "Mark Spitz, the American, wins Olympic Gold".

The journalist who wrote the article, the late Paolo Bugialli, called me to apologize, insisting he'd had nothing to do with the headline, and we became good friends. Several years later, however, when he was stationed in Madrid, I went to visit him and his wife, Serena, and discovered it had probably been his doing all along. I was staying in a hotel but eating all my meals at their place. One day Paolo said to me, "Tonight you'll find a compatriot, a *connazionale*, of yours at dinner," and I thought to myself, "Ah, a fellow American." Guess again! The new guest was a woman from Milan who was... Jewish. And although many, many Italians, especially in big cities like Rome, Milan and

Turin, have some Jewish relatives, there is still a significant amount of low-grade anti-Semitism. At some point during my life here, I remember having decided to avoid mentioning that I was Jewish if it weren't strictly necessary, having gotten tired of hearing supposedly funny quips every time I mentioned something that had to do with money, although to be fair Italians make the same comments about people from Genoa or, alternatively, from Scotland. And what do you say when a friend refers to someone wealthy as a *rabbino,* a rabbi. They don't have the slightest idea that to some the term might be offensive.

The ambivalence of many modern-day Italians towards Jews is probably not hard to explain. Anti-Semitism has profound, historical roots that go back centuries in all of Europe (1492 was not just the year that Columbus discovered America but that in which Spain expelled all its Jews and Arabs). And the English and the French had already done the same thing more than a hundred years earlier. But in Italy, where the Roman Catholic Church was paramount for centuries, a temporal as well as a spiritual power, discrimination against Jews was institutionalized in dogma and to an astounding degree.

In 1555, Pope Paul IV decreed the establishment of the Rome Ghetto and, in a chilling precursor of things to come, ordered that when during the day they were outside the ghetto, Jews wear distinctive yellow hats or shawls to set them apart. That ghetto was the last in Europe to be closed in 1870 (the French Revolution had done away with France's ghettos almost a century earlier), only 135 years ago. And as long as it lasted, Jews were not allowed to own property and could only exercise a very limited number of professions. So however deplorable, might it not be that many Italians were so "used to" anti-Semitic regulations that they didn't really recognize the infamy of the "racial laws" enacted by Mussolini in 1938? And even today, although they surely know that during the war large numbers of Italian Jews, were deported to the Nazi death camps and never returned, there is little acknowledgement of what kind of things went on.

It is often said of the Italians that as a people they have a very short historical memory. And, in fact, there is rarely any talk about the extremely harsh discrimination introduced by those racial laws even before World War II broke out. From one day to the next, Jewish students had to quit their studies, Jewish professionals were barred from working with Gentile clients, Jews could not have non-Jewish domestic help, their names could not be printed in the phone book, they couldn't use public libraries (from which all books by Jewish authors were removed), their property was confiscated, and many were interned. Although many non-Jewish Italians did help and befriend their Jewish friends or neighbors, hiding them after the German occupation, a huge number also took advantage of the cash incentives introduced by the 1938 laws to Italians who provided the names and addresses of anyone who was Jewish.

Most Italian Jews would be horrified to hear themselves compared to today's immigrants, and that is not in fact my intention. But the history of this country's Jews shows that even though the Italians pride themselves at never having arrived at the excesses of Adolf Hitler's Germany (nor have I ever heard of "restricted" resorts or schools that my Jewish parents' generation had to deal with in the United States, even as late as the 1950s), Italians don't have a fantastic track record in dealing with those whom they consider "different".

Another aspect of the "New Italy" that may slow down integration is the fact that almost 50% of the foreigners now living in Italy are in services, a huge proportion being housekeepers – reportedly close to 500,000 compared with only 100,000 or so Italian women or men who still do work of this kind.

Incidentally, in a country where an astounding number of people employ part-time or full-time housekeepers, it is fair to say that if Italians were Americans, practically no one would be eligible to become Attorney General: at some point in time, just about everyone I know had a cleaner who was not legal or for whom he or she did not pay social security. Today, possibly also because of stricter anti-terrorism laws and more stringent tax evasion measures, many people are more reluctant to hire illegals or to cut corners on the social charges.

Furthermore, to get a *permesso di soggiorno* and be truly legal, a foreigner now has to demonstrate that he or she has at least one employer who is paying them a living wage. My housekeeper, a young Filipino man who cleans better than any woman I have known, gets social security from me and another woman and is counting on having a pension someday, although he'll probably have to wait until he is close to 70 years old to get it. But others are not so lucky. An Egyptian I know here worked in a pizzeria for more than ten years without ever being put on the books, although, to be fair, many young Italians find the same problem. They manage to get a job but not from someone who is willing to employ them legally.

Italy's gradual transition into a multiethnic society plus an exponential increase in travel abroad by Italians has had another side effect, that of making the Italians more gastronomically open-minded. When I first moved to Rome in 1972, there was exactly one Chinese restaurant, two French restaurants, one of which was run by nuns, a Lebanese place, an Eastern European Jewish delicatessen, and – in the eighties – a Vietnamese restaurant that profited from the Italian left's forceful opposition to the Vietnamese war. In those days, if you wanted to eat something "different", you went out for Sardinian, Sicilian, Venetian, Bolognese or Tuscan food. Today, instead, there are literally hundreds of Chinese restaurants, about a dozen Japanese restaurants and a smattering of sushi places, a growing number of Indian eateries, as well as Mexican, Thai, Greek, East African, North African and Tex-Mex eateries. Near my house in Trastevere, there is even a Middle Eastern take-out and, amazingly enough, among those eating falafel are as many home-grown *trasteverini* as displaced Egyptians, Lebanese and…. homesick New Yorkers.

But despite all this, for many Italians the perception of immigrants – generally referred to as *extracommunitari* because they come from outside the European Union (which makes me, too, an *extracommunitaria*) – continues to be somewhat negative. To a degree this is understandable: some of the newcomers who don't find jobs (or who, in some cases, don't really want them) turn to crime and at present about a third of the 61,000 occupants of Rome's overcrowded prisons are, in fact, foreigners. But there is more to it than that, not all that surprising if you consider that in most Italian towns anyone who was born elsewhere is forever considered a foreigner. Not long ago in Bolsena, the lake-town where I go on weekends, I was chatting with Gilda, who with her husband, Omero, is the owner of the *frutteria* I generally shop at. Gilda was complaining about the opening of a new (and less expensive) *fruttivendolo* around the corner. "Furthermore," she added with contempt, "they are *forestieri*", which can mean outsiders or even foreigners. "Oh, really?" I said, stupidly imagining the town's first Pakistani residents. "Where are they from?" "From San Lorenzo," she replied, referring to a village merely ten kilometers away.

Chapter 39 – Nicolina

Nicolina is in the hospital and the whole neighborhood, by which I mean the two or three blocks that constitute my immediate *quartiere*, is abuzz. Nicolina, her hair now almost white but still tied back in her signature chignon, is 91 and mentally sharp as a whip. Only a year ago, on May 16, 2005, the neighbourhood feted her for her 90th birthday, but now the situation has deteriorated. Severe pains in her legs led doctors to determine she was suffering from a cracked vertebra caused by osteoporosis and needed to be hospitalized. So for the last month and a half she has been bed-ridden miles away in a sprawling clinic called Villa Pia in an outlying area on the other side of the Janiculum Hill. Since Nicolina has no relatives, save for a half-cracked and possibly dangerous nephew named Armando, this has created considerable problems, and a small, informal neighborhood task force has sprung into being to deal with the emergency, which means visiting her in the hospital, bringing her extra clothing and food there, and speaking with the doctors about her future.

The biggest problem, however, is yet to come. According to health service rules, she can stay in the fourth-floor ward she is currently in for 59 days, after which she has to leave. The next step involves asking the city government for special home-health care for her. If she doesn't qualify, she will have to pay for it herself with her meagre old-age pension or else resign herself to living out her life in a long-term health care facility. The linchpins of this informal support group are Giancarlo and Stella, the dress-alike upholsterers. Giancarlo and Nicolina are not really related – Giancarlo is Armando's cousin, is all – but everyone thinks of him as Nicolina's nephew and as she has gotten older they have become increasingly involved in her care; during an earlier crisis, they bought a trundle bed and took her in to their apartment in the Aurelia neighborhood until she got better. But they are not alone. Pinuccia, an attractive older woman who before retiring worked in the fashion world as a manager, first for Valentino and then for Lancetti, and who until her premature death (from cancer) two years ago lived in the building next to Stella and Giancarlo's atelier, is very involved. As is Anna, the veteran cook at *Cencio La Parolaccia*

("Cencio's Dirty Word" would be the best translation), the restaurant across the street from Nicolona's *basso* – as Italians call a ground-floor shop that has been turned into an apartment. Originally, Nicolina and her sister Ada, Armando's mother, rented this space from a fishmonger who used it to sell his wares only on Tuesdays and Fridays. Then Nicolina bought it so at least no one can kick her out.

Others who have been going to visit her include Fernanda, whose wonderful linen shop, *Mode e Materie*, now closed, was right across the street from Nicolina's *basso*; Danila, the wife of Attilio the greengrocer, who with a 13-year old Down's syndrome son has plenty of her own problems; and Antonio, the delivery man for Pettinicchio, a dairy products company, who has been parking his truck in front of Nicolina's place for years now. Also tangentially involved are Ettore and Paola, whose tiny beauty parlor next to *Cencio La Parolaccia* is also across the street from Nicolina.

It was in fact Ettore's grandfather, Vincenzo, known as Cencio, who founded the restaurant, a popular place that specializes in bawdy Roman songs and subjects its customers to a variety of vulgar epithets that they inexplicably enjoy. When she was younger, Nicolina used to clean *La Parolaccia*, and Cencio's *testamento* included a clause instructing his heirs to make sure she has at least one square meal a day as long as she lives. Ettore and his sister, Simonetta, who now alternate in running the restaurant, have always honored this and in normal times Anna takes lunch across the street to Nicolina every day at around 1:30 p.m. Sometimes Nicolina gets food from *Otello*, another restaurant right across from the bar, for which she used to do various errands or favors. And, of course, in the mornings, fresh *cornetti* from the bar, if she wants them.

This sort of small-town solidarity, in this case right smack in the middle of a major city with myriad problems, is really heart-warming. I get updates on Nicolina's health (editor's note: she was never able to return home and in 2010, at the age of 95, died in a long-term care facility) when, on Friday mornings, I am having my hair washed and blown dry by Paola. Paola and Ettore's establishment could easily be one of the smallest *parrucchiere* or hairdressers in Rome, with only two chairs, one washbasin and one full size hairdryer that no one seems to use. When I first moved into the neighborhood in 1972 this space housed a barbershop, and after Ettore took it over he continued doing men's haircuts so that today it is a real unisex shop. I once would have found this disconcerting, especially now that I use a color rinse one a month that Paola also applies to my eyebrows making me look, I think, something like Zero Mostel or the late English actor, Robert Morley. But you can get used to anything. And even if men did not figure among Paola and Ettore's clients, they, too, would still be stopping by to chat.

This beauty shop is, in some ways, more of a tearoom than a coiffeur. I don't mean that Ettore and Paola serve refreshments; they don't, although they will sometimes bring you a coffee from the bar if you ask them. But often along with the one or two clients, male or female, who are having their hair cut, colored or set you'd be likely to find Carlo, the caretaker at the Museum of Rome in Piazza San Egidio, Wilma, a greying, heavy-set woman with a short, skinny ponytail who could use having her hair done but who comes in only to gossip, Ettore's recently widowed father, Nino, Gianluca, a dark-haired 35-ish man with a goatee who delivers soda, water and beer to many of the restaurants in the area, and Adriano Panatta, the now somewhat hefty former Italian tennis star. When she isn't working as a movie production assistant, Valentina, Paola's daughter, comes by. As do various suppliers for the restaurant and other friends from the neighborhood, although fewer now that the non-smoking law has gone into effect. The phone is also constantly ringing, for the most part masochists wanting to make reservations at *La Parolaccia*.

I have long, dark curly hair with which I've been battling for most of my life. For a while, I gave up trying to keep it straight and wore it shoulder-length curly. I also have always hated spending too much time at beauty parlors, especially fancy ones. But when I discovered that Paola and Ettore would charge me only 13 euros (about $15) to have my hair washed and blown dry, I became a regular. Of course, there are disadvantages. *Trasteverini* by birth (they met when they were teenagers), both Ettore and Paola talk very loudly, even though the store is so small there is no need to yell. And when others, Romans all, join them for chitchat, the din can be unbearable. But I'm the only one who seems to mind. In Trastevere, and elsewhere in Italy, too, people often seem to all talk at the same time, as if it were more important to talk than actually to be listened to. Still, a weekly visit to the place is one way to keep in touch with local developments and, in a small way, to take the pulse of the nation.

Along with Anna, the cook, another one of the apartments above *La Parolaccia* is occupied by Eugenio and Rosina, the couple who for years ran a small housewares shop around the corner in Via della Scala, the kind of store Italians call a *casalinghi*. This was the place to come when you didn't have the time or energy to go to a big hardware store, to the supermarket or to UPIM, the Italian equivalent of a five-and-dime. If you needed anything from toilet paper to flashlight batteries, from a fold-up clothes dryer to use on the terrace to a vacuum-sealed jar in which to store dried porcini mushrooms or muesli, Eugenio had it. His prices, of course, were not competitive. But all the same, it was extremely convenient, not least because if I didn't have my wallet with me, I'd just tell Eugenio to *segnarlo*, to write it down in his book. Once, looking over his shoulder, I realized that after all these years he still didn't know my name. The heading read simply, "*l'americana*".

Although it has always seemed hard to believe (since he has always looked a bit ragged), Eugenio is reportedly very well off, owning a variety of apartments throughout the city. That this is what he chose to do with his savings is not really surprising since Italians have long been convinced that the only good investment is *il mattone* – literally, the brick – or if you prefer, real estate. Whether or not this is true, the family seemed happy. But then disaster struck. The couple's daughter, Gabriella, a lovely young woman who was a bit more modern in attitude than her parents (Eugenio would never accept returns, even if something you bought the day before at his store turned out to be broken) developed a malignant brain tumor and, after a few months, died. Her brother, Massimo, opted for a career in the military and moved out of town.

Rosina, a small, shapeless woman with lifeless short, straight hair and a rather high-pitched voice, has never recovered from her daughter's death and over the years has gotten sicker and sicker. About five years ago she stopped going to the store and retreated to her apartment. Everyone says that Eugenio could have amply afforded to hire a home care worker to take care of her, but he didn't seem to want to spend the money. Eugenio has his own health problems; he has been hospitalized twice with heart ailments of one sort or another and each time has had to close the store because he has no help other than a retired typographer, a white-haired man named Werther (his father loved Goethe) who takes the bus all the way from the other side of Rome to help out. Danilo, Gabriella's son, worked for Eugenio for a while, and everyone thought he could have been trained to take over. But living up to his reputation as a miser, Eugenio paid him so badly that despite the blood relationship Danilo left to take a job in a supermarket. In the winter of 2006, Eugenio was hospitalized again, but unlike Nicolina, there was no one to visit him except the faithful Werther. Afterwards, he decided to close the store, for good. He spends his days taking care of Rosina. Every morning they can be seen sitting at a table in the rear of the bar and having breakfast. The rest of the day he does errands – picks up Rosina's prescriptions, goes to the doctor, makes payments at the Post Office and, when the weather is good enough to have a couple of chairs put out on the sidewalk, sits and chats with Nicolina. He must be lonely, because he has gotten very friendly and always wants to stop and chat.

Another person who went to visit Nicolina regularly is Anna, the bar's afternoon manager. A small-boned and slender Sardinian with wonderful thick, long, black Sardinian hair which she wears in a sort of page-boy with bangs, and who doesn't look a year older than she did 20 years ago, Anna is unhappily married, but hasn't formally separated or divorced. Her two teenage sons, on the other hand, who help out at the bar during the summer, are adorable: good-looking, polite and strangely enough, neatly dressed, shaved and combed. In fact, one of the things that has changed the most in Italy in the years – no, decades – I've lived here, is the physical appearance of Italian men, especially those under 30. Once all Italian males, even teen-agers, were concerned about their appearance and were snappily well-dressed. As one can see from old movies or documentary footage, they tended to have thick beautiful hair – and they shaved every day like their fathers did before them. At some point, however, as if it were a virus, they "caught" the American penchant for casual dress and have interpreted it in the worst way possible, at least from my point of view.

Italian women, too, dress far more casually than they did 15 or 20 years ago – and often – particularly here in Rome – seem to prefer a rather vulgar look. But they still look beautiful, while far too many males have turned into slobs. This means that when I go into the bar in the mornings to have my wake-up *espresso*, especially in the summer, I am forced to share the counter with a series of messy-looking, unshaven men dressed in baggy T-shirts and wide-legged, below-the-knee cargo pants that the Italians call *pinocchietti*, since they somewhat resemble those worn by the cartoon figure, Pinocchio. This may in part be because many of the men who live in Trastevere are either unemployed, self-employed, students, or workmen, rather than

321

bank clerks, civil servants or the Italian equivalent of office nine-to-fivers. But if you go to the bar in the evening when half of Rome's younger population seems to have picked Trastevere as a destination, the dress code situation is similar.

Furthermore, something seems to have happened to Italian men's hair. Some people say it is a result of the 1986 Chernobyl disaster, which sent some contamination westward. My dermatologist blames it on the hormones in beef, but then all Americans would be losing their hair as well.

The fact is that Italy appears to have been struck by a blight of male baldness. A very large number of men under 35 appear to be balding, and many seem to have opted for shaving their heads in the conviction that this way they look better. Furthermore, since most of these men add on goatees with an integrated moustache, there are lot of males running around who to me, at least, look almost identical. And not very attractive, either. It all makes me think of the film *Gigi* and feel like breaking out into a chorus of Maurice Chevalier's wonderful song, "Oh, I'm so glad, that I'm, not young any more!".

Chapter 40 – A Roman Life, 40 Years Later

"**A**ren't you supposed to be getting your hair done this morning?" asks Giancarlo, noisily stacking the espresso cups in the dishwasher after the morning's first customer onslaught. After years of serving me my morning espressos, Giancarlo knows a lot about my habits and sometimes seems to know my schedule – along with that of many other of his clients – as well as he knows his own. It is, in fact, Friday, and for the last several years I have been having my hair done every Friday morning at or around 9:30 by Paola or Ettore, whose tiny hairdresser shop is about 20 steps from the bar. So Giancarlo is wondering why at 10 a.m. I am having coffee rather than sitting in a barber's chair having my long, dark-brown hair washed and blow-dried.

Thirty years after my arrival at Piazza Sant'Egidio in 1972, I decided to *cambiare casa*, change houses, that is, to move. But I haven't gone far, just down the street about 150 yards to trendy Via della Scala where I now have a bit more space and a lovely, 20-square-yard terrace. Along with the original cast of characters who for almost 30 years populated my life, I have acquired a whole new set of neighborhood friends.

Across the street from my new building is Gianni's pizzeria where Gianni, 50, grey hair, a matching moustache, a very heavy Roman accent and unbridled enthusiasm for the A.S.Roma soccer team, sells delicious take-out slices and helped by Fadel and Ali does a flourishing business. Eugenio's shop, more or less next door to Gianni, has been rented to a Peruvian who imports and sells native Peruvian artifacts. And despite a monthly rent of 2,000 euros (about $2,500), the store so far continues to survive. Next door to the Peruvians are Claudio and Sergio, the jeweller brothers who have become good friends of mine and who own their own store. My only beef with them is their inability to conceive of men their age (43 and 45) being attracted to an older woman. I don't take it personally as neither of them appeals to me, but when a 40-year old says "Since my wife is 40, if I'm going to get some on the side it's got to be a 20-year old," it makes my blood boil.

Stefano, part owner of the Caffè della Scala, just to the right of my current *portone*, or front door, found an indelible place in my heart when, after I complained about the thump-thump from the evening's music, he went to enormous lengths to find a new place for the café's hi-fi speakers. He gets me plates or glasses wholesale if I need them, and brings me capers from Pantelleria, the island off Sicily where he vacations every summer. I in turn always bring him something from my trips, be it Greek oregano or Belgian chocolate. On the other side of the *portone* there used to be a picture-frame shop, this one, too, shared by two brothers, Gianni, the *corniciao* (cor-nee-chai-o) or frame maker and his brother, Mario, a gifted painter. But when their lease was up, the landlord, a Croatian man who lives in my new building, kicked them out so he could get a better rent, 3,000 euros per month according to neighborhood chit-chat. Three women's clothing stores, a kebab place and a small cocktail bar have already opened and shut in that locale: probably most people who open shops around here don't appear to do any market research prior to throwing their hat(s) into the ring.

Farther down on Via della Scala, there is the *tabaccheria*, another important fixture in any Italian neighborhood and a place to which someone like me who doesn't smoke nevertheless might go for stamps, notebooks, phone cards, bus tickets, pens, tissues, lottery tickets or batteries. Next to that for many years was my *tintoria*, or drycleaners. This, too, has closed because of an impending rent increase and the tiny shop has been rented to Middle Easterners selling a variety of glass gewgaws. But Rita, a young woman married to a *carabiniere,* who ran the *tintoria* with her mother, did not lose heart. She is now working out of their store in a Rome suburb and has managed to keep a goodly portion of her Trastevere clients. Twice a week she comes our way to deliver or pick up on a door-to-door basis. The only difference is that I can no longer run downstairs and ask her to press a pair of trousers that I need to wear immediately. *Pazienza.* It's still an extremely convenient arrangement.

The rest of the street is a mix of new and old. The "new" prevails – stores selling casual clothing, gewgaws, or Middle Eastern jewellery, a couple of real estate agencies and even a clothing designer who is reportedly doing quite well. Since I first moved to this area, the turnover in the kinds of stores has been significant and seems to have become even more rapid in recent years. In general, it is the artisans and the food shops that (unfortunately) have disappeared. In fact, today the "old" is represented by the tabaccheria, and by Biagio's wine and liquor store, where you can get a glass of wine at any time or else buy over-priced liquors, wines, sodas and water. In the good weather, white-haired Biagio, whom some of you may have seen playing himself in the lovely 2008 Italian film *Mid-August Lunch*, puts a barrel outside and a couple of chairs so that people can sit and sip their drinks. He is pushing 70, although you'd never guess it since he still hand delivers heavy six-packs of water or cartons of wine.

Naturally, I have new neighbors in my current building, a rose-colored construction probably dating back some 150 years with a lovely small, plant-filled inner courtyard with a Roman-style column in the center and a towering magnolia tree. My apartment is on two floors and incorporates a stone arch that is probably very old, although no one is sure just how much so.

The apartment was probably illegally renovated some 35 years ago and to avoid future problems I have taken advantage of a "building amnesty", a *condono edilizio,* and paid a hefty chunk of money to wipe out irregularities for which in my mind I bear no responsibility, except for that of having purchased the apartment, which here in Italy is enough to make me liable. The reader might be interested in knowing, that at current writing, I have been waiting ten years to get the final amnesty papers.

As in the Sant'Egidio building, there are ten apartments, five of which are owner-occupied, four of which are rented out on a more or less long-term basis, and two – soon to be three – that are rented out to tourists on short lets. Although there have been some tense moments – Italian condominiums are famous for their disagreements – at the moment I get along with almost everyone in the building. My best friends in the building are a gay couple, Mimmo, a Neapolitan, and Luca, a Roman, who have been together 25 years and who own three men's clothing stores, two in the center and one in the Parioli residential area.

Before I met them, most of the male homosexuals I knew here were artists, actors, writers and so forth. Coming out must have been difficult for any gay man 20 years ago, but it must have been particularly difficult for these two men to tell their families, both conservative merchant families, that they were gay and going to live together. "My mother still hasn't gotten over it," says Mimmo's sister, Gabriella, who now also lives in Rome. The funniest thing, she adds, speaking of herself and the two other heterosexual siblings, is that the only union to have lasted is Mimmo's with Luca.

Since I arrived here in 1972, the neighborhood has changed significantly. American college students enrolled in the nearby John Cabot University increasingly are a noticeable presence. Breaking with a long-standing Italian tradition, new tourist-oriented restaurants that begin serving at noon and provide meals all day long have sprung up throughout the quarter. There are far too many peddlers selling things you could buy anywhere else in the world. There are too many pubs, too many *gelaterie*, too many fast food places, too many "punks" (called *punkabestie* here because they are generally accompanied by a variety of unappealing dogs), all adding up to the fact that the city government is not on its toes and that the Italian *decoro* police, the city police unit entrusted with making sure that store and restaurant signs and décor are in keeping with the neighborhood's history, have not been doing their job. Furthermore, despite the fact that the garbage is collected daily, Trastevere's streets are dirty and there are still too few Romans with enough civic conscientiousness to scoop up after their dogs.

But not everything has changed. Unbelievably, some 30 years have gone by since I first started having my coffee in what is now Alessandro's bar, 25 of them since Giancarlo started working there. Except for the fact that his once dark blond hair is thinning and his moustache and goatee now show more grey than anything else, at 63 he basically looks the same as ever. True, he is now rather wrinkled, a direct consequence of his ongoing obsession with getting – and keeping – a suntan. And largely because of all those years in the sun, and a refusal to wear sunglasses, he has already had an operation to remove a cataract in the right eye and eventually will have to do the left one as well. Nowadays, at times he complains that his legs hurt, not surprising for someone who spends most of his days on his feet and has been doing so for decades. But he still looks and laughs like the Giancarlo I met back then and continues to turn his razor-sharp wit on one and all. In my case, it is generally my American accent that gets parodied, or I get accused of incipient Alzheimer's because of all the times I lock myself out of my apartment (the bar has long had a set of my keys hidden in a ceramic teapot just for such emergencies).

One frequent butt of Giancarlo's generally good-natured teasing is Loretta, the cashier. One week when she was out for a few days because of an ear infection, Giancarlo kept announcing to the world that "Loretta's gone to the gynecologist." Or else it's "*Buongiorno*, Orietta," based on his assertion that with her well-sprayed, light-brown hair-do and roundish face, Loretta looks a bit like Orietta Berti, an Italian singer popular in the Italian provinces for her sentimental country-style songs and who now, at 60, is a frequent talk show guest. Loretta takes it all with a smile and gives some back as well. And this despite her own not inconsiderable problems: a husband who has fathered a child with another woman but who, so far at least, refused for almost a decade to move out, probably because he didn't want to pay a second apartment rental or be forced to give financial support to the couple's two children.

Giancarlo, in contrast, has gone and gotten married, at least on paper, to a Brazilian woman, whom I myself have never seen. And who hasn't been seen by anyone else for months. As before, he lives alone with his dogs and, since he is known to be gay and hardly high up on the income scale, it is generally assumed that this was some kind of negotiated agreement to enable her to become an Italian citizen in turn for who knows how much cash. Giancarlo is however planning to move to Brazil, specifically to Fortaleza, as soon as he retires because, he says, there's lots of sun and, what's more, he'll be able to live much better there on his small pension than here in Italy.

And what about me? I, too, have changed, or rather my life-style has changed. Although the reader may be surprised to learn that during much of the period that I have lived here, I did have an Italian "significant other" (about whom I have deliberately refrained from writing), at the moment I am now decidedly single although, since hope springs eternal, I admit it would be nice to have a man with whom one could share the greater pleasures of life.

At the end of 2007, I left the Italian newspaper for which I had worked for 16 years and currently do most of my writing – remunerated and not – from my home-office desk or the table on my lovely terrace. I continue to love my Trastevere neighborhood, at least during the day when most of the people around are locals – although the number of tourists is, unfortunately to my mind, rapidly escalating. These days, the early morning generally is spent taking down the garbage, having my first coffee at the *Caffè della Scala* which is right downstairs to the right of my *portone* (I haven't yet tried going down there in my pajamas but it's a temptation), schmoozing with the barman, Fabio, and the other regulars and then, at least four times a week, heading off to the gym.

Having been told repeatedly by orthopedists and radiologists, that my spinal column is one of the ugliest around, from time to time there are also doctors and massage therapists to be seen, most of which are paid for, although perhaps not at 100%, by the generous journalists' insurance plan I still belong to. And since I take a lot of care with my appearance, there is also the hairdresser, the manicurist and the masseur, all services that cost less here in Italy than they do back in the United States. The same goes for the cleaner who comes in two or three times a week and who also can be counted on to go buy heavy items such as cat litter and mineral water, or at least to carry them up the stairs to my apartment if I have brought them home on my trusty 125cc scooter. Often when people ask me whether I plan to move back home, the first thing that comes to my mind is that I simply could not afford it.

Luckily for me, I have a lot of friends, mostly Italians and Americans who, like me, have lived here for a long time and with whom it is possible to speak in a time-effective mix of our two fluent languages. In good weather, a great deal of my social life is consumed at the aperitivo hour at this or that café, since I am far less interested in going out for dinner than I once was. If I go out to eat, I want it to be a special place where I can eat something particular, or else I need to satisfy a craving for one of those pasta dishes that, yes, you could do at home, but it's never quite as good.

After four decades in Italy, the big question might be, would I do it all over again? And the answer is definitely yes. Of course, I have no way of knowing what my life would have been like if I had stayed at home, finished my studies and gotten a good job. I might have been happy, but I doubt I would have had the magical experiences that life as a woman and a journalist in a foreign land has brought me. I've made a life for myself in a country that is on some levels a very frustrating place to be. So much so that a few times I have thought that the most appropriate title for this book would have been: "Italy, a lovely place to visit, but would you really want to live here?" But there are so many compensating factors. As George Bernard Shaw put it: I hear you say "Why?" Always "Why?" You see things; and you say "Why?" But I dream things that never were; and I say "Why not?"

Ciao!

Thanks for reading this! And I do hope you have enjoyed it. As you now know, I have spent a huge chunk of my adult life in Italy and I am really pleased to finally have been able to share with others the experiences of a lifetime in what I like to think of as Stranitalia, a word I made up when I started a newsblog of the same name and which basically means, "strange Italy". I LOVE Italy and I LOVE Rome and if I had to do it all over again, I assure you I would make the same choices: to come here to study and then to work and to stay on and really live a rich and full life here.

But as by now you may have realized, this is a very complex country and while most visitors understandably have a tendency to look at Italy through the rose-colored glasses created by its fantastic physical beauty and its countless art works and monuments (no other country has as many of those), there is also a darker side to Italian life.

Anyway, if you have enjoyed this book, I would greatly appreciate reviews on the Amazon website from people like you. In this era of self-publishing, having a large number of (hopefully favorable) reviews may be the only way to attract attention. It isn't very hard to do. Just go to my book's page on Amazon, click where it says the number of reviews I already have and click again where it says, "Create your own review". People write books so that others will read them and the principal gratification is hearing from you and knowing what you, the reader, thinks.

Mille grazie,

Sari Gilbert

www.myhomesweetrome.com
www.stranitalia.com

Gilbert when she worked for Il Sole 24 Ore

About the Author

Sari Gilbert fell in love with Italy at a tender age and has been living in Rome since the 1970s when she started moved there to complete her graduate studies and then found work there as a reporter and foreign correspondent.

Born and bred in New York City, she graduated, magna cum laude and Phi Beta Kappa, in political science from Syracuse University. The second semester of her junior year was spent at Syracuse University in Florence and after graduation Gilbert retuned to Italy, to the Johns Hopkins School of Advanced International Studies (SAIS) in Bologna.

After a second year at SAIS in Washington D.C., she received an M.A. in International Relations. After a brief stint as Assistant Economist at The Federal Reserve Bank of New York, she returned to SAIS and received her doctorate in International Relations The research for her doctoral theses, 600 pages on Italy's decision to join the NATO alliance in 1949, was done in Rome.

Upon receiving her doctorate, Gilbert returned to Rome with a research grant awarded by the Council on Foreign Relations. She had planned a career in research or university teaching but after an internship at the *New York Times* Rome bureau, she became interested in journalism and started writing for a variety of American and Canadian publications, including the *Washington Post*, Newsweek, and a myriad of other newspapers, journals and magazines. In 1991, Gilbert joined the staff of the short-lived Italian daily, *L'Indipendente*, and then went on to work as a reporter and commentator for the prestigious *Il Sole 24 Ore*.

Over the years, except for fashion shows and soccer games, she covered just about every kind of news story there was to cover in Italy: elections, government crises, Mafia trials, terrorism, papal assassination attempts, immigrant smuggling, political corruption, earthquakes, food, tourism, business and banking, with the result that she knows a great deal about this delightful, frustrating and terribly complicated country. Oh, and that includes men as well. As an attractive, unmarried woman with an important job, she had – shall we say – diverse opportunities to love and be loved.

My Home Sweet Rome: Living (and Loving) in the Eternal City, provides a comprehensive – and entertaining – look at the ins and outs of life in Italy.

You can read more about Sari's continuing adventures on her website and hear about upcoming books and appearances.

www.myhomesweetrome.com